KEEPING
THE CHURCH
IN ITS PLACE

KEEPING
THE CHURCH
IN ITS PLACE

THE CHURCH AS
NARRATIVE CHARACTER
IN ACTS

RICHARD P. THOMPSON

t&t clark

NEW YORK • LONDON

T & T Clark International, 80 Maiden Lane, New York, NY 10038

T & T Clark International, The Tower Building, 11 York Road, London SE1 7NX

T & T Clark International is a Continuum imprint.

Except as otherwise indicated, Scripture is the author's translation. Occasionally cited for comparison: NRSV, NIV.

Cover art: St. Paul Preaching to the Jews in the Synagogue at Damascus. Byzantine Mosaic, end 12th c. Duomo, Monreale, Italy. From Bridgeman-Giraudon/Art Resource, NY.

Cover design: Brenda Klinger

Library of Congress Cataloging-in-Publication Data

Thompson, Richard P.
   Keeping the church in its place : the church as narrative character in the book of Acts / Richard P. Thompson.
      p. cm.
   Includes bibliographical references and index.
   ISBN-13: 978-0-567-02654-5 (hardcover : alk. paper)
   ISBN-10: 0-567-02654-X (hardcover : alk. paper)
   ISBN-13: 978-0-567-02645-3 (pbk. : alk. paper)
   ISBN-10: 0-567-02645-0 (pbk. : alk. paper)
   1. Bible. N.T. Acts – Narrative criticism. 2. Church – Biblical teaching. I. Title.
BS2625.6.C5T46 2006
226.6'066 – dc22

                                                                    2006031959

Printed in the United States of America on Recycled Paper

06   07   08   09   10   10   9   8   7   6   5   4   3   2   1

CONTENTS

❧

v

Abbreviations

AB   Anchor Bible

ACNT   Augsburg Commentary on the New Testament

ANTC   Abingdon New Testament Commentaries

ATR   *Anglican Theological Review*

BAFCS   The Book of Acts in Its First Century Setting

BDAG   W. Bauer, W. F. Arndt, F. W. Gingrich, and F. W. Danker, *Greek-English Lexicon of the New Testament and other Early Christian Literature*, 3rd ed. Chicago, 2000

BBB   Bonner biblische Beiträge

BETL   Bibliotheca ephemeridum theologicarum lovaniensium

BT   *The Bible Translator*

Bib   *Biblica*

BR   *Biblical Research*

BTB   *Biblical Theology Bulletin*

BZ   *Biblische Zeitschrift*

CBQ   *Catholic Biblical Quarterly*

CQ   *Classical Quarterly*

ÉBib   Études bibliques

EKKNT   Evangelisch-katholischer Kommentar zum Neuen Testament

ETL   *Ephemerides theologicae lovanienses*

ÉTR   *Études théologiques et religieuses*

EvT	*Evangelische Theologie*
FRLANT	Forschungen zur Religion und Literatur des Alten und Neuen Testaments
HTKNT	Herders theologischer Kommentar zum Neuen Testament
HTR	*Harvard Theological Review*
ICC	International Critical Commentary
Int	*Interpretation*
IVPNTC	InterVarsity Press New Testament Commentary
JAAR	*Journal of the American Academy of Religion*
JBL	*Journal of Biblical Literature*
JETS	*Journal of the Evangelical Theological Society*
JHS	*Journal of Hellenic Studies*
JSNT	*Journal for the Study of the New Testament*
JSNTSup	Journal for the Study of the New Testament: Supplement Series
JTS	*Journal of Theological Studies*
LCBI	Literary Currents in Biblical Interpretation
LCL	Loeb Classical Library
LD	Lectio divina
LEC	Library of Early Christianity
LSJ	H. G. Liddell, R. Scott, H. S. Jones, *A Greek-English Lexicon.* 9th ed. Oxford, 1940
NIB	*New Interpreter's Bible*
NCB	New Century Bible
NIBC	New International Bible Commentary
NICNT	New International Commentary on the New Testament
NovT	*Novum Testamentum*
NIV	New International Version

NRSV	New Revised Standard Version
NT	New Testament
NTD	Das Neue Testament Deutsch
NTS	*New Testament Studies*
OBO	Orbis biblicus et orientalis
OBT	Overtures to Biblical Theology
OT	Old Testament
ÖTNT	Ökumenischer Taschenbuch-Kommentar zum Neuen Testament
PerRS	*Perspectives in Religious Studies*
RB	*Revue biblique*
RevistB	*Revista bíblica*
RSR	*Recherches de science religieuse*
SANT	Studien zum Alten und Neuen Testament
SBLDS	Society of Biblical Literature Dissertation Series
SBLMS	Society of Biblical Literature Monograph Series
SBLSP	*Society of Biblical Literature Seminar Papers*
SNTSMS	Society for New Testament Studies Monograph Series
SP	Sacra pagina
ST	*Studia theologica*
SUNT	Studien zur Umwelt des Neuen Testaments
SwJT	*Southwestern Journal of Theology*
TDNT	*Theological Dictionary of the New Testament*. Edited by G. Kittel and G. Friedrich. Translated by G. W. Bromiley. 10 vols. Grand Rapids, 1964–1976
THKNT	Theologischer Handkommentar zum Neuen Testament
TLZ	*Theologische Literaturzeitung*
TNTC	Tyndale New Testament Commentaries

TS	*Theological Studies*
TZ	*Theologische Zeitschrift*
WUNT	Wissenschaftliche Untersuchungen zum Neuen Testament
WW	*World and World*
ZBK	Zürcher Bibelkommentare

INTRODUCTION

The subject of the Christian community or the church is not an unfamiliar one within New Testament studies. The recognition that most biblical texts addressed early Christian groups and selected issues that those early Christians faced lies behind much of this interest about first-century churches. Thus, many scholarly studies have sought answers to important historical questions about the situation and contexts from which and to which the respective texts were written. In other words, such questions have focused on those historical matters that lie *behind* the text. Out of this concern has come an abundance of scholarly attempts to discover historical information about the respective group or church that each writing or author originally addressed.[1] Although one must avoid the problems of "mirror reading" in such historical endeavors,[2] many historical-critical studies have proved to be insightful attempts to uncover and decipher textual clues about the first-century churches to which the various New Testament writings were addressed.

Although these studies of most New Testament writings have sought to answer historical questions about respective Christian communities or churches, the Acts of the Apostles has received little attention on this

---

1. In Pauline studies, representative works include Wayne A. Meeks, *The First Urban Christians* (New Haven: Yale University Press, 1983); and Gerd Theissen, *The Social Setting of Pauline Christianity,* trans. John H. Schutz (Philadelphia: Fortress, 1982). In Johannine studies, representative works include Raymond E. Brown, *The Community of the Beloved Disciple* (New York: Paulist Press, 1979); David Rensberger, *Johannine Faith and Liberating Community* (Philadelphia: Westminster, 1988); and D. Moody Smith, *Johannine Christianity: Essays on Its Setting, Sources, and Theology* (Columbia: University of South Carolina Press, 1984). In Matthean studies, representative works include David L. Balch, ed., *Social History of the Matthean Community: Cross-Disciplinary Approaches* (Minneapolis: Fortress, 1991); Stephenson H. Brooks, *Matthew's Community: The Evidence of His Special Material,* JSNTSup 16 (Sheffield: JSOT Press, 1987); and J. Andrew Overman, *Matthew's Gospel and Formative Judaism: The Social World of the Matthean Community* (Minneapolis: Fortress, 1990).

2. For a discussion of the problems associated with mirror reading in Pauline studies, see George Lyons, *Pauline Autobiography: Toward a New Understanding,* SBLDS 73 (Atlanta: Scholars Press, 1985), 75–121.

subject. The traditional view of Acts perceives the book as "the first history of the Christian church"; yet the churches as described there and their possible narrative functions have received little serious scholarly attention.[3] Critical study has largely relegated the Lukan descriptions of these various Christian groups to one of two basic roles. On the one hand, many have given the book of Acts and these descriptions a supplemental role by gleaning historical background information from the work for the sake of studying Christian communities in *other* New Testament writings, especially the Pauline letters.[4] This supplemental use of the Acts narrative does not consider *that* text's unique contributions, however, and minimizes the potential functions of those descriptions within that narrative. On the other hand, when many *do* study the statements about or descriptions of Christian communities in Acts for their contributions to the book or to Lukan thought, such studies usually examine these statements and descriptions with regard for certain historical questions and *without* regard for the narrative context in which one finds such literary elements.[5] Both approaches to the study of the churches in

---

3. See Philip Francis Esler, *Community and Gospel in Luke-Acts: The Social and Political Motivations of Lucan Theology*, SNTSMS 57 (Cambridge: Cambridge University Press, 1987), which is a notable exception, although narrative function is not a consideration in that study.

4. Because of discrepancies between Acts and the Pauline letters in historical details, debate over the historical reliability of Acts has attracted considerable attention. For a variety of perspectives, see, e.g., W. Ward Gasque, *A History of the Interpretation of the Acts of the Apostles* (Peabody, MA: Hendrickson, 1989); Colin J. Hemer, *The Book of Acts in the Setting of Hellenistic History* (Winona Lake, IN: Eisenbrauns, 1990); John Knox, *Chapters in a Life of Paul*, rev. ed. (Macon, GA: Mercer University Press, 1987), 3–90; Gerd Lüdemann, *Early Christianity according to the Traditions in Acts: A Commentary*, trans. John Bowden (Philadelphia: Fortress, 1989), 1–18; Eckhard Plümacher, *Lukas als hellenisticher Schriftsteller: Studien zur Apostelgeschichte*, SUNT (Göttingen: Vandenhoeck & Ruprecht, 1972); and Philipp Vielhauer, "On the 'Paulinism' of Acts," in *Studies in Luke-Acts*, ed. Leander E. Keck and J. Louis Martyn (Philadelphia: Fortress, 1980), 33–50.

5. E.g., attention has been given to the summary statements about the Jewish believers in Acts 2:41–47; 4:32–37; and 5:12–16; see Alan C. Mitchell, "The Social Function of Friendship in Acts 2:44–47 and 4:32–37," *JBL* 111 (1992): 255–72; Gregory E. Sterling, "'Athletes of Virtue': An Analysis of the Summaries in Acts (2:41–47; 4:32–35; 5:12–16)," *JBL* 113 (1994): 679–96; Maria Anicia Co, "The Major Summaries in Acts: Acts 2,42–47; 4,32–35; 5,12–16 Linguistic and Literary Relationship," *ETL* 68 (1992): 49–85; Henry J. Cadbury, "The Summaries in Acts," in *The Beginnings of Christianity*, ed. F. J. Foakes-Jackson and Kirsopp Lake, 5 vols. (London: Macmillan, 1933), 5:392–402; and Pierre Benoit, "Remarques sur les 'sommaires' de Actes 2. 42 à 5," in *Aux sources de la tradition chrétienne: Mélanges offerts à M. Maurice Goguel* (Paris: Neuchâtel, Delachaux & Niestlé, 1950): 1–10. One finds similar problems in redaction-critical works, such as Hans Conzelmann, *The Theology of St. Luke*, trans. Geoffrey Buswell (Philadelphia: Fortress, 1961), 207–34.

the Acts of the Apostles have provided helpful answers to important historical questions. However, these approaches alone are not sufficient for the study of the churches in Acts because they have extracted textual materials about the various local churches from their narrative places.[6]

The suggestion that one must examine the descriptions of the different groups of Christians or Christian communities within the context of the Acts narrative, however, does not raise historical questions but literary ones. Since historical-critical approaches to biblical studies have dominated the scholarly landscape during the last two centuries, the absence until recently of studies that interpret Acts or a Gospel as an integrated, holistic narrative comes as no surprise. Historical-critical studies have analyzed and dissected portions of textual materials in pursuing an understanding of earliest Christianity, but such works reflect little concern for the integrity of the entire literary composition.[7] Thus, historical criticism may identify *what* literary conventions an author used in textual composition, but literary criticism also asks *how* and *why* the author may have used these particular tools and not others. These basic distinctions between historical-critical and literary-critical approaches do not imply that one approach is more appropriate or useful than another.[8] Rather, one should recognize that the study of a narrative must closely consider the literary phenomena within that narrative since it, on the one hand, invites its readers or audience into its *narrative* world and, on the other hand, does not address its readers directly in their *everyday* world (e.g., like a letter).

The study of the churches in the Acts of the Apostles, then, requires one to raise literary questions rather than historical ones. Since these various groups of Christian believers appear among the characters or actors[9] in

---

6. Cf. Meir Sternberg, *The Poetics of Biblical Narrative: Ideological Literature and the Drama of Reading*, Indiana Literary Biblical Series (Bloomington: Indiana University Press, 1985), 2: "Elements thus get divorced from the very terms of reference that assign to them their role and meaning: parts from wholes, means from ends, forms from functions."

7. See Beverly Roberts Gaventa, "Toward a Theology of Acts: Reading and Rereading," *Int* 42 (1988): 146–57; and Mary Ann Tolbert, *Sowing the Gospel: Mark's World in Literary-Historical Perspective* (Minneapolis: Fortress, 1989), 21–27.

8. See Pheme Perkins, "Crisis in Jerusalem? Narrative Criticism in New Testament Studies," *TS* 50 (1989): 296–313, for an excellent treatment concerning both the distinctiveness and compatibility of narrative criticism in relation to historical criticism.

9. This understanding of characters as "actors," which may include individuals or groups, is consistent with Aristotle's description of tragic characters (see *Poetics* 6.5, 8, 21; 8:1). Cf. Malcolm Heath, "The Universality of Poetry in Aristotle's Poetics," *CQ* 41 (1991): 389.

the narrative, one must assess relevant issues of Lukan characterization concerning those groups.[10] What ancient literary concepts and conventions shaped the Lukan composition and its descriptions of the earliest churches? How does the narrative text depict these character groups, and why does that text present these characters in the ways that it does? How do they interact and compare with other characters? What narrative roles do the churches as characters play in Acts? How do the various portrayals of the Christian communities relate to one another? How do these characters contribute to the narrative's rhetoric?[11] While some Lukan scholars have addressed similar literary concerns regarding other characters in Luke or Acts or both, these scholars have given little or no attention to the Christian communities in Acts.[12] This lack of attention is rather puzzling when one considers that one group, the Jerusalem believers, stands prominently among the cast of characters in the first seven chapters.[13] If one takes seriously the different characters that appear on the Acts narrative stage, then one must also keep and analyze the different portrayals of these churches or Christian communities in their respective narrative places.

The focus of this work, therefore, is the Lukan characterization of churches, Christian communities, or groups of believers in the Acts of the Apostles. This study will try to analyze the different portrayals of these early Christian communities in the Acts narrative, to delineate potential roles of these descriptions in that narrative, and to answer preliminary questions regarding both the ancient rhetoric of Acts and the potential responses that it may evoke. Such an attempt requires a working understanding of ancient literary practices and a literary assessment of the

---

10. See Gaventa, "Toward a Theology of Acts," 152, who asks, "Do the communities (e.g., Christians in Jerusalem, Jewish leaders) function as characters?" Cf. Mark Allan Powell, "The Religious Leaders in the Gospels of Luke: A Literary-Critical Study," *JBL* 109 (1990): 94, who suggests that a character group "implies that they [i.e., the group members] function as a single character in the narrative."

11. See Hubert Cancik, "The History of Culture, Religion, and Institutions in Ancient Historiography: Philological Observations concerning Luke's History," *JBL* 116 (Winter 1997): 673–95.

12. See, e.g., Robert C. Tannehill, *The Narrative Unity of Luke-Acts*, 2 vols. (Philadelphia/Minneapolis: Fortress, 1986–90), 2:43, 81, who minimizes the role of the church descriptions in the opening chapters of Acts.

13. See Richard P. Thompson, "Believers and Religious Leaders in Jerusalem: Contrasting Portraits of Jews in Acts 1–7," in *Literary Studies in Luke-Acts: Essays in Honor of Joseph B. Tyson*, ed. Richard P. Thompson and Thomas E. Phillips (Macon, GA: Mercer University Press, 1998), 327–44.

passages in the Acts narrative that contribute pictures of these earliest churches. As recognized later, both the composition of a text and the role of the reader in the reading process preclude an assertion that only this reading is a valid one. Therefore, this study seeks to provide an alternative reading of Acts that accounts for the prominent, recurrent portraits of Christian believers among the narrative characters — a reading that keeps these churches in their places within the narrative text.

ONE

ANCIENT NARRATIVES, CHARACTERIZATION, AND THE ACTS OF THE APOSTLES

The designation "literary criticism" implies that the biblical text itself is the focus of critical reflection and analysis as a *literary* text. Such an assertion does not imply, however, that studying a text from a literary perspective is limited merely to the elements of that text. To approach the Acts narrative from a literary perspective means that one perceives the text both as a creation of an author and as a means of communication between that author and some reader. Such an approach recognizes that both the text and its reader contribute to the reading process and to the understanding of that text. Thus, a basic premise of literary criticism is that all texts, both ancient and modern ones, have a potential rhetorical function. Even ancient historical narratives such as the Acts of the Apostles[1] were composed with the purpose of affecting their respective

---

1. The narrative similarities among generic options for Acts provide a more useful context for study than a lengthy argument about genre. For the relationship of historiography, biography, and novel in the Greco-Roman era, see Charles William Fornara, *The Nature of History in Ancient Greece and Rome*, Eidos: Studies in Classical Kinds (Berkeley: University of California Press, 1983), 184–87; J. B. Bury, *The Ancient Greek Historians* (London: Macmillan, 1909), 224–41; and Arnaldo Momigliano, *The Development of Greek Biography: Four Lectures* (Cambridge, MA: Harvard University Press, 1971), 101–4. For studies identifying Luke-Acts or Acts as historiography, see, e.g., David E. Aune, *The New Testament in Its Literary Environment*, LEC 8 (Philadelphia: Westminster, 1987), 77–115; Hubert Cancik, "The History of Culture, Religion, and Institutions in Ancient Historiography: Philological Observations concerning Luke's History," *JBL* 116 (Winter 1997): 673–95; Colin J. Hemer, *The Book of Acts in the Setting of Hellenistic History* (Winona Lake, IN: Eisenbrauns, 1990); Gregory E. Sterling, *Historiography and Self-Definition: Josephus, Luke-Acts and*

implied audiences or readers,[2] not with the purpose of merely record-
ing what happened.[3] A literary-critical approach to the Acts narrative,
therefore, will consider *what* Acts seems to convey (i.e., the *story*), *how*
the narrative conveys that story (i.e., its discourse), and *how* one may
interpret or experience that narrative.[4] Such approaches should include,
among other things, specific consideration of the included characters:
the presentation of those characters, and the function of those characters within the rhetorical context of the Acts narrative. Therefore, an
adequate understanding of a narrative like Acts, including its characterization, must account for both the creative presentation of the ancient
text and the reading process in which the reader interacts with that text
and to which that one contributes.

Apologetic Historiography (Leiden: Brill, 1992); and Eckhard Plümacher, *Lukas als hellenistischer Schriftsteller: Studien zur Apostelgeschichte,* Studien zur Umwelt des Neuen Testaments
(Göttingen: Vandenhoeck & Ruprecht, 1972). For studies identifying Acts as historical monograph, see Darryl W. Palmer, "Acts and the Ancient Historical Monograph," in *The Book
of Acts in Its Ancient Literary Setting,* ed. Bruce W. Winter and Andrew D. Clarke, BAFCS
(Grand Rapids: Eerdmans, 1993), 1–30; and Eckhard Plümacher, "Die Apostelgeschichte als
historische Monographie," in *Les Actes des Apôtres: Traditions, rédaction, théologie,* ed. Jacob
Kremer, BETL 48 (Leuven: Leuven University Press, 1979), 457–66. For studies identifying
Luke-Acts as biography, see, e.g., L. C. A. Alexander, "Acts and Ancient Intellectual Biogra-
phy," in *The Book of Acts in Its Ancient Literary Setting,* ed. Bruce W. Winter and Andrew D.
Clarke, BAFCS (Grand Rapids: Eerdmans, 1993), 31–63; Vernon K. Robbins, "Prefaces in
Greco-Roman Biography and Luke-Acts," *PerRS* 6 (Summer 1979): 94–108; and Charles H.
Talbert, *Literary Patterns, Theological Themes, and the Genre of Luke-Acts,* SBLMS 20 (Mis-
soula, MT: Scholars Press, 1974), 125–40. For a study identifying Acts as novel, see Richard I.
Pervo, *Profit with Delight: The Literary Genre of the Acts of the Apostles* (Philadelphia:
Fortress, 1987).

2. The term "reader" (the common designation in most current literary discussions) is
used here to denote the one who seeks to understand a text. However, the original recipients
were most likely "hearers" (i.e., an audience) and not "readers." This and other expectations of
the implied reader or audience will be reflected, at least in part, by the text. For two discussions
about implied readers, see, e.g., Wayne C. Booth, *The Rhetoric of Fiction,* 2nd ed. (Chicago:
University of Chicago Press, 1983), 138; and Wolfgang Iser, *The Act of Reading: A Theory of
Aesthetic Response* (Baltimore: Johns Hopkins University Press, 1978), 34.

3. Cf. John A. Darr, *On Character Building: The Reader and the Rhetoric of Characterization in Luke-Acts,* LCBI (Louisville: Westminster/John Knox, 1992), 17; Meir Sternberg, *The
Poetics of Biblical Narrative: Ideological Literature and the Drama of Reading,* Indiana Literary Biblical Series (Bloomington: Indiana University Press, 1985), 15; and Robert C. Tannehill,
Luke, ANTC (Nashville: Abingdon, 1996), 31.

4. See Seymour B. Chatman, *Story and Discourse: Narrative Structure in Fiction and Film*
(Ithaca, NY: Cornell University Press, 1978), for his influential distinction between "story" and
"discourse." However, this distinction is artificial, since the reader only has access to the story
through discourse.

ANCIENT NARRATIVE TEXTS, READERS,
AND THE READING PROCESS

Ancient and modern literary theorists alike emphasize both the ways in which literary texts may affect their respective readers and the creative textual elements that function to achieve such ends.[5] On the one hand, ancient literary discussions stress the potential power of the spoken word, although such discussions reflect strong disagreement about the use of words. Although Plato based his indictment against poetry on poetry's appeal to the passions and emotion rather than reason,[6] Aristotle and Longinus stressed the appropriateness of emotion in the stimulation of human interest, which is critical to a given work's potential provocation of thought and persuasiveness.[7] On the other hand, both ancient and modern literary discussions also stress the role of literary creativity in the composition of a given text.[8] For instance, Greco-Roman discussions on the art of literary composition emphasize the importance of the textual elements that best contribute to the potential reception of a respective work. Although emotional effects or entertainment were not the ultimate concern in ancient historiography, those historians recognized that the narrative characters and events of the historical text must come to life in the imaginations of the text's recipients if its potential beneficial effects would materialize.[9] Only by creating interest or stirring emotions in the readers would a text like Acts present a narrative world that those readers may imagine in their minds: to "see" the characters, to "hear"

---

5. See Stephen D. Moore, *Literary Criticism and the Gospels: The Theoretical Challenge* (New Haven: Yale University Press, 1989), 96, who rightly observes that classical and contemporary discussions generally have one significant difference: classical discussions emphasize the *affective*, emotional experience of reading, whereas contemporary discussions emphasize the *cognitive* experience.

6. See Plato, *Republic* 10.602c–608c.

7. See Aristotle, *Poetics* 4.2–5; 6.2; 14.1–9. See also Longinus, *On the Sublime* 15.1–2. Cf. Paul Woodruff, "Aristotle on *Mimēsis*," in *Essays on Aristotle's Poetics*, ed. Amélie Oksenberg Rorty (Princeton: Princeton University Press, 1992), 86.

8. Cf. Dionysius, *On Literary Composition*; Booth, *The Rhetoric of Fiction*, 68; and Iser, *The Act of Reading*, 35.

9. See, e.g., Polybius, *The Histories* 1.4.11; 15.36.3. See Frank W. Walbank, "Profit or Amusement: Some Thoughts on the Motives of Hellenistic Historians," in *Purposes of History: Studies in Greek Historiography from the 4th to the 2nd Centuries B.C.*, ed. Herman Verdin, Guido Schepens, and Eugénie de Keyser, Studia hellenistica 30 (Leuven: Lovanii, 1990), 260–62; and V. D'Huys, "Κρήσιμον καὶ τερπνόν in Polybios' Schlachtschilderungen: Einige literarische Topoi in seiner Darstellung der Schlacht bei Zama (XV 9–16)," in Verdin et al., *Purposes of History*, 267–88.

them speak, to become involved in the unfolding story.[10] The imaginatively composed text, then, invites the reader into its presented narrative world and not another; the reader has access to that world only through that text's creative presentation. The narrative elements, taken together to make up the whole text, potentially guide the reader through that text toward response.[11]

Although here one cannot examine every possible textual element either that contributes to the reading of the Acts narrative or that critics (both ancient and modern ones) have discussed, two general categories of significant elements stand prominently within literary discussions pertaining to ancient historical narratives such as Acts: the creative arrangement of the literary work, and the artistic techniques used within that work. Ancient literary theorists typically emphasized the necessity of unity in a literary work, which they linked to the "plot" or ὁ μῦθος. Aristotle emphasized that the plot, as the arrangement of incidents in poetry, includes a well-planned arrangement that joins all parts of the work, much like a living organism.[12] Historians such as Dionysius and Polybius contended that the consistency and unity of the historical narrative depend on a synthesis of selected events and persons.[13] The creative arrangement of the historical narrative, therefore, potentially focuses the reader's attention not only on the events but also on the relationship of those events.[14] The *connection* of those historical episodes, not the episodes themselves, is the significant element of an ancient narrative such as Acts.[15]

The precise literary arrangement of the various textual parts is critical to the whole process of reading the Acts narrative. Dionysius stressed the

---

10. Cf. Dionysius, *On Thucydides* 15, 23; and Longinus, *On the Sublime* 7.3.

11. Cf. Wolfgang Iser, *The Implied Reader: Patterns of Communication in Prose Fiction from Bunyan to Beckett* (Baltimore: Johns Hopkins University Press, 1974), 274–88.

12. Aristotle, *Poetics* 7.1–10; 8.1–4.

13. See Dionysius, *Letter to Gnaeus Pompeius* 3; and *On Literary Composition* 6. See also Polybius, *The Histories* 1.4.2–3; 1.4.11; and 3.32.2; also Kenneth Sacks, *Polybius on the Writing of History*, University of California Publications in Classical Studies 24 (Berkeley: University of California Press, 1981), 108–9; and Frank W. Walbank, *Polybius*, Sather Classical Lectures 42 (Berkeley: University of California Press, 1972), 67.

14. Cf., e.g., Herodotus, *Histories* 1.1; Thucydides, *History of the Peloponnesian War* 1.23.6; Dionysius, *Roman Antiquities* 1.5.1–3; and Josephus, *The Jewish War* 1.9–12. See Paul Pedech, *La méthode historique de Polybe*, Collection d'études anciennes (Paris: Les Belles Lettres, 1964), 210.

15. Justus Cobet, *Herodots Exkurse und die Frage der Einheit seines Werkes*, Historia Einzelschriften 17 (Wiesbaden: Franz Steiner, 1971), 140.

importance of the narrative's ability to coax its recipients along through the course of events so that they would not become wearied or bored.[16] Obviously, the attentiveness of the reader is critical to the narrative experience, especially when one considers the importance of *each* selected narrative episode. Since a random presentation of events — a presentation that did *not* potentially lead the reader to the next event — was considered to be deficient and ineffective, one cannot overemphasize the importance of the reader's attention.[17] Therefore, the arrangement of narrative events in Acts functions in two ways: the development of the thematic or conceptual unity of the historical work, and the concern for the reader's response to the narrative presentation.

These concerns for literary arrangement are not confined only to matters of holding the reader's interest. We find the effectiveness of the ancient historical text in what one may describe as "the narrative process." The description of one event does not provide the basis for history, nor does it alone deliver the potential benefits of the historical text to the reader. However, single events, linked in an interrelated work of art, contribute cumulatively to the potential benefits and function of ancient history. The Acts narrative directs the reader toward its ultimate aim by taking one step-by-step through the selected events, thereby urging the reader to make one's own judgments based on tentative interpretations from the presentation of previous narrative episodes.[18] Descriptions of narrative events and the effect on readers depend on those readers' involvement in and judgments of earlier episodes. Only in the narrative process, through which the reader accumulates impressions and makes judgments along the way, may the reader advance to an understanding and perception of what the narrative depicts. This cumulative effect is what Longinus perceived in the presentation of narrative events — an effect through αὔξησις or "amplification."[19] Thus, the historical text was expected to offer sequentially only one episode at a time and to distinguish the depiction of each episode with clarity and completeness. Lucian advised the historian to introduce the subsequent episode only after

---

16. Dionysius, *On the Style of Demosthenes* 45.

17. See Aristotle, *Poetics* 9.11.

18. Cf. Chaim Perelman and L. Olbrechts-Tyteca, *The New Rhetoric: A Treatise on Argumentation*, trans. John Wilkinson and Purcell Weaver (Notre Dame, IN: University of Notre Dame Press, 1969), 491. See Iser, *The Implied Reader*, 275, 288; and *The Act of Reading*, 112.

19. Longinus, *On the Sublime* 11.1–12.2; cf. 23.1, where Longinus also described the effectiveness of "accumulation" (ἀθροισμοί) in terms of effect. Cf. the use of αὔξησις by Dionysius, *On Thucydides* 19.

finishing the first one, thus allowing each episode to contribute to the narrative as a whole.[20] These historians compared their work with drama or tragedy; they visualized individual episodes like scenes of a play.[21] Each part contributes to the whole but does not contribute equally. Through a combination of literary patterns and the creative episodic arrangement, a historical narrative such as Acts escorts its reader to a potential point of final judgment and response.

The creative arrangement of the historical narrative of Acts, therefore, serves to bring clarity and interest to what that narrative describes. The narrative plot, not the chronological account of a certain historical period, dictates the arrangement of the Acts events or episodes.[22] That is, chronology does not explain anything by itself and is not always easy to follow.[23] Thus, Lucian suggested that the historian give considerable attention to the arrangement of the narrative and emphasized the importance of the progression and smoothness of the narrative's flow.[24] The ancient historians were expected to arrange their works with the plot, theme, and potential effects in mind. The historical narrative thereby presents the selected events as connected by these judgments rather than by chronological sequence.

The other major category by which the author's creative contributions are often recognized in ancient historiography is the use of artistic techniques. The importance of artistic technique to such history writing parallels Greco-Roman educational and rhetorical interests in literary style and technique. Just as Greco-Roman education emphasized the reading of classical literature and the imitation of literary style, so also

---

20. Lucian, *How to Write History* 55.

21. Fornara, *The Nature of History in Ancient Greece and Rome*, 171–72.

22. E.g., Josephus promised to write κατὰ τὴν οἰκείαν τάξιν, "according to the proper order" (*Jewish Antiquities* 1.17), which he clarified later as τὸ κατὰ γένος ἕκαστα τάξαι, "the arrangement according to subject" (ibid., 4.197). Cf. Luke 1:3. See Shaye J. D. Cohen, *Josephus in Galilee and Rome: His Vita and Development as a Historian*, Columbia Studies in the Classical Tradition 8 (Leiden: Brill, 1979), 3–23, 66–67; and Tessa Rajak, *Josephus: The Historian and His Society* (Philadelphia: Fortress, 1983), 144–73.

23. See Aristotle, *Poetics* 9.3; 23.2. See also Dionysius, *On Thucydides* 9; and idem, *Letter to Gnaeus Pompeius* 3. Cf. Donald Lateiner, *The Historical Method of Herodotus* (Toronto: University of Toronto Press, 1989), 120; also Kurt von Fritz, *Die griechische Geschichtsschreibung*, 2 vols. (Berlin: Walter de Gruyter, 1967), 1 (part 1): 780–84, who concludes that Thucydides employed a chronological *sequence* but not a chronological *scheme* in his work.

24. Lucian, *How to Write History* 47–48, 55. Lucian stressed the importance of the connection of the narrative episodes so that the narrative *as a whole* is not disjointed.

did history writers look to the study of literature for technical assistance in creating a narrative that would potentially evoke a positive response. Discussions about literary techniques include everything from word choice to word order and from different writing styles to vividness in description.[25] Lucian stated that literary techniques are helpful to τὴν προσήκουσαν, "the one who heard" or the one the narrative addressed, not for the creation (ποίησις) of the work itself.[26] Thus, all literary devices or techniques must assist in fulfilling that function. The primary aim of ancient historiography was not the demonstration of the author's literary skill but the work's potential beneficial effect on its readers.[27] Longinus contended that the effect or greatness of any literary text depends not on exquisite style or literary technique but on "the mere force of composition and verbal carpentry."[28] Dionysius's criticism against the work of the historian Thucydides implies similar sentiments: Thucydides often lapsed into a literary style that was inaccessible to his audience, and this habit resulted in a limited potential function of his literary composition.[29]

The reception of historiography and other literary works including Acts requires a covert quality of artistic composition.[30] Thus, the historian, as *author* of the historical narrative, served as the creative composer of the text. The historian decided which events to develop or magnify as matters of importance (e.g., through repetition) and which events to treat scantily, as of lesser importance.[31] Certain events, individuals, or groups

---

25. For Greco-Roman discussions on literary techniques, see, e.g., Aristotle, *Poetics* and *Rhetoric*; Demetrius, *On Style*; Dionysius, *The Critical Essays*; and Longinus, *On the Sublime*.

26. Lucian, *How to Write History* 35.

27. This is not to say, however, that there was *no* concern for literary technique or dramatic presentation. Cf. P. A. Brunt, *Studies in Greek History and Thought* (Oxford: Clarendon, 1993), 181–82, who suggests that historians *did* seek to outshine their predecessors in their dramatic and often sensational descriptions, but that did not eradicate the beneficial aim of history.

28. Longinus, *On the Sublime* 40.1–2.

29. Dionysius, *On Thucydides* 51–52. Cf. G. M. A. Grube, *The Greek and Roman Critics* (London: Methuen, 1965), 229; and Emilio Gabba, *Dionysius and the History of Archaic Rome*, Sather Classical Lectures 56 (Berkeley: University of California Press, 1991), 67–69.

30. See Dionysius, *On Thucydides* 51, who stressed that history "should contain an element of artistry; and yet it should not be entirely artificial" (LCL; ἀλλ᾽ ἔχουσάν τι καὶ ποιητικόν· οὔτε παντάπασι ποιητικήν); Demetrius, *On Style* 1.19, who advised that the writing of narrative not "seem rhetorical and unconvincing through its moulded shapeliness" (LCL); and Longinus, *On the Sublime* 17.2.

31. See Dionysius, *On Thucydides* 13–18, who reprimanded Thucydides for his lack of care in the development (ἐξεργασία) of certain episodes, either by allotting too much space to

may receive greater emphasis through amplification or artistic embellishment, as the narrative imaginatively depicts selected scenes or individuals to accentuate what is significant.[32] Polybius often depicted characters or events by using common literary forms, or *topoi*, creating through familiarity a certain impression in the minds of the reader while attempting to underscore the notable.[33] Others also used literary topoi to describe scenes or individuals in early sections of the historical narrative, thus providing the reader with literary patterns or allusions by which to judge or evaluate later narrative episodes or characters.[34] Dionysius stressed that the description and arrangement of narrative materials in two contrasting groups, especially regarding significant characters in the work, was a forceful means by which to create the desired effect. By focusing on the contrast between two character groups rather than a description of every "trivial matter" (μικρολογῶν), Dionysius suggested that the author could powerfully emphasize the "whole *thesis*" (ὅλη τῇ θέσει) with the "whole *antithesis*" (ὅλην τὴν ἀντίθεσιν; emphases added).[35] However the author composed the work, the use of artistry for the sake of emphasis requires restraint through moderation. Excessive literary creativity may diminish the potential effect on the reader.[36] The desired effect of that creative presentation depends on the narrative *experience* shared by that reader.

---

the unimportant or by hurrying over matters of greater importance. See also Lucian, *How to Write History* 32, 56. Cf. Dionysius, *On the Style of Demosthenes* 18; and Longinus, *On the Sublime* 23.4, who disagree concerning *how* the historian should emphasize certain matters. Dionysius suggested that *artistic* elaboration or adornment emphasizes matters of importance. Longinus, however, suggested emphasis through *quantitative* amplification or accumulation.

32. See Fornara, *The Nature of History in Ancient Greece and Rome*, 136; and Brunt, *Studies in Greek History and Thought*, 181–209, esp. 188, 202–4.

33. See Polybius, *The Histories* 15.9.1–15.16.6; and D'Huys, "Κρήσιμον καὶ τερπνόν in Polybios' Schlachtschilderungen," 267–88. See also Herodotus, *Histories* 1, where his portrayal of Croesus provides the paradigm for the five Persian rulers that follow him; cf. Charles Rowan Beye, *Ancient Greek Literature and Society*, 2nd ed. (Ithaca, NY: Cornell University Press, 1987), 208–13; and von Fritz, *Die griechische Geschichtsschreibung*, 1 (part 1): 466.

34. Cf. Peter Toohey, *Reading Epic: An Introduction to the Ancient Narratives* (New York: Routledge, 1992), 14, who suggests that parallel scenes in epics provide their thematic bases.

35. Dionysius, *On the Style of Demosthenes* 21. Cf. Robert L. Brawley, *Centering on God: Method and Message in Luke-Acts*, LCBI (Louisville: Westminster/John Knox, 1990), 67–85.

36. See Dionysius, *On the Style of Demosthenes* 18: "Isocrates does not always strike the right note for the occasion. This is because he insists on making his language colorful and showy at all costs, believing that in literature pleasure should reign supreme. Consequently he sometimes fails to achieve the required effect, since not all subjects demand the same manner of expression" (LCL). See also Longinus, *On the Sublime* 16–29. Cf. D. A. Russell, *Criticism in Antiquity* (Berkeley: University of California Press, 1981), 146.

Thus, the possible effects of ancient historiography limit such artistic and creative elements to those that would potentially achieve such ends.

Because the original recipients of ancient texts such as Acts listened to the public reading of those texts, these historical narratives reflect the aural character of that audience. The oral presentation or reading of the ancient literary text demands an arrangement and clarity that allows for an audience's hearing, interest, involvement, and response *without* the privilege of reviewing the *textual* accounts that a reader would have encountered previously.[37] To fulfill the obligation to a listening audience, a narrative must present potential themes or purposes of the work clearly, convincingly, and *simply*; readings based on complex analyses often ignore the aural nature of the ancient text. By encouraging the audience's involvement, the Acts narrative potentially guides listeners in forming their own judgments, both by what is presented and by what is not.[38] The textual elements combine the evidence of each event with the stimulation of the audience's interest and emotions so that an appropriate and beneficial response may result at its conclusion. Thus, the whole Acts narrative potentially compels its recipients to draw benefit from the encounter and experience of that text, but does so with elements appropriated for a listener rather than a reader.

The assumption behind these ancient discussions of literary composition is that the reader's encounter with the narrative text has a cumulative effect: the imaginative combination of episodic arrangement and order, literary patterns and emphases, character depictions, descriptive allusions and repetition, and other textual elements potentially usher that reader to a point of final judgment and response. Obviously, these concerns for the effect of such textual elements on the reader of Acts suggest that one must not ignore the role of that reader. On the one hand, in the reading process the reader progressively encounters and must account for what Wolfgang Iser identifies as the repertoire and strategies

---

37. See Moore, *Literary Criticism and the Gospels*, 84–88, who correctly warns about the failure to recognize the differences between *reading* the text and *hearing* it read.

38. See Demetrius, *On Style* 4.222, who credits Theophrastus with the important consideration that "not all points should be punctiliously and tediously elaborated, but some should be left to the comprehension and inference of the hearer, who when he perceives what you have left unsaid becomes not only your hearer but [also] your witness, and a very friendly witness too. For he thinks himself intelligent because you have afforded him the means of showing his intelligence. It seems like a slur on your hearer to tell him everything as though he were a simpleton" (LCL).

of the text: the text's repertoire as those intertextual and extratextual historical and social concepts, values, and practices (including literary conventions) with which the reader may or may not be familiar;[39] and the text's strategies as those intratextual connections between various parts of that text.[40] Thus, scholars generally turn to the text's repertoire to define the "implied reader"[41] but turn to the text's strategies to identify its internal logic or rhetoric. To be sure, the Acts narrative provides — either explicitly or implicitly or both — much of what the reader needs to know and numerous textual elements, connections, and clues from that which one reads and therefore begins to build consistency.

On the other hand, the wide range of what may be included in the textual repertoire and strategies still forces the reader to select from all the possible meanings that Acts allows.[42] The reader, not the text alone, decides which meaning will be realized and which possible meanings will be excluded.[43] Since no text provides the reader with all the information or connections necessary for its realization, these textual indeterminacies or "gaps" stimulate the reader's imagination so that one fills in those gaps in ways that build a consistent reading.[44] These interpretive or reading activities, whether conscious to the reader or not, bring the Acts text to life, and without them the text remains lifeless and meaningless.[45] One is aware, however, that one's reading of the biblical text does not exhaust all possible readings, since other possibilities remain that one's own reading inevitably excludes.[46] Thus, while one may seek to read a text like Acts in ways that build consistency out of the textual elements,

---

39. Iser, *The Act of Reading*, 68–85, 152. Cf. Darr, *On Character Building*, 22–23; and Mary Ann Tolbert, *Sowing the Gospel: Mark's World in Literary-Historical Perspective* (Minneapolis: Fortress, 1989), 54.

40. Iser, *The Act of Reading*, 86–103.

41. For different definitions of "implied reader," see Booth, *The Rhetoric of Fiction*, 138; and Iser, *The Act of Reading*, 34. For brief discussions on the Lukan implied reader, see, e.g., Joseph B. Tyson, *Images of Judaism in Luke-Acts* (Columbia: University of South Carolina Press, 1992), 19–41; Darr, *On Character Building*, 23–29; Tannehill, *Luke*, 24–27; and William S. Kurz, *Reading Luke-Acts: Dynamics of Biblical Narrative* (Louisville: Westminster/John Knox, 1993), 12–16.

42. Iser, *The Act of Reading*, 122–25.

43. Iser, *The Implied Reader*, 280.

44. Iser, *The Act of Reading*, 163–231; and Sternberg, *The Poetics of Biblical Narrative*, 235–37.

45. Cf. Iser, *The Implied Reader*, 275: "The convergence of text and reader brings the literary work into existence."

46. See ibid., 280.

one also recognizes that such a reading does not exclude other possible readings that also seek to do the same thing.[47]

One must stress, then, that neither the biblical text nor the reader controls the reading process. On the one hand, the text leads, summons, and coaxes the reader along the way with various literary elements.[48] The text places a kind of accountability on the reader but gives no assurances that the reader either will recognize every possible textual connection and clue or will discover the significance of every textual element. On the other hand, no text including Acts provides all the necessary clues and information for a consistent reading. Thus, this lack of textual provision leaves to the reader the process of filling in textual indeterminacies in ways that are consistent with what the text states or describes. The reader's encounter with a text like Acts leaves much to one's imagination, which the text itself stimulates and provokes. Nonetheless, the text does not and cannot control one's reading or interpretation; with reading come both responsibility and freedom for the interpretive responses.[49]

READING CHARACTERS IN ANCIENT NARRATIVES

The importance of characters to historiography is related to the very essence of a narrative like Acts. If ancient historiography, like poetry, includes plot as a *mimesis* of human action (πρᾶξις),[50] then human beings and groups, the characters of the story, are critical to that presentation and its potential readings. However, the suggestion that one can legitimately study these characters by themselves (i.e., apart from other

---

47. See Robert C. Tannehill, "'Cornelius' and 'Tabitha' Encounter Luke's Jesus," *Int* 48 (1994): 347–56, who shows how two different persons in ancient times may have understood certain parts of Luke's Gospel.

48. Cf. Stephen D. Moore, "Deconstructive Criticism: The Gospel of the Mark," in *Mark and Method: New Approaches in Biblical Studies*, ed. Janice Capel Anderson and Stephen D. Moore (Minneapolis: Fortress, 1992), 93: "The critic, while appearing to comprehend a literary text from a position outside or above it, is in fact being comprehended, being grasped, by the text. He or she is unwittingly acting out an interpretive role that the text has scripted, even dramatized, in advance."

49. See Robert C. Tannehill, "Freedom and Responsibility in Scripture Interpretation, with Application to Luke," in *Literary Studies in Luke-Acts: Essays in Honor of Joseph B. Tyson*, ed. Richard P. Thompson and Thomas E. Phillips (Macon, GA: Mercer University Press, 1998), 265–78.

50. Gerald F. Else, *Plato and Aristotle on Poetry* (Chapel Hill: University of North Carolina Press, 1986), 80–81.

narrative elements) is an overstatement.[51] If one takes seriously the reading process mentioned above, then the reader does not merely explore characterization as a feature inherent to the literary text itself. Rather, the reader also constructs and evaluates characters whom one encounters in the progressive reading of that narrative.[52] The reader of the Acts narrative, then, must build the Lukan characters in ways that account for both the text's repertoire (i.e., those intertextual and extratextual elements) and strategies (i.e., those intratextual elements). In the study of Greco-Roman literature, one finds several general features or aspects of character depiction that become useful tools in the building and evaluation of characters through one's reading of Acts: indirect or implicit description, direct or explicit description, the manner or categories by which the text depicts characters, the accumulation of pictures and effect, and the interaction and interplay among characters in the narrative.[53]

Indirect Description

One aspect of character depiction in Greco-Roman literature is related to the prominent focus on human action. The indirect description (or implicit presentation) of a character through human action is the dominant means of presenting characters, both in Greco-Roman literature and in Acts.[54] This attention on the action of characters as an indirect means of depicting them does not ignore the ancient understanding of the relation between human action and human "character," ἦθος.[55] Aristotle stressed the subordination of ἦθος to the plot because no "character" exists apart from action. One can only appeal to "character" that is observable in action.[56] By telling about the action of the literary character, the author

---

51. See C. Garton, "Characterisation in Greek Tragedy," *JHS* 77 (1957): 247.

52. Cf. Darr, *On Character Building*, 37; and William H. Shepherd Jr., *The Narrative Function of the Holy Spirit as a Character in Luke-Acts*, SBLDS 147 (Atlanta: Scholars Press, 1994), 80–82.

53. Cf. Sternberg, *The Poetics of Biblical Narrative*, 476–80, who gives a list of fifteen devices for characterization; and David B. Gowler, *Host, Guest, Enemy and Friend: Portraits of the Pharisees in Luke and Acts*, Emory Studies in Early Christianity 2 (New York: Peter Lang, 1991), 55–75.

54. Cf. Robert Alter, *The Art of Biblical Narrative* (New York: Basic Books, 1981), 116–17; Gowler, *Host, Guest, Enemy and Friend*, 130; Shepherd, *The Narrative Function of the Holy Spirit*, 88; and Darr, *On Character Building*, 44.

55. For the sake of clarity, ἦθος or "character" will specifically depict the Greek term. The word character (without quotation marks) pertains to individuals or groups of a literary work.

56. See Aristotle, *Poetics* 6.8. Cf. Marguerite Deslauriers, "Character and Explanation in Aristotle's Ethics and Poetics," *Dialogue* 29 (1990): 83.

reveals that person's ἦθος implicitly because ἦθος not only is related to the *cause* of action but also is *developed* through action.[57] Thus, πρᾶξις sufficiently identifies or signifies ἦθος in cases where the person's choice or προαίρεσις is exposed, even though action and not "character" is the point of significance.[58] The ancient understanding of "character" included choice, rationality, and human responsibility, which influence the actions of all persons.[59]

The interrelation of action and ἦθος as portrayed in the literary text helps to explain why the direct or explicit description of ἦθος was often unnecessary. The narrative depicts selected actions of a chosen group of interacting characters, actions that often reveal the ἦθος of each character or group and actions that ἦθος informs.[60] Ancient literary practice tends to reflect this connection between human activity and ἦθος through the implicit contrast and comparison of the depicted *action* of various characters, not of the characters per se.[61] The narrative frequently shows

---

57. In *Poetics* 6.7, Aristotle states that "character and thought are the natural causes of any action" (LCL); πέφυκε δ' αἴτια δύο τῶν πράξεων εἶναι, διάνοιαν καὶ ἦθος. In his *Nicomachean Ethics*, Aristotle considers the relation between human activity and ἕξις, in that one's actions develops ἕξις or "disposition" (2.2.1). At the same time, one's ἕξις also determines the motives for one's actions (3.5.17). The individual's προαίρεσις or "choice" between good and evil provides the basis for the moral development of ἕξις (3.2.11). The two concepts of ἕξις and ἦθος are interrelated in that both are acquired and realized in action. However, ἕξις is the disposition or "habit" to act in a certain way, whereas ἦθος is the ethical quality of that action. Thus, the actions or dialogue of the literary text best revealed a person's ἦθος if they indicate some kind of προαίρεσις (*Poetics* 15.2). If προαίρεσις is not indicated, two scenarios are possible. One scenario suggests that the person or group might reflect a developed disposition or ἕξις in a given action but not reflect precisely the ἦθος or ethical quality of that action (cf. *Nicomachean Ethics* 3.2.1). A second scenario suggests that the action is not of a moral nature, not demanding a choice between "good" and "evil." Cf. Stephen Halliwell, *Aristotle's Poetics* (Chapel Hill: University of North Carolina Press, 1986), 150–51; and Lionel Pearson, "Characterization in Drama and Oratory — *Poetics* 1450a20," CQ 18 (1968): 76–83.

58. Halliwell, *Aristotle's Poetics*, 164.

59. See Stephen Halliwell, "Traditional Greek Conceptions of Character," in *Characterization and Individuality in Greek Literature*, ed. Christopher Pelling (Oxford: Clarendon, 1990), 35: "The chief elements [of the traditional conceptions of character] I have in mind are as follows: first, a basic recognition of the psychological identity of individuals, which is not to be equated with a theory of individualism and which does not override social or status-based components of identity; second, the ascription to individuals of at least some powers of choice and self-directed agency; third, the existence of criteria, however rudimentary, of rationality (in particular, criteria bearing on the *reasons* which can be given for choices of action); fourth, some conception of human responsibility, involving a sense of standards of applicability of praise and blame to agents and their actions."

60. Christopher Pelling, "Conclusion," in Pelling, *Characterization and Individuality in Greek Literature*, 256.

61. See Dionysius, *On the Style of Demosthenes* 21.

the reader these characters by describing their actions with literary topoi or social ideals, often portraying two different characters so that the reader may compare and contrast them.[62] A narrative focus on characters' actions provides little explicit information about those characters themselves; the narrative merely tells selectively about what they do. Nonetheless, the reader must actively make judgments and decisions about those characters from the information that the text provides.[63]

Through the employment of indirect description, the portrayed actions of narrative characters implicitly attribute certain features to them. Ancient historical narratives, including Acts, often include speeches and dialogue by one or more characters in describing narrative action.[64] These speeches and dialogue reflect the respective character's mind or point of view and frequently function as vehicles through which the narrator may subtly guide the judgments and understanding of the reader regarding the character.[65] The words of a reliable character often function as implicit commentary for the narrator and potentially provide assistance to the reader in one's perceptions of preceding and subsequent events and characters.[66] Thus, an aspect of character depiction for which one's reading of Acts and its characters must account is the employment of indirect description: the description of characters that selectively focuses on what the reader oneself would see if witnessing the event firsthand.

Direct Description

A second aspect of character depiction in Greco-Roman literature is the use of direct description (or explicit presentation) in portraying characters. The ancient employment of indirect description or implicit

---

62. Cf. Plümacher, *Lukas als hellenistischer Schriftsteller*, 16; and David A. Holgate, *Prodigality, Liberality and Meanness: The Prodigal Son in Greco-Roman Perspective*, JSNTSup 187 (Sheffield: Sheffield Academic Press, 1999), 92–99. See Pericles and Cleon in Thucydides, *History of the Peloponnesian War*; also Beye, *Ancient Greek Literature and Society*, 231.

63. An excellent example of a Greek historiographer who relied on indirect description is Thucydides. See Henry D. Westlake, *Individuals in Thucydides* (Cambridge, UK: Cambridge University Press, 1968).

64. Cf. E. Auerbach, *Mimesis: The Representation of Reality in Western Literature* (Princeton: Princeton University Press, 1953), 39.

65. Cf. Alter, *The Art of Biblical Narrative*, 117; and David B. Gowler, "Characterization in Luke: A Socio-Narratological Approach," *BTB* 19 (April 1989): 56.

66. See Virginia J. Hunter, *Thucydides: The Artful Reporter* (Toronto: Hakkert, 1973); and Henry R. Immerwahr, *Form and Thought in Herodotus* (Cleveland: Western Reserve University Press, 1966), who stress the use of speeches to anticipate future narrative events in ancient historiography. See also Kurz, *Reading Luke-Acts*, 135–55.

presentation does not exclude the use of direct descriptions or explicit statements that tell the reader about certain characters.[67] Historical narratives from the Greco-Roman era often appropriate explicit statements of judgment or description in the portrayal of certain characters that provide additional information the reader may need to evaluate those characters' actions.[68] These explicit statements or descriptions may reveal motives, emotions, or thoughts that the reader may not observe oneself if witnessing the event firsthand. Such statements may also take the form of a summary that directly informs the reader about certain actions and may offer some basic conclusions about them. Given the dominance of the use of indirect description, however, these explicit statements about a character suggest the narrator's concern that the reader understand correctly the respective action and its related "character."[69] That is, by telling the reader directly about the character, the narrator seems to limit somewhat the reader's role in making the necessary connections and judgments. The narrative portrayal of the story's actors, however, usually does not fully develop those characters.[70] Such representation reflects the influence of orality in Greco-Roman culture.[71] While ancient historical narratives may describe some circumstances or events in significant detail, the descriptions of characters are usually limited to a few details necessary to envisage the situation and persons.[72] Simplicity in character portrayal is a representative feature of Greco-Roman literature.[73] Whether the description is direct or indirect, such

---

67. See Booth, *The Rhetoric of Fiction*, 3–20.

68. E.g., on the character Pericles, see Thucydides, *History of the Peloponnesian War* 1.127.3; 1.139.4; 2.65.5–13. On Cleon, see ibid., 3.36.6; 4.21.3. See also "Explicit Judgements on Ability and Character," in Westlake, *Individuals in Thucydides*, 5–19. On Polybius, see Walbank, *Polybius*, 92. See, e.g., Polybius, *The Histories* 10.26.9, who stated that his practice was not to describe an individual in a general way when that one first appeared in the narrative, but to make comments on "character" and to pass moral judgments on each separate incident.

69. See Meir Sternberg, *Expositional Modes and Temporal Ordering in Fiction* (Baltimore: Johns Hopkins University Press, 1978), 93–102; and Alter, *The Art of Biblical Narrative*, 117.

70. Consider the tendency of ancient literary practice to present characters that are not as fully developed as characters in modern literary works.

71. Cf. Werner H. Kelber, *The Oral and the Written Gospel: The Hermeneutics of Speaking and Writing in the Synoptic Tradition, Mark, Paul, and Q* (Philadelphia: Fortress, 1983), 69.

72. See Garton, "Characterisation in Greek Tragedy," 249; and Simon Goldhill, "Character and Action, Representation and Reading: Greek Tragedy and Its Critics," in Pelling, *Characterization and Individuality in Greek Literature*, 102.

73. Cf. Pelling, "Conclusion," in Pelling, *Characterization and Individuality in Greek Literature*, 246–47.

literature typically provides *relevant* information about the narrative's characters, so that it may in certain ways coax along the reader's attempt to make the necessary judgment and connections. However, because of the scarcity of information about the characters, the potential for a significant number of textual gaps exists. Thus, a reading of Acts requires not only the consideration of the depicted character's actions and implications, but also due regard for what the narrative states either directly or indirectly about them.[74]

The Manner or Categories of Character Depiction

A third aspect of character depiction in Greco-Roman literature is the manner or categories by which the narrative text presents the respective characters. That is, the reader of Acts should consider not only the indirect or direct descriptions of the characters within the text (including intratextual connections) but also the categories or manner (including both intertextual and extratextual connections) by which the narrative presents those characters and from which that reader constructs and evaluates them. A critical issue concerning character depiction in Greco-Roman literature, articulated most distinctively in several essays by Christopher Gill, focuses on two categories of character portrayal: characters as typical figures, and characters as individual personalities.[75]

The depiction of characters as typical figures focuses on those narrative descriptions that employ (either indirectly or directly) common social categories. The "character-viewpoint," to use Gill's designation, describes narrative participants as those who reflect or violate typical social behavior. These characters are often depicted in similar ways, so that the individuality of the character may seem to be lost.[76] However, the important distinction here is not necessarily the *degree* to which characters are depicted in typical social categories, but the *evaluative framework* by which these characters are presented and through which the reader may assess them.[77] Gill suggests that this way of depicting character reflects normative assumptions about human nature and behavior:

---

74. Ibid., 248–49.

75. See Christopher Gill, "The Question of Character-Development: Plutarch and Tacitus," *CQ* 33 (1983): 469–87; idem, "The *Éthos/Pathos* Distinction in Rhetorical and Literary Criticism," *CQ* 34 (1984): 149–66; idem, "The Question of Character and Personality in Greek Tragedy," *Poetics Today* 7 (1986): 251–73; and idem, "The Character-Personality Distinction," in Pelling, 1–31.

76. Cf. Beye, *Ancient Greek Literature and Society*, 17.

77. Cf. Holgate, *Prodigality, Liberality and Meanness*, 92–99.

The person is, typically, treated as a "moral agent," responsible for his actions and their consequences, and also responsible, at some level, for his feelings, and, at some other level, for the qualities or character-traits expressed in those actions and feelings. Typically too, the person is treated as, in principle at least, a rational being, whose actions derive from his beliefs and desires and reflect his intentions and motives.[78]

The narrative participants, therefore, are characterized by means of social conventions and norms.[79] This narrative presentation of persons or groups from a character-viewpoint allows for an assessment of such characters based on these social categories rather than individuality. Thus, this means of characterization allows for the comparison and contrast of characters by use of similar social categories, thereby affirming the characters who reflect traits acceptable to society.[80] For the reader to participate in the narrative, however, one must identify to some extent the social conventions of that narrative world: the social structure, values, and attitudes that a character's described behavior and inner thoughts suggest.[81] Thus, this portrayal of characters within the narrative potentially leads the reader to evaluate and make judgments about those characters based on these conceptual and descriptive categories.

The depiction of characters as individual personalities focuses on the narrative description of certain characters as unique individuals. Unlike the character-viewpoint, the "personality-viewpoint" does not place (either explicitly or implicitly) the person in an evaluative context but examines the person according to that character's distinctiveness as a unique personality. Although both viewpoints use descriptive statements to express the respective concerns, the latter is less evaluative. More common for the personality-viewpoint are statements and events that invite the reader either to share or try to understand the character's point of view.[82] Feelings and access to the character's mental processes are more

---

78. Gill, "The Question of Character and Personality in Greek Tragedy," 252.

79. See Aristotle, *Poetics* 15.2, where the tragic hero must be judged as good, implying some standard by which one might evaluate the character. See Gill, "The Question of Character and Personality in Greek Tragedy," 260.

80. Cf. Gill, "The Question of Character and Personality in Greek Tragedy," 257.

81. See P. E. Easterling, "Constructing Character in Greek Tragedy," in Pelling, *Characterization and Individuality in Greek Literature*, 88; Gill, "The *Éthos/Pathos* Distinction in Rhetorical and Literary Criticism," 164–65; and Halliwell, "Traditional Greek Conceptions of Character," 45, 50.

82. Gill, "The Question of Character and Personality in Greek Tragedy," 253.

common than a focus on the action.[83] However, the emotions of the characters themselves are not the primary concern; the concern is the arousal of the *reader's* emotions.[84] The personality-viewpoint does not confirm social attitudes and assumptions, but often questions their validity.[85] The danger that Plato identified in poetry reflects this idea of personality-viewpoint, for he feared poetry's power to induce listeners to share a character's emotions or to respond with empathy to that character rather than to guide them in making judgments about the character.[86] The depiction of characters as unique personalities, however, parallels more closely the Aristotelian concern that the tragic character be one with whom the audience may identify.[87] Thus, the portrayal of characters from a personality-viewpoint usually does not prompt judgment, but understanding.[88]

The distinctions made between character-viewpoint and personality-viewpoint provide useful ideas for the study of characterization in Acts.[89] These two viewpoints assist the reader in the delineation of character depiction in three areas: the explanation of actions, the evaluation of those characters and their actions, and the adoption of a particular perspective.[90] On the one hand, the character-viewpoint explains the reasons for the actions of a character as an active moral agent. This means of characterization identifies a framework of social conventions for the appraisal of the character. The character-viewpoint takes no special account of the perspective of the persons involved and may even be described as

---

83. Ibid., 256.

84. Cf. Gill, "The *Éthos/Pathos* Distinction in Rhetorical and Literary Criticism," 151–53. See Aristotle, *Poetics* 17.

85. Gill, "The Character-Personality Distinction," 6–7.

86. Plato, *The Republic* 10.605c–d. See Gill, "The Question of Character and Personality in Greek Tragedy," 258–59; and "The *Éthos/Pathos* Distinction in Rhetorical and Literary Criticism," 164–65. Cf. Booth, *The Rhetoric of Fiction*, 377–78.

87. Aristotle, *Poetics* 15.5.

88. However, Aristotle (*Poetics* 15.2) did prompt judgment, since only the depiction of a good man was appropriate for the tragedy, since the audience identified and empathized with him.

89. Halliwell, "Traditional Greek Conceptions of Character," 56–59, makes similar distinctions, categorizing two modes of characterization: the descriptive or narrative, and the dramatic. For Halliwell, the descriptive or narrative mode "tends to give us more 'distanced,' sometimes moralistic, images of individuals, set firmly in the terms of general ethical categories" (58). The dramatic mode, in contrast, places characters "dramatically before our eyes, to let them speak for themselves, even, at the extreme, to give us privileged access to the workings of their minds" (58).

90. Cf. Gill, "The Character-Personality Distinction," 3–6.

impartial. On the other hand, the personality-viewpoint explains the causes of action directed toward the passive character. This means of characterization appraises the character through that one's individuality or distinctiveness and tends to identify with the perspective of a specific character, which in some instances may be a character group (i.e., several persons who function in the narrative as one character). These distinctions suggest not only different *aspects* or elements of character depiction in Greco-Roman literature but also different *kinds* of depiction in terms of focus and function. Each distinctive manner or kind of character portrayal brings and evokes certain assumptions, so that one must account for these different categories of portrayal in seeking to construct and evaluate respective characters within the Acts narrative.

The evidence from ancient thinkers and literature suggests that Greco-Roman audiences would have expected both kinds of character depiction. Generally, these two varieties of portraying characters correspond to ancient generic categories. On the one hand, the character-viewpoint, or the narrative means of character depiction, dominates the portraits in history and oratory.[91] On the other hand, the personality-viewpoint, or the dramatic means of character depiction, dominates the portraits of poetry and drama, particularly tragedy.[92] One must not insist on making distinct boundaries of demarcation, however, since ancient literary principles and practices do not adhere to these strict distinctions. Ancient literature often includes *both* kinds of the portrayal of characters within a given work.[93] Characterization in ancient literature fluctuates insofar as one may discover *degrees* of character depiction.[94] The significance lies, however, in the distinctive *function* of these two categories

---

91. See Gill, "The Question of Character-Development," 472; and Halliwell, "Traditional Greek Conceptions of Character," 58.

92. Gill, "The Question of Character and Personality in Greek Tragedy," 269–71, suggests that Aristotle adopted the character-viewpoint for tragedy, since the emotional reactions depend on the moral judgment that the tragic character is good. See also Halliwell, "Traditional Greek Conceptions of Character," 58.

93. See Gill, "The Question of Character and Personality in Greek Tragedy," 251–73; and "The Character-Personality Distinction," 1: "Greek tragedies are typically designed to invite a mixture of these types of response [responses relating to the character-viewpoint and the personality-viewpoint]; and that, at certain key moments, the audience is invited to shift from a character-viewpoint to a personality-viewpoint."

94. Cf. Adele Berlin, *Poetics and Interpretation of Biblical Narrative* (Sheffield: Almond Press, 1983), 32; Sternberg, *The Poetics of Biblical Narrative*, 321–64; and Fred W. Burnett, "Characterization and Reader Construction of Characters in the Gospels," *Semeia* 63 (1993): 15–19.

of portrayal. Failure to distinguish between these two ways of depicting narrative characters in Acts potentially leads to incorrect conclusions on issues such as function, theme, and point of view, if one takes seriously the expectations inherent to the narrative text itself.

The Accumulation of Pictures and Effect

A fourth aspect of character depiction in Greco-Roman literature is the accumulation of pictures and effect through the successive or progressive reading of the narrative. That is, the reader's construction and evaluation of characters in Acts depend on the accumulation of images and effect in the encounter of such characters through that narrative's sequential reading. To be sure, a tension exists between the sense of completeness in the narrative depiction of a particular episode or character and the cumulative effect of the *whole* narrative. As mentioned earlier, each narrative scene should reflect a sense of completeness and contribution.[95] On the one hand, the presentation of each episode invites the reader to make judgments, based on the experience of the depicted event and the characters involved. On the other hand, the narrative process that guides the reader from one event to another also reflects an evolutionary quality, in which effect and judgment are cumulative and redefined by the experience of each pericope. Since the actions that the Acts narrative depicts infer possible "character" traits or motives of the characters, these portrayals function within the narrative much like the specific episodes: each incidental depiction of a character contributes cumulatively to the narrative plot and to that character's portrayal in the narrative.[96]

This cumulative aspect of characterization in Greco-Roman literature is critical to the rhetorical nature of these ancient texts. Although action signified and strengthened the ἦθος of the character, ancient theorists recognized that one isolated act may occasionally deceive the observer since a person's actions may not *always* reflect that one's ἦθος.[97] One individual act may indicate one thing about that someone's ἦθος, but several examples of similar action provide substantiation.[98] The building and evaluation of a narrative's characters, whether they are individuals or groups, rely on a cumulative effect, through the presentation of several

---

95. Cf. Aristotle, *Poetics* 8.4.

96. Cf. Darr, *On Character Building*, 42–43.

97. Aristotle, *Nicomachean Ethics* 3.2.1.

98. Aristotle (*Rhetoric* 1.9.31) stressed that several examples of the good man acting according to προαίρεσις were necessary to substantiate the praise of that one.

selected examples of that character's actions, through a character's inter-action with other characters, and through the comparison or contrast between them. A character is not only inseparable from the narrative events or actions, but also is typically identifiable through interaction with other characters.[99] The accumulation of pictures and impressions within the narrative context invites appropriate and particular judgments from the reader along the way — judgments that, after retrospection, may even require revision of ones made earlier in the narrative process.[100] Ignoring the dynamic nature of the reading process, through which the reader encounters and experiences the textual elements progressively and sequentially, may cause the reader or critic to distort the function of those elements within the Acts text itself.[101]

The Interaction and Interplay between Narrative Characters

One final aspect of character depiction in Greco-Roman literature (men-tioned above) includes the interaction and interplay between narrative characters. Perhaps the most basic and important element in the por-trayal of the Acts characters is the web of relationships within which one finds all narrative actors.[102] The reader encounters any given char-acter within a narrative context that is itself defined and shaped by other characters and thereby builds and evaluates that character in light of the others. In part, narrative characters often "reveal *other* characters — to make, by their own choices and acts, rhetorical judgments on the choices and acts of others."[103] Both ancient and modern literary discus-sions recognize that the interaction and the interplay between characters potentially stimulate the reader to compare and contrast them within the overall rhetoric of the literary work.[104] Similarities and differences,

---

99. See Easterling, "Constructing Character in Greek Tragedy," 88.

100. Pelling, "Conclusion," in Pelling, *Characterization and Individuality in Greek Litera-ture*, 102, interprets ἦθος not as "a whole personality" but as a set of attitudes recognized in a particular course of action. Cf. Iser, *The Implied Reader*, 287–88; and *The Act of Reading*, 112.

101. Contra Moore, *Literary Criticism and the Gospels*, 15, whose understanding of char-acterization in the Gospels as "static" rather than "dynamic" does not lend itself to the cumulative nature of ancient characterization. Cf. Shepherd, *The Narrative Function of the Holy Spirit*, 77; and Gowler, *Host, Guest, Enemy and Friend*, 80–84.

102. See Darr, *On Character Building*, 41–42.

103. Mary D. Springer, *A Rhetoric of Literary Character: Some Women of Henry James* (Chicago: University of Chicago Press, 1978), 191.

104. See, e.g., Dionysius, *On the Style of Demosthenes* 21; and W. J. Harvey, *Character and the Novel* (Ithaca, NY: Cornell University Press, 1965), 53.

harmony and conflict, and support and opposition between different characters all offer the reader significant images from which to develop and appraise the characters in a given text.[105] The portrayals of narrative characters in Acts, then, are interdependent; the reader builds and assesses a character both in light of other Acts participants and in light of that character's narrative function.

CHARACTERIZATION AND THE ACTS OF THE APOSTLES

A study of characters, such as the churches or groups of Christian believers in Acts, must critically consider the contributions of both the text and the reader. Characterization, as presented in this study, refers *both* to the textual images and descriptions of characters *and* to the reader's construction, evaluation, and reevaluation of those characters as one reads progressively and sequentially through the narrative. While contributing to the building of certain Acts characters in the reading of that New Testament book, the reader must account for the textual features and clues that reflect the nature and expectations of a Greco-Roman historical narrative, including the aspects of character depiction in such ancient literature as mentioned above. A literary assessment of both the various portraits of churches or groups of Christian believers in the Acts of the Apostles and the function of those portraits requires critical attention to these literary features. It is to that task that this study now turns.

---

105. See Cancik, "The History of Culture, Religion, and Institutions in Ancient Historiography," 695.

T W O

THE JERUSALEM CHURCH
AS NARRATIVE CHARACTER
(ACTS 1:1–8:3)

The purpose of this study is to examine critically the different portrayals of churches or groups of Christian believers within the ancient narrative context of the book of Acts. This examination utilizes basic ancient literary conventions and concerns that are common to Greco-Roman historiography with a specific objective: to provide a reading of the book of Acts that considers the narrative function of these portrayals within the rhetorical presentation of that biblical text.

To fulfill this purpose, each of the next three chapters (including the current one) assesses the descriptions of early Christian groups or communities and their respective function in one of three units of the Acts narrative: 1:1–8:3; 8:4–12:25; and 13:1–28:31.[1] This study focuses on

---

1. Scholars offer many different options for the identification of basic narrative units in Acts. E.g., many commentators identify the first break between Acts 5 and 6 [see, e.g., F. F. Bruce, *The Book of the Acts*, rev. ed., NICNT (Grand Rapids: Eerdmans, 1988), viii; and I. Howard Marshall, *The Acts of the Apostles*, TNTC (Leicester: Inter-Varsity, 1980), 51]. Others identify the first major break between Acts 12 and 13 [see, e.g., William Neil, *Acts*, NCB (Grand Rapids: Eerdmans, 1973), 152–53; and Joseph B. Tyson, *Images of Judaism in Luke-Acts* (Columbia: University of South Carolina Press, 1992), 130]. The reasons for delineating the major narrative units as 1:1–8:3; 8:4–12:25; and 13:1–28:31 are as follows:

  1. The unit of 1:1–8:3 focuses exclusively on events in Jerusalem and the developing Jerusalem church until the Christians are scattered to other areas. Cf. Robert C. Tannehill, "The Composition of Acts 3–5: Narrative Development and Echo Effect," in *SBLSP* (1984), 218.

  2. The unit of 8:4–12:25 focuses on the gospel's initial spread to non-Jewish persons outside Jerusalem. Thus, the geographical circle widens as the Samaritans and Gentiles initially receive the gospel. The narrative focuses on some difficulties that arise for the Christian community with this broadening context.

29

those descriptions of the churches or respective groups of Christians that contribute to a narrative scene as a character.[2] Because characterization in ancient historiography relies significantly on the cumulative effect of descriptions, this reading of Acts will examine each description according to its sequential location within the narrative. For each examined description, the inclusion of three elements is essential to preserve the specific focus and the ancient narrative form of the text. One element is a basic summary of the narrative context, including a summary of the narrative sequence, depictions, and emphases leading up to the passage in question. The second and most comprehensive element is a literary analysis of the narrative event or scene, an analysis that centers specifically on the characterization of the specific early Christian group or church and its role both in the respective scene and in the narrative as that character interacts, compares, and contrasts with other characters.[3] The third element is an initial assessment of the specific instance of characterization as part of the Acts narrative, drawing out its potential function and implications for this reading of the book of Acts.

THE EARLIEST BELIEVERS AFTER
JESUS' ASCENSION (ACTS 1:12–26)

The Literary Context (Acts 1:1–11)

The first description of a group of Christian believers is located in Acts 1, a literary context framed by the ascension of Jesus and the extraordinary

---

3. The unit of 13:1–28:31 focuses on events connected with Paul's ministry to both Jews and Gentiles of the Roman Empire, including his arrest and "trials." In this unit, the Christian community deals with an increasing Gentile presence among what initially has been a group of Jewish believers.

For the purposes of this study, however, the precise identification of distinct literary units is not as significant as the recognition of the progressive and cumulative nature of the narrative and, more specifically, the characterization of churches or groups of Christians as one textual component.

2. Since Luke does not use consistent terminology in naming the Christians (see 11:26), this study includes significant references to what one may call a group of Christian believers (i.e., more than two). For convenience, in this study "believers," "Christians," and "church" will be most commonly used to designate those who are part of the Christian community, although the latter two designations do not initially appear. However, these designations are not intended to refer to an institution separate from Judaism.

3. As this study will indicate, the character of the Christian church consistently and most prominently interacts and contrasts with Jewish characters in the Acts narrative.

events that the narrative presents as occurring on the day of Pentecost. Although the prologue of the book provides a link between the narratives of the Lukan Gospel and Acts,[4] the first eleven verses may serve as a transitional section, which reviews the conclusion of the Lukan Gospel and prepares the readers and hearers for the narrative that follows.[5]

This beginning section of the Acts narrative includes two scenes, both of which include statements by Jesus. After summarizing a period of forty days after Jesus' resurrection[6] as a time in which he taught the apostles about the "kingdom of God,"[7] the narrative describes Jesus as giving them orders (παρήγγειλεν; 1:4). Two infinitival phrases explicate these orders more fully: the apostles are not to leave Jerusalem (ἀπὸ Ἰεροσολύμων μὴ χωρίζεσθαι), and they are to wait for the Father's promise (περιμένειν τὴν ἐπαγγελίαν τοῦ πατρός). Jesus' words (1:5) further delineate something about that promise: *the apostles* would soon

---

4. On the one hand, the prologue explicitly refers to "the first work" (τὸν μὲν πρῶτον λόγον), which describes what "Jesus began both to do and teach" (ἤρξατο ὁ Ἰησοῦς ποιεῖν τε καὶ διδάσκειν; Acts 1:1). Cf., e.g., Alfons Weiser, *Die Apostelgeschichte*, 2 vols., ÖTNT (Würzburg: Echter, 1986), 1:47–48; and Hans Conzelmann, *Acts of the Apostles*, trans. James Limburg et al., Hermeneia (Philadelphia: Fortress, 1987), 3–4. Contra Marie-Émile Boismard and A. Lamouille, *Les Actes des deux Apôtres*, 3 vols., ÉBib (Paris: Gabalda, 1990), 2:11. On the other hand, the prologue and the beginning of Acts are neatly woven together, providing a smooth transition from Luke's Gospel to Acts. See Lucian, *How to Write History 55*; and Jacques Dupont, "La question du plan des Actes des Apôtres à la lumière d'un texte de Lucien de Samosate," in *Nouvelles études sur les Actes des Apôtres*, LD 118 (Paris: Éditions du Cerf, 1984), 27–29.

5. See Luke T. Johnson, *The Acts of the Apostles*, SP 5 (Collegeville, MN: Liturgical Press, 1992), 28. Cf. Bruce, *The Book of the Acts*, 28; and Robert C. Tannehill, *The Narrative Unity of Luke-Acts: A Literary Interpretation*, 2 vols. (Philadelphia/Minneapolis: Fortress, 1986–90), 2:9–25.

6. "Forty days" contrasts with the inference in Luke 24 that in *one* day Jesus appears two times after his resurrection, clarifies what has occurred in the previous few days, and states his intention to send "the promise of the Father" (τὴν ἐπαγγελίαν τοῦ πατρός; 24:49), the same expression as in Acts 1:4. Cf., e.g., Conzelmann, *Acts of the Apostles*, 5–6; Ernst Haenchen, *The Acts of the Apostles: A Commentary*, trans. Bernard Noble and Gerald Shinn (Philadelphia: Westminster, 1971), 140–41; Gerhard Krodel, *Acts*, ACNT (Minneapolis: Augsburg, 1986), 56; Neil, *Acts*, 64; and Tannehill, *The Narrative Unity of Luke-Acts*, 2:10. However, the emphasis on the "promise" and other similarities link this section to Luke 24. See Tannehill, *The Narrative Unity of Luke-Acts*, 1:295–98 for an explanation of the literary connections between these two chapters. Cf. Johnson, *The Acts of the Apostles*, 25; and Rudolf Pesch, *Die Apostelgeschichte*, 2 vols., EKKNT 5 (Zürich: Neukirchener Verlag, 1986), 1:65.

7. In Luke, Jesus proclaims the "kingdom of God" as a significant theme of his message (4:43; 6:20; 7:28; 9:2, 11, 60, 62; 10:9, 11; 11:2, 20; 12:31–32; 13:18, 20, 28–29; 14:15; 16:16; 17:20–21; 18:16–17, 24–25, 29; 19:11; 21:31; 22:16, 18, 29–30; 23:42). In Acts, the apostles continue to proclaim this message (8:12; 14:22; 19:8; 20:25; 28:23, 31).

(οὐ μετὰ πολλὰς ταύτας ἡμέρας) be baptized[8] with the Holy Spirit.[9] Thus, the beginning of this narrative creates a sense of anticipation in the readers, as the first scene (1:1–5) urges them to expect the imminent fulfillment of that divine promise.

The second narrative scene (1:6–11) also stresses the coming of the Holy Spirit. The narrative grammatically connects this scene to the previous scene, as μὲν οὖν indicates.[10] When the apostles "come together,"[11] they ask Jesus about the future restoration of the kingdom to Israel. This question reflects some confusion in their understanding of Jesus' teaching about the kingdom of God (1:3).[12] Jesus responds, however, by affirming emphatically that the apostles *themselves* will receive δύναμις when the Holy Spirit comes upon them (λήμψεσθε δύναμιν ἐπελθόντος τοῦ ἁγίου πνεύματος ἐφ᾽ ὑμᾶς; 1:8). This δύναμις, or power, will enable them to be Jesus' witnesses (1:8).[13] Although the apostles' question reflects their confusion by equating the kingdom that to be restored *to Israel* and the kingdom *of God*, Jesus' response indicates that the *real* issue in this section is the kingdom that belongs to God and has God as its creator and source. The narrator provides implicit commentary to the readers through Jesus' words by describing this kingdom as the future

---

8. Two matters concerning this Greek construction are worth noticing. First, the emphatic second-person plural pronoun (ὑμεῖς ... βαπτισθήσεσθε) stresses that these apostles will receive the promise. Second, the passive indicative stresses that some other party besides the apostles will be responsible for this "baptism" (an example of the "divine passive").

9. See William H. Shepherd Jr., *The Narrative Function of the Holy Spirit*, SBLDS 147 (Atlanta: Scholars Press, 1994), who contends that the Holy Spirit functions in Luke-Acts as the OT Spirit of prophecy and empowers the main characters of the unified narrative as prophets.

10. The particle μέν and the conjunction οὖν indicate continuation, which suggests that this new scene is both distinct from and yet connected with the previous scene. Cf. Conzelmann, *Acts of the Apostles*, 6; and Haenchen, *The Acts of the Apostles*, 142.

11. The aorist participle συνελθόντες emphasizes the activity of gathering or assembling as a group.

12. Cf. Johnson, *The Acts of the Apostles*, 29: "The question of the disciples concerning the restoration of the kingdom to Israel (Acts 1:6) follows naturally on Jesus' discourse concerning 'the kingdom of God' (1:3). We are equally curious: what is the relationship between these kingdoms, and how do they connect to the kingship of Jesus that Luke has been so concerned to establish in the latter portion of his Gospel?" Cf. also Haenchen, *The Acts of the Apostles*, 141–43; and Tannehill, *The Narrative Unity of Luke-Acts*, 2:14, who stress that this functions not to highlight the apostles' ignorance, but clarifies what "the kingdom" means.

13. Cf. C. K. Barrett, *A Critical and Exegetical Commentary on the Acts of the Apostles*, 2 vols., ICC (Edinburgh: T&T Clark, 1994–98), 1:78–79; Joseph A. Fitzmyer, *The Acts of the Apostles: A New Translation with Introduction and Commentary*, AB (New York: Doubleday, 1998), 200; and Charles H. Talbert, *Reading Acts: A Literary and Theological Commentary on the Acts of the Apostles*, Reading the New Testament (New York: Crossroad, 1997), 26–27.

fulfillment of a divine promise through the Holy Spirit's coming. This fulfilled promise will enable the gospel message to spread beyond the geographical boundaries of Israel "to the end of the earth" (ἕως ἐσχάτου τῆς γῆς; 1:8).[14] Once the Lukan narrator clarifies through Jesus' words what is about to happen to the apostles, the narrative briefly describes Jesus' ascension.[15] This narrative scene ends with the apostles alone and somewhat perplexed,[16] but they also receive a promise of Jesus' return to add to the promises that Jesus has previously given them (1:11; cf. 1:4–5, 8).

The Characterization of the Group of Believers in Acts 1:12–26

The first picture of the earliest Christians in the book of Acts describes their initial response to Jesus' instructions. Once Jesus has ascended to heaven, the narrative presents the apostles, who subsequently[17] return to Jerusalem (1:12), implying an obedient response to Jesus' instructions given before his ascension (e.g., 1:4).[18] The description of the characters themselves is insubstantial; the text merely lists the names of the eleven remaining apostles (1:13). Luke mentions no other characters. The descriptive material of verse 12 focuses only on the location from which they travel and on that location's distance from Jerusalem.[19] That the entire group of eleven apostles returns to Jerusalem and goes to τὸ ὑπερῷον, "the upper room" or room in the attic,[20] implies a collective

14. See Brian Rosner, "The Progress of the Word," in *Witness to the Gospel: The Theology of Acts*, ed. I. Howard Marshall and David Peterson (Grand Rapids: Eerdmans, 1998), 219, who argues that this statement, following the Lukan Gospel, anticipates the universalization of the Christian movement.

15. See Jürgen Roloff, *Die Apostelgeschichte*, NTD 5 (Göttingen: Vandenhoeck & Ruprecht, 1981), 25, who sees similarities between the ascension descriptions of Jesus and certain Greco-Roman heroic or sovereign figures; and Talbert, *Reading Acts*, 20–21, who sees both Greco-Roman and Jewish literary influences.

16. The participle ἀτενίζοντες suggests that the apostles are so startled and perplexed at what they have seen that they continue to gaze intently into the sky, which implies that they hope to figure out what has just happened.

17. The correlative adverb τότε indicates the subsequent action of the apostles.

18. Cf. Gerhard Schneider, *Die Apostelgeschichte*, 2 vols., HTKNT 5 (Freiburg: Herder, 1980–82), 1:205.

19. Ibid., 1:205 stresses that this places the ascension near the theological center of this work: Jerusalem.

20. See the use of this term in Josephus, *Life* 146; Acts 9:37, 39 (where Tabitha's dead body is placed); and 20:8 (where a group of believers have met together). Cf. Barrett, *The Acts of the Apostles*, 1:86–87; James D. G. Dunn, *The Acts of the Apostles*, Narrative Commentaries (Valley Forge, PA: Trinity Press International, 1996), 15–16; Roloff, *Die Apostelgeschichte*, 27–28; and Talbert, *Reading Acts*, 28.

activity. *Together* they return; *together* they go to this small, secluded location; *together* they stay in this place. An additional description of the room, provided by the phrase οὗ ἦσαν καταμένοντες (where they were staying), is an imperfect periphrastic construction emphasizing that they have been staying there.[21] Luke states nothing explicitly about the apostles' motives or thoughts; he records no speech or conversation. Rather, this simple description in 1:12–13 provides only a brief account of what they do after Jesus disappears. They do as Jesus has instructed them, and the implication is that they obey these instructions *exactly*. The first impression from this description is positive: those who are the witnesses to Jesus' resurrected life and his ascension are also faithful respondents to his teaching.

The next verse stands as an important description of these early Christians. Whereas verses 12 and 13 focus one's attention on the implicit obedience as seen in the apostles' actions, verse 14 describes *explicitly* not only their actions but also their communal focus.[22] Luke summarizes, οὗτοι πάντες ἦσαν προσκαρτεροῦντες ὁμοθυμαδὸν τῇ προσευχῇ (these all were constantly devoting themselves together to prayer; 1:14). If the audience has any doubts about the social bond among these persons as described implicitly in verses 12 and 13, this summary statement — a direct description of the believers — presents this bond among them in three distinct ways. First, the use of the third-person pronoun οὗτοι (these) along with πάντες (all) emphasizes that all eleven apostles are participants in the described event.[23] Second, Luke characteristically uses the adverb ὁμοθυμαδόν (together) to depict positively the corporate activity and focus of these apostles along with others.[24] Third, the imperfect

---

21. The periphrastic construction is a typical Lukan literary feature. Here one finds an imperfect construction, which expresses the action's durative nature. Thus, ἦσαν καταμένοντες stresses that the apostles are staying there. In addition, the intensive verb καταμένω emphasizes that they "stayed put." Cf. Barrett, *The Acts of the Apostles*, 1:87.

22. Cf. Schneider, *Die Apostelgeschichte*, 1:207, who suggests that this verse offers *"eine ideale Zustandsbeschreibung "* (a description of an ideal state of affairs).

23. The imperfect periphrastic construction, ἦσαν προσκαρτεροῦντες, states that the apostles are "devoting themselves." In addition, οὗτοι πάντες places direct emphasis on the apostles devoting themselves *as a group*.

24. The adverb ὁμοθυμαδόν is found eleven times in the NT, ten in Acts (1:14; 2:46; 4:24; 5:12; 7:57; 8:6; 12:20; 15:25; 18:12; 19:29). All six uses describing the unanimity of an early Christian group are positive (1:14; 2:46; 4:24; 5:12; 8:6; 15:25), whereas the three occurrences describing opponents to Christians (7:57; 18:12; 19:29) focus on the united opposition against one or more believers. Cf. Ben Witherington III, *The Acts of the Apostles: A Socio-Rhetorical Commentary* (Grand Rapids: Eerdmans, 1998), 113; Fitzmyer, *The Acts of the Apostles*, 215;

periphrastic construction stresses the continuous activity of devotion among these followers of Jesus.[25] The text provides more than a description of a continuous *activity*; a continuous inner *compulsion* or devotion energizes this activity. The narrator states that this continuous devotion is observable in these earliest Christians' practice of prayer.[26] If one considers the connection of prayer and the Holy Spirit in the Gospel of Luke, this first mention of prayer in Acts implicitly enhances the sense of anticipation in the readers that the Holy Spirit, already promised in 1:1–11 and expected imminently, will soon come.[27] Thus, this direct description assists the readers by highlighting the positive, communal bonds of these earliest Christians.[28]

One additional presentation of these earliest Christians in Acts 1 is found in the narrative scene in which the believers select another individual to replace Judas Iscariot as a member of the twelve apostles. The size of the group that is meeting has changed since the previous description of the apostles' return to Jerusalem. Luke states that the crowd has increased to about 120 persons (1:15).[29] The narrator explicitly stresses the group's positive characteristics of "togetherness" and unity (ἐπὶ τὸ αὐτό; 1:15) and implicitly reaffirms those qualities with Peter's opening words that address the group as "brothers" (1:16).[30] After Peter's

and Hans Wolfgang Heidland, "ὁμοθυμαδόν," in *TDNT*, 5:185–86, who ignores the Lukan use of the term to describe certain opponents of the Christians.

25. For this construction describing the believers, see also 2:42. The participle appears alone to describe the earliest Christians in 2:46. Cf. Walter Grundmann, "προσκαρτερέω," in *TDNT*, 3:618–19; and Barrett, *The Acts of the Apostles*, 1:88.

26. Cf. David John Williams, *Acts*, NIBC 5 (Peabody, MA: Hendrickson, 1990), 30, who stresses that praying together expresses unity. See also Robert W. Wall, "The Acts of the Apostles: Introduction, Commentary, and Reflections," in *NIB*, 10:44; and Beverly Roberts Gaventa, *The Acts of the Apostles*, ANTC (Nashville: Abingdon, 2003), 68.

27. Cf. Pesch, *Die Apostelgeschichte*, 1:80–82; Fitzmyer, *The Acts of the Apostles*, 215; and also Roloff, *Die Apostelgeschichte*, 29, who suggests that the central characteristics of the first Christian community are its persistence in prayer and its united corporate life.

28. Cf. Walter Schmithals, *Die Apostelgeschichte des Lukas*, ZB (Zürich: Theologischer Verlag, 1982), 25, who contends that the Lukan emphasis on the Christians' unity reflects a historical situation in which heresy threatens a Christian community's unity. However, one must not assume that the narrative world and the audience's "real world" are identical.

29. Both the larger size of the group in Jerusalem and the scene's opening phrase (καὶ ἐν ταῖς ἡμέραις ταύταις) suggest a possible change of location. This phrase links the previous section to this one, but it need not suggest the same location. Cf. Schmithals, *Die Apostelgeschichte des Lukas*, 25; and Paul Zingg, *Das Wachsen der Kirche: Beiträge zur Frage der lukanischen Redaktion und Theologie*, OBO (Göttingen: Vandenhoeck & Ruprecht, 1974), 165.

30. Or, more precisely, in both the Greco-Roman context and in the context of Acts 1, ἀδελφός may be translated "brothers and sisters," which Luke uses to refer to a person's relatives, Jews, or Jewish believers in Acts 1–14 (14:2 may be an exception). Beginning with the

appeal that one from their group must "become a witness with us" to Jesus' resurrection (1:22), the group responds by presenting two persons for consideration (1:23). The narrative then tells the readers that these believers pray, and included here is a brief account of what they pray (1:24–25). They seek divine guidance in the selection of Judas's replacement and characterize Judas as breaking from their ranks (i.e., from their "community") for *his own* (ἴδιον) concerns.[31] This description functions potentially to heighten within the readers a sense of anticipation for what God might do. Thus, this last narrative scene before the account of the Pentecost events also presents these earliest Christians as those who prayed and were joined together by a common bond.

An Assessment of the Characterization of the Believers in Acts 1:12–26

In the opening chapter of the book of Acts, the narrative places before the imaginative vision of the readers several images of a group of the earliest Christians. Specifically, Luke paints a word picture that highlights the obedience, the prayerfulness, and the corporate activity of this group. After Jesus' ascension and the resultant initial perplexity, Luke positively but briefly presents in both implicit and explicit ways these Christians as those who respond faithfully and expectantly as followers of Christ. In so doing, this initial characterization of a group of earliest believers

---

"Apostolic Decree," ἀδελφός refers to Christian groups consisting of Jews *and* Gentiles (e.g., 15:23, 32, 33, 36, 40; 16:2, 40; 17:6, 10, 14; 18:18, 27), to Jewish believers (e.g., 15:23; 21:7, 17), or to a Jewish audience (who probably are not believers; e.g., 23:5). One may tentatively conclude, then, that the Jerusalem Council serves as a significant turning point for the Christian movement, as a common social bond between Jewish and Gentile believers is identified that is similar to the *religious, ethnic* bond of the Jews.

In narrating this event, Luke states that "Peter, arising among the brothers and sisters, said" (ἀναστὰς Πέτρος ἐν μέσῳ τῶν ἀδελφῶν εἶπεν; 1:15), and he begins Peter's address with the expression ἄνδρες ἀδελφοί, literally, "men brothers." This latter expression appears 14 times in the NT, all in Acts (1:16; 2:29, 37; 7:2, 26; 13:15, 26, 38; 15:7, 13; 22:1; 23:1, 6; 28:17). The expression is a more formal address spoken by the Christian believers to other Jewish people; only three times does Luke ascribe ἄνδρες ἀδελφοί to others (2:37; 7:26; 13:15). In all instances, the expression stresses some common social bond between the speaker and the audience. Thus, these Christians in Acts express the positive nature of this bond and commonality between either the speaker and the Jewish believers (1:16; 15:7, 13) or the speaker and a Jewish audience that may not be characterized as believers (2:29; 7:2; 13:26, 38; 22:1; 23:1, 6; 28:17). Conversely, once Luke describes the violent reaction against Paul and Barnabas beginning with 13:50, others outside of the group of believers (e.g., the Jews) never express this positive bond within Acts.

31. Cf. Schneider, *Die Apostelgeschichte*, 1:220, who stresses that this is the community's prayer.

develops an expectation within the readers, as they begin to anticipate what will happen as the narrative unfolds.

THE GATHERED BELIEVERS AND THE COMING OF THE HOLY SPIRIT AT PENTECOST (ACTS 2:1–13)

The Literary Context

As already stated, the first chapter of Acts prepares readers for the following narrative events. In Acts 1, two related themes or images dominate the narrative: the promise of the coming of the Holy Spirit, and the united community of obedient believers, who are presumably praying for that promise to become reality. The narrative creates within the readers a sense of anticipation of what might happen next. Acts 2 describes the extraordinary fulfillment of what has been promised to the narrative characters in the previous chapter and what the readers are encouraged to expect.

The Characterization of the Group of Believers in Acts 2:1–13

The narration of what happens on the day of Pentecost begins and ends with scenes that focus largely on the portrayal of the Christian community in its early stages. The major portion of this narrative section, however, is devoted to Peter's explanatory speech to the people who have gathered (which functions as implicit commentary on the Pentecost events). These two portraits, then, are central elements of the text's description both of what happens that requires Peter's interpretation and of the results of this event and interpretation.[32]

The first thirteen verses of Acts 2 describe the extraordinary event that occurs on that day. The conjunction καί connects this account of the Pentecost event with the narrative events of the previous chapter.[33] The only human characters or actors in the first four verses of chapter 2 are the believers; those who hear the gospel message enter the narrative section

---

32. Cf. Beverly Roberts Gaventa, "Toward a Theology of Acts: Reading and Rereading," *Int* 42 (1988): 154–56, who suggests that Luke uses a pattern of *event, interpretation,* and *response* in Acts 2–5. The first portrayal of the Christians in Acts 2, then, is associated with the event, and the second portrayal shows the response.

33. Luke uses the conjunction καί a total of seven times in 2:1–4 to connect this narrative event with the narrative happenings of Acts 1. See Weiser, *Die Apostelgeschichte,* 1:77, who suggests that the conjunction καί in 2:1–4 is conspicuously absent in 2:5–13. See also Stephen H. Levinsohn, *Textual Connections in Acts,* SBLMS 31 (Atlanta: Scholars Press, 1987), 103–6.

in the later verses as they respond to what has happened. The narrative presents these believers, though, as continuing in what they have been doing. Luke's brief summary about these people (2:1) reflects the images of togetherness, oneness, and unity that have characterized them earlier, particularly in the main part of the sentence: ἦσαν πάντες ὁμοῦ ἐπὶ τὸ αὐτό (they were all together in the same place). The use of πάντες suggests that the *entire* group has continued to meet and pray together in continuity with the images of Acts 1.[34] The phrase ἐπὶ τὸ αὐτό, already used in describing the earliest Christians (1:15), appears again, suggesting that the readers are to associate this narrative scene and character group with the scene involving the 120 believers in the previous chapter. If, however, Luke's depiction does not highlight these matters sufficiently, the adverb ὁμοῦ helps to complete this brief sketch and makes the point that this group of early Christians is continuing *together* in devotion to prayer when the day of Pentecost comes.[35] Although Luke does not explicitly state why this corporate quality is important or how these believers concretely demonstrate such a quality, such an emphasis suggests that this characteristic is critical both to the narrative and potentially to what follows. Given these qualities, however, this group of Jesus' followers is not described explicitly as existing separately from the Jewish people; these followers are found in Jerusalem, possibly praying at the temple.[36]

The narrated events that follow leave little doubt for the reader about what happens. Using metaphorical language, Luke describes a scene in

---

34. One might question whether πάντες refers to the 120 or only to the apostles. The context suggests that πάντες refers to the 120. Cf. Dunn, *The Acts of the Apostles*, 18; Fitzmyer, *The Acts of the Apostles*, 238; Haenchen, *The Acts of the Apostles*, 167; Marshall, *The Acts of the Apostles*, 68; Neil, *Acts*, 72; Pesch, *Die Apostelgeschichte*, 1:103; Schneider, *Die Apostelgeschichte*, 1:247; and Williams, *Acts*, 39–40. However, since πάντες refers to the apostles in 1:14, one may conclude that πάντες refers to the apostles here also. Cf. Roloff, *Die Apostelgeschichte*, 40; Michael L. Sweeney, "The Identity of 'They' in Acts 2.1," *BT* 46 (April 1995): 247; and Talbert, *Reading Acts*, 40. Nonetheless, *in both cases* the focus is on the togetherness of a group of believers.

35. The compound verb συμπληρόω suggests that the emphasis on "being together" is found here. Cf. Schneider, *Die Apostelgeschichte*, 1:248, who suggests that this verb does not hint about the fulfillment of a promise.

36. For understanding the location as the upper room, see, e.g., Dunn, *The Acts of the Apostles*, 24; Fitzmyer, *The Acts of the Apostles*, 213; Kirsopp Lake, "The Communism of Acts II. and IV.–V. and the Appointment of the Seven," in *The Beginnings of Christianity*, ed. F. J. Foakes-Jackson and Kirsopp Lake, 5 vols. (London: Macmillan, 1933), 5:140; Boismard and Lamouille, *Les Actes des deux Apôtres*, 2:31–32; Marshall, *The Acts of the Apostles*, 68; and Pesch, *Die Apostelgeschichte*, 1:103.

which the promise given to the apostles in Acts 1 is divinely fulfilled.[37] One of the first phrases in this description, ἐκ τοῦ οὐρανοῦ (from heaven; 2:2), suggests that this event has its source in God. The description of the sound (ἦχος) from heaven is ὥσπερ φερομένης πνοῆς βιαίας (like a rushing, violent wind; 2:2) and infers the overpowering force of that divine presence.[38] Visible to those present are διαμεριζόμεναι γλῶσσαι ὡσεὶ πυρός (divided tongues as of fire), which sit on each person there (2:3). Thus, this description uses imagery that alludes to divine presence and purity.[39] Finally, Luke describes explicitly what he has just depicted: the coming of the Holy Spirit to the believers, as ἐπλήσθησαν πάντες πνεύματος ἁγίου (they all were filled with the Holy Spirit; 2:4).[40] This direct description of what has taken place among the believers, which the reader may not otherwise realize, provides an explanation for the unusual phenomenon that occur next. The narrator observes that the believers begin to speak ἑτέραις γλώσσαις (in other languages), an event correlated again with the coming of the Holy Spirit.[41]

---

37. Observe the use of comparative particles to describe this event: ὥσπερ (2:2), ὡσεί (2:3), and καθώς (2:4). Cf. Marshall, *The Acts of the Apostles*, 68; and Williams, *Acts*, 40.

38. Marshall, *The Acts of the Apostles*, 68, sees this symbolism as reminiscent of OT theophanies (e.g., 1 Sm 22:16; Job 37:10; Ezek 13:13). Other examples are found in Josephus, *Jewish Antiquities* 3.79–82; 7.71–77. Cf. also Barrett, *The Acts of the Apostles*, 1:113; Bruce, *The Book of the Acts*, 50; Roloff, *Die Apostelgeschichte*, 41; Gottfried Schille, *Die Apostelgeschichte des Lukas*, THKNT 5 (Berlin: Evangelische Verlagsanstalt, 1983), 94; Schneider, *Die Apostelgeschichte*, 1:248–49; and Williams, *Acts*, 40.

39. Fire is a motif found in OT theophany stories (e.g., Gen 15:17; Exod 3:2; 13:21–22; 14:24, 19:18; Isa 66:15, 18). Cf. Johnson, *The Acts of the Apostles*, 42, who observes the combination of "sound" and "fire" in Ps 29:7; and Schneider, *Die Apostelgeschichte*, 1:249, who sees the comparative ὡσεὶ πυρός as reflecting apocalyptic imagery and, along with 2:2, referring to the messianic Spirit-baptism that John the Baptist announced (Luke 3:16). Cf. also Marshall, *The Acts of the Apostles*, 68–69; Neil, *Acts*, 72–73; Pesch, *Die Apostelgeschichte*, 1:103; Talbert, *Reading Acts*, 41–42; and Weiser, *Die Apostelgeschichte*, 1:83–84. For Hellenistic references to wind and fire as signs of divine presence, see Pieter W. van der Horst, "Hellenistic Parallels to the Acts of the Apostles (2.1–47)," *JSNT* 25 (1985): 49–50.

40. The verb πίμπλημι, which appears 22 times in Luke-Acts, refers to "filling up" or to fulfillment. See Schmithals, *Die Apostelgeschichte des Lukas*, 30, who describes this gift of the Holy Spirit as "democratic," in that *all* and not only certain persons in hierarchical positions receive this gift. Cf. Witherington, *The Acts of the Apostles*, 133.

41. While many translations prefer to render ἑτέραις γλώσσαις literally (in other tongues), the narrative context (2:1–13) suggests that γλῶσσαι refers figuratively to different languages (see the term διάλεκτος in 2:6, 8), but this term may have been used to correlate this phenomenon with διαμεριζόμεναι γλῶσσαι (2:3). Cf. Fitzmyer, *The Acts of the Apostles*, 239; Johnson, *The Acts of the Apostles*, 42; Roloff, *Die Apostelgeschichte*, 42; Shepherd, *The Narrative Function of the Holy Spirit*, 162n27; Weiser, *Die Apostelgeschichte*, 1:85; Williams, *Acts*, 41; and Witherington, *The Acts of the Apostles*, 133. See van der Horst, "Hellenistic Parallels to the

In the first part of Acts 2, the reader discovers two distinct pictures. The first picture is of the group of gathered believers, which the narrative consistently depicts with unanimity and a bond of "togetherness." The second picture comes out of the first one: a picture of the fulfillment of the Jesus' promise to his apostles, as the Holy Spirit comes to that same group of believers in extraordinary ways.[42] Clearly, the narrative links both pictures together. While one finds no direct statements that join these two pictures, the clear implication is that the coming of the Holy Spirit is closely associated with the specific depiction of this unanimous, praying group.

While the narrative text of 2:1–4 provides a variety of descriptions and connections that assist readers in making initial judgments about the believers and the extraordinary phenomenon just mentioned, those persons in Jerusalem who notice something of what is happening do not have such "inside information." Thus, the text of 2:5–13 provides additional clarification about what the text has just summarily described.[43] However, the readers' focus is redirected from the gathered Christians to the crowd of Jewish people who have witnessed the event.[44] Although the crowd does not yet interact with the Christians, the Lukan characterization of this Jewish crowd stands in juxtaposition with that of the believers. These Jewish people, "from every nation" (2:5), have *themselves* gathered together, but have done so out of confusion concerning what they have heard.[45] Through this group Luke provides more details of what has happened as those in the crowd converse about this unexplainable scene in which they all hear the believers speaking in their own respective dialect (ἕκαστος τῇ ἰδίᾳ διαλέκτῳ; 2:6, 8).[46] What

---

Acts of the Apostles (2.1–47)," 50–52, for Hellenistic references discussing and/or describing divinely inspired speech.

42. Cf. Krodel, *Acts*, 71–72, who points to this description of the "filling with the Holy Spirit" (2:4) as the center and emphasis of an *a-b-a* structure.

43. The conjunction δέ in 2:5 functions not as an adversative but indicates that the following material is explanatory.

44. Tannehill, *The Narrative Unity of Luke-Acts*, 2:28–29, states that the crowd becomes a "focalizing character," as the reader has access to the event through the experiences, thoughts, and perceptions of the crowd.

45. In 2:6, the two compound verbs that specify something about the crowd, συνέρχομαι (to gather together) and συγχέω (to confuse/trouble), both suggest a subtle emphasis on "being together" here.

46. Krodel, *Acts*, 77, reminds us that Luke does *not* give other information, such as how each heard these languages. See van der Horst, "Hellenistic Parallels to the Acts of the Apostles (2.1–47)," 52–54, who compares the list of languages in 2:5 with a similar list from the Homeric *Hymn to Apollo*.

Luke explicates through the questions and comments of the crowd is the diversity among the Jewish people who have gathered (2:9–11). The extraordinary speaking in other languages,[47] due to the coming of the promised Holy Spirit, brought this diverse group together, so that readers may infer that *all* the Jewish people, even those of the Diaspora, hear the message.[48] At the same time, Luke describes two responses to what they have witnessed: some respond out of amazement and confusion (2:12; cf. 2:7–8), and some respond with ridicule and mockery (2:13).[49] Readers, then, are left with an ambiguous picture of the Jewish people who witness the extraordinary events. On the one hand, these diverse Jewish people have come together as witnesses of the phenomenon. On the other hand, the response is mixed.[50]

An Assessment of the Characterization of the Believers in Acts 2:1–13

The characterization of the Christian believers in this section of Acts corresponds to and depends on that which the readers find in Acts 1. In the previous chapter, Luke depicts the apostles and other followers of Jesus as those who obediently and prayerfully gather together in the expectation that the promised Holy Spirit will soon come. In the beginning verses of Acts 2, that sense of expectation and togetherness among

---

47. See Haenchen, *The Acts of the Apostles*, 174; Johnson, *The Acts of the Apostles*, 46; Roloff, *Die Apostelgeschichte*, 40–41; Schmithals, *Die Apostelgeschichte des Lukas*, 31; and Talbert, *Reading Acts*, 43, who identify links between this event and a Jewish tradition that describes the proclamation of the Jewish law on Mt. Sinai in seventy languages (see *Exodus Rabbah* 5:9; *b. Sabbat* 88b).

48. Cf. Gerhard Lohfink, *Die Sammlung Israels: Eine Untersuchung zur lukanischen Ekklesiologie*, SANT (Munich: Kösel, 1975), 48–49; Karl Löning, "Das Verhältnis zum Judentum als Identitätsproblem der Kirche nach der Apostelgeschichte," in *"Ihr alle aber seid Brüder": Festschrift für A. Th. Khoury zum 60. Geburtstag*, ed. Ludwig Hagemann and Ernst Pulsfort (Würzburg: Echter, 1990), 306–8; Fitzmyer, *The Acts of the Apostles*, 243; and Tannehill, *The Narrative Unity of Luke-Acts*, 2:27.

49. The intensive verb διαχλευάζω (to mock) contrasts those who respond with ridicule (2:13) and those who are confused but seek an explanation (2:12). Since the narrative already states that the Holy Spirit has given the believers such ability, the mocking is a derisive response to the Holy Spirit's activity. This depiction, then, suggests a division of the πάντες (2:13). See van der Horst, "Hellenistic Parallels to the Acts of the Apostles (2.1–47)," 54–56, for Hellenistic references to responses of mockery or derision and to comparisons of ecstatic behavior to drunkenness.

50. Cf. Haenchen, *The Acts of the Apostles*, 171–75; Krodel, *Acts*, 77, who states that these two reactions are "Luke's literary devices" that prepare the way for Peter's speech; and Marshall, *The Acts of the Apostles*, 71, who only emphasizes the reaction of "incomprehension."

these people is reiterated before the vivid description of the Pentecost scene.[51] The initial result of this event, then, is twofold: the promise is fulfilled among those who are praying and expecting together, and what takes place brings together those who witness the phenomenon as recipients of the spoken message. Although the initial response is mixed and complete comprehension is lacking, this narrative section clearly indicates that the message from these gathered followers of Jesus addresses the Jewish people and uniquely brings them together, although they have come from various parts of the Greco-Roman world. Thus, the Lukan narrator positively depicts this group of gathered believers as the proclaimers of that divine message, as those who have experienced the fulfillment of the awaited promise.[52]

THE COMMUNITY OF BELIEVERS AND THE AFTERMATH OF THE PENTECOST EVENTS (ACTS 2:42–47)

The Literary Context (Acts 2:14–41)

The mixed reaction of the Jewish people who witness the spectacular phenomenon of the Christians' proclamation of the gospel message in languages unfamiliar to the speakers results in a speech to these people by the Apostle Peter. This speech, found in 2:14–36, functions similarly for both the narrative level of the event and the communicative level of the text: the speech explains what has just occurred. The use of speeches as narrative explanations for the assistance of the implied audience (or reader) was a common technique of Greco-Roman historiography.[53] Speeches function within the historiographical text as useful

---

51. Haenchen, *The Acts of the Apostles*, 173: "[Luke] had to depict it vividly so that it would rise unforgettably before the eyes of his readers. But that was not enough: he would not have succeeded in his task unless at the same time the *meaning* of this incident was plain to them."

52. Cf. Johnson, *The Acts of the Apostles*, 45: "Luke's point is not the pyrotechnics of theophany, but spiritual transformation. The real 'event' of Pentecost is the empowerment of the disciples by the Holy Spirit."

53. The classic discussions comparing the speeches of Acts with those of ancient historiography are by Martin Dibelius, "The Speeches in Acts and Ancient Historiography," in *Studies in the Acts of the Apostles*, trans. Mary Ling (London: SCM, 1956), 138–85; and Henry J. Cadbury, "The Speeches in Acts," in *The Beginnings of Christianity*, ed. F. J. Foakes-Jackson and Kirsopp Lake, 5 vols. (London: Macmillan, 1933), 2:489–510. Also cf. F. F. Bruce, "The Significance of the Speeches for Interpreting Acts," *SwJT* 33 (Fall 1990): 21–28; Henry J. Cadbury, *The Making of Luke-Acts*, 2nd ed. (London: SPCK, 1958), 184–93; G. H. R. Hors-

tools to direct implicitly the reader's attention and understanding and to provide necessary interpretations of previous and subsequent episodes. Peter's speech in Acts 2, then, appears as a major narrative component in the first pivotal event in the book and functions as implicit commentary to the readers from a reliable character.[54]

As Peter speaks to the bewildered crowd of Jewish people, the main thesis is that the event that has just occurred is the divine fulfillment of what the Scriptures have declared. The narrative speech ascribed to Peter joins the prophetic promise of a divine outpouring of the Spirit to the contemporary event that the people have witnessed.[55] References to scriptural passages dominate the speech recorded in 2:14–36, passages that Peter asserts are fulfilled by the event.[56] The speech, in turn, highlights three points in proving that thesis.[57] First, the Lukan Peter contends that the Jews themselves bear responsibility for the crucifixion of Jesus,[58] although that execution was carried out "by the hands of the

---

ley, "Speeches and Dialogue in Acts," *NTS* 32 (October 1986): 609–14; Johnson, *The Acts of the Apostles*, 53–55; Plümacher, *Lukas als hellenistischer Schriftsteller*, 38–72; Eckhard Plümacher, "Die Missionsreden der Apostelgeschichte und Dionys von Halikarnass," *NTS* 39 (April 1993): 161–77; Stanley E. Porter, "Thucydides 1.22.1 and Speeches in Acts: Is There a Thucydidean View?" *NovT* 32 (1990): 121–42; Eduard Schweizer, "Concerning the Speeches in Acts," in *Studies in Luke-Acts*, ed. Leander E. Keck and J. Louis Martyn (Philadelphia: Fortress, 1980), 208–16; and Robert C. Tannehill, "The Functions of Peter's Mission Speeches in the Narrative of Acts," *NTS* 37 (July 1991): 400–414.

54. See Löning, "Das Verhältnis zum Judentum," 162, 166; Haenchen, *The Acts of the Apostles*, 212; Talbert, *Reading Acts*, 44; and Tannehill, "The Functions of Peter's Mission Speeches," 404.

55. At the beginning of Peter's speech, the same promise from God is twice given: ἐκχεῶ ἀπὸ τοῦ πνεύματός μου (I will pour out my Spirit; 2:17–18). Near the speech's end, Peter asserted: ἐξέχεεν τοῦτο ὃ ὑμεῖς [καὶ] βλέπετε καὶ ἀκούετε ([Jesus] has poured this [the promised Holy Spirit] out which you see and hear; 2:33). In this latter reference, the same verb from the promise (ἐκχέω) appears but now in the aorist tense, which associates the scriptural promise of Joel 2:28–29 and the historical event. See Williams, *Acts*, 53, who rightly observes that God would act in the quotation from Joel, whereas Jesus acted on God's behalf (2:33). Cf. Johnson, *The Acts of the Apostles*, 52; and Shepherd, *The Narrative Function of the Holy Spirit*, 163–67.

56. More specifically, 2:17–21, 25–28, 31, and 34b–35 are all references to the Scriptures.

57. For a look at the similarities in the Petrine speeches in Acts 1–5, see Tyson, *Images of Judaism in Luke-Acts*, 103–9; Bruce, *The Book of the Acts*, 63; and Dibelius, "The Speeches in Acts and Ancient Historiography," 165.

58. Two verbs describing Jesus' death (2:23) are significant. First, the verb ἀναιρέω refers to those whom Peter addressed in this speech, namely ἄνδρες Ἰσραηλῖται (you Israelites; 2:22), and emphasizes the violence of killing, execution, or murder. Second, the participle προσπήξαντες seems to be used as a word picture, as Jesus is literally "fixed up on to" the cross, distinguishing the actual death. Cf. Johnson, *The Acts of the Apostles*, 51.

lawless" (2:23).[59] Second, in contrast to the crucifixion, God has raised Jesus from the dead (2:24, 31–32) in fulfillment of the scriptural message (2:25–28, 31).[60] Third, the resurrected Jesus has received the promised Holy Spirit from the Father (τὴν τε ἐπαγγελίαν τοῦ πνεύματος τοῦ ἁγίου λαβών) and then "poured out" (ἐξέχεεν) the promise, as Peter's audience has witnessed (2:33). The narrated speech concludes with an affirmation to "the whole house of Israel": God's activity has made Jesus both Lord and Christ (2:36).[61] By including this speech, then, Luke provides for the reader a clear connection between the Pentecost event and the divine promise, a promise that Jesus has affirmed in Acts 1, that the Scriptures have declared, and that only God can fulfill.[62]

Although Luke provides Peter's speech as the dominant, explanatory element of the Pentecost scene, he also briefly describes the Jewish people's response to that speech.[63] The response is one of sorrow and remorse, not offense over what Peter has said about Jesus or their role in his death.[64] Thus, the Jewish crowd's initial response is positive, as demonstrated both by the affirmation of their ethnic bond with the apostles and by their question about what they should do (2:37).[65] Peter, in turn, tells the crowd that, by repenting and being baptized in the name of Jesus

---

59. Tyson, *Images of Judaism in Luke-Acts*, 106: "As a word used by a Jew in speaking to a Jewish audience, *anomos* would almost certainly signify Gentiles, those without Torah, and hence would serve to remind the reader that...Pilate acceded to the wishes of the Jewish priests and others and permitted the crucifixion of Jesus."

60. In 2:24, the mention of the resurrection functions within the speech to describe Jesus of Nazareth (2:22) within the larger sentence structure of verses 22–24: ὃν ὁ θεὸς ἀνέστησεν λύσας τὰς ὠδῖνας τοῦ θανάτου (whom God raised up by freeing him from the birthpains of death). In 2:32, God is the subject, although Jesus is clearly the emphasis: τοῦτον τὸν Ἰησοῦν ἀνέστησεν ὁ θεός (*this Jesus* God raised up [emphasis added]).

61. This affirmation is directed to *Israel*, πᾶς οἶκος Ἰσραήλ. The expression may be either an explication of the "house" (2:2) or a wordplay on οἶκος. Luke's use of this term (2:2, 36) suggests that these early Christians are not separate from Israel at all. Thus, the promise's fulfillment is not for the believers alone but for all of Israel.

62. Cf. Max Turner, "The 'Spirit of Prophecy' as the Power of Israel's Restoration and Witness," in Marshall and Peterson, *Witness to the Gospel*, 334–35, 348.

63. Cf. Gaventa, "Toward a Theology of Acts," 154–56.

64. Literally, Luke states that "they were cut to the heart" (κατενύγησαν τὴν καρδίαν) when they heard the speech. This expression indicates the people's deep conviction for their involvement in Jesus' death. Cf. Haenchen, *The Acts of the Apostles*, 183n6, who states that the verb expresses emotional stress; and Johnson, *The Acts of the Apostles*, 56–57. Luke, however, states nothing of a negative reaction concerning the identification of Jesus as "both Lord and Christ" (καὶ κύριον . . . καὶ Χριστόν; 2:36). Cf. Gaventa, "Toward a Theology of Acts," 156.

65. By addressing Peter and the apostles as ἄνδρες ἀδελφοί, the Jewish audience affirms the religious and ethnic bond and not separation between them and the apostles. Cf. Haenchen, *The Acts of the Apostles*, 183–84.

Christ, they *too* will receive the promise given to the believers: "the gift of the Holy Spirit" (2:38–39).[66] Luke's brief statement that mentions "those who welcomed his message" and are baptized (2:41) concludes the scene, but with an obvious hint about what has occurred. The narrator leaves the reader to conclude that those who are baptized *do* receive the same promise, as Peter's instructions in 2:38 clearly state.[67] The addition of approximately three thousand persons suggests that the Jewish people in Jerusalem responded in an overwhelmingly positive way to the Christian message and a sense of divine blessing.[68]

The Characterization of the Group of Believers in Acts 2:42–47

Although Luke narrates the basic elements of the Pentecost event, including Peter's speech, he concludes this section by summarizing some results from what has just occurred.[69] Here the narrative shifts from the narrator

66. The gift of the Holy Spirit (τὴν δωρεὰν τοῦ ἁγίου πνεύματος; 2:38) is identified as "the promise" (ὑμῖν γάρ ἐστιν ἡ ἐπαγγελία; 2:39). See Conzelmann, *Acts of the Apostles*, 22, who claims that the accent of this verse is on the promise; Johnson, *The Acts of the Apostles*, 57, who stresses that the Holy Spirit is epexegetical (as *being* the gift itself); and Tannehill, *The Narrative Unity of Luke-Acts*, 2:36, who observes that the emphatic position of ὑμῖν balances the emphatic pronoun of the accusation of 2:36 (whom *you* crucified), so that the speech directs *both* the accusation *and* the promise toward the narrative audience.

67. See van der Horst, "Hellenistic Parallels to the Acts of the Apostles (2.1–47)," 58, for parallel references in Hellenistic sources to ἀποδέχεσθαι τὸν λόγον (2:41).

68. The aorist passive form of προστίθημι, suggests more than simple addition; it includes association with certain persons or causes (2:41). Luke does not state to *what* or to *whom* the 3,000 were added, although these were probably added to the 120 who were already believers. However, the consensus is that the large numbers of persons joining the believers is indicative of divine blessing. See, e.g., Fitzmyer, *The Acts of the Apostles*, 267; Krodel, *Acts*, 91–92; Schmithals, *Die Apostelgeschichte des Lukas*, 38; and Johnson, *The Acts of the Apostles*, 61. Contra Lohfink, *Die Sammlung Israels*, 62. However, scholars have raised many questions concerning the purpose and historical accuracy of the large numbers of Jews in Jerusalem that the narrative presents as responding favorably to the Christian message. For a comprehensive treatment of this subject, see Zingg, *Das Wachsen der Kirche*, who focuses on the Lukan theological intent of showing divine blessing. Cf. Wolfgang Reinhardt, "The Population Size of Jerusalem and the Numerical Growth of the Jerusalem Church," in *The Book of Acts in Its Palestinian Setting*, ed. Richard Bauckham, BAFCS (Grand Rapids: Eerdmans, 1995), 237–65, who focuses on the historical reliability of the Lukan figures; and Boismard and Lamouille, *Les Actes des deux Apôtres*, 2:150–51, who assert that 2:41 and other growth statements allude to the Hebrew population during the Exodus. See Haenchen, *The Acts of the Apostles*, 184–85: "The question whether such a mass-baptism was at that time possible in Jerusalem . . . is alien to the nature of the presentation."

69. See Lucian, *How to Write History* 55. Cf. Dupont, "La question du plan des Actes des Apôtres," 28–29. For studies of the Lukan summaries, see Pierre Benoit, "Remarques sur les 'sommaires' de Actes 2. 42 à 5," in *Aux sources de la tradition chrétienne: Mélanges offerts à M. Maurice Goguel*, Bibliothèque théologique (Neuchâtel: Delachaux & Niestlé, 1950), 1–10;

showing the reader what has happened to the narrator *telling* about what happens next. This shift moves largely from implicit to explicit description. Nonetheless, this section is joined to the preceding narrative, as the grammatical connections[70] and recurrent imagery[71] clearly indicate. The paragraph summarizes certain communal dynamics among the believers after the Pentecost event.[72] This description, however, is not of an isolated historical event.[73] Rather, the shift from the aorist tense in previous and subsequent sections to the imperfect tense in the summary indicates that the described dynamics are ongoing, continual characteristics, which Luke highlights as results of the fulfilled promise of the Holy Spirit's coming.[74]

The first statement in this narrative section provides the initial depiction of those who now constitute the ones who have responded favorably to the Christian message. Luke states, ἦσαν δὲ προσκαρτεροῦντες τῇ διδαχῇ τῶν ἀποστόλων καὶ τῇ κοινωνίᾳ, τῇ κλάσει τοῦ ἄρτου καὶ ταῖς προσευχαῖς (they constantly devoted themselves to the apostles' teaching and the fellowship, to the breaking of bread and the prayers; 2:42). Just as the first description in Acts of the apostles and others emphasizes

---

Henry J. Cadbury, "The Summaries in Acts," in Foakes-Jackson and Lake, *The Beginnings of Christianity*, 5:392–402; Maria Anicia Co, "The Major Summaries in Acts: Acts 2,42–47; 4,32–35; 5,12–16 Linguistic and Literary Relationship," *ETL* 68 (1992): 49–85; Gregory E. Sterling, " 'Athletes of Virtue': An Analysis of the Summaries in Acts (2:41–47; 4:32–35; 5:12–16)," *JBL* 113 (Winter 1994): 679–96; and H. Alan Brehm, "The Significance of the Summaries for Interpreting Acts," *SwJT* 33 (Fall 1990): 29–40.

70. See Zingg, *Das Wachsen der Kirche*, 169; and Co, "The Major Summaries in Acts," 59, both of whom emphasize that the conjunction δέ grammatically links the summary to the narrative events that precede it.

71. E.g., the imperfect periphrastic ἦσαν προσκαρτεροῦντες of 1:14 recurs in 2:42 and links these two narrative sections together. Also, the imagery of 2:47 clearly imitates the description of 2:41, in that persons are added (προστίθημι in both cases) to the group. Thus, one may see 2:41 and 2:47 forming an *inclusio* by these references to the group's growth. Cf. Luke T. Johnson, *The Literary Function of Possessions in Luke-Acts*, SBLDS 39 (Missoula, MT: Scholars Press, 1977), 185n2; and Schmithals, *Die Apostelgeschichte des Lukas*, 38.

72. Cf. Gaventa, *The Acts of the Apostles*, 81. See Schneider, *Die Apostelgeschichte*, 1:284, who identifies an a-b-a-b structure: (a) the life of the community (2:42), (b) the effect on outsiders (2:43), (a) the life of the community (2:44–47a), (b) the effect on outsiders (2:47b–c).

73. E.g., descriptions of several characters use aorist verbs: Peter (ἐπῆρεν τὴν φωνὴν αὐτοῦ καὶ ἀπεφθέγξατο αὐτοῖς; 2:14), the Jewish people (κατενύγησαν τὴν καρδίαν εἶπόν; 2:37), Peter again (διεμαρτύρατο; 2:40), and the 3,000 (ἐβαπτίσθησαν καὶ προσετέθησαν; 2:41). In contrast, all the indicatives in 2:42–47 use the imperfect tense. Cf. Co, "The Major Summaries in Acts," 59.

74. Cf. Weiser, *Die Apostelgeschichte*, 1:101; and Lake, "The Communism of Acts II. and IV.–V. and the Appointment of the Seven," 5:141.

their continual devotion to prayer (1:14), this description also emphasizes the continual devotion of this larger group of believers, among
whom are other Jewish people who have responded positively to the
Pentecost speech.[75] By using the same imperfect periphrastic construction in depicting both groups, the reader is encouraged to link these two
groups together and to perceive this expanded Jewish group as similar
to those who *together* have been obedient and devoted to prayer.[76]

In this statement (2:42), however, Luke expands the description
of that to which this large group is devoted by providing two pairs
of elements in the believers' activity and practice, presenting them
grammatically as parallel constructions:

τῇ διδαχῇ τῶν ἀποστόλων καὶ τῇ κοινωνίᾳ,
τῇ κλάσει τοῦ ἄρτου καὶ ταῖς προσευχαῖς.

The scholarly consensus is that Luke provides a list of the four
basic elements of early Christian practice or liturgy.[77] Given the parallel construction of these two phrases, however, one may modify such
a conclusion. Rather than seeing this Lukan description as *four* basic
elements of early Christian activity, one may perceive the close association of two general kinds of corporate activities: those related to *worship*
practices toward God, and those related to *social* practices among believers.[78] The first phrase indicates such an association. On the one hand,
these believers are devoted to "the apostles' teaching" (τῇ διδαχῇ τῶν
ἀποστόλων), which refers to their ongoing practice of reflection on the

---

75. Cf. Schmithals, *Die Apostelgeschichte des Lukas*, 38, who suggests that the narrative
stresses the unanimity of the Christians and the Jews. However, the narrative has not indicated
any separation of the believers from the general Jewish populace.

76. However, the phrase of 2:42 does not duplicate the "togetherness" emphasis. See
Zingg, *Das Wachsen der Kirche*, 147, who sees this repeated description as an expression of
an intensive community experience.

77. For the more general understanding, see, e.g., Conzelmann, *Acts of the Apostles*, 23;
Haenchen, *The Acts of the Apostles*, 191; Johnson, *The Literary Function of Possessions in
Luke-Acts*, 185; William J. Larkin Jr., *Acts*, IVPNTC (Downers Grove, IL: InterVarsity, 1995),
61; Roloff, *Die Apostelgeschichte*, 65; Schmithals, *Die Apostelgeschichte des Lukas*, 38; and
Weiser, *Die Apostelgeschichte*, 1:103–5. For understanding the list as the four elements of early
Christian meetings or liturgy, see Boismard and Lamouille, *Les Actes des deux Apôtres*, 2:152;
Marshall, *The Acts of the Apostles*, 83; Schille, *Die Apostelgeschichte des Lukas*, 115; and
Williams, *Acts*, 59.

78. Cf. Barrett, *The Acts of the Apostles*, 1:162, 164–66; Pesch, *Die Apostelgeschichte*,
1:30; Schneider, *Die Apostelgeschichte*, 1:286; and Witherington, *The Acts of the Apostles*,
160.

testimony about Jesus' ministry and resurrection (cf. 1:21–22; 2:32).[79] On the other hand, these believers are devoted simultaneously to "the fellowship" (τῇ κοινωνίᾳ), a term that has a wide range of meaning in the Greco-Roman world and that refers to the relation between two or more individuals.[80] The term κοινωνία was itself associated with, among other contexts, Greco-Roman political thought and the concept of friendship, in which certain friendships are described as "partnerships" between friends.[81] Here, the articular form of κοινωνία seems to refer not only to the bond between a few persons but also within the entire group.[82] In this first phrase, then, Luke joins the implications of this reflective activity with a bond created among the believers, suggesting that such a positive, social bond has developed in the context of such reflective and worshipful activity.

If the first phrase joins the activities of worship and community, the second parallel construction may also emphasize similar points. Whereas a general consensus connects the believers' devotion "to the prayers" (ταῖς προσευχαῖς) with descriptions of the believers (1:14) and of the subsequent activity of Peter and John (3:1),[83] no consensus exists regarding the expression "the breaking of bread" (τῇ κλάσει τοῦ ἄρτου). More specifically, one must consider whether this Lukan expression reflects early eucharistic activity or the eating of a meal together.[84] Considering

---

79. Cf., e.g., Bruce, *The Book of the Acts*, 73; Krodel, *Acts*, 92; and Williams, *Acts*, 59.

80. Contra Marshall, *The Acts of the Apostles*, 83.

81. Scholars have acknowledged an apparent Lukan appeal to Greco-Roman friendship traditions. Cf. Alan C. Mitchell, "The Social Function of Friendship in Acts 2:44–47 and 4:32–37," *JBL* 111 (Summer 1992): 255–72; Conzelmann, *Acts of the Apostles*, 23–24, 36; Jacques Dupont, "La communauté des biens aux premiers jours de l'Église (Actes 2,42.44–45; 4,32.34–35)," in *Études sur les Actes des Apôtres*, LD 45 (Paris: Éditions du Cerf, 1967), 503–19; Luke T. Johnson, *Sharing Possessions: Mandate and Symbol of Faith*, OBT 9 (Philadelphia: Fortress, 1981), 119–27; Tannehill, *The Narrative Unity of Luke-Acts*, 2:45; and Weiser, *Die Apostelgeschichte*, 1:104. See Fitzmyer, *The Acts of the Apostles*, 270, who points to a Jewish understanding rather than a Greco-Roman one.

82. Cf. Jacques Dupont, "L'union entre les premiers Chrétiens dans les Actes des Apôtres," in *Nouvelles études sur les Actes des Apôtres*, LD 118 (Paris: Éditions du Cerf, 1984), 298–99; and Johnson, *The Acts of the Apostles*, 58. Contra Williams, *Acts*, 59, who understands κοινωνία to occur between God and the believers.

83. Cf. Boismard and Lamouille, *Les Actes des deux Apôtres*, 2:151.

84. For those who interpret this eucharistically, see, e.g., Boismard and Lamouille, *Les Actes des deux Apôtres*, 2:152; Bruce, *The Book of the Acts*, 73; Fitzmyer, *The Acts of the Apostles*, 270–71; Johnson, *The Acts of the Apostles*, 58; Krodel, *Acts*, 93; Marshall, *The Acts of the Apostles*, 83; and Williams, *Acts*, 60. For those who interpret this as a shared meal, see, e.g., Dunn, *The Acts of the Apostles*, 35; Erwin R. Goodenough, "The Perspective of Acts," in Keck and Martyn, *Studies in Luke-Acts*, 52; David Peterson, "The Worship of

the Lukan association of worship and social activities, as well as the subsequent reference to people breaking bread from house to house (κλῶντές τε κατ᾽ οἶκον ἄρτον; 2:46), the "breaking of bread" seems to refer to the eating of meals together but with both social and religious overtones. That is to say, Luke does not make a concrete distinction between eucharistic activity and a common meal, which suggests to the readers that the meals together among the believers are characterized by the same gospel that the eucharistic ritual enacts.[85] Luke's summary does not lend itself to detailed description regarding these so-called elements of early Christian activity. However, the text *does* suggest to the reader that the coming of the promised Holy Spirit results in a communal bond among the believers that is evident in a close if not inseparable relationship between worship and social practices.

The first statement of the summary at the end of the Pentecost narrative event suggests, therefore, that the fulfilled promise of the Holy Spirit so affects the rapidly growing group of believers that they are much like the smaller group of believers that gathered after Jesus' ascension. The narrative thus encourages the reader to correlate this larger group with the smaller group of believers that has already been characterized positively, thereby adding to the cumulative effects of these images. Consequently, this correlation presents a positive picture of this character group. Even though this group of more than three thousand persons has apparently come from a diversity of backgrounds within Judaism, the fulfilled divine promise enables communal bonds to form among them.[86] This initial description of the Christian believers after the Pentecost event, therefore, directly correlates the divine activity and presence among the believers with the positive, communal ties among them.

One should not interpret the description of 2:42, however, in isolation from the remainder of the summary or from the entire narrative. Though this beginning statement provides a brief outline of those communal dynamics among the Christian believers, the next five verses contribute to

---

the New Community," in Marshall and Peterson, *Witness to the Gospel*, 392; Schille, *Die Apostelgeschichte des Lukas*, 116; and Schneider, *Die Apostelgeschichte*, 1:286.

85. Cf. Conzelmann, *Acts of the Apostles*, 23; and Haenchen, *The Acts of the Apostles*, 191, 584. See also Barrett, *The Acts of the Apostles*, 1:164–66; Pesch, *Die Apostelgeschichte*, 1:130; and Witherington, *The Acts of the Apostles*, 161.

86. Cf. Daniel Marguerat, "La mort d'Ananias et Saphira (Ac 5.1–11) dans la stratégie narrative de Luc," *NTS* (1993): 213; and Zingg, *Das Wachsen der Kirche*, 144–45.

that description by adding several more "details."[87] Acts 2:43 forms an *inclusio* (envelope) by the use of ἐγίνετο to begin and conclude the sentence. The focus of this sentence is φόβος, a sense of religious awe that everyone (πάσῃ ψυχῇ)[88] experiences because the apostles work "many wonders and signs" (πολλά τε τέρατα καὶ σημεῖα), which the readers should perceive as demonstrations of divine power.[89] The next description, found in 2:44–47a, explains more fully the relationship of the communal and worship activities of the believers.

The first part of this additional description of the "post-Pentecost" Christians (2:44–45) focuses the readers' attention on some specific ways in which the believers continually associate as κοινωνία.[90] At the beginning of this description, the narrator directs readers' attention explicitly to the togetherness of the believers: πάντες δὲ οἱ πιστεύοντες ἦσαν ἐπὶ τὸ αὐτό (all who believed were together; 2:44a). Here both πάντες and the phrase ἐπὶ τὸ αὐτό emphasize a sense of togetherness and unity, the same expressions also used in the previous, positive depiction of the waiting Christians just before the extraordinary Pentecost happenings (cf. 1:15; 2:1).[91] The next phrase further emphasizes these positive, communal bonds among the Christians: εἶχον ἅπαντα κοινά (they held all things in common; 2:44b). This expression has affinity with positive qualities affirmed in Greco-Roman traditions concerning political ideals and friendship.[92] Here is the second description in this summary that reflects the ancient concepts that stressed and described (in ideal or actual

---

87. Cf. Johnson, *The Literary Function of Possessions in Luke-Acts*, 185n2, who suggests that these verses amplify 2:42; and Benoit, "Remarques sur les 'sommaires' de Actes 2. 42 à 5," 4, who argues that 2:43–45 interrupts the continuity between 2:42 and 2:46–47 and introduces themes developed in subsequent summaries.

88. It is unclear whether "everyone" refers to the Christian believers or to everyone in Jerusalem. The large increase implies that all Jerusalem responds favorably to the gospel message; "everyone" may refer to the Christian crowd while giving the allusion that religious awe has filled all Jerusalem. Cf. Christoph Zettner, *Amt, Gemeinde und kirchliche Einheit in der Apostelgeschichte des Lukas* (New York: Peter Lang, 1991), 260–261. Contra Haenchen, *The Acts of the Apostles*, 191–92; Krodel, *Acts*, 93; Marshall, *The Acts of the Apostles*, 84; and Williams, *Acts*, 60, who understand this as a reference to the nonbelievers of Jerusalem.

89. Johnson, *The Literary Function of Possessions in Luke-Acts*, 185–86; and Pesch, *Die Apostelgeschichte*, 1:131. See Benoit, "Remarques sur les 'sommaires' de Actes 2. 42 à 5," 5, who suggests that a later redactor was added this to prepare the reader for 5:11–12.

90. This description (2:44–45) includes four imperfect indicatives: ἦσαν, εἶχον, ἐπίπρασκον, and διεμέριζον. Cf. Barrett, *The Acts of the Apostles*, 1:169.

91. Cf. Witherington, *The Acts of the Apostles*, 161.

92. Barrett, *The Acts of the Apostles*, 1:167–69, also points to Jewish influences.

terms) the social bond and relationship among individuals in society.[93] The text concretizes such affirmed qualities of the Spirit-induced unanimity by depicting the sharing of possessions (2:45),[94] which stresses the customary actions of persons selling possessions (τὰ κτήματα καὶ τὰς ὑπάρξεις ἐπίπρασκον) and distributing (or "dividing," διεμέριζον) the proceeds to anyone who was in need (πᾶσιν καθότι ἄν τις χρείαν εἶχεν).[95] This practice, summarized here with language reflecting certain Greco-Roman traditions, suggests that the willingness of certain believers leads to them giving resources for needs within the Christian group.[96]

Because of the brevity of this description, questions abound regarding how readers should interpret these dynamics among the Christian believers as described thus far in the summary. Some have contended that the Lukan summary depicts the Christian community with a primitive

---

93. Various writers use the expression ἅπαντα κοινά (cf. 2:44), including Plato, *Critias* 110c. Others write κοινὰ πάντα, including Aristotle, *Nicomachean Ethics* 8.1.4; Iamblichus, *Life of Pythagoras* 168; and Lucian, *On Salaried Posts in Great Houses* 19–20. For other references of ancient authors using these expressions, see Dupont, "La communauté des biens aux premiers jours de l'Eglise," 505–9; and Plümacher, *Lukas als hellenistischer Schriftsteller*, 17–18. See also van der Horst, "Hellenistic Parallels to the Acts of the Apostles (2.1–47)," 59–60, for other Hellenistic references to "collective property." Of particular interest are the following references to the Essenes as having everything in common: Philo, *Every Good Man Is Free* 86; and Josephus, *The Jewish War* 2.122–23; idem, *Jewish Antiquities* 18.20. Cf. Dupont, "La communauté des biens aux premiers jours de l'Eglise," 518–19, who concludes that, while this summary incorporates Greco-Roman concepts and literary themes relating to friendship, the evidence is not completely convincing. Of particular importance is that the summary never describes these earliest Christians as "friends" or "brothers," but simply as "believers."

94. Marguerat, "La mort d'Ananias et Saphira," 213.

95. Cf. Schmithals, *Die Apostelgeschichte des Lukas*, 38–39; and Johnson, *The Acts of the Apostles*, 59, who states that the lack of details directs one's attention to "the sharing of possessions as a spontaneous outgrowth of the Spirit." Cf. also S. Scott Bartchy, "Community of Goods in Acts: Idealization or Social Reality?" in *The Future of Early Christianity: Essays in Honor of Helmut Koester*, ed. Birger A. Pearson (Minneapolis: Fortress, 1991), 312–15, who suggests that Luke describes a "fictive-kinship relationship" among the believers.

96. Many have suggested that Luke is depicting a primitive form of communism. Cf., e.g., Brian Capper, "The Palestinian Cultural Context of Earliest Christian Community of Goods," in Bauckham, *The Book of Acts in Its Palestinian Setting*, 323–56; Joseph A. Fitzmyer, "Jewish Christianity in Acts in Light of the Qumran Scrolls," in Keck and Martyn, *Studies in Luke-Acts*, 242–44; and Marshall, *The Acts of the Apostles*, 84. Cf. also Dupont, "La communauté des biens aux premiers jours de l'Eglise," 511–12, who reminds that, since a common ancient literary device was to impute the actions of a few to everyone, one should not be mistaken about what this generalization suggests; and Johnson, *Sharing Possessions*, 21, who states that this practice of selling possessions was not absolute, as the description of breaking bread in their homes (2:46) implies.

communism or an early form of Christian social welfare.[97] Others have
debated whether this picture of the early Christians is historically accurate or an idealistic description based on ancient utopian ideals.[98]
However, the affinity in these descriptions to social and political concepts from the Greco-Roman world suggests that one must consider
their potential effect on an implied audience that might be familiar
with such concepts.[99] If Luke uses social ideals or conventions to characterize these early believers,[100] an adequate analysis of this depiction
requires a brief exploration of the Greco-Roman concepts of the *polis*
and friendship.[101]

Central to both the Greco-Roman political ideals and friendship traditions was the concern for social cohesiveness. Plato, for instance,
articulated an understanding of the ideal *polis* (city-state) that was anal-
ogous to a human individual.[102] In an important discussion concerning
this ideal found in *Republic 5*, Plato stresses that cohesion and unity are
much better than division and fragmentation within the ideal *polis*.[103]
The destruction of political cohesion occurs when individuals dispute

---

97. See, e.g., Boismard and Lamouille, *Les Actes des deux Apôtres*, 2:31; Haenchen, *The Acts of the Apostles*, 233–35; Martin Hengel, *Property and Riches in the Early Church: Aspects of a Social History of Christianity* (Philadelphia: Fortress, 1974), 31–34; and Lake, "The Communism of Acts II. and IV.–V.," 5:140–51.

98. See, e.g., Bartchy, "Community of Goods in Acts," 309–18; François Bovon, "Israel, die Kirche und die Völker im lukanischen Doppelwerk," *TLZ* 108 (1983): 403–14; Capper, "The Palestinian Cultural Context of Earliest Christian Community of Goods," 323–56; Johnson, *The Acts of the Apostles*, 61–62; David L. Mealand, "Community of Goods and Utopian Allusions in Acts II–IV," *JTS* 28 (April 1977): 97; Pesch, *Die Apostelgeschichte*, 1:184–94; Plümacher, *Lukas als hellenistischer Schriftsteller*, 17–18; Daniel R. Schwartz, "The End of the Line: Paul in the Canonical Book of Acts," in *Paul and the Legacies of Paul*, ed. William S. Babcock (Dallas: Southern Methodist University Press, 1990), 16; and Weiser, *Die Apostelgeschichte*, 1:102–3.

99. Cf. Mitchell, "The Social Function of Friendship in Acts 2:44–47 and 4:32–37," 257, who correctly warns: "To grasp Luke's meaning it is not enough to say that he appealed to the well-known Greco-Roman tradition of friendship.... His interest lies not primarily in friendship but in using the notion of friendship for another purpose."

100. The use of such social ideals and conventions to describe the believers is an excellent example of characterization from a character-viewpoint, as described in chapter 1 (above).

101. See Wall, "The Acts of the Apostles," in *NIB*, 10:72, who sees these ideals "more deeply rooted in the prophetic typology of Jubilee."

102. Plato, *Republic* 2.368a–369c.

103. See, e.g., ibid., 5.462b: Ἔχομεν οὖν τι μεῖζον κακὸν πόλει ἢ ἐκεῖνο, ὃ ἂν αὐτὴν διασπᾷ καὶ ποιῇ πολλὰς ἀντὶ μιᾶς; ἢ μεῖζον ἀγαθὸν τοῦ ὃ ἂν ξυνδῇ τε καὶ ποιῇ μίαν; (Do we know of any greater evil for a state than the thing that distracts it and makes it many instead of one, or a greater good than that which binds it together and makes it one? [LCL])

over "mine" and "not mine."[104] Concern over distinctions of possession and rights militate against the cohesion of the *polis* because that concern creates dissension and arguments.[105] Conversely, Plato emphasizes that, when devotion to a common interest characterizes the citizens, they all share one another's feelings of joy and sorrow or of pleasure and pain, just as the whole person suffers from pain in one finger.[106] The greatest good of the *polis*, then, is unanimity, for its realization fulfills the basic needs of all persons.[107] Thus, Plato's positive depiction of the ideal *polis* focuses on unanimity as indicative of two things: the elimination of self-interest, and the affirmation of the collective interest of the *polis*.

The friendship traditions within the Greco-Roman culture also emphasized some important, positive aspects of social cohesion. Although these traditions were somewhat diverse in delineating the role of friendship within the social structure, the Aristotelian discussions in *Nicomachean Ethics* 8–9 and in *Eudemian Ethics* 7 provide an adequate background and delineation of several significant emphases of this traditional concept.[108] Aristotle states that φιλία (friendship) holds the *polis* together[109] and defines φιλία as κοινωνία, in which friends are like siblings and "have all things in common," which the summary of Acts 2 reflects.[110] The term φιλία, however, is applicable to a variety of personal

---

104. Ibid., 5.462c.

105. Ibid., 5.464c–e.

106. Ibid., 5.463c–464b.

107. Ibid., 5.464b.

108. For studies dealing with the concept of friendship in Aristotle's writings, see Julia Annas, "Plato and Aristotle on Friendship and Altruism," *Mind* 86 (October 1977): 532–52; Cooper, "Aristotle on Friendship," 301–40; W. W. Fortenbaugh, "Aristotle's Analysis of Friendship," *Phronesis* 22 (1975): 51–62; Horst Hutter, *Politics as Friendship: The Origins of Classical Notions of Politics in the Theory and Practice of Friendship* (Waterloo, ON: Wilfrid Laurier University Press, 1978); Richard Kraut, *Aristotle on the Human Good* (Princeton: Princeton University Press, 1989), 109–54; Geoffrey Percival, *Aristotle on Friendship* (Cambridge: Cambridge University Press, 1940); A. W. Price, *Love and Friendship in Plato and Aristotle* (Oxford: Clarendon, 1989); and A. D. M. Walker, "Aristotle's Account of Friendship in the *Nicomachean Ethics*," *Phronesis* 24 (1979): 180–96.

109. Aristotle, *Nicomachean Ethics* 8.1.4.

110. Ibid., 8.9.1–2; cf. 9.8.2. In Aristotle's writings, the references to "common property" between friends suggests a modified view that differs from Plato's understanding, since Aristotle rejects common *ownership* of property in the polis, which he sees as creating division (*Politics* 2.1.8–2.2.9). Cf. Mitchell, "The Social Function of Friendship in Acts 2:44–47 and 4:32–37," 260–63. Cf. Plato, *Republic* 4.449c: κοινὰ τὰ φίλων ἔσται (the possessions of friends will be in common [LCL]). That both Plato and Aristotle refer to proverbial statements about friends and property suggests a common tradition.

relationships,[111] so Aristotle believes that one's understanding of φιλία must take these different relationships into account.[112] Aristotle observes that three primary characteristics are common to the various kinds of φιλία or friendship: (1) εὔνοια, usually translated "goodwill,"[113] yet also connotes the active seeking for what is good or beneficial for another; (2) recognition that someone has acted out of εὔνοια toward another person; and (3) reciprocity, which stresses that the recipient of an act of εὔνοια responds with a mutual act of εὔνοια.[114] In all friendships, Aristotle contends that friends will enjoy a unique bond between them because they seek the other's good for that friend's sake alone. A person thus did not act in friendship out of self-interest but self-*dis*interest for the sake of one's friend.[115] In such a reciprocal relation, such selfless activity toward a person will create a "chain reaction" of beneficial activity between these friends — activity based on the attitude of εὔνοια only for the friend's sake.[116] This selfless activity, therefore, provides the social cohesion necessary for the *polis* to exist and function, in contrast to the στάσις created by self-serving activity.[117] Although Aristotle does not agree with Plato on certain aspects of political philosophy, they both positively affirm that the activity of friendship, based on one's interest

---

111. According to Aristotle (*Nicomachean Ethics* 8.2.1–8.3.9; *Eudemian Ethics* 7.2.1–23), three kinds of friendships correspond to three reasons for liking something: utility or usefulness, pleasure, and virtue.

112. Aristotle, *Nicomachean Ethics* 8.4.4. Unlike Plato, Aristotle was interested in describing, as he understood it, the basic social bond that held diverse people together.

113. The term εὔνοια is not adequately translated by the term "goodwill," because the Greek term refers to "mind" (-νοια) rather than "will." Thus, the term is left untranslated in the present work.

114. See, e.g., Aristotle, *Nicomachean Ethics* 8.2.3–4; 9.5.3; and *Eudemian Ethics* 7.2.8; 7.7.3.

115. Thus, one does not act out of selfishness in the case of utility in order to gain some benefit from that act; rather, it is εὔνοια and, therefore, evidence of friendship because that one acts for the friend's sake alone. See Cooper, "Aristotle on Friendship," 301–40, esp. 311 for a thorough examination of the role of disinterestness in Aristotle's understanding of εὔνοια in relation to all three kinds of friendship. Contra Hutter, *Politics as Friendship*, 108; and Price, *Love and Friendship in Plato and Aristotle*, 155–57.

116. Contra Mitchell, "The Social Function of Friendship in Acts 2:44–47 and 4:32–37," 264–66; and A. R. Hands, *Charities and Social Aid in Greece and Rome* (Ithaca, NY: Cornell University Press, 1968), 26, who sees a giver's action as "self-regarding." For similar conclusions about the patron-client relationship, see John E. Stambaugh and David L. Balch, *The New Testament in Its Social Environment*, LEC 2 (Philadelphia: Westminster, 1986), 63–67.

117. Cf. Aristotle, *Politics* 1.1.8–12, who states that persons are part of a *polis* because they are not self-sufficient; a chief good of the *polis* is the self-sufficiency of those joined in κοινωνία.

in the well-being of others rather than on self-interest, enables the *polis* to fulfill its potential social function.

While definitive evidence of literary dependence on the Greco-Roman friendship traditions or political thought is not available,[118] the brief descriptions of 2:42, 44–45 indicate a conceptual affinity with such social ideals or concepts.[119] The Lukan depiction of the Christians with friendship and utopian imagery assumes that the readers will recognize the positive traits now attributed to the believers: traits of unanimity and selfless activity for the sake of one another — traits that lead to reciprocated action among them.[120] By characterizing the believers from a character-viewpoint, the narrator directs the readers' attention to the specific traits that are highlighted explicitly. Such a depiction uses these affirmations from Greco-Roman traditions of friendship and politics to present a positive image of this group of Christian believers: an image of a community, which the Holy Spirit has created, that reflects the highest ideals and expectations of that era's political and social thought.

The last two verses of this narrative summary, 2:46–47, form a literary section that provides additional description of the communal dynamics of those early Christians already described in 2:42–45. The phrase καθ' ἡμέραν (daily) stands both at the beginning of these two verses and at the end, which suggests an emphasis on the recurring, daily activity of those who constitute the group of believers. Two foci are present here in these verses: the primary narrative focus is on the activity of the believers themselves, and the secondary focus is on the activity of God.

The major portion of 2:46–47 focuses on the activity of the Christians. The grammatical structure of this description places one activity at the center, with four participial phrases modifying the main verb. Two

---

118. Cf. Plümacher, *Lukas als hellenistischer Schriftsteller*, 17–18, who recognizes the difficulties in identifying the Lukan sources for such traditions.

119. Conceptual *affinity* must not be confused with conceptual *identity*. See Dupont, "L'union entre les premiers Chrétiens dans les Actes des Apôtres," 303; and "La communauté des biens aux premiers jours de l'Eglise," 519.

120. Cf. Mitchell, "The Social Function of Friendship in Acts 2:44–47 and 4:32–37," 264–72, who contends that Luke has "contextualized the maxim so to question the social order of his day." However, if the distinctions between characterization from a character-viewpoint and that from a personality-viewpoint are valid ones in Greco-Roman literature, one would question Mitchell's conclusion here, since social conventions and ideals are not used to *question* them but to *affirm* them within the narrative experience.

participial phrases precede and two participial phrases follow the main verb, as shown below:

Participial phrase #1: τε προσκαρτεροῦντες ὁμοθυμαδὸν ἐν τῷ ἱερῷ,

Participial phrase #2: κλῶντές τε κατ᾿ οἶκον ἄρτον,

Main clause: μετελάμβανον τροφῆς ἐν ἀγαλλιάσει καί ᾿ἀφελότητι καρδίας

Participial phrase #3: αἰνοῦντες τὸν θεὸν καὶ

Participial phrase #4: ἔχοντες χάριν πρὸς ὅλον τὸν λαόν.

The imperfect indicative μετελάμβανον defines the construction's main action. The verb implies more than simply "receiving" food or nourishment (τροφῆς; 2:46), which relates to the distribution of verse 45. The prepositional phrase following the main verb, ἐν ἀγαλλιάσει καὶ ἀφελότητι καρδίας (with gladness and simplicity of heart), provides a direct description of the believers' inner motives for the readers, who cannot make such a conclusion about those motives or attitudes without such information being given directly.[121] Clearly, the narrator presents the believers as those who by joyful benevolence, not by coercion, participate in this group that meets the human needs of others.

The first two participial phrases that modify μετελάμβανον reflect positive imagery that the reader has already encountered in Acts. The first participle προσκαρτεροῦντες describes the noteworthy, continual devotion of the believers, just as is denoted earlier (1:14; 2:42).[122] Alongside the participle is the adverb ὁμοθυμαδόν, the same term used to describe affirmatively the "togetherness" or unanimity of the Christians who return obediently to Jerusalem after Jesus' ascension (1:14).[123] This time, however, the narrator describes these characteristics of devotion and togetherness in the context of the temple, a description that stresses the

---

121. The NRSV translation of ἐν ἀγαλλιάσει καὶ ἀφελότητι καρδίας (2:46), "with glad and generous hearts," loses a distinct element of the phrase: the "gladness" (ἀγαλλιάσει) and "simplicity" (ἀφελότητι) are the means by which the "sharing together" occurs, rather than καρδίας, which modifies ἀγαλλιάσει καὶ ἀφελότητι.

122. The only difference in the use of the participle προσκαρτεροῦντες (2:46), when compared to 1:14 and 2:42, is that it does not form an imperfect periphrastic construction.

123. Cf. Schmithals, *Die Apostelgeschichte des Lukas*, 39; and Fitzmyer, *The Acts of the Apostles*, 272.

continued importance of worship and Christian practices in continuity with Judaism.[124] The second participial expression, κλῶντές ... ἄρτον, also appears in verse 42 to depict the believers' communal practices. The clear connections between these participles and verse 42, which itself correlates divine presence and activity among the believers with the communal ties among them, reflect the same positive images in the main action of 2:46.

The two participial phrases of 2:47 that subsequently modify μετελάμβανον also contribute to the cumulative picture of the early Christians in the narrative summary (2:42–47). The first phrase, which briefly describes the believers continually "praising God" (αἰνοῦντες τὸν θεόν), suggests that humanitarian interests did not create this unique experience of a utopian community. Rather, the mention of this activity, directed toward and in response to God, recognizes the relation between the fulfillment of the divine promise and the communal concern for one another. The nature of those communal bonds among the believers cannot be divorced from the fulfillment of the divine promise, the coming of the Holy Spirit.

The second participial phrase, ἔχοντες χάριν πρὸς ὅλον τὸν λαόν, is a bit more ambiguous. Modern translations typically identify ὅλον τὸν λαόν as the source of χάριν, as one finds in the NRSV: "having the goodwill of all the people." Such a translation conveys a positive image of the believers, to be sure: it implies that these believers enjoyed an impressive reputation with all the λαός, the term that Acts typically reserves to speak of the Jewish people as *God's* people.[125] However, one significant problem with this typical translation is that it does not fit the literary context well, in which the believers are described largely as the *actors*

---

124. The continual devotion ἐν τῷ ἱερῷ suggests no separation between the believers and Judaism. This emphasis also compares to the depiction in Acts 2 of the fulfilled promise to Israel through the Holy Spirit's coming and of Jerusalem "bursting at the seams" with believers, who are Jews themselves. Cf. Haenchen, *The Acts of the Apostles*, 192; Peterson, "The Worship of the New Community," 375; Schille, *Die Apostelgeschichte des Lukas*, 121–22; Williams, *Acts*, 61–62; and Zingg, *Das Wachsen der Kirche*, 159.

125. See Joseph B. Tyson, "The Jewish Public in Luke-Acts," *NTS* 30 (October 1984): 574–83; and Johnson, *The Acts of the Apostles*, 59–60. Luke never uses λαός to describe a crowd of Gentiles. Luke uses the term λαός 47 times in Acts, describing mostly the Jewish people or Israel (cf., e.g., 4:27; 13:17; 21:28; 26:17, 23); the only explicit use of λαός in a different manner (15:14) describes a people of God taken from among the Gentiles. In 18:10, λαός refers to "my [God's] people," but it is not certain whether this refers *only* to Jews. See also Lohfink, *Die Sammlung Israels*, 49; and Zingg, *Das Wachsen der Kirche*, 147–48.

rather than the *receivers* of human action.[126] Considering the various uses of the preposition πρός with the accusative, including its possible function of indicating the direction of an action *toward* the preposition's object, a reconsideration of the translation is necessary.

In his article on this participial phrase, T. David Andersen reexamines the phrase by considering evidence from Jewish writings and from general usage in Greco-Roman literature.[127] A significant element of Andersen's brief work is a study of the potential meaning of a grammatical construction in which χάρις precedes the preposition πρός. Though that construction only appears here in the New Testament, it appears six times in Josephus's works and three times in Philo's works.[128] In every reference χάρις refers to an attitude of favor or goodwill directed *toward* the person designated by the preposition πρός.[129] In addition, the Liddell-Scott-Jones lexicon identifies the usage of the preposition πρός with the accusative in literary contexts dealing with "intercourse or reciprocal action," including contexts dealing with εὔνοια, ἔχθρα, and φιλία, important themes in Greco-Roman friendship traditions and political philosophy.[130] Finally, since the narrative uses other prepositions to express the meaning of "having favor with," the use of a preposition that usually communicates the opposite meaning would be most surprising.[131] Considering these factors, the participial phrase seems to direct the reader's attention to the believers having or expressing favor *toward* the people, rather than to the goodwill or favor coming *from* the people to the believers.[132] Thus,

---

126. The typical translation of the apostles and Christians as the recipients of χάρις fits the literary context, where the people respond positively to Peter's speech (2:41). However, within 2:42–47 the believers are described explicitly as givers of χάρις and only implicitly as recipients of χάρις, and this occurs within the context of other Jewish-Christian believers.

127. T. David Andersen, "The Meaning of ΕΧΟΝΤΕΣ ΧΑΡΙΝ ΠΡΟΣ in Acts 2.47," *NTS* 34 (1988): 604–10.

128. The six references in Josephus's work are *Life* 252, 339; *Jewish Antiquities* 6.86; 12.124; 14.146, 148. The three references in Philo's works are *Confusion of Tongues* 116; *On Abraham* 118; and *Embassy to Gaius* 296.

129. Andersen, "The Meaning of ΕΧΟΝΤΕΣ ΧΑΡΙΝ ΠΡΟΣ in Acts 2.47," 607. Cf. Fitzmyer, *The Acts of the Apostles*, 272–73.

130. LSJ, 1498. Cf. Andersen, "The Meaning of ΕΧΟΝΤΕΣ ΧΑΡΙΝ ΠΡΟΣ in Acts 2.47," 608–9.

131. Andersen, "The Meaning of ΕΧΟΝΤΕΣ ΧΑΡΙΝ ΠΡΟΣ in Acts 2.47," 609. For other Lukan references conveying the sense of "having favor with," see, e.g., Luke 1:30; 2:52; and Acts 7:46. In these cases, the prepositions παρά or ἐνώπιον are used.

132. In a society of reciprocity, the believers' goodwill may be reciprocated, so that they will also enjoy favor *from* the people, but that is not the primary emphasis here. Contra Co, "The Major Summaries in Acts," 75n67.

the believers are the ones who respond positively, act as friends toward those of Jerusalem, and create an atmosphere of unity.

This revised understanding of the participial phrase ἔχοντες χάριν πρὸς ὅλον τὸν λαόν enhances the developing portrait of the earliest Christians in 2:42–47. The narrative does not concentrate directly on the interaction between the Jewish Christians and the rest of the Jewish people of Jerusalem. Rather, Luke directs the reader's attention to the communal dynamics both *among* believers and now *from* believers to others. Clearly, one is left with the distinct impression that these Christians are not becoming isolated or limited in their spirit of sharing only to those in their group; instead, they extend such positive communal attitudes and actions to others within Jerusalem.

The final statement within the narrative summary of 2:42–47 concludes the smaller section of 2:46–47. The conjunction δέ connects this sentence grammatically to the summary's previous descriptions of the Christians. However, whereas the previous section focuses on the believers' daily activity, this sentence presents God's recurrent activity among them. The subject is ὁ κύριος,[133] and ὁ κύριος continually adds τοὺς σῳζομένους to that group.[134] Luke modifies what he has depicted as divine activity (conveyed by the verb προσετίθει) with the phrase ἐπὶ τὸ αὐτό, the same phrase used in 1:15 and 2:1 to affirm the unity of the believers.[135] This phrase provides the last image of this statement and narrative summary, leaving the reader with a lasting impression that the unanimity, communal dynamics, and growth among the Christians are

---

133. The difficulty in interpreting ὁ κύριος is that the narrative uses this designation in Acts 2 to refer both to God *and* to Jesus (cf. 2:25, 34, 36, 39). See David P. Moessner, "*Two Lords 'at the Right Hand'? The Psalms and an Intertextual Reading of Peter's Pentecost Speech (Acts 2:14–36)*," in *Literary Studies in Luke-Acts: Essays in Honor of Joseph B. Tyson*, ed. Richard P. Thompson and Thomas E. Phillips (Macon, GA: Mercer University Press, 1998), 215–34.

134. The indicative προσετίθει of 2:47 creates a possible *inclusio* with 2:41, emphasizing the group's growth as a result of divine activity. Cf. Johnson, *The Literary Function of Possessions in Luke-Acts*, 185n2. Cf. also Co, "The Major Summaries in Acts," 60, who sees ὁ κύριος linking to 2:39 (κύριος ὁ θεός) and τοὺς σῳζομένους linking to 2:40 (σώθητε), thus identifying other textual links between 2:42–47 and preceding events.

135. Although textual variants of 2:47 either substitute or add τῇ ἐκκλησίᾳ, sufficient evidence does not exist to consider these alternatives seriously. Nonetheless, the NRSV and NIV translation of ἐπὶ τὸ αὐτό (to their number) weakens the sense of unanimity and togetherness that accompanies the connections between this statement, 1:15, and 2:1. Cf. Dupont, "L'union entre les premiers Chrétiens dans les Actes des Apôtres," 304–8; Johnson, *The Literary Function of Possessions in Luke-Acts*, 187, 189; and Pesch, *Die Apostelgeschichte*, 1:132.

all directly related to the divine activity and presence that the narrative explicitly describes.[136]

An Assessment of the Characterization of the Believers in Acts 2:42–47

As Luke concludes the Pentecost narrative, he describes in a brief summary what has happened to the group of believers because of the extraordinary events and Peter's explanation to the Jews who were present. The characterization of the believers in 2:42–47 is not merely one of Luke's "little cameos of life in the early church, intended... as models for the church of his own day."[137] This concluding summary coaxes the reader to connect this consummate portrait of the Christians to other narrative images and events in the first two chapters of Acts. The extraordinary events and results of Pentecost spill over onto the expanding group of believers. The narrative describes both implicitly and explicitly this group — a group expanding in diversity and number — in terms of unanimity, fulfillment of the divine promise, and continuity with Judaism. Such descriptions utilize some of the same imagery, words, and expressions found in prior narrative depictions of believers to show that these believers are much like the "pre-Pentecost" ones. These images, however, do not suggest that the "church" is at this time created as a new group separate from Judaism.[138] These Jewish believers maintain complete continuity with Judaism and its practices, as God fulfills God's promise to Israel among them. Nothing indicates any negative reaction to these believers.[139] At the same time, Luke depicts these believers as responding spontaneously in unanimity and active goodwill toward others. Thus, a positive picture of this group begins to emerge from one's reading of the Acts narrative — a group that fulfills the essence of Greco-Roman political and social ideals because of divine activity.[140]

---

136. Cf. Marguerat, "La mort d'Ananias et Saphira," 215–16; Zingg, *Das Wachsen der Kirche*, 169; and Schmithals, *Die Apostelgeschichte des Lukas*, 38, who sees the growth descriptions (2:41, 47b) as providing the context in which the believers are depicted in 2:42–47a.

137. Williams, *Acts*, 59.

138. Cf. Löning, "Das Verhältnis zum Judentum," 309; and Zingg, *Das Wachsen der Kirche*, 159.

139. Cf. Tannehill, *The Narrative Unity of Luke-Acts*, 2:47.

140. Luke describes the activity of goodwill predominantly within the believers, but the participial phrase ἔχοντες χάριν πρὸς ὅλον τὸν λαόν indicates that the believers respond similarly to *all* in Jerusalem.

The summary of 2:42–47 and, more specifically, its characterization of the church or Christian community do not function in this narrative context to provide specific directions for the religious or social program of the Christian church, either in Luke's day or in modern times.[141] Rather, the characterization of the believers in 2:42–47 contributes to the cumulative, positive portrait in the narrative in four distinct ways: (1) by reaffirming the qualities of unanimity and togetherness in the midst of rapid growth and increasing diversity, (2) by presenting images that suggest continuity with Judaism in the fulfillment of God's promise to Israel, (3) by depicting the fulfillment of Greco-Roman social ideals, and (4) by linking these positive traits to divine blessing and activity.[142]

THE PRAYING BELIEVERS
AFTER INITIAL PERSECUTION (ACTS 4:23–31)

The Literary Context (Acts 3:1–4:22)

After the extraordinary events of Pentecost and the positive results as attested by the communal dynamics of the growing group of believers, Luke narrates a healing scene, which correlates with the summary statement of 2:43 that "many wonders and signs occurred through the apostles."[143] In this account, Peter and John encounter a lame man as they enter the temple at the time of prayer (3:1–3), a practice consistent with the previous summary descriptions of believers who "devoted themselves to…the prayers" (2:42; cf. 1:14) and "daily spent much time together in the temple" (2:46).[144] Peter commanded the lame man to stand up and lifted him up, and Luke states that "immediately his feet

---

141. Contra, e.g., Krodel, *Acts*, 95; Mitchell, "The Social Function of Friendship in Acts 2:44–47 and 4:32–37," 272; Schmithals, *Die Apostelgeschichte des Lukas*, 39; John T. Squires, "The Plan of God," in Marshall and Peterson, *Witness to the Gospel*, 38–39; and Williams, *Acts*, 59.

142. Cf. Pesch, *Die Apostelgeschichte*, 1:132–33, who suggests that this unanimous community is identified here as the eschatological people of God. Cf. also Tannehill, *The Narrative Unity of Luke-Acts*, 2:46–47; Weiser, *Die Apostelgeschichte*, 1:101–2; and David Seccombe, "The New People of God," in Marshall and Peterson, *Witness to the Gospel*, 355–56.

143. See van der Horst, "Hellenistic Parallels to Acts (Chapters 3 and 4)," *JSNT* 35 (1989): 37–41, for parallel references in Hellenistic sources to different matters in the description of this healing scene and subsequent speech.

144. The healing scene at the temple also reaffirms the idea that the believers, as a character group in the narrative, are not to this point distinct or separate from Judaism. See Barrett, *The Acts of the Apostles*, 1:177–78, who states that the imperfect indicative ἀνέβαινον (3:1) also stresses the believers' ongoing faithfulness to Judaism.

and ankles were strengthened" (3:6–7), a point made obvious by the healed man's actions: "and jumping up, he stood and began to walk, and he entered with them into the temple, walking and jumping and praising God" (3:8).[145] The narrated event continues by emphasizing three different results of this healing: (1) the man's walking and his response of praise to God (3:8–9), which is the same description previously ascribed to the believers (cf. 2:47),[146] (2) the astonishment of the people (λαός)[147] and their earnest pursuit of Peter and John in search of an explanation (3:9–11; cf. 3:12),[148] and (3) Peter's explanation (3:12–26).[149] In the speech, Luke presents Peter as explaining what has occurred; Peter functions implicitly as Luke's spokesperson while reiterating similar themes to those of his previous speech, including the death and resurrection of Jesus (cf. 2:14–40).[150] However, this speech intensely calls for repentance and paradoxically stresses both the audience's responsibility for Jesus' death (3:13–15, 17; cf. 2:23) and its involvement in the promised blessing.[151]

The narrative creates a sense of anticipation that, like the response to the Pentecost speech, repentance and further evidence of God working among the believers will result. The mood changes at this point, however,

---

145. The two participles, ἐξαλλόμενος and ἀλλόμενος, have a common root. Along with four occurrences of περιπατέω in 3:6–9, the repetition emphasizes the dramatic event: a man lame from birth now walks (and more)! Cf. Johnson, *The Acts of the Apostles*, 66; and Tannehill, "The Composition of Acts 3–5," 219.

146. The narrator describes the man as "walking and jumping and praising God" (περιπατῶν καὶ ἀλλόμενος καὶ αἰνῶν τὸν θεόν; 3:8), which is repeated in the report of what the people saw (περιπατοῦντα καὶ αἰνοῦντα τὸν θεόν; 3:9) and also repeats a prior description of the believers (αἰνοῦντα τὸν θεόν; 2:47). Cf. Johnson, *The Acts of the Apostles*, 64–66. See Haenchen, *The Acts of the Apostles*, 200–201.

147. The people's initial reaction, mentioned three different times in 3:10–12, is similar to that described of the Pentecost crowd (2:7, 12). In all these descriptions, one (two in 2:7) of three "amazement" terms — ἐξίστημι, θάμβος, or θαυμάζω — is used, suggesting that readers should perceive the similarity of these initial reactions.

148. The verb συντρέχω is an interesting choice of words for two reasons: (1) the term connotes both "running together" or "gathering together" and close association or agreement, and (2) the possible wordplay with συνέδριον that also gathers together out of concern for the apostles' actions rather than out of "amazement" (cf. 4:15; 5:21, 27, 34, 41; also 6:12, 15).

149. According to Gaventa ("Toward a Theology of Acts," 154), Peter's response interprets the event within a threefold literary pattern of event, interpretation, and response.

150. Cf. Tannehill, "The Functions of Peter's Mission Speeches," 404–5.

151. See Tannehill, "The Composition of Acts 3–5," 220–21, who states that the vivid accusations about Jesus' death and the emphatic second-person plural pronouns (3:19–26) stress the audience's involvement in God's work, both negatively and positively. Cf. Tyson, *Images of Judaism in Luke-Acts*, 110–11.

as the temple authorities (the priests, the captain of the temple, and the Sadducees) are "greatly annoyed" (διαπονούμενοι; 4:2) with Peter and John and arrest them because the apostles were teaching about Jesus' resurrection in the temple, the location of the Sadducees' authoritative, priestly role.[152] The narrator briefly describes the circumstances in which conflict first arises in the Acts narrative, as these authority figures, not the believers, initiate that conflict and opposition.[153] Luke continues to present this surprising picture by describing these who have violated the harmonious atmosphere of the Christians as themselves gathering *together* with other religious leaders (4:5).[154] The ones who have come together because of their opposition (τὸ συνέδριον; 4:15), however, are also "astonished" (ἐθαύμαζον; 4:13) as they witness the boldness of Peter and John.[155] The duo's narrated boldness coincides with Luke's direct description of Peter as "filled with the Holy Spirit" (πλησθεὶς πνεύματος ἁγίου; 4:8).[156] In contrast, the narrator describes the council as resorting to verbal threats in their attempts to squelch the apostles' voices, even though Peter and John have openly acknowledged God's role both in the healing and in the subsequent message.[157]

---

152. The narrator's brief explanation (4:2; cf. 4:18) suggests that readers may not recognize why the temple authorities have arrested Peter and John. Cf. 23:1–10 (esp. 23:8), where the narrator provides a similar explanation about the Sadducees. Cf. Johnson, *The Acts of the Apostles*, 76. See Conzelmann, *Acts of the Apostles*, 32.

153. Regarding the plot function of arrests in Acts, see Richard I. Pervo, *Profit with Delight: The Literary Genre of the Acts of the Apostles* (Philadelphia: Fortress, 1987), 19–24.

154. Luke uses the verb συνάγω in two distinct ways: (1) to describe *positively* a gathering together of believers or, at least, "interested observers" (cf. Acts 4:31; 11:26; 13:44; 14:27; 15:6, 30; 20:7, 8); (2) to describe *negatively* the gathering of Jesus' opponents (cf. Luke 22:66; Acts 4:26, 27). Cf. Tyson, *Images of Judaism in Luke-Acts*, 110, who sees the apostles opposed by the temple priests, just as Jesus was.

155. The narrator describes this amazement similarly to the amazement of the Pentecost crowds and of the people at the temple the previous day. However, unlike the other two scenes, the council is in no mood to listen with an open mind (4:14, 16). Cf. Krodel, *Acts*, 98; Pervo, *Profit with Delight*, 43; and Bruce, *The Book of the Acts*, 96.

156. The description of Peter as "filled with the Holy Spirit" refers the reader to the Pentecost event and the Holy Spirit's coming (cf. 2:1–4). Cf. Shepherd, *The Narrative Function of the Holy Spirit*, 168; and Dunn, *The Acts of the Apostles*, 52–53.

157. This contrast between the apostles (where God is at work) and the council is subtly linked to God's earlier activity in adding to the believers, as suggested by the use of σῴζω both in 2:47 (τοὺς σῳζομένους) and in Peter's explanation about the lame man's healing (σέσωται; 4:9; cf. 4:12, σωθῆναι). Cf. Bruce, *The Book of the Acts*, 78–79, 94–96; Krodel, *Acts*, 110–11; Tannehill, "The Functions of Peter's Mission Speeches," 407; and Pervo, *Profit with Delight*, 43: "Their opponents are a pack of fascist clowns, reduced to silence with a few inspired words."

The problem for these religious leaders was that, while they are attempting to silence the apostles' message about Jesus, the people (λαός) respond favorably to what they have seen and heard.[158] The narrative emphasizes the affirmative response of the Jewish people, both from the outset of the opposition (4:4) and at the scene's end, when the authorities release the two apostles (4:21). The lasting image of this context is one of a split or division over the response to the gospel message.[159] On the one hand, the Jewish people respond positively and overwhelmingly in belief and praise to God, thereby acknowledging God's activity (4:4, 21; cf. 2:47). On the other hand, the temple authorities reject that message and respond negatively in staunch opposition, thereby renouncing what the narrative clearly presents as God's activity. This narrative scene, therefore, depicts a divided response to the gospel message, a division created by the religious leaders who respond and act separately from the believers, the Jewish people, and God.[160]

The Characterization of the Group of Believers in Acts 4:23–31

The next narrative section chronologically follows the account of the lame man's healing and the apostles' subsequent arrest. Both the participle ἀπολυθέντες and the conjunction δέ connect these two literary sections sequentially, so that what follows here in 4:23–31 is dependent on prior episodes.[161] In describing what happens next, Luke states that the two apostles report what the temple authorities have told them to τοὺς ἰδίους (their own), which apparently refers to a gathering of believers (4:23).[162] Although the ambiguous expression τοὺς ἰδίους does not directly indicate whether this gathering includes only the apostles or a

---

158. Cf. Lohfink, *Die Sammlung Israels*, 62, who stresses that this success maintained continuity between the "old" people of God and the church as the "new" people of God; and Jack T. Sanders, *The Jews in Luke-Acts* (Philadelphia: Fortress, 1987), 236–38, who suggests that this favorable Jewish response does not correlate with the speeches in Acts that represent the Jewish people as "Christ-killers."

159. See Johnson, *The Acts of the Apostles*, 80–82; Zettner, *Amt, Gemeinde und kirchliche Einheit*, 261; and Gaventa, "Toward a Theology of Acts," 155. Cf. Jacob Jervell, *Luke and the People of God: A New Look at Luke-Acts* (Minneapolis: Augsburg, 1972), 47; and Lohfink, *Die Sammlung Israels*, 50–51.

160. Contra Jacob Jervell, *The Theology of the Acts of the Apostles* (Cambridge, UK: Cambridge University Press, 1996), 34–43.

161. Forms of ἀπολύω (4:21, 23) are used to refer to the council members' action. See Schneider, *Die Apostelgeschichte*, 1:354, for a list of literary connections between 4:23–31 and the previous scene. Cf. Barrett, *The Acts of the Apostles*, 1:242; Schille, *Die Apostelgeschichte des Lukas*, 138; and Weiser, *Die Apostelgeschichte*, 1:131–32.

162. The brief statement about the report relies on the previous scene rather than repetition.

larger group of believers, these individuals obviously are not mere acquaintances.[163] These persons are almost like family, indicating a close, personal relationship, just as the previous descriptions of groups of Christians have depicted.[164] The narrative implies that Peter and John, as all persons would do, return to those who will support and encourage them, in stark contrast to those who have just opposed and threatened them.

As one examines this narrative section, Luke condenses his description to focus the reader's attention on the collective response of these believers. The narrator states that the ones who hear (οἱ . . . ἀκούσαντες) the report "together raised their voices to God" (ὁμοθυμαδὸν ἦραν φωνὴν πρὸς τὸν θεόν; 4:24; cf. 4:31). This description of the believers' action depends on two aspects of their portrayal already encountered in earlier sections of Acts. One aspect of that portrayal reaffirmed here is the unanimity or togetherness of those who compose the group of believers. The term ὁμοθυμαδόν, which Luke has already appropriated in the positive depiction of the Christians (cf. 1:14; 2:46), highlights again the unity that holds these believers together, even in the face of the reported intimidation and opposition.[165]

The other aspect of that portrayal of the believers is the focus on their unified activity of prayer.[166] Just as the narrative has previously presented the believers as those who pray to God — for the fulfillment of the divine promise (cf. 1:14), for guidance (cf. 1:24), and in worship

---

163. The connection between the request to do σημεῖα καὶ τέρατα (4:30) and the apostles' activity including these very things (cf. 2:43; 5:12) suggests that τοὺς ἰδίους refers to the apostles. In addition, Luke is probably not stating that *all* the believers were present. See Jacques Dupont, "La prière des apôtres persécutés (Actes 4,23–31)," in *Études sur les Actes des Apôtres*, LD 45 (Paris: Éditions du Cerf, 1967), 521–22; Co, "The Major Summaries in Acts," 61–62; and Johnson, *The Literary Function of Possessions in Luke-Acts*, 193. For interpretations of τοὺς ἰδίους as a general group of believers, see, e.g., Barrett, *The Acts of the Apostles*, 1:243; Bruce, *The Book of the Acts*, 98; Dunn, *The Acts of the Apostles*, 57; Haenchen, *The Acts of the Apostles*, 226; Pesch, *Die Apostelgeschichte*, 1:175; Roloff, *Die Apostelgeschichte*, 86; Schneider, *Die Apostelgeschichte*, 1:356; and Williams, *Acts*, 87.

164. The term ἴδιος appears 22 times in Luke-Acts, but only four of these references are plural (Luke 18:28; Acts 4:23; 21:6; 24:23). In Luke 18:28 and Acts 21:6, the form is τὰ ἴδια, which apparently refers to "home" (including both possessions and family). See BDAG, 467; LSJ, 818; and Schneider, *Die Apostelgeschichte*, 1:356n16.

165. Cf. Fitzmyer, *The Acts of the Apostles*, 307; Pesch, *Die Apostelgeschichte*, 1:175–76; Roloff, *Die Apostelgeschichte*, 86; and Schille, *Die Apostelgeschichte des Lukas*, 143. Cf. also Schmithals, *Die Apostelgeschichte des Lukas*, 52, who states that Luke is addressing a problem of heresy, suggesting that any who destroy unanimity stand outside the Christian community.

166. Cf. Fitzmyer, *The Acts of the Apostles*, 307.

(cf. 2:42) — so also these believers turned to God in this troubling time with a *single* voice, recognizing God in united fashion as the sovereign creator (cf. 4:24, 28).[167] The prayer's content, as the narrative presents it, centers on two basic themes. On the one hand, their prayer articulates briefly an understanding of the similarities between the situation just described and the circumstances surrounding the death of Jesus, as persons ironically united (literally, "gathered together") in opposition against him.[168] On the other hand, their prayer requests not deliverance but divine provision to accomplish more of what the narrative has just recounted (4:29–30).[169] Luke does not characterize the group through the provision of explicit information from the vantage point of an omniscient narrator. Rather, readers are allowed to listen to the believers' prayer, which gives them indirect access to their feelings and thoughts (i.e., from more of a personality-viewpoint). Through that prayer, the reader sees that those who unite together in prayer exude a confident expectation that God will continue to give them what they need in the face of the united opposition against them. Just like the anticipation

---

167. The narrator states that they raise *a* voice (φωνήν; 4:24), not voices (plural) as the NRSV and NIV suggest. This emphasis on their unity, however, does not suggest that they all are praying the same thing at the same time. Cf. Schneider, *Die Apostelgeschichte*, 1:356–57; Marshall, *The Acts of the Apostles*, 103; and Williams, *Acts*, 87. Contra Haenchen, *The Acts of the Apostles*, 226, who states: "The forms of worship of Luke's own day must have acquainted him with prayers spoken aloud by the whole congregation."

168. In 4:27, several persons and/or groups are mentioned in this united front against Jesus, including Herod, Pontius Pilate, the Gentiles, and "the peoples of Israel" (λαοῖς Ἰσραήλ). Although both the Lukan Gospel and Peter's speeches place the responsibility for Jesus' death on the Jewish people, this designation is rather puzzling here for two reasons: (1) at this point the λαός sides with the apostles; (2) the term here is plural, which seems unusual if Israel understands itself as *the* people of God. The prayer may function, among other things, as a narrative hint about what will eventually happen to the believers in relation to the Jewish people. See van der Horst, "Hellenistic Parallels to Acts (Chapters 3 and 4)," 44, for similar Hellenistic parallels to the expression σὺν ἔθνεσιν καὶ λαοῖς.

169. The believers' request to God in the prayer (4:29–30) has three parts, which have narrative connections to the prior events that presented the believers most favorably (3:1–4:22): (1) ἔπιδε ἐπὶ τὰς ἀπειλὰς αὐτῶν links to the council's threats that contrast with the believers' determination to obey God (cf. 4:17–21); (2) δὸς τοῖς δούλοις σου μετὰ παρρησίας πάσης λαλεῖν τὸν λόγον σου links to the boldness of their speech as observed by the council (cf. 4:13); (3) ἐν τῷ τὴν χεῖρά [σου] ἐκτείνειν σε εἰς ἴασιν καὶ σημεῖα καὶ τέρατα γίνεσθαι διὰ τοῦ ὀνόματος τοῦ ἁγίου παιδός σου Ἰησοῦ links to the healing of the lame man and their explanation of what had happened (cf. 3:1–4:12), as well as to earlier descriptions of the apostles doing πολλά τε τέρατα καὶ σημεῖα (2:43). See Tannehill, *The Narrative Unity of Luke-Acts*, 2:63, who asserts that the "signs and wonders" are considered important as indicators of Jesus' saving power. Cf. Pesch, *Die Apostelgeschichte*, 1:177–78; Schmithals, *Die Apostelgeschichte des Lukas*, 51; and Schneider, *Die Apostelgeschichte*, 1:355.

created by the mention of the believers' prayerful activity in Acts 1, here the believers' prayerful requests potentially create a similar sense of expectation in the readers.

The final element in the description of this group meeting after the incarceration and interrogation of Peter and John is a summation that contributes to the developing portrait of these early Christians. In closing this literary section, Luke summarizes the three things that happen after the believers have finished their prayerful request (4:31).[170] The first thing that Luke mentions is that "the place in which they were gathered together was shaken." The shaking of a building or the earth, a common motif in ancient literature signifying divine assent or presence, indicates divine approval of the request from these united believers.[171] In contrast to the council that has "gathered together" in opposition to those whom Luke implicitly describes as merely responding obediently to God, these believers, who have themselves "gathered together," are the ones among whom God's presence is demonstrated.[172]

The other two descriptions of the believers that conclude this narrative scene allude to the extraordinary Pentecost events. Luke states explicitly that "they all were filled with the Holy Spirit."[173] The narrator uses the identical depiction of what has happened to the believers on Pentecost to describe what occurs to the believers here.[174] In addition, the last description in this sentence, ἐλάλουν τὸν λόγον τοῦ θεοῦ μετὰ παρρησίας

---

170. The verb δέομαι refers more specifically to the aspect of requesting something in prayer. Cf. Schneider, *Die Apostelgeschichte*, 1:360n59, who identifies this term as a *"lukanisches Vorzugswort."*

171. See van der Horst, "Hellenistic Parallels to Acts (Chapters 3 and 4)," 44–45, for references that include this motif. Cf. Fitzmyer, *The Acts of the Apostles*, 311; Haenchen, *The Acts of the Apostles*, 228; Marshall, *The Acts of the Apostles*, 107; Pesch, *Die Apostelgeschichte*, 1:179; Schmithals, *Die Apostelgeschichte des Lukas*, 51–52; Schneider, *Die Apostelgeschichte*, 1:360–61; Weiser, *Die Apostelgeschichte*, 1:134; and Witherington, *The Acts of the Apostles*, 204.

172. Luke specifically states that the place shaken is where the believers ἦσαν συνηγμένοι, a perfect periphrastic construction of the verb συνάγω, the same term that describes the united opposition to Jesus and the apostles (4:5; cf. also 4:26, 27).

173. See Roloff, *Die Apostelgeschichte*, 87, who rightly observes that Pentecost is not repeated, but the event serves to confirm the believers in a new situation. Contra Dupont, "La prière des apôtres persécutés (Actes 4,23–31)," 522, who calls this *"la petite Pentecôte."* Cf. Bruce, *The Book of the Acts*, 100; Conzelmann, *Acts of the Apostles*, 35; William S. Kurz, *Reading Luke-Acts: Dynamics of Biblical Narrative* (Louisville: Westminster/John Knox, 1993), 81; and Shepherd, *The Narrative Function of the Holy Spirit*, 169–70.

174. The description in 4:31 is practically identical to that in 2:4. Cf. Pesch, *Die Apostelgeschichte*, 178.

(they were speaking the word of God with boldness) links to three parts of the narrative: (1) the believers' speaking on Pentecost as the Holy Spirit enabled them, (2) the boldness of Peter and John as observed by the council, and (3) the believers' request for such boldness.[175] Such similarity in description suggests that this group, now having faced their first test from opposition, still enjoys the fulfillment of the divine promise that God has given for all of Israel.[176] This positive image, however, contrasts significantly with the contextual image of the Jewish leaders, who have appeared as opponents to the believers and, implicitly, to the God whom Luke depicts as present among those believers.

An Assessment of the Characterization of Believers in Acts 4:23–31

The characterization of the early Christians in 4:23–31 does not depict the actual interaction of the believers with other narrative characters. However, this depiction of the believers within its narrative context depends on the interaction between the two apostles and the Jewish leaders in the previous section. Taken together with that section, the Lukan description of the believers suggests an obvious contrast between these believers and the Jewish leaders, a contrast observable in three ways. First, Luke uses the motif of unanimity to contrast the Jewish *believers* and Jewish *leaders*. On the one hand, the narrator describes the Jewish believers in terms of unanimity and togetherness, images that link the group to similar, positive traits in earlier portraits of the believers. On the other hand, the narrator describes the Jewish leaders also as gathering together, but makes it clear that opposition to the teaching of Peter and John motivates that action.

Second, Luke uses the motif of continuity and consistency. The Jewish believers maintain continuity with Judaism; their activity remains

---

175. Observe the similarities to other parts of the Acts narrative: (1) both the believers in the Pentecost event and the believers here began to speak as the Holy Spirit enables them; (2) the council sees in Peter and John τὴν ... παρρησίαν (4:13), which is the same term used to describe the believers' speech here; (3) the boldness of 4:31 is described similarly in the believers' prayerful request (4:29), suggesting that what is described is the fulfillment of that request (cf. Johnson, *The Acts of the Apostles*, 85). See John A. Darr, *On Character Building: The Reader and the Rhetoric of Characterization in Luke-Acts*, LCBI (Louisville: Westminster/John Knox, 1992), 148–49, who states that, by the time one has encountered this prayer early in Acts, the narrative has already established the ideal of boldness.

176. Cf. Turner, "The 'Spirit of Prophecy' as the Power of Israel's Restoration and Witness," 329–30.

consistent with earlier depictions of them, and the general Jewish populace responds favorably to the Christian message.[177] The Jewish leaders also maintain continuity, but the narrator suggests through the believers' prayer that these leaders' continuity is in terms of consistent opposition to the Christian message (cf. 4:26, 27).

Third, Luke uses the motif of divine presence and activity in relation to the believers. He consistently depicts the believers in ways indicative of divine blessing and approval: the continuing growth of the group of believers, the statements from the apostles that they must obey God, the united prayer to God, and the answer to their prayer.[178] This portrait of the Jewish believers contrasts significantly with the portrait of the Jewish leaders, who oppose these believers, whom the narrator depicts as obviously blessed and affirmed by God. This contrast, which portrays the early Christians affirmatively, develops from the traits already highlighted in the previous glimpses of this group. Although the narrator describes a contrasting picture of Jewish leaders who are united in opposition to the believers, the image of the latter group is still consistent with their positive qualities as depicted thus far in the narrative — a picture of unanimity and of divine blessing maintained by worship, prayer, and obedience.[179] Thus, the amazing scene at the end of this narrative section leaves the reader with a sense of expectation and excitement, as the Holy Spirit provides the believers with what is needed to face their opposition.

THE COMMUNITY OF BELIEVERS AFTER PERSECUTION AND DIVINE AFFIRMATION (ACTS 4:32–37)

The Literary Context

The prior narrative scene depicts the believers' response to the Jewish leaders' opposition. The narrator gives no indication of doubt on the part of those believers. Rather than describing the shaking of their confidence, Luke describes the shaking of the place where they have gathered together in unanimity. This picture confirms to the reader that the divine

---

177. Cf. Schmithals, *Die Apostelgeschichte des Lukas*, 52, who suggests that the OT references also indicate this continuity.

178. The group's continuing growth and its obedience to God are part of the literary context and not part of the characterization in 4:23–31. However, the characterization in 4:23–31 depends on the narrative context of 3:1–4:22.

179. Cf. Peterson, "The Worship of the New Community," 393–94.

activity that characterizes these believers in the midst of the excitement
of the extraordinary Pentecost events continues to characterize them in
the midst of intimidation and opposition. Thus, the narrator directs the
reader's focus to the Christians' united and faithful response to God and
to the proclamation of the gospel.

The Characterization of the Group of Believers in Acts 4:32–37

The narrative section of 4:32–37 retains the focus of attention on the
Christians. Like 2:42–47, one may categorize this section as a narrative summary: the narrator does not describe a specific scene in which
the believers' actions are observed. In four statements Luke selectively
summarizes specific aspects of the life of the Christian community that
contribute significantly to the narrative plot and its potential effect on
the reader. With this summary, Luke returns the depiction of that group
to an overview of certain common practices among the believers. As the
shift from the aorist tense of the previous narrative section to the imperfect tense in this passage indicates, these descriptions illustrate once again
the ongoing, communal dynamics that characterize the believers.[180] At
the same time, the conjunction δέ makes the grammatical connection,
linking this description of the communal dynamics to the previous narrative scene. In this way, the narrative leaves the reader with obvious
signs of divine blessing both before and after the experience of persecution.[181] The literary section of 4:32–37, therefore, functions similarly
to the summary description at the conclusion of the Pentecost narrative
by explicitly highlighting particular aspects of communal life that are
significant within a literary context emphasizing divine activity.[182]

The beginning of this narrative section (4:32–35)[183] consists of a two-
part general statement (4:32) about the believers' communal practices
or, more literally, "the crowd of those who believed" (τοῦ δὲ πλήθους
τῶν πιστευσάντων; 4:32).[184] The subject of the first part, however, is

---

180. Cf. Krodel, *Acts*, 116; Pesch, *Die Apostelgeschichte*, 1:180; and Schneider, *Die
Apostelgeschichte*, 1:363.

181. Cf. Roloff, *Die Apostelgeschichte*, 88.

182. The similarities between 2:42–47 and 4:32–37 do not suggest that one should ignore
their *respective* functions within their *respective* narrative contexts. See Johnson, *The Literary
Function of Possessions in Luke-Acts*, 1–12.

183. See Wall, "The Acts of the Apostles," in *NIB*, 10:96, who identifies these verses as a
chiastic structure.

184. See Marshall, *The Acts of the Apostles*, 108, who suggests that the word choice reflects
the group's numerical growth (cf. 2:6).

not the believers; rather, the subject is καρδία καὶ ψυχὴ μία (one heart and soul). With the expression ψυχὴ μία, the narrator borrows friendship imagery to convey explicitly the communal relationship that unites them.[185] This phrase, however, is not the same one found in Acts 2; ψυχὴ μία focuses more specifically on the basis of this communal bond or friendship than on its manifestation.[186] Here, ψυχὴ μία describes the unanimity that is the foundational element of the group and that results in outward expressions. With the inclusion of καρδία with ψυχὴ μία, the narrator combines the Hellenistic imagery of friendship with either common Septuagint expressions that link καρδία and ψυχή in stressing the total person's response to God or Jewish expressions of unity.[187] This direct description by Luke, using social ideals undoubtedly familiar to his

---

185. The proverbial Greek expression ψυχὴ μία is found in the works of Aristotle (*Nicomachean Ethics* 9.8.2), Plutarch (*On Brotherly Love* 478c), and Iamblichus (*Life of Pythagoras* 168). See van der Horst, "Hellenistic Parallels to Acts (Chapters 3 and 4)," 46, for a list of references that use this expression to describe real friendship; also Dupont, "La communauté des biens aux premiers jours de l'Eglise," 513–14. Cf., e.g., Johannes Joachim Degenhardt, "Die ersten Christen und der irdische Besitz," in *Die Freude an Gott — unsere Kraft*, ed. Johannes Joachim Degenhardt (Stuttgart: Verlag Katholisches Bibelwerk, 1991), 150–56; Johnson, *The Acts of the Apostles*, 86; Pesch, *Die Apostelgeschichte*, 1:184–94; Talbert, *Reading Acts*, 63–64; and Weiser, *Die Apostelgeschichte*, 1:136–37. Contra Williams, *Acts*, 92, who sees καρδία καὶ ψυχὴ μία as a "typically Hebraic turn of phrase indicating their complete accord."

186. Aristotle states that μία ψυχή is an acceptable expression to describe the basis of friendship, because person A's attitude of active goodwill toward a friend will reflect person A's attitude toward oneself. Thus, one's attitude toward oneself provides the model for friendship with others (*Nicomachean Ethics* 9.8.2). Aristotle suggests, though, that the friend can be perceived as an "other self" (ibid., 9.4.5; 9.9.10) in that the same strong feelings of friendship or affection for oneself are also reflected toward the friend. Thus, two friends desire a common good and are united with each other because their common interests and ideals indicate a similarity of mind or reason. This unity between friends creates κοινωνία by what they hold in common. See Annas, "Plato and Aristotle on Friendship and Altruism," 542; and Kraut, *Aristotle on the Human Good*, 132–33.

187. The expression linking καρδία and ψυχή to the total person's response to God is frequent in the LXX. For example, these two concepts are linked 12 times in Deuteronomy (4:29; 6:5, 6; 10:12; 11:13, 18; 13:4; 26:16; 28:65; 30:2, 6, 10) and express the highest ideals of the people of Israel in relation to God. Cf. Haenchen, *The Acts of the Apostles*, 230–33; Gerd Lüdemann, *Early Christianity according to the Traditions in Acts: A Commentary*, trans. John Bowden (Philadelphia: Fortress, 1989), 60–61; and Pesch, *Die Apostelgeschichte*, 1:181–82. See Dupont, "La communauté des biens aux premiers jours de l'Eglise," 513, who suggests, however, that these expressions in Deuteronomy have no connection with unanimity, which he sees as Luke's emphasis here. Rather, he sees the Hebrew expression לֵב אֶחָד (one heart; 1 Chr 12:39) as expressing the concept more readily, which the LXX translates as ψυχὴ μία. See also Boismard and Lamouille, *Les Actes des deux Apôtres*, 2:160; and Johnson, *The Literary Function of Possessions in Luke-Acts*, 4, 199.

implied audience (though probably unfamiliar to modern readers) and following the narrative events immediately preceding this summary, suggests that what has created this unanimity is not the bond of friendship per se but the divine presence and the believers' faith in God.[188] This faith in God is a trait that, above all else, determines their "character" as a group, even though opposition has arisen.

The second part of the general statement of verse 32 continues with a brief description of a consequence of this unanimity. Luke describes this consequence both in negative and positive forms. On the one hand, οὐδὲ εἷς, in the emphatic position, claims that one's possessions are ἴδιον (one's own), a subtle contrast to Judas's actions as described in the believers' prayer of Acts 1.[189] On the other hand, the expression ἦν αὐτοῖς ἅπαντα κοινά uses the same proverb found in 2:44, where Luke favorably depicts the believers' willingness to provide for one another's needs.[190] The link between these two passages encourages the reader to transfer the same positive traits to these believers. Although the prior description did not include all of these believers, all are now forced to come to grips with the reality of opposition.

The second statement in the narrative summary of 4:32–37 highlights the divine role in the life of the believers. Even though the Jewish leaders in a previous scene have warned Peter and John against their speaking or teaching about Jesus (cf. 4:18), Luke states that the apostles do *exactly* what they were warned against doing: "they continually gave their testimony" (ἀπεδίδουν τὸ μαρτύριον; 4:33) to the resurrection of Jesus.[191] Luke, however, places an additional element of direct description in the

---

188. See Dupont, "L'union entre les premiers Chrétiens dans les Actes des Apôtres," 305, who sees the community of possessions as a consequence of the Christians' unanimity. Cf. Pesch, *Die Apostelgeschichte*, 1:187–88, who reminds that their "*eschatologisches Erfüllungsbewußtsein*" and faith created the unanimity. Cf. Boismard and Lamouille, *Les Actes des deux Apôtres*, 2:160, who see this as an allusion to Jer 32:39 and Ezek 11:19.

189. The believers' prayer for guidance before electing Judas's replacement ends by referring to him as going εἰς τὸν τόπον τὸν ἴδιον (1:25). See Johnson, *The Literary Function of Possessions in Luke-Acts*, 199.

190. See Mitchell, "The Social Function of Friendship in Acts 2:44–47 and 4:32–37," 261–62, who sees tension in the use of property: that which is common (κοινός) versus that which is private (ἴδιος). Cf. Mealand, "Community of Goods and Utopian Allusions in Acts II–IV," 96–99; and Schneider, *Die Apostelgeschichte*, 1:365.

191. See Tannehill, *The Narrative Unity of Luke-Acts*, 2:64: "This pattern of reduplication contributes to the story of the developing conflict between the church and the Sanhedrin. It helps to build suspense as the resolve of both parties to the conflict is tested under increasing pressure."

emphatic position, thereby stressing that the apostles acted "with great power" (δυνάμει μεγάλη)[192] and creating an allusion to the resurrected Jesus' promise of power (1:8; cf. 2:22; 3:12; 4:7).[193] This imagery also correlates with the power and boldness underscored in earlier scenes of healing, interrogation, and the coming of the Holy Spirit (cf. 3:12; 4:7, 13, 29–31).[194] In addition, Luke provides additional information to his readers, showing that *all* the believers (πάντας αὐτούς)[195] are under the influence of χάρις μεγάλη, an explicit statement that accentuates God's activity in their lives together.[196] The summary's arrangement places the apostles' activity of proclamation at the center of the united group of believers, a group described in ideal imagery immediately after the narrative affirmation that God has blessed these believers (cf. 4:31).[197]

The third statement of this narrative summary, 4:34–35, returns to the imagery of a group of persons who share their possessions for the sake of others. However, the narrative does not suggest a significant shift in emphasis, since the following descriptions of the dynamics among the believers is grammatically joined to the previous declaration that "great grace was upon them all" (4:33b).[198] The statement explaining that "there was no needy person among them" (4:34a) proceeds from the imagery of a community of grace. The precise wording of this brief statement reflects possible connections to Deuteronomy 15:4, where the

---

192. See Schille, *Die Apostelgeschichte des Lukas*, 145, who observes that the dative case makes this information supplemental to the main emphasis, which is the proclamation of the gospel.

193. See Pesch, *Die Apostelgeschichte*, 1:181–82, who sees the mention of power tied to the previous emphasis of heart and soul (4:32) and reflecting the Shema of Deut 6:5, which in the LXX uses the same three nouns (καρδία, ψυχή, δύναμις) in the same order to describe how one is to love God.

194. See Johnson, *The Literary Function of Possessions in Luke-Acts*, 199; Pesch, *Die Apostelgeschichte*, 1:182–83; and Schneider, *Die Apostelgeschichte*, 1:365. Cf. Weiser, *Die Apostelgeschichte*, 1:137.

195. The designation πάντας αὐτούς is rather ambiguous; grammatically, it seems to refer to the apostles (4:33). However, the conjunction γάρ in 4:34 connects these two sentences, and the pronoun αὐτοῖς there seems to refer to the believers in general. Cf., e.g., Haenchen, *The Acts of the Apostles*, 231; Johnson, *The Acts of the Apostles*, 86; Krodel, *Acts*, 117; and Marshall, *The Acts of the Apostles*, 109.

196. Contra Gaventa, *The Acts of the Apostles*, 100, who interprets χάρις μεγάλη as a reference to the favor of the Jerusalemites toward the believers.

197. Cf. Johnson, *The Acts of the Apostles*, 86, 90; Krodel, *Acts*, 116–18; and Roloff, *Die Apostelgeschichte*, 88. Contra Lüdemann, *Early Christianity according to the Traditions in Acts*, 61, who sees 4:33 as an interruption.

198. See note 195 regarding the conjunction γάρ in 4:34.

elimination of need with the people of God indicates God's blessing.[199] This elimination of need within the Christian community occurs, according to the narrator, because (γάρ) certain persons of wealth[200] have from time to time sold some property they owned and brought the proceeds (τὰς τιμάς) to the apostles for community use.[201] The inclusion of this particular practice explicitly contributes to the favorable portrait of these believers, providing what readers may see as an example of the Christian community's uniqueness. Only the unanimity, the καρδία καὶ ψυχὴ μία among the believers, will cause wealthier members to cross social boundaries and to provide for persons with whom they have not closely associated in their culture, resulting in the elimination of need and an obvious sign of divine blessing.[202] The placing of the proceeds παρὰ τοὺς πόδας τῶν ἀποστόλων paints a picture of humility, as those who possessed τὰς τιμάς kneel before the apostles, who serve as believers' representatives and leaders by virtue of their role as witnesses to Jesus' resurrection (cf. 1:22; 4:33).[203] As the result of such responsiveness, resources are made available καθότι ἄν τις χρείαν εἶχεν (as anyone had

---

199. The expression οὐδὲ ... ἐνδεής τις ἦν ἐν αὐτοῖς (4:34), is quite similar to Deut 15:4 (οὐκ ἔσται ἐν σοὶ ἐνδεής [LXX]; cf. Deut 15:7). For an interpretation that Luke is depicting the fulfillment of God's promise to Israel, see J. J. Degenhardt, "Die ersten Christen und der irdische Besitz," 151; Johnson, *The Acts of the Apostles*, 86–87; and Schneider, *Die Apostelgeschichte*, 1:365.

200. The description of such persons as κτήτορες χωρίων ἢ οἰκιῶν ὑπῆρχον implies that they were wealthy. Since only wealthy persons owned property, these with greater financial resources provided for the needy within the Christian community. On social and economic status in the first century CE, see, e.g., Ramsay MacMullen, *Roman Social Relations: 50 B.C. to A.D. 284* (New Haven: Yale University Press, 1974), 88–120; Wayne A. Meeks, *The First Urban Christians* (New Haven: Yale University Press, 1983), 20–22, 53–55; and Stambaugh and Balch, *The New Testament in Its Social Environment*, 63–81.

201. The imperfect tense of this sentence's five verbs refers to typical, continuing activity within the community. Cf. Haenchen, *The Acts of the Apostles*, 231; Roloff, *Die Apostelgeschichte*, 89; Weiser, *Die Apostelgeschichte*, 1:137; and Williams, *Acts*, 93–94.

202. Cf. Mitchell, "The Social Function of Friendship in Acts 2:44–47 and 4:32–37," 272, who highlights the social implications of friendship imagery but lapses into mirror reading in defining the social and historical context to which Luke wrote. Cf. also Hans-Joachim Degenhardt, *Lukas, Evangelist der Armen: Besitz und Besitzverzicht in den lukanischen Schriften* (Stuttgart: Verlag Katholishes Bibelwerk, 1965), 182–83; Haenchen, *The Acts of the Apostles*, 233; and Schmithals, *Die Apostelgeschichte des Lukas*, 54–55.

203. By placing τὰς τιμάς at the apostles' feet, these persons relinquished their cultural and individual rights for the use of the community. Cf. Halvor Moxnes, "Patron-Client Relations and the New Community in Luke-Acts," in *The Social World of Luke-Acts: Models for Interpretation*, ed. Jerome H. Neyrey (Peabody, MA: Hendrickson, 1991), 265; and also Johnson, *The Literary Function of Possessions in Luke-Acts*, 200–203.

need; 4:35), the same positive description found in 2:45. This generosity in giving for the needy within the Christian community is not the central point of this part of the narrative, however, nor is that generosity the creating force of that community. The sharing of goods or possessions actualizes the unanimity among believers as stressed in 4:32 and results in persons responding for the sake of one another.[204]

The fourth and final statement in the narrative summary of 4:32–37 describes the noteworthy actions of one individual, Joseph, or Barnabas, as Luke calls him in subsequent parts of the narrative. Although Luke characterizes Barnabas as a separate character, his initial depiction in the narrative functions both to describe the exemplary behavior of one believer and to furnish supplemental characterization of the church or Christian community. By directly furnishing personal information about Barnabas in the translation of his name as "son of encouragement,"[205] the narrator makes an obvious attempt to convince the reader that Barnabas responds out of generosity and humility, just as others have done. The reader is to judge Barnabas's response as an act motivated by grace, just like the generous activity that the narrative has depicted generally.[206] The brief narrative recounting of Barnabas's action, consistent with the information given about him, concretizes the description of the believers' general practice.[207] The initial portrait of Barnabas, therefore, is positive and has two functions. On the one hand, it introduces a character who will appear later in the narrative. On the other hand, it provides a specific example of an individual who responds favorably to a need within the community of believers as a result of the oneness or the καρδία καὶ ψυχὴ μία created among them by the presence and blessing of God.[208]

---

204. See Co, "The Major Summaries in Acts," 73. Cf. J. J. Degenhardt, "Die ersten Christen und der irdische Besitz," 151–53; and Schneider, *Die Apostelgeschichte*, 1:365.

205. The narrator appears to provide adequate information to the reader for judging the positive nature of Barnabas's action. On the use of narrative asides in Luke-Acts, see Steven M. Sheeley, *Narrative Asides in Luke-Acts*, JSNTSup 72 (Sheffield: JSOT Press, 1992).

206. The three verbal forms used to describe Barnabas's action are variations of the same verbs used to describe the general practice in 4:34–35 but are now in the aorist tense, signifying a specific act. See Marguerat, "La mort d'Ananias et Saphira," 211–13, who suggests that the aorist tense indicates that 4:36–37 is *not* part of this summary. Cf. Pesch, *Die Apostelgeschichte*, 1:180, 184; and Schneider, *Die Apostelgeschichte*, 1:363.

207. Cf. Mitchell, "The Social Function of Friendship in Acts 2:44–47 and 4:32–37," 269, who sees this description as a striking reversal in social roles; Bartchy, "Community of Goods in Acts," 315; Barrett, *The Acts of the Apostles*, 1:258, 260; and Fitzmyer, *The Acts of the Apostles*, 322.

208. Cf. Pesch, *Die Apostelgeschichte*, 1:18; and Talbert, *Reading Acts*, 65.

An Assessment of the Characterization of the Believers in Acts 4:32–37

The narrative summary of 4:32–37 has obvious similarities to the narrative summary of 2:42–47.[209] Both summaries immediately follow the outpouring of the Holy Spirit, thereby joining the communal dynamics to God's activity among the believers.[210] Both descriptions follow positive responses by the Jewish people to the gospel message. These summaries explicitly depict the Christian community as unanimous and united together because of God, which results in a greater concern for the welfare of one another than for the private use of possessions.[211] Both narrative sections mention little if any interaction with other characters. The duplication of imagery in the latter portrait of this Christian group suggests that Luke is trying to emphasize certain aspects in the life of these believers that contribute to the narrative plot, while also building on these images as that plot unfolds.[212]

The Lukan characterization of the Christian community continues to evolve, however, as the reader's attention is drawn to the additional narrative actions and direct descriptions that contribute to that picture.[213] While the narrator links these favorable pictures together with common descriptions and affirmations, he employs these commonalities in the inclusion of additional narrative elements that intensify the cumulative image of the believers and that image's potential effect on the readers.[214]

---

209. See Johnson, *The Literary Function of Possessions in Luke-Acts*, 9–11, for questions about the similarities of 4:32–37 and 2:42–47: (1) "Why are there two passages describing the community of goods in Luke-Acts, and only two? Why do they occur where they do?" (2) "Why does the community's practice in regard to possessions receive such attention in these descriptions of the inner life of the community in the first place?" (3) "What are we to make of the differences?" (4) "What is the relation of 4:34ff. to its immediate and broader contexts?"

210. Shepherd, *The Narrative Function of the Holy Spirit*, 170. Cf. Seccombe, "The New People of God," 355–56.

211. See Thomas Wieser, "Community — Its Unity, Diversity and Universality," *Semeia* 54 (1985): 88, who suggests that this sharing was "the only logical alternative to the mimetic rivalry that pervades every other human community and which ultimately leads to its destruction."

212. See Tannehill, *The Narrative Unity of Luke-Acts*, 2:67–79, for a discussion of the role of redundancy and repetition in Acts 1–5; and Johnson, *The Acts of the Apostles*, 91: "After having read this much of Luke-Acts, we are no longer surprised to find him using his favorite symbolism for relationships and power, the use of possessions."

213. Cf. Tannehill, *The Narrative Unity of Luke-Acts*, 2:63–64.

214. Cf. ibid., 2:76–77: "When a narrator emphasizes certain images and patterns through repeated use, much will depend on the capacity of the selected material to grow in significance as the narrative progresses. Repetition without growth soon becomes monotonous."

Thus, this latter narrative summary describes the unanimity of the believers, not merely in the context of celebration (i.e., the day of Pentecost) but also in the context of opposition. The last description of the believers not only shows the provision for the needy in the context of their unanimity but also shows the *elimination* of need, which demonstrates that this community of grace fulfills certain aspects of both Greco-Roman and Jewish (biblical) ideals of community. The narrative summary of 4:32–37, therefore, directs the reader's attention more specifically to this unanimous community of faith within a narrative context of initial opposition. Divine grace characterizes these believers, as seen in the spontaneous activity of selflessly sharing possessions for the sake of others. For the narrator, such activity is not noteworthy merely as a model that every congregation should implement. Rather, the narrative context suggests that the communal atmosphere of unanimity that induces such selfless activity and results indicates God's blessing and grace.

The Church and the Incident
with Ananias and Sapphira (Acts 5:1–11)

The Literary Context

The affirmative depiction of the Christian community, even after the initial episode of opposition, portrays a unanimous group of believers as a community of grace because of the spontaneous and selfless sharing of possessions for one another's sake. The Lukan description of a typical response includes selling a piece of property, bringing the proceeds for use by the community, and placing them at the apostles' feet. The example of Barnabas concretizes this generalized yet direct description of the believers, as Luke provides explicit information about him to prompt the readers to appropriate conclusions regarding his act of generosity.

The Characterization of the Church or Group of Believers in 5:1–11

The incident that Ananias and Sapphira create is significant for the Lukan characterization of the church or Christian community. Although the group itself is only mentioned briefly at the end of this narrative section, the descriptive material in this pericope correlates with the depiction of the believers in Acts 1–4.[215] The couple's actions, as one reads the narrative, appear to reflect many characteristics of the early believers.[216] Thus, the Lukan depiction of these the couple within the context of the Christian community potentially contributes to the Lukan portrait of that group and, more important, to the narrative plot.[217]

The narrative event itself relies on prior action taken by Ananias and Sapphira. Like Barnabas and others who have sold something of value, Ananias also sells a piece of property (5:1; cf. 2:45; 4:34, 37).[218] Like Barnabas and others who have placed the proceeds at the apostles' feet, the narrator tells the reader that Ananias does the same thing (5:2; cf. 4:35, 37).[219] Luke, however, takes on the role of an omniscient narrator by supplying additional information that changes the whole complexion of what initially appears as noteworthy behavior: Ananias withholds some of the proceeds (καὶ ἐνοσφίσατο ἀπὸ τῆς τιμῆς) by bringing only "a part" (μέρος τι; 5:2). The verb νοσφίζομαι, used here to explain what Ananias has done, negatively connotes embezzlement or misappropriation and is the same verb used in the Septuagint translation of Joshua 7:1 to describe Achan's sin.[220] Hence, the narrator explicitly shows the reader that Ananias's actions are not as they may initially appear.[221] The Lukan narrator also reveals that Ananias is not alone in this scheme, for he has done so σὺν Σαπφίρῃ τῇ γυναικὶ αὐτοῦ, (with his wife Sapphira;

---

215. The conjunction δέ suggests that this episode is linked to prior scenes. Cf. Kurz, *Reading Luke-Acts*, 82; Corina Combet-Galland, "Actes 4/32–5/11," *ETR* 52 (1977): 548–53, who sees 4:32–5:11 as one section with three parts; Marguerat, "La mort d'Ananias et Saphira," 211–13; and Marshall, *The Acts of the Apostles*, 111.

216. Cf. Williams, *Acts*, 100–101. See Marguerat, "La mort d'Ananias et Saphira," 218, who observes that the "horizon of narration" comes from an insider perspective.

217. Contra Neil, *Acts*, 94: in complimenting Luke's honesty in telling the story "like it was," Neil implies that Luke had no other reasons for including this narrative event.

218. The same verb describes the selling actions of both Barnabas and others. However, κτῆμα, the term for what was sold in 2:45, does not appear in 4:32–37. Cf. Kurz, *Reading Luke-Acts*, 82; and Barrett, *The Acts of the Apostles*, 1:264–65.

219. While the descriptions are similar, there is no definitive evidence that Ananias and Sapphira desire the praise or positive impression made by Barnabas's act. For an interpretation that Ananias and Sapphira *do* have such selfish desires, see Roloff, *Die Apostelgeschichte*, 93.

220. Cf. Barrett, *The Acts of the Apostles*, 1:265; Boismard and Lamouille, *Les Actes des deux Apôtres*, 2:164–65; Robert L. Brawley, *Centering on God: Method and Message in Luke-Acts*, LCBI (Louisville: Westminster/John Knox, 1990), 177; Bruce, *The Book of the Acts*, 102–103; Fitzmyer, *The Acts of the Apostles*, 322; Haenchen, *The Acts of the Apostles*, 237, 239; Johnson, *The Acts of the Apostles*, 88; Weiser, *Die Apostelgeschichte*, 1:144–45; and Williams, *Acts*, 96. See Marguerat, "La mort d'Ananias et Saphira," 222–26, who suggests that Luke is alluding to the fall in Gen 3 by describing the "original sin" of the church.

221. Cf. Aristotle, *Nicomachean Ethics* 3.2.1; idem, *Rhetoric* 1.9.31.

5:1), more specifically "with his wife's knowledge" (συνειδυίης καὶ τῆς γυναικός; 5:2). The precise wording in these first two verses explicitly implicates both Ananias and Sapphira since they had knowingly joined together in the action.[222] This husband and wife — who probably are associating with the believers, as one's initial observation of their actions suggests — have united together in action that paradoxically opposes an essential element of that unanimous group.[223] As Luke Johnson suggests, these two characters provide a narrative "counter-community of avarice" opposite the "spirit-community" that shares its possessions.[224]

The narrative account of what transpires after Ananias places the money at the apostles' feet omits numerous details that the reader's imagination may fill.[225] For instance, the author provides no information about who witnesses these events. No explanation is provided for Peter's extraordinary insight into Ananias's mind, insight that functions to confirm through a reliable character what the narrator has already explicitly stated about Ananias's actions.[226] Peter, who functions both as the narrator's spokesperson and as the representative for the believers, not only accuses Ananias of withholding part of the proceeds but also contrasts Ananias with the characterization of the believers in Acts in three ways. First, Peter states that Satan and not the Holy Spirit has filled (ἐπλήρωσεν; 5:3) Ananias.[227] Second, Peter informs Ananias that he has lied to the Christian community and the God whose blessing has characterized them (5:4; cf. 5:3).[228] Third, Peter identifies the center of his dishonesty as *his* heart (ἐν τῇ καρδίᾳ σου; 5:4) in distinction to the

---

222. Both συνειδυίης (5:2) and the σύν prepositional phrase (5:1) suggest collaboration. Cf. Barrett, *The Acts of the Apostles*, 1:265; and Johnson, *The Acts of the Apostles*, 87.
223. Cf. Combet-Galland, "Actes 4/32–5/11," 551; Weiser, *Die Apostelgeschichte*, 1:146–47; and Joseph B. Tyson, "Acts 6:1–7 and Dietary Regulations in Early Christianity," *PerRS* 10 (Spring 1983): 148–49, who sees this action as a threat to the church, within a four-part pattern of peace, threat, resolution, and restoration.
224. Johnson, *The Acts of the Apostles*, 87.
225. Cf. Wall, "The Acts of the Apostles," in *NIB*, 10:98.
226. The opening chapters of Acts present Peter as a reliable character, so readers should also see Peter's evaluation of Ananias as reliable. Cf. Schneider, *Die Apostelgeschichte*, 1:374.
227. Cf. Fitzmyer, *The Acts of the Apostles*, 323; and Talbert, *Reading Acts*, 66.
228. Peter serves as Luke's spokesperson by accusing Ananias of lying to the Holy Spirit (5:3) and to God (5:4), not merely to "men" (ἀνθρώποις). However, since Luke does not state explicitly *how* Ananias lied, readers are left to make sense of this accusation. Cf. Brawley, *Centering on God*, 178; Dunn, *The Acts of the Apostles*, 64; Fitzmyer, *The Acts of the Apostles*, 323; Haenchen, *The Acts of the Apostles*, 237; Marguerat, "La mort d'Ananias et Saphira," 221; and Schneider, *Die Apostelgeschichte*, 1:372.

single heart (καρδία καὶ ψυχὴ μία; 4:32) that unites the fellow believers.[229] Even the description of Ananias's subsequent death, almost immediately after hearing Peter's accusations, contrasts Ananias with the ψυχὴ μία that characterizes the believing group (5:5).[230] Peter, however, does not pronounce judgment; the implicit cause of Ananias's death is divine justice.[231] As a result, ἐγένετο φόβος μέγας ἐπὶ πάντας τοὺς ἀκούοντας (5:5), a description that alludes to the fear or sense of religious awe mentioned earlier, after the Pentecost narrative (cf. 2:43).[232]

The narrative description of the scene as Peter questions Sapphira also excludes significant details. Luke includes no explanation for Sapphira's lack of awareness of what has happened, including not only the death but also the burial of her husband.[233] Peter's question to Sapphira implicitly suggests that she could renounce her part of the scheme. However, Sapphira herself confirms Peter's earlier accusation of lying (5:8), an obvious point due to the previous scene with Ananias and Peter.[234] Luke does not depict Peter as repeating the same accusations against Sapphira. Peter's discernment serves again to confirm the narrator's initial judgment: Ananias and Sapphira have agreed together (συνεφωνήθη ὑμῖν) to test the "Spirit of the Lord" (5:9), a *unity* of dishonest and deceptive action that contradicts the *unanimity* of the community of grace.[235]

---

229. Cf. Combet-Galland, "Actes 4/32–5/11," 551; and Marguerat, "La mort d'Ananias et Saphira," 221.

230. In another subtle wordplay, the narrator states that Ananias πεσὼν ἐξέψυξεν (fell down and died; 5:5). The verb ἐκψύχω is a compound verb derived from the prefix ἐκ (out) and the noun ψυχή (soul/life). Unlike the community of believers that possesses ψυχὴ μία among them (4:32), Ananias is now ψυχή-less. See Barrett, *The Acts of the Apostles*, 1:267–68, who notices that the only three occurrences of this verb in Acts (cf. 5:9; 12:23) refer to the sudden or unpleasant death of the wicked.

231. Ananias's death indicates his sin. Cf., e.g., Brawley, *Centering on God*, 176–78; Fitzmyer, *The Acts of the Apostles*, 324; Philippe-H. Menoud, "La mort d'Ananias et de Saphira (Actes 5. 1–11)," in *Aux sources de la tradition chrétienne: Mélanges offerts à Goguel*, 146–54; Schille, *Die Apostelgeschichte des Lukas*, 148–49; and Wieser, "Community," 88.

232. The addition of the adjective μέγας to the noun φόβος (5:11), following the adjective's usage to describe the power of the apostles' testimony and the grace upon the believers (4:33), may indicate both plot intensification and a common source (God) for the power, grace, and fear. The phrase ἐπὶ πάντας τοὺς ἀκούοντας apparently extends to other persons and is not limited to the believers. Cf. Combet-Galland, "Actes 4/32–5/11," 549.

233. Cf. Bruce, *The Book of the Acts*, 106; Roloff, *Die Apostelgeschichte*, 94; Schille, *Die Apostelgeschichte des Lukas*, 150; and Schneider, *Die Apostelgeschichte*, 1:376.

234. Cf. Johnson, *The Acts of the Apostles*, 92; and Weiser, *Die Apostelgeschichte*, 1:143–44.

235. Luke uses a verb with the σύν prefix, συμφωνέω (5:9), for the united action of Ananias and Sapphira in contrast to the believers' unanimity. Cf. Johnson, *The Acts of the Apostles*, 89.

The narrative description of the deaths of Ananias and Sapphira, therefore, vividly contrasts these negative examples to the life of the Christian
community.[236]

Luke concludes this unpleasant narrative event within the community
of believers by describing the reaction to what has taken place. Just as the
statement in verse 5 mentions that "great fear" seizes everyone who hears
about what has happened to Ananias, verse 11 repeats the same description.[237] However, in the middle of the latter statement, the narrator adds
the prepositional phrase ἐφ' ὅλην τὴν ἐκκλησίαν (upon the whole church),
the first time the term ἐκκλησία appears in Acts.[238] In the Septuagint
ἐκκλησία typically refers to the assembly of God's people.[239] The believers, as well as everyone else who hears what happened, are overwhelmed
by the realization of the nature of the Christian community—a response
with which readers may readily identify.[240] Although the episodes of Acts
4 clearly differentiates between the Jewish people and their leaders, the
designation ἡ ἐκκλησία (the Jewish believers) alongside the other Jewish
people who simply hear about these events provides an explicit narrative
distinction between these latter groups.[241] The narrative clearly characterizes these believers, united together by the Holy Spirit, with reference
to God's presence, so that even lying to the community is lying to God

---

236. One additional descriptive element that Luke includes here is that, when she dies, she
falls down πρὸς τοὺς πόδας αὐτοῦ (5:10), which may allude to Ananias's placing of their partial
gift πρὸς τοὺς πόδας τῶν ἀποστόλων (5:2). Cf. Combet-Galland, "Actes 4/32–5/11," 549; and
Schneider, *Die Apostelgeschichte*, 1:377.

237. Cf. Fitzmyer, *The Acts of the Apostles*, 325; Lüdemann, *Early Christianity according to
the Traditions in Acts*, 64; Schmithals, *Die Apostelgeschichte des Lukas*, 57; and Witherington,
The Acts of the Apostles, 219.

238. Cf. Marguerat, "La mort d'Ananias et Saphira," 216; and Barrett, *The Acts of the
Apostles*, 1:270–71.

239. Of the 103 appearances of ἐκκλησία and 22 appearances of ἐκκλησιάζω in the LXX,
the typical reference is the assembly of the people (λαός) or Israel, either in worship or as a
nation (e.g., Deut 4:10, 23:9, 31:30; Judg 20:2; 2 Chr 30:2, 4, 13, 17, 23–25; Ezra 10:1, 8,
12, 14). Cf. Karl Ludwig Schmidt, "ἐκκλησία," in *TDNT*, 3:501–26; Johnson, *The Acts of the
Apostles*, 89; Fitzmyer, *The Acts of the Apostles*, 325; Krodel, *Acts*, 122; and Witherington,
The Acts of the Apostles, 219–20.

240. Contra Barrett, *The Acts of the Apostles*, 1:270; Bruce, *The Book of the Acts*, 107;
and Kurz, *Reading Luke-Acts*, 82, who suggests that this fear of the community "is meant to
typify fear of the readers to commit similar sins against their spirit-filled authorities," and that
the fate of Ananias and Sapphira is to be a lesson for the implied readers.

241. The overwhelming response in Acts 1–4 implies that almost *everyone* becomes a
believer. However, 5:11 distinguishes between the Jewish believers and nonbelievers. See Marguerat, "La mort d'Ananias et Saphira," 214, who states that the Christians no longer meet at
the temple, against 5:12, 21.

(cf. 5:4, 9).[242] For Luke to call these Christians ἡ ἐκκλησία suggests that this *negative* event in Acts actually *affirms* in almost stunning imagery the divine presence in this group of Jewish believers, a presence that expels those who are not καρδία καὶ ψυχὴ μία.[243] The term ἐκκλησία, therefore, depicts the Christian community both similarly to and in distinction from the other Jewish people who also understand themselves as ἡ ἐκκλησία.[244]

An Assessment of the Characterization of the Church or Group of Believers in Acts 5:1–11

In the narrative context following the exemplary response of Barnabas, the story of the apparent generosity of Ananias and Sapphira surprises the readers. The narrator explicitly renounces this story as a shocking example of deception and disunity in a group characterized by unanimity.[245] Up to this point in the narrative, the narrator has combined both indirect and direct descriptions, including the use of social ideals and imagery to characterize the Christian community in overwhelmingly positive terms. The inclusion of the Ananias and Sapphira incident suggests, however, that idealistic concepts do not control Luke's portrait of the early Christians.[246] Rather, these ideals serve to convey particular images of this group to the readers, and this particular narrative section draws on some of those images. In the narrative's arrangement, the description of this incident following the brief account of Barnabas's generosity, when one also considers the explicit characterization of both Barnabas and the couple Ananias and Sapphira, creates an unexpected but obvious contrast both to the example of Barnabas and to the community of believers at large.[247] Although the believers as a group are more passive

---

242. Cf. Brawley, *Centering on God*, 178; and Marguerat, "La mort d'Ananias et Saphira," 221.

243. Cf. Bartchy, "Community of Goods in Acts," 316; Marguerat, "La mort d'Ananias et Saphira," 217; and Marshall, *The Acts of the Apostles*, 114.

244. The narrative provides textual clues for the reader to perceive the believers through positive imagery that has been reserved for *all* Israel as the people of God. However, one should not confuse this imagery's *use* in relation to the Christian community with the church's *replacement* of Israel as the "new Israel." Cf. Marguerat, "La mort d'Ananias et Saphira," 216–17, who does not understand the use of the term ἐκκλησία as "theologically loaded."

245. The explicit renunciation of Ananias's and Sapphira's actions may explain why Luke explicitly characterizes Barnabas by providing the "son of encouragement" translation.

246. Cf. Bruce, *The Book of the Acts*, 104.

247. Cf. Tannehill, *The Narrative Unity of Luke-Acts*, 2:79; and Pesch, *Die Apostelgeschichte*, 1:196.

than active in this narrative section, the contrasts of this scene function within the narrative to contribute significantly to a developing picture of the Christian community in Acts.

The narrative event about Ananias and Sapphira hinges on a paradoxical representation of the recurring qualities of the community of believers. The believers are favorably characterized by a unanimity of purpose and existence, divine presence and grace, and the resultant sharing of resources when others have need. The depiction of Ananias and Sapphira also presents the couple as united together and sharing resources, and yet this portrayal counters the positive characterization of the early Christians. This husband and wife, who appear as insiders in the Christian community, are ironically presented as outsiders by their deceptive behavior, by which they try to convey their oneness and unity with the rest of the group. Their misconception of the Christian community as a group identified by God's presence contributes to their infraction against it and results in the sudden deaths that implicitly confirm that divine presence.[248] This couple, in their indivisibility and oneness, ironically threaten to destroy the unanimity of the believers by creating a *partial* unity that denies the *complete* unity of the group.[249] The narrator's perspective concerning the Christian community, therefore, has focused on the "inside" threat to that group's unanimity, which he has depicted as the sign of divine blessing.[250] What readers often see as harshness toward Ananias and Sapphira serves implicitly to depict the Christian community in terms of the divine elimination of divisive and destructive behavior.[251] The church's response of "great fear," therefore, confirms their recognition of God's activity within them, which Ananias and Sapphira have obviously failed to recognize. This narrated image dramatically suggests that the God who is present among the believers in Acts 1–4 continues to be demonstrably involved among them as ἡ ἐκκλησία, the assembly of God's people, a group distinct from the Jewish nonbelieving population.

---

248. See Henriette Havelaar, "Hellenistic Parallels to Acts 5.1–11 and the Problem of Conflicting Interpretations," *JSNT* 67 (Summer 1997): 63–82.

249. Cf. Combet-Galland, "Actes 4/32–5/11," 552–53.

250. Cf. Krodel, *Acts*, 122, whose attention to the *specific* ethical issues mentioned in the narrative misses the Lukan central and *general* concern for the unanimity of believers.

251. Cf. Marguerat, "La mort d'Ananias et Saphira," 217–18.

The Church after the Incident
with Ananias and Sapphira (Acts 5:12–16)

The Literary Context

The narrative depiction of the incident with Ananias and Sapphira defines more distinctly the nature of the church, or Christian community. The drastic action against these two persons who threaten the community's unanimity indicates that a violation against the essential character of the group is also a violation or sin against God. The scene offers to the reader a picture of a group of persons who, in some measure, are identified with God. What has happened to Ananias and Sapphira represents the failure to understand the nature of the church.[252] The "great fear" that the text mentions twice (5:5, 11) does not describe the beginning of an atmosphere of terror but the recognition of God's presence and activity found within the group.

The Characterization of the Church or Group of Believers in 5:12–16

The narrative section of 5:12–16 continues to keep the attention of the reader on the extraordinary nature of the Christian community. Like the passages of 2:42–47 and 4:32–37, this passage is a narrative summary, as the Lukan narrator explicitly shows to readers certain practices and responses of the believers that are potentially important to the narrative plot.[253] After the stunning turn of the previous events, Luke depicts different kinds of interaction with the Jewish people in Jerusalem. Given the "great fear" (5:11) that seizes nearly everyone in the previous scene because of all that has occurred, this summary directly shows or describes how the social interactions both within the Christian community and between the Jewish believers and the Jewish people are affected.[254]

The first statement briefly describes what the apostles do in the midst of the Jewish people (ἐν τῷ λαῷ; 5:12a). The narrative presents this activity as σημεῖα καὶ τέρατα πολλά, and this statement immediately follows

---

252. See Gaventa, "Toward a Theology of Acts," 155, who suggests that within the cycle of event, interpretation or proclamation, and response, this incident functions as the interpretation or proclamation, in that it comes in the form of a narrated story accentuating the consequences of lying to the community and the Holy Spirit.

253. As in the narrative summaries of 2:42–47 and 4:32–37, the narration shifts to the imperfect tense, thus indicating an explicit description of general, ongoing matters.

254. The typical Lukan use of the conjunction δέ in grammatically linking narrative sections provides the implicit connection between this summary and the "great fear" of the prior scene.

the "great fear" that the previous incident provoked. This arrangement suggests that the reader should recognize the literary allusion to earlier positive descriptions of the early Christians, in which everyone has "fear" because of the πολλά τε τέρατα καὶ σημεῖα that the apostles have done.[255] While the φόβος in 2:43 is associated with the apostles' activity and the φόβος μέγας of 5:11 is associated not directly with the apostle's activity but with the previous event, the juxtaposition of these motifs clearly draws on the positive imagery from the earlier summary.[256] These "signs and wonders" also implicitly reflect another answer to an earlier prayer of a group of believers. After the initial incarceration and interrogation by the Jewish leaders, these believers request that God would grant them the privilege of doing σημεῖα καὶ τέρατα through Jesus' name (4:29–30), a request apparently answered, as these actions attest.[257] This subsequent picture of the apostles' extraordinary activity explicitly shows the Jewish people as witnessing public displays of divine power, which is similar to what the readers encountered following that earlier prayer.[258] This depiction of the Christians, then, suggests that the same Christian activity continues among the Jewish people as before the incident with Ananias and Sapphira.

The second statement within the narrative summary of 5:12–16, found in 5:12b–13, ambiguously describes three aspects of the communal relations among the believers themselves and between these Jewish believers and the Jewish people. The first part of this statement, καὶ ἦσαν ὁμοθυμαδὸν ἅπαντες ἐν τῇ Στοᾷ Σολομῶντος (5:12b), affirms the unanimity of the believers, as Luke relies once more on the adverb ὁμοθυμαδόν and the term ἅπαντες to stress the togetherness of *all* the believers.[259]

---

255. Cf. Co, "The Major Summaries in Acts," 49–85, esp. 63. Contra Benoit, "Remarques sur les 'sommaires' de Actes 2. 42 à 5," 5, who sees this connection as evidence of redaction.

256. Co, "The Major Summaries in Acts," 63. Contra Fitzmyer, *The Acts of the Apostles*, 325.

257. This apparent answer to the prayer of 4:29–30 suggests that those described in 4:23–31 may have been the apostles. See Tannehill, *The Narrative Unity of Luke-Acts*, 2:63, who stresses the importance of "signs and wonders" in demonstrating Jesus' saving power. Cf. Conzelmann, *Acts of the Apostles*, 39; Pesch, *Die Apostelgeschichte*, 1:206; Schneider, *Die Apostelgeschichte*, 1:379; and Weiser, *Die Apostelgeschichte*, 1:149.

258. Cf. Marguerat, "La mort d'Ananias et Saphira," 214, who stresses that Luke abandons the theme of sharing possessions for one of miraculous activity.

259. This is the fourth appearance of the adverb ὁμοθυμαδόν in Acts; all four depict the positive aspect of unanimity or togetherness among the believers (cf. 1:14; 2:46; 4:24). It is unclear whether ἅπαντες refers to the apostles, the believers, or the Jewish people (5:12). However, given the size of this part of the temple, the entire Christian community probably

Moreover, Luke informs the reader that this unanimity occurs in the context of Solomon's Portico, the same part of the temple where Peter spoke to the people after his healing of the lame man (cf. 3:11–12).[260] The apostles' activity ἐν τῷ λαῷ, along with the earlier scene in which Peter spoke to πᾶς ὁ λαός at Solomon's Portico (3:11–26), suggests that this picture of united believers places them amiably among the λαός, the Jewish people. The second part of this statement supports that picture and initially asserts that the Jewish people "held them in high regard" (5:13b).[261] The remainder of this statement, however, describes a different response within this scene: τῶν δὲ λοιπῶν οὐδεὶς ἐτόλμα κολλᾶσθαι αὐτοῖς (no one from the rest dared to join them; 5:13a). The infinitive κολλᾶσθαι implies an intimate attachment, which appears to be the connotation in most occurrences of the term in Luke-Acts.[262] Although the narrator positively depicts the believers in continuity with Judaism and as a well-respected part of the Jewish people, others who are unidentified except that they are τῶν λοιπῶν refuse to join ranks with the believers, perhaps because of what has happened to Ananias and Sapphira.[263] What Luke explicitly describes as happening among the believers clearly indicates both to the Jewish people and to the reader that God is at work. However, the described response is mixed, so that the narrative

could not meet there at the same time, although the narrative seems to present that image. Cf. Haenchen, *The Acts of the Apostles*, 242; Krodel, *Acts*, 123; Marshall, *The Acts of the Apostles*, 115; Roloff, *Die Apostelgeschichte*, 97; and Schneider, *Die Apostelgeschichte*, 1:380. Contra Fitzmyer, *The Acts of the Apostles*, 328; Johnson, *The Literary Function of Possessions in Luke-Acts*, 195n1; and Pesch, *Die Apostelgeschichte*, 1:206, who see this referring to the apostles.

260. This is the same location for Peter's and John's prior arrest (cf. 4:1–3). Cf. Pesch, *Die Apostelgeschichte*, 1:206; and Schmithals, *Die Apostelgeschichte des Lukas*, 58.

261. The Jewish people's high esteem for the believers does not coincide with 2:47a. Rather, considering the important role of reciprocity in Greco-Roman society, one may understand this as part of the reciprocal action of the Jewish people to the "goodwill" and wonders that have been actively demonstrated among them. Contra Co, "The Major Summaries in Acts," 75; and Fitzmyer, *The Acts of the Apostles*, 328. Cf. also Roloff, *Die Apostelgeschichte*, 98.

262. The term κολλᾶσθαι appears in Luke 10:11; 15:15; Acts 8:29; 9:26; 10:28; and 17:34. One appearance (Acts 8:29) uses the term to refer to one's approach to another. The other references connote a close attachment. See Daniel R. Schwartz, "Non-Joining Sympathizers (Acts 5, 13–14)," *Bib* 64 (1983): 552–53; and Witherington, *The Acts of the Apostles*, 225.

263. Cf. Barrett, *The Acts of the Apostles*, 1:274; Dunn, *The Acts of the Apostles*, 65–66; Marguerat, "La mort d'Ananias et Saphira," 214; Schneider, *Die Apostelgeschichte*, 1:380–81; and Schwartz, "Non-Joining Sympathizers (Acts 5, 13–14)," 550–51. Contra Pesch, *Die Apostelgeschichte*, 1:206; and Witherington, *The Acts of the Apostles*, 225–26, who see "the rest" as the remaining believers; and Bruce, *The Book of the Acts*, 109, who suggests that the incident "scared off all but the totally committed."

again depicts two distinct groups within the Jewish people: those who are believers through whom God is working, and those Jewish persons who do not believe.[264] The negative response, inserted within an *inclusio* of positive acceptance by the Jewish people, implies that the believers continued to proclaim the gospel message effectively.[265]

The third statement (5:14–15) of this narrative summary highlights the positive responses to the believing community and its message. Luke tells the reader that believers (πιστεύοντες; 5:14) are continually being added (προσετίθεντο), the same verb found in earlier depictions of divine blessing and tremendous growth of the believing group (cf. 2:41, 47).[266] Although the dative τῷ κυρίῳ may be grammatically linked with either προσετίθεντο or πιστεύοντες, the Lukan literary tendencies suggest that τῷ κυρίῳ be connected with προσετίθεντο, thus affirming the continuing growth of the group of believers as the direct result of God's activity.[267] Closely correlated with this continued growth (ὥστε; 5:15) is a brief description of sick persons who are carried out and placed in the streets so that healing might occur if Peter's shadow falls on them.[268] This response to the believers, apparently colored by ancient beliefs in the magical powers of one's shadow,[269] reinforces the idea of

---

264. Cf. Jervell, *Luke and the People of God*, 47; and Sanders, *The Jews in Luke-Acts*, 240. Contra Schwartz, "Non-Joining Sympathizers (Acts 5, 13–14)," 553–55, who identifies "the rest" as "all non-Christians, including those who will come to praise and believe."

265. This contrast, however, does not suggest hostility. Cf. Schneider, *Die Apostelgeschichte*, 1:381; Weiser, *Die Apostelgeschichte*, 1:150; and Co, "The Major Summaries in Acts," 79. Contra Neil, *Acts*, 95, who understands "the rest" as the apostles' opponents.

266. The term πλήθη also contributes to this picture of tremendous growth (5:16; cf. 2:6; 4:32). Cf. Boismard and Lamouille, *Les Actes des deux Apôtres*, 2:165–66; Haenchen, *The Acts of the Apostles*, 245; Pesch, *Die Apostelgeschichte*, 1:206; and Williams, *Acts*, 103.

267. The absolute use of a participle of πιστεύω in Acts (as in 5:14) is a common designation for Christians (e.g., 2:44; 4:32; 15:5; 18:27; 19:18; 21:20, 25) and is rarely modified by a dative noun. See Co, "The Major Summaries in Acts," 77–78. For others who link τῷ κυρίῳ with προσετίθεντο, see Barrett, *The Acts of the Apostles*, 1:275; Haenchen, *The Acts of the Apostles*, 243; Gerhard Schneider, *Lukas, Theologe der Heilsgeschichte: Aufsätze zum lukanischen Doppelwerk*, BBB 59 (Königstein: Peter Hanstein, 1985), 213–25; and Zingg, *Das Wachsen der Kirche*, 30. For examples of those who also link τῷ κυρίῳ with πιστεύοντες, see Fitzmyer, *The Acts of the Apostles*, 328–29; Johnson, *The Acts of the Apostles*, 95; Roloff, *Die Apostelgeschichte*, 96; and Weiser, *Die Apostelgeschichte*, 1:104.

268. See Conzelmann, *Acts of the Apostles*, 39; and Schneider, *Die Apostelgeschichte*, 1:381–82, who state that ὥστε (5:15) presents what follows as a consequence of 5:12–13, not of 5:14.

269. Cf. Johnson, *The Acts of the Apostles*, 96; Marshall, *The Acts of the Apostles*, 115–16; Pesch, *Die Apostelgeschichte*, 1:207; Roloff, *Die Apostelgeschichte*, 98; Schmithals, *Die Apostelgeschichte des Lukas*, 57; and Williams, *Acts*, 103.

the people's recognition that God is blessing the believers and working in extraordinary ways through the apostles (cf. 5:12).[270]

The final statement (5:16) of the narrative summary of 5:12–16 explicitly underscores the magnitude of what is taking place. Not only are the Jerusalemites responding to the obvious signs that God is working through the apostles and the church; large numbers of people (τὸ πλῆθος) from towns near Jerusalem (τῶν πέριξ πόλεων Ἰερουσαλήμ) also typically come together (συνήρχετο) and bring those who need healing.[271] The narrative scene gives the impression that persons from beyond Jerusalem gather at the temple, where all the believers are.[272] Although the narrator focuses on these people as the actors in the last part of this section, they respond to what the text states at the summary's beginning (5:12a): from the hands of the apostles (διὰ τῶν χειρῶν τῶν ἀποστόλων) are "many signs and wonders" (σημεῖα καὶ τέρατα πολλά). The conclusion of the summary includes the term ἅπαντες, emphasizing that *all* receive healing. Thus, Luke places the believers' action at the center of the exciting things that are happening, and this activity brings people together to the temple, even those from surrounding towns.[273]

An Assessment of the Characterization of the Church or Group of Believers in Acts 5:12–16

Some have suggested that the narrative summary of 5:12–16 offers nothing new to the book of Acts and its plot.[274] Such a conclusion need not be negative, since repetition is a common literary convention of ancient historiography.[275] Another suggestion posits that the Lukan narrator is much too obvious in his affirmation and colorful depiction of the

---

270. Cf. Barrett, *The Acts of the Apostles*, 1:276–77; Haenchen, *The Acts of the Apostles*, 243; Krodel, *Acts*, 123–24; and Pesch, *Die Apostelgeschichte*, 1:207–8.

271. The imperfect tense of συνήρχετο signifies that this scene is not atypical (5:16). Luke again uses a compound verb with the prefix σύν, suggesting the coming *together* of different persons because of what is happening.

272. See Schneider, *Die Apostelgeschichte*, 1:382, who observes that the "geographical horizon" has now widened beyond Jerusalem.

273. Cf. Schmithals, *Die Apostelgeschichte des Lukas*, 58, who suggests that these "editorial moves" depict the Christians as "the true, spiritual Israel."

274. See Schmithals, *Die Apostelgeschichte des Lukas*, 57; and Schneider, *Die Apostelgeschichte*, 1:378.

275. See Tannehill, *The Narrative Unity of Luke-Acts*, 2:67–79, for a discussion of repetition and redundancy in Acts 1–5; and idem, "The Composition of Acts 3–5," 229–37, for a discussion of the role of "echo effect" in Acts.

apostles as though they possess "superhuman" powers.[276] In this summary the Lukan characterization of the Christian community is, to be sure, a positive one that directly describes the believers largely through their actions and through the response of others to them. The description does not stand in isolation from the previous images of the believers but alludes to other statements and narrative matters that positively create a developing portrait of these believers in Jerusalem. Thus, the narrator again explicitly shows that the believers are unanimous and avid participants in Jewish religious practice. This narrative summary, however, does not return to the imagery of friendship and sharing found in the previous summaries of 2:42–47 and 4:32–37. Rather, one discovers that the narrative summary of 5:12–16, more than the two previous summaries, depicts the Jewish believers in relation to extraordinary events that sensationally indicate divine presence and activity among them.[277] The dramatic event dealing with Ananias and Sapphira along with the resultant "great fear" can have lasting effects, either positively or negatively, on the ongoing growth and communal dynamics of the Christian community. The different responses of "great fear," as Luke briefly describes them, suggest that with the continuing success also comes a response of apprehension that leads to separation rather than the building of community. Both the associated success among the Jewish people and the response of apprehension prepare readers for subsequent narrative events. The drama and excitement of these narrative events continue to build and potentially create feelings within the readers similar to the emotions depicted in the narrative, as the narrative confronts them with these developing images of the church or Christian community.

THE PROCLAIMING BELIEVERS AND INCREASING PERSECUTION (ACTS 5:17–42)

The Literary Context

The narrative events after the arrest and interrogation of Peter and John depict the Christian community as continuing in growth and divine blessing. Neither the hollow threats of the Jewish authorities nor the subtle

---

276. Johnson, *The Literary Function of Possessions in Luke-Acts*, 195. Cf. Schmithals, *Die Apostelgeschichte des Lukas*, 57.

277. Cf. Marguerat, "La mort d'Ananias et Saphira," 214.

threats of deceptive persons within their group can hamper the spread of the gospel message. The close identification of the Christian church with God, the favorable response by large numbers of Jewish people, and the dramatic scenes of extraordinary activity all combine to create an atmosphere of excitement and expectation, as the reader awaits the next narrative unit.

The Characterization of the Church or Group of Believers in Acts 5:17–42

The narrative events after the summary of 5:12–16 stand as a surprising reversal to the continuing growth and public affirmation that the believers have enjoyed. The episodes of 5:17–42 show an intensification of the negative response to the Jewish believers by the Jewish leaders. This negative response, however, is directed not toward the group of believers at large but toward the apostles, whom Luke depicts as representatives of the church.[278] In the Lukan narration, the Jewish leaders confront the apostles in hostile opposition. The narrative presents this confrontation in four basic scenes that contrast the apostles, as the representatives of the Christian community, with these Jewish leaders.

Luke begins his explanation of what happens by explicitly stating that the Sadducees are "filled with jealousy" (ἐπλήσθησαν ζήλου; 5:17), apparently over the response of the Jewish people toward the apostles.[279] This description provides "inside information" concerning their negative motives and contrasts with two positive aspects of the cumulative narrative portrait of the Christians: (1) the motives seen in Christians who share their possessions for the benefit of others,[280] and (2) the Christians being

---

278. Although the apostles are a group *within* the Christian community and are depicted with specific roles, they still contribute to the characterization of the church for two reasons: (1) as a group, their actions are depicted as similar to the larger group of believers, and (2) the unanimity that Luke accents within the Christian community joins this "select" group to the entire group of believers. This inclusion, however, contrasts significantly with the relation between the Jewish leaders and the Jewish people, which Acts 3–4 depicts as divided.

279. The typical Lukan grammatical connection of narrative sections by the conjunction δέ links the "success" and growth imagery with the arrest motivated out of jealousy (5:17–18).

280. The jealousy motive contrasts with the friendship motif used in the description of the Christians, since jealousy is thought to incite murderous impulses. For a list of references referring to the dangers of jealousy, see Johnson, *The Acts of the Apostles*, 96; and Shepherd, *The Narrative Function of the Holy Spirit*, 173n65. Cf. Haenchen, *The Acts of the Apostles*, 248; and Williams, *Acts*, 105–6. Contra Talbert, *Reading Acts*, 68, who translates ζῆλος to mean that the Sadducees acted *zealously*, not *jealously* (5:17).

"filled with the Holy Spirit" (cf. 2:4; 4:30).[281] This jealousy leads to the apostles' arrest apparently while they are at the temple.[282] The description of the apostles' prompt prison escape, due to their release by an angel of the Lord, affirms that God is clearly on the apostles' side (5:18–19).[283] The reader continues to find the apostles depicted as obedient to divine instructions when they return to the temple to teach, as the angel instructs them (5:20–21).[284] After the Jewish council[285] that has been called together (συνεκάλεσαν; 5:21) cannot find the apostles when the council seeks to interrogate them, the council embarrassingly receives the news that the apostles are back, teaching in the temple. This news confirms what the narrator has already told the readers about the apostles' escape and makes these authorities appear extremely foolish (5:21–26).[286] This second arrest, ironically, is not a violent one, for those who order the arrest fear that "the people" (τὸν λαόν; 5:26) might react violently in the apostles' defense.[287] Thus, the first narrative scene prepares for the subsequent interrogation and depicts the apostles with imagery reflective of earlier images of the believers: the working of God on their behalf, their obedience to God, and their positive reputation with the Jewish people. The Sadducees and the council, however, are portrayed with dangerous motives and as opponents to the apostles and God's purposes.[288]

---

281. Notice the contrast between the believers and these opponents: believers are frequently described as "filled with the Holy Spirit" (2:4; 4:8, 31), but these opponents are "filled with jealousy" (5:17). Cf. Dunn, *The Acts of the Apostles*, 67.

282. Cf. Gaventa, "Toward a Theology of Acts," 154; and Marguerat, "La mort d'Ananias et Saphira," 215.

283. See Pervo, *Profit with Delight*, 21–23, who relates this scene to similar stories in aretalogical literature. Cf. Bruce, *The Book of the Acts*, 110; Johnson, *The Acts of the Apostles*, 97; and Marshall, *The Acts of the Apostles*, 118.

284. Cf. Williams, *Acts*, 107; and Fitzmyer, *The Acts of the Apostles*, 335.

285. Literally, "the council and the whole body of the elders of Israel" (τὸ συνέδριον καὶ πᾶσαν τὴν γερουσίαν τῶν υἱῶν Ἰσραήλ; 5:21b).

286. Luke uses an unidentified person to confirm the sensational story (5:25) and to announce that the apostles are teaching in the temple, which is further confirmed by ὁ στρατηγὸς σὺν τοῖς ὑπηρέταις, who rearrest them (5:26). Luke describes the Jewish leaders, however, as clueless about what is happening. Cf. Haenchen, *The Acts of the Apostles*, 250; Krodel, *Acts*, 126–27; Marguerat, "La mort d'Ananias et Saphira," 214–15; and Tannehill, *The Narrative Unity of Luke-Acts*, 2:65: "[The scene] focuses on the reports of messengers who tell the Sanhedrin what readers already know, provoking smiles at their surprise and confusion."

287. Cf. Tyson, "The Jewish Public in Luke-Acts," 580, who stresses that this continuing positive response by the Jewish people is consistent with Luke's depiction of the initial acceptance of the Jewish people in Luke's gospel.

288. Cf. Johnson, *The Acts of the Apostles*, 102; Lohfink, *Die Sammlung Israels*, 50; Tannehill, "The Composition of Acts 3–5," 227.

The second narrative scene describes the actual interrogation of the apostles by the high priest. The high priest confirms both what Peter and John have been instructed *not* to do during their previous encounter (cf. 4:17–18) and what the apostles have done anyway: πεπληρώκατε τὴν Ἰερουσαλὴμ τῆς διδαχῆς ὑμῶν (5:28).[289] Thus, the high priest functions as a narrative character (although he may be seen as unreliable) who verifies what Acts has already told. The apostles' response also strengthens the narrator's reliability by affirming their obedient loyalty to God and by stating in concise fashion the major themes found in the three Petrine speeches of Acts 2–4.[290] The council's narrated reaction of fury (διεπρίοντο; 5:33)[291] and murderous intent,[292] however, stands in severe contrast to the apostles. The interrogation scene, therefore, continues to contrast the apostles with the Jewish leaders: the apostles insist on obedience to God by proclaiming Jesus' resurrection, and the Jewish leaders insist on the cessation of such activity and are willing to resort to murder in order to silence them.[293]

The third narrative scene provides information about a closed-door meeting of the council. The description of this meeting introduces another character, who calls for the private session and whose speech dominates the entire discussion.[294] The character, Gamaliel, is initially described by Luke as a Pharisee who is "respected by all the people" (παντὶ τῷ λαῷ; 5:34).[295] The narrator's explicit characterization of

---

289. Once again, the "filling" imagery confirms what Luke has described thus far: the Jewish people are responding favorably and in large numbers to the gospel message.

290. The brief speech to the council concludes with an affirmation that God has given the Holy Spirit "to those who obey him" (5:32), which basically attributes the Holy Spirit to their own lives as believers since they have already testified that they themselves "obey God" (5:29). By now, the apostles are reliable characters and important contributors to the narrator's perspective. Cf. Shepherd, *The Narrative Function of the Holy Spirit*, 174; Johnson, *The Acts of the Apostles*, 98; Krodel, *Acts*, 128; and Williams, *Acts*, 110–11.

291. The intensive verb διαπρίω suggests that their rage or anger is consuming them. Cf. Tannehill, *The Narrative Unity of Luke-Acts*, 2:65, who flags the strong emotion of this verb, which in 7:54 connotes both the rage and murderous inclinations of the opponents; Haenchen, *The Acts of the Apostles*, 251; Barrett, *The Acts of the Apostles*, 1:291–92; and Witherington, *The Acts of the Apostles*, 233.

292. The verb ἀναιρέω connotes violent killing in battle, by execution, or by murder. See BDAG, 64; and LSJ, 106. See also Barrett, *The Acts of the Apostles*, 1:292, who states that the imperfect indicative ἐβούλοντο (5:33) indicates the planning has begun.

293. Cf. Krodel, *Acts*, 127–28.

294. The council's private meeting removes the apostles for its duration. However, the apostles remain the object of the council's (and the reader's) attention.

295. Scholars have debated whether this characterization of Gamaliel is positive or negative. See John A. Darr, "Irenic or Ironic? Another Look at Gamaliel before the Sanhedrin (Acts

Gamaliel may explain why the council listens to this person: the people *respect* Gamaliel, and the council is *afraid* of the people.[296] The main emphases of the speech indicate, nonetheless, that Gamaliel indirectly serves as a spokesperson for the narrator, ironically allowing one of the council members to articulate some of the critical issues.[297]

Although the speech as Luke presents it does not focus on matters of justice, it does predict that the Christian "movement" will fizzle out if it is merely a human phenomenon — an impossibility considering the prison rescue in 5:19–20.[298] The speech's conclusion, therefore, focuses on a second possibility in discerning the Christian activity: if "this work" (τὸ ἔργον τοῦτο;) has God as its source, the council's response can best be characterized as impotent.[299] This consideration of God as the source of this Christian work, however, implicitly confirms what the Jewish authorities have already tried but failed to do (5:21–26; cf. 4:5–22).[300] Gamaliel's warning, that the council's opposition could make them θεομάχοι, those who fight against God (5:39), again suggests implicitly yet ironically what the reader has already seen in the first five chapters.[301] On the one hand, the apostles and believers enjoy the presence and blessing of God. On the other hand, the Jewish

---

5:33–42)," in Thompson and Phillips, *Literary Studies in Luke-Acts*, 121–39. For studies that present differing views of the Lukan characterization of the Pharisees, see Darr, *On Character Building*, 85–126; and Gowler, *Host, Guest, Enemy and Friend*.

296. Darr, *On Character Building*, 118. See Fitzmyer, *The Acts of the Apostles*, 339, who states that the council listens to Gamaliel because of his authority within the council. Cf. William John Lyons, "The Words of Gamaliel (Acts 5.38–39) and the Irony of Indeterminacy," *JSNT* 68 (December 1997): 45–46.

297. The character expresses some aspect of the narrator's perspective. Cf. Tannehill, *The Narrative Unity of Luke-Acts*, 2:67; and Kurz, *Reading Luke-Acts*, 83: "Letting an opponent express what the narrator holds as the truth provides a strong ironic twist and is a powerful way to identify the Christian movement with God's action."

298. To the reader, Gamaliel's comparison of Theudas and his group of around 400 men to the believers, given the narrator's description of extraordinary growth and numbers exceeding 5,000 men (2:41; 4:4; not counting the growth reported in 5:14), seems laughable, only to be surpassed by the council being convinced by it (cf. Darr, "Irenic or Ironic?" 135–36)! However, the references to some sort of scattering in the examples of Theudas and Judas (cf. 5:36–37) may anticipate the scattering of the church in Acts 8. Cf. Lohfink, *Die Sammlung Israels*, 86–87.

299. Cf. Lohfink, *Die Sammlung Israels*, 87–88, who stresses that the word τὸ ἔργον is used elsewhere in Acts for what God is doing among the Christians (cf. 13:2, 41; 14:26; 15:38).

300. Cf. Tannehill, *The Narrative Unity of Luke-Acts*, 2:67; Darr, "Irenic or Ironic?" 136–38; and Brian Rapske, "Opposition to the Plan of God and Persecution," in Marshall and Peterson, *Witness to the Gospel*, 237.

301. See Johnson, *The Acts of the Apostles*, 100–101, for a list of references in which the term θεομάχοι is found. Cf. Zettner, *Amt, Gemeinde und kirchliche Einheit*, 263.

leaders are becoming increasingly hostile toward the apostles, which suggests that they also are opposing God.[302] The speech distinguishes between human and divine activity, a distinction already made clear in the narrative observations about the apostles and, more generally, the believers.

The fourth narrative scene concludes this section by describing both the results of the meeting and the interrogation of the apostles. The hands-off policy that Gamaliel's speech advocates saves the day for the apostles, as Gamaliel persuades the council members *not* to react as they desire.[303] The council calls the apostles back into the meeting and has them beaten (δείραντες) without any explicit rationale given for such treatment, as Luke continues to develop a picture of communal disruption created by these Jewish leaders. Luke states that these authority figures order the apostles μὴ λαλεῖν ἐπὶ τῷ ὀνόματι τοῦ Ἰησοῦ, using terminology that alludes to their previous, unsuccessful attempts to silence them (cf. 4:17–20, 31).[304] What Luke describes next is not at all surprising, however, given the characterization of the believers that has accumulated through the narrative and one's reading to this point. As the apostles leave the council after their beatings and orders to be silent, Luke calls them οἱ χαίροντες (the rejoicing ones; 5:41). The council has instructed the apostles to silence their message, but the narrative section ends instead with a brief description that highlights the apostles' teaching and proclamation (5:42).[305] Gamaliel has warned the council members that they will be unable to stop the work of the believers if God is the source of their activity. And Luke clearly depicts that the apostles continue — "every day" (πᾶσάν ἡμέραν), never ceasing (οὐκ ἐπαύοντο) — to do what has been prohibited, even in the temple (5:42).[306] The reader is left with an image of the unceasing activity of the believers in the proclamation of the gospel message, a clear sign that this Christian work and

---

302. Cf. Kurz, *Reading Luke-Acts*, 146.

303. See Tannehill, *The Narrative Unity of Luke-Acts*, 2:66, who finds two rescues in Acts 5: one by an angel, one by Gamaliel. See Johnson, *The Acts of the Apostles*, 101, who highlights the scene's irony: "The Sanhedrin heeds Gamaliel, which means that they 'obey humans rather than God.' Gamaliel's superficially benign statement is in effect a self-condemnation."

304. See Dunn, *The Acts of the Apostles*, 73: "The high priestly opposition (5:40) is reduced to repetition of the old threats."

305. See Gaventa, "Toward a Theology of Acts," 156.

306. Cf. Johnson, *The Acts of the Apostles*, 101; Dunn, *The Acts of the Apostles*, 74; Fitzmyer, *The Acts of the Apostles*, 342; and Peterson, "The Worship of the New Community," 375.

community truly does have its source in God. However, with that image comes the anticipation of future clashes with the Jewish leaders.[307]

An Assessment of the Characterization of the Church or Group of Believers in Acts 5:17–42

The narrative events of 5:17–42 are strikingly similar to episodes found in Acts 4.[308] The repetitive nature of this section, in relation to Acts 4 as well as to the rest of Acts 1–4, assists the reader in linking important themes, recognizing narrative unity, and accumulating significant images for the book's unfolding plot and rhetoric.[309] Nevertheless, the literary means by which the Lukan narrator describes the Christian community in the narrative section of 5:17–42 are somewhat different from what one has found in previous sections of the Acts narrative.

Four particular aspects of the characterization of Christian community stand out in the narrative section of 5:17–42 within the developing plot of Acts 1–5. One aspect of this characterization is the specific focus on the apostles as a "select" group within the larger group of believers. Luke thus depicts the apostles with imagery consistent with the larger group as presented in Acts 1–5. A second aspect is the increasingly hostile confrontation of the apostles by the Jewish leaders because of the Jewish people's positive response. Such hostilities both sharpen the contrast between these Jewish believers and the Jewish leaders and create a vivid picture of division within the Jewish people generally. Another aspect of the characterization of the Christian community is the obvious divine role and the identification of God with the apostles. This narrative image is also consistent with the portrayal of the larger group of believers as depicted thus far in the narrative. The fourth aspect in the characterization of the Christian community is the ironic role of Gamaliel as a Lukan spokesperson, who implicitly identifies both the unstoppable activity of the Christians with God and the council as θεομάχοι. These four aspects of the Lukan characterization of the believers clearly identify this group with God, as the apostles stand confidently in a dangerous situation filled with jealous opposition, interrogation, murderous rage, and abuse.

---

307. Cf. Barrett, *The Acts of the Apostles*, 1:301, who states: "The preachers were thus disobedient to the Council, and were asking for trouble."

308. Cf. Haenchen, *The Acts of the Apostles*, 254.

309. Cf. Tannehill, *The Narrative Unity of Luke-Acts*, 2:75–77.

THE EARLIEST BELIEVERS AND
THE PROBLEM WITH THE WIDOWS (ACTS 6:1–7)

The Literary Context

The previous narrative section of 5:17–42 clearly depicts the Christians in terms of divine activity, which is evident in the unceasing proclamation of the gospel message despite the growing hostility and murderous inclinations of the Jewish leaders. Although the reader does not find the recurrent imagery of unanimity explicitly present there, the imagery of division takes a significant role in those depicted events, as the contrast between the Jewish leaders and the apostles clearly indicates.[310] That lingering image of divine activity, both corresponding with the associated proclamation of the gospel message and contrasting with the expected continuation of hostilities and division, creates in readers a sense of anticipation as to what will happen next in the developing Christian church or community in Jerusalem.

The Characterization of the Church or Group of Believers in Acts 6:1–7

The narrative scene that follows the hostile atmosphere of the apostles' arrest and persecution returns the reader's focus to internal matters within the church.[311] Luke conjoins this narrative section and the preceding narrative sequence both by grammatical and chronological connections, which potentially coax the reader to perceive this section as a continuation of the story.[312] The narrator also links this particular scene to the depiction of the Christian community in Acts 1–5 by directly describing the group's growth both at the beginning (6:1) and at the end (6:7) of this section in ways that remind the reader of earlier images that have linked such growth to divine activity and

---

310. The naming of Peter and the apostles as the speakers of the "defense speech" (5:29–32) suggests a degree of unanimity, in that they must speak with one voice. However, one cannot make a strong argument here.

311. That the narrative returns the action to internal, communal matters after scenes of arrest and interrogation duplicates a basic "pattern" found also in Acts 4.

312. The typical Lukan grammatical connection δέ combines with the chronological phrase ἐν ταῖς ἡμέραις ταύταις to assist the reader in making the necessary connections (6:1; cf. 1:15). Cf. Earl Richard, *Acts 6:1–8:4: The Author's Method of Composition*, SBLDS 41 (Missoula, MT: Scholars Press, 1978), 216; Haenchen, *The Acts of the Apostles*, 260; Fitzmyer, *The Acts of the Apostles*, 346; and Lüdemann, *Early Christianity according to the Traditions in Acts*, 74. Contra Kurz, *Reading Luke-Acts*, 83; and Edvin Larsson, "Die Hellenisten und die Urgemeinde," *NTS* 33 (1987): 205, who stress that this section starts a new phase in Acts.

blessing.[313] The repetitive use of growth imagery, then, takes on an important role in the narrative sequence by explicitly affirming the continued growth and divine blessing in this scene following the apostles' persecution.

The narrative account concentrates on a polemical problem that arises among the Jerusalem believers. The controversy is between two groups within the church, which Luke identifies as the Hellenists and the Hebrews.[314] Unfortunately, Luke provides no further details in describing these two groups, so that the reader may realistically conclude that the distinction refers to language and not to race or theology.[315] However, although the scarcity of information leaves a number of gaps or unanswered questions, the narrator directs the reader's attention to the immediate problem. Luke describes the Hellenists as complaining (γογγυσμός; 6:1) against their Hebrew counterparts within the Christian community. The use of the noun γογγυσμός reflects poorly on

---

313. In 6:1 the genitive absolute πληθυνόντων τῶν μαθητῶν seems to clarify when the event takes place (cf. Johnson, *The Acts of the Apostles*, 105; Schille, *Die Apostelgeschichte des Lukas*, 167; and Larsson, "Die Hellenisten und die Urgemeinde," 205). In 6:7, however, this growth imagery is the statement's subject: ἐπληθύνετο ὁ ἀριθμὸς τῶν μαθητῶν ἐν Ἰερουσαλὴμ σφόδρα. Thus, these two forms of the verb πληθύνω frame the action of this account and create an *inclusio* (cf. Krodel, *Acts*, 131–32; Richard, *Acts 6:1–8:4*, 217; Tyson, "Acts 6:1–7 and Dietary Regulations in Early Christianity," 152; and Weiser, *Die Apostelgeschichte*, 1:167).

314. The term Ἑλληνιστής (6:1) does not appear in Greek literature prior to the book of Acts, but it also describes groups of people in 9:29 and 11:20. See Bruce M. Metzger, *A Textual Commentary on the Greek New Testament* (New York: United Bible Societies, 1971), 386–89; Johnson, *The Acts of the Apostles*, 105; and Witherington, *The Acts of the Apostles*, 240–47.

315. The narrative has maintained the reader's focus on the believers in Jerusalem. Thus, race or ethnicity does not seem to be the issue, as the narrator clearly depicts the *Jewish* Christian community in Acts 1–5 (contra Henry J. Cadbury, "The Hellenists," in Foakes-Jackson and Lake, *The Beginnings of Christianity*, 5:59–74; and Tyson, "Acts 6:1–7 and Dietary Regulations in Early Christianity," 155–58, who is now less convinced; see idem, *Images of Judaism in Luke-Acts*, 112, 127n16). Many scholars see a distinction in language (a conflict between Jewish Christians who speak Hebrew or Greek); see, e.g., Fitzmyer, "Jewish Christianity in Acts in Light of the Qumran Scrolls," 233–57; Haenchen, *The Acts of the Apostles*, 260–61; Craig C. Hill, *Hellenists and Hebrews: Reappraising Division within the Earliest Church* (Minneapolis: Fortress, 1992); Larsson, "Die Hellenisten und die Urgemeinde," 205–25; Marshall, *The Acts of the Apostles*, 125–26; Roloff, *Die Apostelgeschichte*, 108–9; Tyson, *Images of Judaism in Luke-Acts*, 111–12; and Williams, *Acts*, 117–18. Scholars often understand the division over language as a division over ideology. For a brief overview of the history of this understanding and a critical reappraisal of that position, see Hill, *Hellenists and Hebrews* (esp. 5–17); and Larsson, "Die Hellenisten und die Urgemeinde," 205–25. Contra Haenchen, *The Acts of the Apostles*, 266–69; Pervo, *Profit with Delight*, 40; Schmithals, *Die Apostelgeschichte des Lukas*, 63–65; and Nikolaus Walter, "Apostelgeschichte 6.1 und die Anfänge der Urgemeinde in Jerusalem," *NTS* 29 (July 1983): 374.

the Hellenistic Christians, since the term has negative connotations of intense grumbling and strong dissatisfaction due to disobedience in its Septuagintal occurrences.[316] This grumbling, however, is provoked by the Hellenists' widows being consistently overlooked in the daily distribution of food (6:1).[317]

The narrative only presents the problem in generalities and thereby leaves gaps about the precise nature of this apparent system of care and the reasons for such neglect.[318] One must recognize that the failure to provide for the needs of *all* threatens the believers' unanimity and counters earlier descriptions of the needy receiving necessary provisions (cf. 2:44–45; 4:32, 34–35), descriptions that the readers have been encouraged to link with the Christians' unity and the presence of God.[319] The reality of the problem threatens the ideals of a community that the narrative characterizes as a κοινωνία of friends established by God's activity and their common belief (cf. 2:42, 44; 4:32). In this passage the initial depiction of the Jerusalem church, therefore, is one of irony: the Jewish leaders' jealous reactions cannot threaten them, but a basic communal issue does threaten the church's existence! Neither the Greek-speaking Christians nor the Hebrew-speaking Christians stand out as affirmative

---

316. See Karl Heinrich Rengstorf, "γογγύζω...." in *TDNT*, 3:728–37. The 15 occurrences of γογγύζω and 10 occurrences of διαγογγύζω in the LXX predominantly refer to grumbling or complaining due to guilty unbelief and disobedience. Cf. Johnson, *The Acts of the Apostles*, 105; and Walter, "Apostelgeschichte 6.1 und die Anfänge der Urgemeinde in Jerusalem," 373.

317. The imperfect tense, παρεθεωροῦντο, suggests that this consistently happens. Cf. Tyson, "Acts 6:1–7 and Dietary Regulations in Early Christianity," 158; Haenchen, *The Acts of the Apostles*, 268; and Johnson, *The Acts of the Apostles*, 105.

318. See Walter, "Apostelgeschichte 6.1 und die Anfänge der Urgemeinde in Jerusalem," 370–93, who argues that the synagogues provide for widows, but that the Hellenistic Jews are overlooked because they are not originally from the area; and F. Scott Spencer, "Neglected Widows in Acts 6:1–7," *CBQ* 56 (October 1994): 715–32. Cf. Haenchen, *The Acts of the Apostles*, 261–62; Krodel, *Acts*, 132–33; Lüdemann, *Early Christianity according to the Traditions in Acts*, 75–76; and Schille, *Die Apostelgeschichte des Lukas*, 168. See also Joseph B. Tyson, "The Emerging Church and the Problem of Authority in Acts," *Int* 42 (1988): 138, who proposes that the role of food may reflect the practice of the common meal that Luke refers to in 2:42, 46. In both of these cases, the problem may be related to cultural differences.

319. Cf. Tannehill, *The Narrative Unity of Luke-Acts*, 2:80. If, as Tyson suggests (*Images of Judaism in Luke-Acts*, 112), this problem is related to the practice of the common meal, which itself reflects the believers' unanimity, the central issue would still remain the same: the peril to the essence of the Christian community. See Spencer, "Neglected Widows in Acts 6:1–7," 729, who argues that readers, following other pictures of widows in the Lukan Gospel, would receive "a surprising jolt" when finding out that *the church* is mistreating these widows.

depictions of the church in the first verse, since both contribute to a problem that endangers the very nature of that community.[320]

Although the Lukan narrator sparsely describes the controversy, the response to the problem stands significantly at the heart of the account. The apostles (οἱ δώδεκα) assemble the believers (τὸ πλῆθος τῶν μαθητῶν)[321] and function as reliable spokespersons for the narrator, as the readers are invited to see and evaluate the situation through the apostles' eyes. Luke includes an ironic twist in the Twelve's response of displeasure (οὐκ ἀρεστόν ἐστιν ἡμᾶς) as they implicitly compare the believers' behavior to the Jewish leaders' threats: both require their abandonment of the proclamation of God's word (6:2; cf. 4:18; 5:40).[322] Conversely, the apostles address the believers as ἀδελφοί, thus affirming the close bond between them. The apostles' recommendation, therefore, returns the problem to the entire group and urges the believers to select seven men for this διακονία.[323] Both the requirement for the seven men to be "full of the Spirit and wisdom"[324] and their responsibility for this specific need of the community (ἐπὶ τῆς χρείας ταύτης)[325] implicitly

---

320. Cf. Schmithals, *Die Apostelgeschichte des Lukas*, 63, who sees Luke reflecting his own ecclesiastical situation.

321. Cf. Schille, *Die Apostelgeschichte des Lukas*, 169. See Tyson, "The Emerging Church and the Problem of Authority in Acts," 137–39, who sees this action as indicative of apostolic authority. See also Johnson, *The Acts of the Apostles*, 106, who stresses that τὸ πλῆθος describes a deliberative body (6:2). However, given the general connotation of the term in most references in Acts, this term may simply create an image of a rather large crowd.

322. The intensive verb καταλείπω has a stronger meaning than translations of "neglect" (NRSV) or "overlooked" (NIV) indicate (6:2). Though Luke implicitly evaluates the believers' actions through the apostles, he gives no rationale for those conclusions. Cf. Johnson, *The Literary Function of Possessions in Luke-Acts*, 212; and Schneider, *Die Apostelgeschichte*, 1:425. Contra Schmithals, *Die Apostelgeschichte des Lukas*, 65, who suggests that Luke plays down the conflict.

323. Cf. Haenchen, *The Acts of the Apostles*, 261.

324. The requirement that the seven men be "full of the Spirit and wisdom" (πλήρεις πνεύματος καὶ σοφίας; 6:3) uses the same imagery that has become commonplace in Acts. The imagery functions to contrast the believers, described positively as "filled with the Spirit" (ἐπλήσθησαν . . . πνεύματος ἁγίου; 2:4; cf. 4:31), and opponents (those who somehow threaten the Christian community), described negatively as filled by Satan (ἐπλήρωσεν ὁ Σατανᾶς; 5:3) or with jealousy (ἐπλήσθησαν ζήλου; 5:17). Cf. Schmithals, *Die Apostelgeschichte des Lukas*, 66.

325. The suggestion to select seven men also has narrative allusions. In the narrative summary of 2:42–47, a common practice that reveals certain aspects of the character of the Christian community is the distribution of proceeds from the sale of personal possessions "as any had need" (πᾶσιν καθότι ἄν τις χρείαν εἶχεν; 2:45). In the apostles' suggestion, these seven men will care for "this need" (ἐπὶ τῆς χρείας ταύτης; 6:3). Cf. Johnson, *The Acts of the Apostles*, 106; and Lüdemann, *Early Christianity according to the Traditions in Acts*, 76.

correspond with prior images of the believers as the center of communal and divine activity.

This recommended course of action implies that the restoration of the positive communal dynamics would ensure the continuation of God's blessing in that community. In addition, this possible solution antici-pates the continuation of the same activities that have characterized the apostles and the entire group from the beginning: ἡμεῖς δὲ τῇ προσευχῇ καὶ τῇ διακονίᾳ τοῦ λόγου προσκαρτερήσομεν (we will devote ourselves to prayer and to the ministry of the word; 6:4).[326] The same continuing de-votion to prayer that has characterized the unanimous believers before and after Pentecost, as well as the implicit devotion that the apostles have demonstrated in the proclamation of the gospel message, is also stressed here.[327] This statement functions like a narrative hinge. On the one hand, the narrated account invites readers to look retrospectively to the various aspects of the Christian community as arranged sequentially in the Acts narrative see thus far. On the other hand, the account also creates a sense of anticipation for what might happen as the believers seek to address the threatening internal problem.

The narrator's description of the community's response provides an important though implicit picture of the believers as a character group in this scene. Contrasting with the apostles' displeasure (οὐκ ἀρεστόν ἐστιν ἡμᾶς; 6:2) in what they have perceived, the apostles' recommendation "pleased the whole community" (καὶ ἤρεσεν ὁ λόγος ἐνώπιον παντὸς τοῦ πλήθους; 6:5).[328] The collective action of the entire community in select-ing seven men implicitly depicts a community acting again out of unity.[329] The observation of the communal confirmation of these men, as they place their hands upon (ἐπέθηκαν αὐτοῖς τὰς χεῖρας)[330] the "appointees"

---

326. See Schneider, *Die Apostelgeschichte*, 1:424–25, who counts this statement as indicat-ing that the apostles' primary concern is proclamation. Cf. Haenchen, *The Acts of the Apostles*, 263. See also Spencer, "Neglected Widows in Acts 6:1–7," 729–30, who sees the apostles' perspective reflecting their same deficient view of social ministry as in the Lukan Gospel.

327. The verb that has previously described the Christians' devotion (προσκαρτερέω) also describes here what the reader and the believers can expect by positively dealing with the problem (6:4). Also, the devotion τῇ διακονίᾳ τοῦ λόγου (6:4) alludes to the unstoppable proclamation of "the word" in earlier narrative scenes.

328. See Richard, *Acts 6:1–8:4*, 217.

329. Cf. Schmithals, *Die Apostelgeschichte des Lukas*, 66. See Witherington, *The Acts of the Apostles*, 250, who states that they decide "to avoid even the appearance of favoritism."

330. See Spencer, "Neglected Widows in Acts 6:1–7," who identifies the irony that the apostles "*lay* their hands on the seven, . . . but they refuse to *lift* their hands personally to help the widows" (6:6).

and pray (προσευξάμενοι; 6:6), reaffirms the believers' unified action and helps readers to link their actions to earlier affirmative pictures of the Christian community.[331] The naming of the seven men, therefore, does not function primarily as an introduction of some characters who will appear later in the narrative. Rather, Luke places the list within the context of the collective, communal activity of the believers, so that the unified community is presented as a narrative actor in problem-solving and in preparation for proclamation.[332]

This narrative section concludes with a brief summary of what happens following the community's action (6:7).[333] Here the narrator explicitly links the following details as the results of that unified action. In particular, the narrator summarizes three continuing results that emphasize the believers' numerical growth, which the reader has already found to be associated with divine blessing and activity (cf. 2:41, 47; 4:4; 5:14).[334] The first result mentioned is that "the word of God continued to increase," an implicit judgment that ὁ λόγος τοῦ θεοῦ is not abandoned, against which the apostles have warned (cf. 6:2).[335] The second result returns to the same imagery of numerical growth found in the first verse by using similar terminology to create an *inclusio* that encloses this narrative scene within the context of divine blessing and

---

331. Two parts of the sentence of 6:5–6 accentuate these connections with the themes and images of the characterization of the Christian community in Acts 1–5. One connection is found in the community's collective action as they select (ἐξελέξαντο) and place (ἐτέθηκαν) their hands on the seven men. The first verb refers to the action of the entire community, although the subject of the second verb is not so clear. Although translations such as the NRSV see the apostles (cf. 6:6) laying their hands on the seven, the apostles do not function as the subject of this extended sentence. The "laying on of hands" is not limited to the apostles in Acts (cf. 9:12, 17; 13:3; 19:6; 28:8). Thus, the emphasis is on the believers' collective action, not the apostles' authoritative role. Cf. Neil, *Acts*, 103; and Williams, *Acts*, 123. Contra Bruce, *The Book of the Acts*, 122; Schneider, *Die Apostelgeschichte*, 1:421, 427; Tyson, "The Emerging Church and the Problem of Authority in Acts," 138–39; and Weiser, *Die Apostelgeschichte*, 1:167.

332. Cf. Bartchy, "Community of Goods in Acts," 318; and Bruce, *The Book of the Acts*, 122.

333. See Bruce, *The Book of the Acts*, 123, who thinks this summary (6:7) interrupts the narrative.

334. The imperfect tense of the three verbs of 6:7 suggests continuing results. See Schneider, *Die Apostelgeschichte*, 1:429–30. Cf. Lohfink, *Die Sammlung Israels*, 52; and Richard, *Acts 6:1–8:4*, 216.

335. See Tannehill, *The Narrative Unity of Luke-Acts*, 2:82; and Zingg, *Das Wachsen der Kirche*, 25, 174, who identify a connection of Acts 6:7 with the Exodus and the promise of Abraham. See also Rosner, "The Progress of the Word," 226, who sees this expression as indicating the beginning movement of the gospel to a "universal context."

activity. Finally, the narrator specifically mentions an overwhelming response of faith even by πολύς τε ὄχλος τῶν ἱερέων, the group most hostile
toward the believers to this point in the narrative.[336] Thus, the narrative
account leaves the reader with positive images both of God's activity and
of the church's continuity with Judaism.[337]

An Assessment of the Characterization of the Church or Group of Believers in Acts 6:1–7

The narrative scene of 6:1–7 contributes to the plot of Acts in several
ways, including the authority of the apostles and the introduction of
Stephen and Philip. While one should not minimize the importance of
these narrative contributions, the described actions and dialogue direct
the reader's attention to the community's actions.[338] That the narrative
account includes no other characters, other than the group of believers
itself, requires reflection only on them. The inclusion of these actions,
before and after the apostles' intervention, functions as an indirect presentation of the Christian community, with only the choice of wording
to provide hints for the reader in evaluating them. The narrator's concluding summary statement, however, serves as a direct means by which
the narrator explicitly gives information that assists the readers in their
continuing construction of the church as a significant character in the
Acts narrative.

The characterization of the Christian community in 6:1–7 both co-
heres with and contributes to the cumulative images presented by the
Acts narrative. Again, the narrative affirms the communal dynamic of
unanimity as an essential characteristic of the church. The narrative
clearly urges the reader to correlate the unanimous character of the
church with the continuation of divine blessing, and this correlation implies that the erosion of unanimity could lead to the disappearance of that
divine presence and the disintegration of the church itself. Also consistent
with the earlier images of the Christian community is the continuity between Judaism and the Christian faith, which the overwhelming response

---

336. See Jervell, *Luke and the People of God*, 46, who suggests that this description indicates that "most Jewish Jews" become believers. Cf. Shepherd, *The Narrative Function of
the Holy Spirit*, 179, who sees this description as a sign of division within the leadership of
Judaism.

337. The priests may be mentioned because of mounting tensions that later lead to Stephen's
death. Cf. Brawley, *Centering on God*, 93; and Sanders, *The Jews in Luke-Acts*, 244.

338. Cf. Weiser, *Die Apostelgeschichte*, 1:164.

of priests indicates. What this picture of the early Christians contributes to the cumulative portrait of the church in Acts is not merely an account of the development of hierarchical or ecclesiastical structures. Rather, the narrative presents to the reader a description of the *entire* community's distinct role in being responsible for one another and in proclaiming the gospel message.

THE SCATTERED BELIEVERS
AFTER THE DEATH OF STEPHEN (ACTS 8:1B–3)

The Literary Context (Acts 6:8–8:1a)

After the meeting of the Jerusalem believers and the problem's successful resolution, the direction of the narrative turns to one of the seven men selected by the church. The narrative employs some of the positive images of the Christian community in characterizing Stephen at the commencement of this narrative section, so that the reader is encouraged to see this individual character as consistent with that larger group. Thus, Stephen is πλήρης χάριτος καὶ δυνάμεως,[339] he performed τέρατα καὶ σημεῖα μεγάλα ἐν τῷ λαῷ (6:8),[340] and his speech reflected "wisdom and the Spirit" (6:10) — qualities that will assist readers in understanding and evaluating the following events.[341]

Conversely, Luke introduces a second group into the narrative and negatively describes its actions — some belonging to the "synagogue of

---

339. The characterization of Stephen as "full of grace" is consistent with earlier descriptions of the believers as having χάρις for all the people (2:47) and as under the influence of χάρις μεγάλη (4:33). The addition of καὶ δυνάμεως to πλήρης χάριτος also links Stephen to the apostles, who have δυνάμει μεγάλη in delivering their testimony or proclamation about Jesus' resurrection (4:33). Cf. Marshall, *The Acts of the Apostles*, 129.

340. The description of Stephen doing τέρατα καὶ σημεῖα μεγάλα ἐν τῷ λαῷ (6:8) alludes to the apostles' activity of doing σημεῖα καὶ τέρατα πολλὰ ἐν τῷ λαῷ (5:12a) and to the prayer requesting that God would grant his servants the ability to do σημεῖα καὶ τέρατα (4:30). Cf. Krodel, *Acts*, 134; and Williams, *Acts*, 124.

341. The term used to describe Stephen as speaking (λαλέω; 6:10) previously refers either to the apostles or the believers (cf. 2:4, 6, 7, 11; 4:1, 17, 20, 29; 5:20, 40), or to God or one of God's messengers of the OT (cf. 2:31; 3:21, 22, 24). That the narrator stresses this speech as reflecting "wisdom and the Spirit" links this character with the stated requirements for the seven, including that they were to be πλήρεις πνεύματος καὶ σοφίας (full of the Spirit and of wisdom; 6:3). Cf. Shepherd, *The Narrative Function of the Holy Spirit*, 177–78, who stresses that the Holy Spirit signals to the audience that what the narrator states is reliable; also Johnson, *The Acts of the Apostles*, 108, 112; and Tannehill, *The Narrative Unity of Luke-Acts*, 2:83.

the Freedmen"[342] who stand up and argue (συζητοῦντες) with Stephen.[343] Luke takes on the role of the omniscient narrator, providing additional negative information about four behind-the-scenes maneuvers by these opponents, about which readers would otherwise not know. According to Luke, these persons secretly convince (ὑπέβαλον; 6:11)[344] others to accuse Stephen of blasphemy against Moses and God, an accusation that the readers will see as out of character, considering Stephen's depiction as one of the believers.[345] These opponents stir up (συνεκίνησαν)[346] not only the elders and the scribes but also τὸν λαόν (6:12), as the narrator seems to blame these persons for the first sign of a breach between the Jewish *people* and the Jewish *believers*.[347]

A third act that Luke includes in the narrative is the opponents' confrontation as they seize (συνήρπασαν)[348] Stephen and take him to the council, apparently the same council that has twice interrogated the apostles (cf. 4:5–22; 5:17–40). The last maneuver by these opponents is their production of μάρτυρας ψευδεῖς, whose accusations the readers

---

342. This synagogue is probably for Greek-speaking Jews, so that these opponents are not the ones found in Acts 4–5. Cf. Bruce, *The Book of the Acts*, 124–25; Conzelmann, *Acts of the Apostles*, 47; Johnson, *The Acts of the Apostles*, 108; Lüdemann, *Early Christianity according to the Traditions in Acts*, 82–85; Marshall, *The Acts of the Apostles*, 129; Neil, *Acts*, 105–6; Tannehill, *The Narrative Unity of Luke-Acts*, 2:84; and Williams, *Acts*, 127.

343. The verb συζητέω ("to dispute" or "to argue with") is found in Acts only here (6:9) and in 9:29, where Saul disputes with "Hellenists." The noun συζήτησις ("discussion" or "dispute") is found in 15:2, 7; and 28:29. Cf. Tannehill, *The Narrative Unity of Luke-Acts*, 2:84, who suggests that the plot follows the same course here as in Acts 4–5: after performing signs and wonders, the witnesses of Jesus are arrested and interrogated by the council.

344. The verb ὑποβάλλω (6:11) has a negative connotation when it refers to the interaction between persons. See, e.g., Josephus, *The Jewish War* 5.439; and idem, *Jewish Antiquities* 20.200. Cf. Conzelmann, *Acts of the Apostles*, 47.

345. Cf. Jacob Jervell, "The Acts of the Apostles and the History of Early Christianity," *ST* 37 (1983): 17. Contra Sanders, *The Jews in Luke-Acts*, 246; and Tyson, *Images of Judaism in Luke-Acts*, 113.

346. The verb συγκινέω (6:12) negatively connotes the creation of a "community" of commotion, as the prefix σύν added to the verb κινέω (to stir up/incite) suggests. Cf. Barrett, *The Acts of the Apostles*, 1:326, who sees this as "a large-scale, rabble-rousing activity."

347. To this point in the narrative, Luke has described the λαός as associating with the believers, responding favorably, and providing protection in numbers (cf. 4:21; 5:26). Although some persons refuse to associate with them (cf. 5:13), only the Jewish *leaders* respond negatively. This is the first reference to the Jewish *people* responding negatively. Cf. Sanders, *The Jews in Luke-Acts*, 245; Conzelmann, *Acts of the Apostles*, 47–48; Fitzmyer, *The Acts of the Apostles*, 359; and Tannehill, *The Narrative Unity of Luke-Acts*, 2:84.

348. The verb συναρπάζω (6:12) denotes a violent act of seizure (cf. Luke 8:29; Acts 19:29; 27:15). The prefix σύν also suggests that this violent seizure was by those who joined together against another (cf. Acts 19:29). Cf. Haenchen, *The Acts of the Apostles*, 271; and Sanders, *The Jews in Luke-Acts*, 246, who observes that the citizens make this arrest.

would dismiss as ridiculous in light of both the explicit description and what they have encountered earlier in the narrative (6:13–14).[349] This thoroughly negative depiction of these Jewish opponents ends, however, not with the narrator's observations of these opponents, but with the council members' (πάντες οἱ καθεζόμενοι ἐν τῷ συνεδρίῳ) observation of Stephen: "his face was like the face of an angel" (6:15).[350] In other words, what the reader has seen through the eyes and understanding of the Lukan narrator is confirmed by what the council members see. On the one hand, the believer Stephen reflects all the characteristics of those in the Christian community, particularly the divine presence and power, and implicitly the unanimous and communal attitude toward others that has been associated with God's activity. On the other hand, the opponents behave deceivingly and divisively against Stephen and implicitly do so against God, exactly what Gamaliel had warned against doing (cf. 5:39).

A council meeting provides the narrative setting in which Luke inserts a speech attributed to Stephen and his defense of the charges against him. In actuality, the speech functions little as a response to the charges and more as a narrative explanation implicitly to direct the attention and understanding of readers, so that they may make the necessary interpretations of both prior and subsequent narrative scenes. The speech briefly recites the history of Israel, focusing predominantly on the activity of God as seen in the lives of Abraham (7:2–8), the patriarchs (7:9–16), and Moses (7:17–43).[351] In the latter stages of this historical synopsis, the accent is placed on the rebellious response of the Jewish people to God or, more specifically, οἱ υἱοὶ Ἰσραήλ toward Moses, God's spokesperson (cf. 7:25–29, 39–41).[352] The speech strongly implicates the council's current behavior as consistent with the historical, negative response to God by the Jewish people or Israelites; it "functions as a prophecy for the narrative" because it reveals the attitude behind the

---

349. Contra Lüdemann, *Early Christianity according to the Traditions in Acts*, 82, who claims that Luke represents these charges as accurate ones against a radical Stephen.

350. See Johnson, *The Acts of the Apostles*, 110, who states that this change of countenance indicates that Stephen is an authoritative spokesperson of God.

351. One may attribute the dominant role of Moses in the speech to the fact that he was credited with the Jewish law and the tent of testimony, precursor to the temple. The Jewish law and the temple are at the center of the charges against Stephen.

352. See Tannehill, *The Narrative Unity of Luke-Acts*, 2:86–92, who interprets this as a "tragic reversal." Cf. Bruce, *The Book of the Acts*, 130–31; Haenchen, *The Acts of the Apostles*, 295; Hill, *Hellenists and Hebrews*, 75; and Richard, *Acts 6:1–8:4*, 325.

subsequent events.[353] Stephen emphatically calls them opposers of the Holy Spirit, which in the narrative implicitly contrasts them with the Christian community (7:51; cf. 7:52).[354] Stephen concludes, therefore, that the council members, whom he pointedly associates with perpetrating persecution and murder against persons (i.e., prophets, the Righteous One) sent by God (7:52),[355] are guilty of not keeping (οὐκ ἐφυλάξατε) the law that was ordained by the angels (εἰς διαταγὰς ἀγγέλων; 7:53).[356]

The narrated response to Stephen's speech places a graphic picture of a mob scene in the reader's mind.[357] Although Stephen's speech clearly declares his innocence, the council reacts in an uncontrollable rage (διεπρίοντο ταῖς καρδίαις αὐτῶν; 7:54) that surpasses their earlier negative response to the apostles (cf. 5:33).[358] In complete contrast to the council, the narrator directly describes Stephen as πλήρης πνεύματος ἁγίου, an affirmation that the divine presence that characterizes the Christian community also characterizes him (7:55).[359] The mention of Stephen's heavenly vision merely prepares the reader for Stephen's words

353. Johnson, *The Literary Function of Possessions in Luke-Acts*, 76.

354. The main part of the sentence in 7:51, ὑμεῖς ἀεὶ τῷ πνεύματι τῷ ἁγίῳ ἀντιπίπτετε ὡς οἱ πατέρες ὑμῶν καὶ ὑμεῖς, has three distinct elements: (1) the statement's emphatic nature, with the pronoun ὑμεῖς and its repetition in the ὡς clause; (2) the present tense of ἀντιπίπτω, which in Num 27:14 (LXX) describes the rebellion of the congregation (τὴν συναγωγήν) against God, suggesting that such opposition continues; and (3) the opposition against the Holy Spirit in contrast to the Spirit's active role in the Christian community as found in Acts 1–7. Cf. Shepherd, *The Narrative Function of the Holy Spirit*, 178; and Marshall, *The Acts of the Apostles*, 147.

355. The pronoun ὑμεῖς stresses that Stephen's audience is guilty of murder (φονεῖς; 7:52), which is similar to the emphases in Peter's earlier speeches (cf. 2:36; 3:14–15). One should also recognize, however, the striking differences between this speech and those Petrine speeches. Cf. Tannehill, *The Narrative Unity of Luke-Acts*, 2:85–87.

356. The description of the law as "ordained by angels" (7:53) subtly links the speaker, whose face appears "as the face of an angel" (6:15), with that law and suggests to the reader that the charges against Stephen are invalid.

357. See Tannehill, *The Narrative Unity of Luke-Acts*, 2:97, who correctly observes that this violent reaction is not the only possibility available to the opponents (cf. 2:36–41).

358. Although Luke describes the earlier response as διεπρίοντο καὶ ἐβούλοντο ἀνελεῖν αὐτούς (5:33), now the council's response is described as διεπρίοντο ταῖς καρδίαις αὐτῶν καὶ ἔβρυχον τοὺς ὀδόντας ἐπ' αὐτόν (7:54), the former phrase denoting a *consuming* rage and the latter phrase denoting a *violent* rage. See Barrett, *The Acts of the Apostles*, 1:382, who mentions the imperfect tense of both verbs. Cf. Haenchen, *The Acts of the Apostles*, 291; Marshall, *The Acts of the Apostles*, 148; Schneider, *Die Apostelgeschichte*, 1:472; Tannehill, *The Narrative Unity of Luke-Acts*, 2:86; and Witherington, *The Acts of the Apostles*, 275. Contra Hill, *Hellenists and Hebrews*, 31, who contends that Stephen dies as a direct result of unrest within the Greek-speaking Jewish community, not caused by the council.

359. The conjunction δέ functions adversatively (7:54), contrasting the council members, who are consumed with rage and described as opponents of the Holy Spirit, and Stephen, who

and leads to the final irony of this ugly scene. Those who hear Stephen unite together against him, screaming with a single voice (φωνῆ μεγάλη) and rushing toward him (7:57). The term ὁμοθυμαδόν, which has described the unanimity of the believers, now describes the unanimity of those held together by their rage and opposition.[360] Luke concludes his depiction of this violent scene against an innocent believer by stating simply that Stephen dies after praying for his killers' forgiveness (7:60). Conversely, the council members fulfill Stephen's characterization of them (cf. 7:52) and their prior murderous wishes (cf. 5:33)[361] with the approval (συνευδοκῶν; 8:1a)[362] of one named Saul. The vivid pictures — of the innocent, "angelic" Stephen, who belongs to the community united by the Holy Spirit, and of the Jewish leaders united in uncontrollable rage and uncivilized mayhem against Stephen and God — close the narrative scene with an emotional climax and create a sense of anticipation about what will happen next to the church.[363]

The Characterization of the Church or Group of Believers in Acts 8:1b–3

The anticipation created in the readers by the emotion-charged scene describing the horrendous murder of Stephen leads to a brief narrative description focusing on what happens to the Jerusalem Christians. These verses conclude the first major narrative unit of the book of Acts. After the emotional tone in the depiction of the previous scene, this small section seems almost anticlimactic. However, the characterization of the Christian community after this tragic execution functions significantly in the narrative plot and sequential reading of Acts.

---

is "filled with the Holy Spirit." Cf. Johnson, *The Acts of the Apostles*, 139; and Krodel, *Acts*, 155.

360. Cf. Dunn, *The Acts of the Apostles*, 100; Haenchen, *The Acts of the Apostles*, 292; Johnson, *The Acts of the Apostles*, 140; and Schneider, *Die Apostelgeschichte*, 1:475–76. Contra Heidland, "ὁμοθυμαδόν," 5:185–86, who ignores the use of this term here.

361. The noun ἀναιρέσις (8:1a) is derived from the verb ἀναιρέω, which previously describes the murderous wishes of the council members (5:33). Cf. Williams, *Acts*, 145.

362. The imperfect periphrastic construction, ἦν συνευδοκῶν, suggests that Saul for some time has been in approval with all that happens in confronting and killing Stephen (8:1a). The prefix σύν again highlights that Saul joins with others in consenting to the violence against Stephen. See Johnson, *The Acts of the Apostles*, 141, who observes the use of the same term in 22:20. Cf. Haenchen, *The Acts of the Apostles*, 293; and Barrett, *The Acts of the Apostles*, 1:388.

363. Cf. Pervo, *Profit with Delight*, 66.

The narrative sequence in the first seven chapters has typically included either an event or a summary that positively depicts the Christian community after some threat. The narrative includes a positive depiction of the believers after each of the two threats by the Jewish leaders (cf. 4:21–23; 5:41–42) and after each of the two internal threats to the unity of the Christian community (cf. 5:12–16; 6:7). On the one hand, one expects the continuation of such a pattern, which would result in continued increases in the number of believers living in Jerusalem. On the other hand, the division and hostility created by the Jewish leaders have now escalated to a dangerous level: the murder of an innocent person. Thus, what one finds in this section is not a description of continued success but intense hostilities, linked chronologically in the narrative to what has happened in the prior scene.[364] The description of a "great persecution against the church in Jerusalem" (διωγμὸς μέγας ἐπὶ τὴν ἐκκλησίαν τὴν ἐν Ἱεροσολύμοις) encapsulates the action of this brief section.[365] The depiction of the church here is not active but passive, so that the narrative implicitly presents a picture of the Christian community through the opponents' actions. Once again, the reader discovers a number of narrative gaps: many details are absent in the description of these events.[366] Nonetheless, the narrative does state that because of this persecution (πάντες), presumably the entire community of believers with the exception of the apostles (πλὴν τῶν ἀποστόλων), are scattered (διεσπάρησαν) throughout the region of Judea and Samaria (8:1b).[367] That the apostles remain in Jerusalem while such intense opposition exists is apparently not an important issue in the narrator's attempt to create this picture of the scattered church.[368] These opposing actions against the church, after

---

364. The phrase ἐγένετο δὲ ἐν ἐκείνῃ τῇ ἡμέρᾳ (8:1b) functions as a narrative connection between the previous scene and the current literary section.

365. See Richard, *Acts 6:1–8:4*, 51, who refers to the connection in wording between the Jewish people's response to the church and their response to the prophets (cf. 7:52). Cf. Tannehill, *The Narrative Unity of Luke-Acts*, 2:97; and Marshall, *The Acts of the Apostles*, 151.

366. E.g., how were all the Christians except the apostles scattered? From where did the Christians mentioned later (Acts 15; 21) come? Cf. Conzelmann, *Acts of the Apostles*, 60–61.

367. See Hill, *Hellenists and Hebrews*, 32–40, for a discussion concerning the questions of who was persecuted, who did the persecuting, and who was scattered. Cf. Barrett, *The Acts of the Apostles*, 1:391; Bruce, *The Book of the Acts*, 162; Haenchen, *The Acts of the Apostles*, 293, 297; Krodel, *Acts*, 157–58; Lüdemann, *Early Christianity according to the Traditions in Acts*, 91–92; Schneider, *Die Apostelgeschichte*, 1:478–79; and Williams, *Acts*, 151.

368. See Schmithals, *Die Apostelgeschichte des Lukas*, 76, who stresses the importance of the apostles remaining in Jerusalem so as to imply no fracture between Christianity and Judaism. Cf. Bruce, *The Book of the Acts*, 162–63.

the horrifying scene of Stephen's murder, signify the broadening scope of that opposition and the continued division among the Jewish people caused by the leaders' rejection of the gospel message.[369]

The narrator substantiates the contrasting nature of this harsh opposition or persecution against the Christian community by specifically mentioning the actions of Saul, the one introduced briefly in the scene of Stephen's murder. Saul's actions, described as a continuing assault on the church (ἡ ἐκκλησία), present a negative image of outrage, abuse, and destructive behavior as he lashes out against the believers.[370] The apostles' earlier imprisonments become narrative precursors for this man described as searching diligently for Christians (κατὰ τοὺς οἴκους εἰσπορευόμενος), capturing those he found, and "dragging" them off to prison (8:3), with inhumane treatment of those captured.[371] Although the council's actions against the apostles and Stephen are completed events, Saul's actions persist, as the imperfect tense of the verbs ἐλυμαίνετο and παρεδίδου suggests. That these actions continue insinuates that the picture of the Christian community remains in stark contrast to the image implied by its opponents' action. The continuing response of the opponents not only functions as an indirect negative presentation of these characters but also implies that such actions are reactions against the Christian community, which reflects the same positive characteristics depicted thus far in the book of Acts. Nonetheless, readers will potentially perceive the outlook for the believers in the narrative as growing increasingly bleak, perhaps a low point for the church in the Acts narrative.[372]

In the middle of this description of persecution, which implicitly contrasts the Christian community with its hostile and divisive opponents, the narrator inserts a statement that offers a glimmer of hope in the

---

369. See Dunn, *The Acts of the Apostles*, 104–5, who sees hints of division within the church.

370. The verb λυμαίνομαι denotes harshness and injury (8:3). See Bruce, *The Book of the Acts*, 163n14, who mentions that this verb refers to the ravaging of a body by a wild animal. Cf. Barrett, *The Acts of the Apostle*, 1:392–93; Conzelmann, *Acts of the Apostles*, 61; Johnson, *The Acts of the Apostles*, 142; and Williams, *Acts*, 152.

371. The verb σύρω (8:3) describes the violent action of one party in capturing another or in removing the corpse of someone despised. Of its five occurrences in the NT, only in Acts does it refer to a human being as the object of such action (cf. 14:19; 17:6). See Josephus, *The Jewish War* 1.452; 2.491; and idem, *Jewish Antiquities* 20.136. Cf. Johnson, *The Acts of the Apostles*, 142; and Barrett, *The Acts of the Apostle*, 1:393.

372. See Tannehill, *The Narrative Unity of Luke-Acts*, 2:100. Cf. Schneider, *Die Apostelgeschichte*, 1:479.

depicted darkness. Luke tells about ἄνδρες εὐλαβεῖς who, like those on the day of Pentecost (8:2; cf. 2:5), respond to the events that occur in the midst of the believers. Apparently, these men are not believing Jews, since the Christians have left Jerusalem, except for the apostles.[373] In this case, these persons respond by burying Stephen and by lamenting greatly (κοπετὸν μέγαν; 8:2) for him.[374] The inclusion of this depicted response implies that some openness and sympathy toward the believers and the gospel message remains.[375] Even in the death of a witness to the gospel, the council cannot stop that message! While the division created by the hostilities of the Jewish leaders against the believers is immense and the outlook for them is dismal, the narrator subtly offers readers a ray of hope, which may conceive in them a new sense of anticipation concerning what may lie ahead for the church that has been scattered.[376]

An Assessment of the Characterization of the Church or Group of Believers in Acts 8:1b–3

The characterization of the Christian community in this concluding passage of the larger narrative unit of 1:1–8:3 is much different from what one finds in earlier narrative sections. The Lukan narrator typically describes the church in either summary statements or in narrative scenes though which readers may observe the believers' actions and make judgments concerning them. In this brief passage, however, Luke relies on both implicit and explicit contrasts between the characters of the previous narrative events to create an image of the church. Those obvious contrasts, along with the emotion and horror created by the described mob violence that led to Stephen's arrest, shape the perspective

---

373. Contra Dunn, *The Acts of the Apostles*, 106; Marshall, *The Acts of the Apostles*, 151–52; Schneider, *Die Apostelgeschichte*, 1:479; Williams, *Acts*, 151; and Witherington, *The Acts of the Apostles*, 277, who interpret "devout men" as a reference to Christians.

374. The verb συγκομίζω (8:2) has typical meanings of "carry together" or "collect" and uncommonly refers to burial. See LSJ, 1666.

375. See Bruce, *The Book of the Acts*, 162; Haenchen, *The Acts of the Apostles*, 293–94; Tannehill, *The Narrative Unity of Luke-Acts*, 2:101; and Schneider, *Die Apostelgeschichte*, 1:479, who observes that *m. Sanhedrin* 6.6 mentions that there was no public lamentation for anyone executed. As Tannehill states, if this applies to Stephen's death, this description of Stephen's burial implies both sympathy for Stephen and a protest against the council's hostile action. Cf. Schmithals, *Die Apostelgeschichte des Lukas*, 76–77, who stresses that this scene indicates a split between the Jewish leaders and the Jewish people rather than between the Jewish people and the believers.

376. Cf. Williams, *Acts*, 152.

by which readers may view the church.[377] Luke describes no action by the Christian community; rather, the believers are indirectly presented by the negative, contrasting action of their Jewish opponents.[378] Thus, the narrator implicitly describes the Christian community in ways that correspond with earlier images and in contrast with the Jewish leaders: divine presence rather than opposition toward God, bold proclamation rather than attempts to silence it, and conduct that fulfills the ideals of community rather than divisive and destructive behavior.[379] The violent opposition also identifies the Christian community with the prophets and spokespersons of God who were rejected throughout the history of Israel.[380] The rejection image in the overall depiction of the Christian community functions not only as an implicit validation of its roles of witness and proclaimer, but also as an indication that the blessing of God is found ironically in the persecuted, scattered church.

THE CHARACTERIZATION OF THE CHURCH OR GROUP OF BELIEVERS IN JERUSALEM (ACTS 1:1–8:3)

The beginning unit of the book of Acts, encompassing a little over seven chapters, describes the initial stages of selected events after Jesus' ascension. The narrator clearly directs the reader's attention to the activity of God on behalf of God's people, as God fulfills God's promise to Israel. The Christian community appears collectively as a central character in the narrative plot of these chapters, as that community (or a smaller group from within that community) has a dominant role in most of the narrative scenes. The characterization of the Christian church, as discovered in the snapshots that this study has examined thus far, presents a developing picture of a group whose attitudes, atmosphere, and activities all indicate that God has fulfilled that promise, in this group itself. In concluding the study of this characterization in 1:1–8:3, we should briefly assess the literary means by which this portrait is presented, the basic components of that portrait, and the function of that portrait in that narrative unit.

---

377. Cf. Lohfink, *Die Sammlung Israels*, 47–62, who rightly sees a dramatic shift toward negative images of the Jewish people here.

378. Cf. Tyson, *Images of Judaism in Luke-Acts*, 116.

379. See Lohfink, *Die Sammlung Israels*, 58, who sees the image as the divorce between faithful Israel and unrepentant Israel.

380. Cf. Johnson, *The Acts of the Apostles*, 143.

As we assess the characterization of the church or group of believers in Jerusalem, we find that the Lukan narrator uses a variety of literary conventions typically associated with Greco-Roman historiography. The predominant perspective of the narrative is that of the third-person narrator. The appearance of summary statements or descriptions in key junction points within the Acts narrative (e.g., 2:42–47; 4:32–37; 5:12–16) is evidence for that narrator's use of explicit characterization in relation to the Christian community. In these summaries, the narrator typically describes actions in generalities, accentuating specific aspects of that group's attitudes and actions that contribute significantly to the plot, such as the unanimity of the believers, their camaraderie, and their devotion. Other evidence for the use of explicit characterization is the narrator's direct statements or descriptions that show or provide insight *into* the character (e.g., "filled with the Spirit"; 2:4; 4:31). The explicit characterization of the believers, therefore, influences how the reader may judge much of the believers' actions, which the narrator frequently describes with imagery reminiscent of other positive descriptions. These various depictions, both direct and indirect, also significantly utilize imagery of or make extratextual connections with social conventions and ideals with which a Greco-Roman audience would identify and affirm (e.g., friendship; cf. 2:42, 44–45; 4:32). Such imagery helps readers to make conclusions about the various characters of the narrative. These intratextual and extratextual traits of the Acts narrative, therefore, reflect the use of literary conventions common to the characterization found in Greco-Roman historiography.

That the first part of the Acts narrative provides evidence of the use of such literary conventions is an important consideration, because characterization functions significantly within the narrative plot. The narrator has selected the included events and summaries in this first major unit, as well as the specific images and allusions in the characterization of the Christian community, to contribute to an unfolding narrative plot. This chapter has identified several positive aspects of the characterization of the church or Christian community that the Lukan narrator has highlighted and placed before the reader:

1. the unanimity of the believers;

2. the coming of the Holy Spirit as the fulfillment of God's promise to Israel and the continuing blessing of God within that group;

3. the communal dynamics of sharing and friendship for one another;

4. the continuity of the Christian community with Judaism;

5. the seemingly unstoppable proclamation of the gospel message (the message that God has fulfilled God's promise through Jesus);

6. the great success of that message among the Jewish people; and

7. the scattering of the church due to hostile opposition.

The unfolding of the narrative plot of Acts includes the relationship of selected narrative components, such as this positive characterization of the believers, and the arrangement of the components that guide readers through the text. Such elements of the book of Acts reflect similarly what one finds in examples of Greco-Roman historiography that focus on the history of an institution.[381]

These literary aspects of ancient historiography are of vital importance for understanding not only how the narrator presents the first Christians in Jerusalem, but also how this characterization functions in reading the Acts narrative. The positive depiction of the Christian community does not stand alone within the book of Acts; it contributes with other characters in acting out the narrative plot. Thus, one must also assess how that specific portrayal functions within the narrative sequence of the unfolding plot. This chapter has observed that, alongside this picture of the Christian church, the narrative sequence also includes an increasingly contrasting portrait of the Jews, in which the narrator described the following:

1. the initial positive acceptance by the λαός, the Jewish people;

2. the initial division between the Jewish people and the Jewish leaders who reject the gospel message;

3. the increasing division as the Jewish leaders become more hostile because of their jealousy of the positive response of the people to the gospel;

4. the beginning of opposition from the Jewish leaders *and* the λαός; and

5. the ever-widening division created by the harsh and murderous actions of some of the Jewish people.

---

381. Cf. Hubert Cancik, "The History of Culture, Religion, and Institutions in Ancient Historiography: Philological Observations concerning Luke's History," *JBL* 116 (Winter 1997): 673–95.

These two contrasting images dominate the action of this first major unit of the Acts narrative and provide a picture that vividly portrays the Christian community and its antithesis.[382] What we may offer as a general observation of these two contrasting images is that the Lukan narrative presents a developing story in which the growth of the church or Christian community in Jerusalem is accompanied by a corresponding growth of hostility.[383]

The narrative clues and imagery call for a bit more explication. On the one hand, the Christian community is depicted as united, as acting in ways that develop communal bonds and relations, as the group in which God's blessing is found (cf., e.g., 2:1–4, 42–47; 4:32–5:16), and as initially having wholesome relations with the Jewish people (cf. 2:47; 4:21; 5:26). On the other hand, there are two narrative depictions of the Jews. One picture is of the Jewish people, who initially respond favorably to the believers but who, in chapter 6, respond to Stephen in deceptive, underhanded schemes that include destructive communal conduct (6:9–15). The other picture is of the Jewish leaders, as they reject the gospel message and its emphasis on what God has done.[384] They reflect several traits that lead to the destruction of communal or social bonds: jealousy, rage, murderous desires, and murderous action. The disparity of these portraits occurs on two distinct yet interrelated levels: the social level, dealing with communal relations and social behavior; and the religious level, dealing with issues of God's blessing and presence. The division, both socially and religiously, is created by the Jewish leaders who themselves divide the Jewish people by rejecting God and God's promise; oneness and unity, both socially and religiously, are created by the *acceptance* of God and God's promise.[385]

The disappearance in the narrative of what one has aptly called the "Jerusalem springtime"[386] occurs not because of the inadequacies of God or of the Christian community, but because the unbelieving Jews reject God and divide the Jewish people. Although Israel identifies itself as the people of God, the beginning unit of the Acts narrative depicts

---

382. Cf. Dionysius, *On the Style of Demosthenes* 21.
383. Cf. Gaventa, "Toward a Theology of Acts," 154; and Marguerat, "La mort d'Ananias et Saphira," 215.
384. Cf. Jervell, *Luke and the People of God*, 44.
385. Cf. Jervell, *The Theology of the Acts of the Apostles*, 34–43. See Cancik, "The History of Culture, Religion, and Institutions in Ancient Historiography," 673–95.
386. Lohfink, *Die Sammlung Israels*, 55.

some Jewish people who violently oppose God and demonstrably contradict that claim. The depiction of the Jerusalem church, in contrast, includes those of the Jewish people who believe the gospel message and demonstrably confirm God's blessing upon them through their communal unanimity and unceasing proclamation. The Lukan narrative presentation of two contrasting images of division and unanimity in 1:1–8:3, therefore, creates two differing paradigms for those who claim to be God's people. These contrasts function rhetorically to assist the reader in identifying potentially the church or Christian community rather than its opponents (the Jewish leaders and finally the Jewish people) as a people that belongs to God, ἡ ἐκκλησία. With such an affirmative portrayal of the church, the narrative effects of the onslaught of persecution and scattering (8:1b–3) will create a sense of anticipation in readers, who may expect something much different at this point in the story. However, readers may only recognize such portraits, their function, and their accompanying effects when they keep the church in its rightful place as a prominent character in these chapters of the book of Acts.

THREE

THE CHURCHES IN JERUSALEM AND BEYOND AS NARRATIVE CHARACTERS (ACTS 8:4–12:25)

The beginning unit of the Acts narrative describes the church or Christian community within the city of Jerusalem, the center of Judaism. Paul Zingg suggests that Jerusalem provides the connection between the church and Israel, so that these early Christians are depicted as those who are faithful to Jewish practices and represents those in whom God's promises are being fulfilled.[1] In Acts 1:1–8:3, all the narrative action occurs in or around Jerusalem; all characters are Jewish, including those who comprise the church. Thus, the Acts narrative depicts the Christian community in continuity with Judaism. The narrator presents an ideal portrait of these Jewish believers as embodying the promises that God has given to Israel, a portrait contrasting with the portraits of the Jewish leaders and some of the Jewish people. The concluding image of the scattered believers throughout Judea and Samaria (8:1b), however, presents a shift in the narrative's geographical focus. The narrative depiction of believers no longer confines them to Jerusalem.[2] Now the narrative in increasing fashion begins to describe the believers' activities within broader geographical and ethnic settings.[3] Therefore, in this literary unit the nar-

---

1. Paul Zingg, *Das Wachsen der Kirche: Beiträge zur Frage der lukanischen Redaktion und Theologie,* OBO (Göttingen: Vandenhoeck & Ruprecht, 1974), 143–44.
2. Cf. Jack T. Sanders, *The Jews in Luke-Acts* (Philadelphia: Fortress, 1987), 251.
3. See Joseph B. Tyson, *Images of Judaism in Luke-Acts* (Columbia: University of South Carolina Press, 1992), 117.

rator depicts the church in selected locations, both within and outside Jerusalem, as the believers begin to proclaim the gospel message in other locales.

THE JEWISH BELIEVERS
OUTSIDE OF JERUSALEM (ACTS 8:4)

The Literary Context

The prior scene of persecution against the Jewish believers, which concludes the larger narrative unit of Acts 1:1–8:3, arises out of the larger narrative context of Stephen's trial and execution by a mob of enraged Jews. Both Stephen's murder and the believers' persecution present a contemptible picture of Jewish persons who react in seething violence against those from their own people — reactions that the reader will conclude to be unwarranted and in opposition against God. The image of the resultant scattering of the entire church (8:1b) tells the reader about the severity of the negative response toward the believers, as potential imprisonment and death threatens them all.

The Characterization of the Church or Group of Believers in Acts 8:4

The narrative unit of Acts 8:4–12:25 begins with a brief statement about the believers. This statement, found in 8:4, joins grammatically the new narrative scene with the previous sections about Stephen and the persecution of the church, as the conjunction μὲν οὖν indicates.[4] An additional textual connection between this statement and the previous section is identifiable in the specific reference to the Jewish believers as οἱ διασπαρέντες (the scattered ones), which is derived from the same term that previously described the scattering of the believers (πάντες δὲ διεσπάρησαν; 8:1b).[5] Thus, the narrator makes a direct connection between those whom he describes in 8:4 and those who receive the hateful persecution. The reader is thereby invited to see the narrative's continuity, although the geographical location has shifted.

---

4. Cf. Ernst Haenchen, *The Acts of the Apostles: A Commentary*, trans. Bernard Noble and Gerald Shinn (Philadelphia: Westminster, 1971), 301.

5. Cf. Gerd Lüdemann, *Early Christianity according to the Traditions in Acts: A Commentary*, trans. John Bowden (Philadelphia: Fortress, 1989), 94; Walter Schmithals, *Die Apostelgeschichte des Lukas*, ZB (Zurich: Theologischer Verlag, 1982), 77; and David John Williams, *Acts*, NIBC 5 (Peabody, MA: Hendrickson, 1990), 153.

The characterization of the believers in this passage centers on only one activity. According to the Lukan narrator, the scattered believers pass throughout the aforementioned areas (i.e., Judea and Samaria; Acts 8:1b) because of the hostile activity in Jerusalem, but they are also "proclaiming the word" (εὐαγγελιζόμενοι τὸν λόγον). In this specific description of what happens to the believers because of the persecution in Jerusalem, Luke implicitly suggests that the believers continue in the same, unstoppable practices that have characterized them earlier. Just as the apostles never stopped proclaiming (οὐκ ἐπαύοντο ... εὐαγγελιζόμενοι; 5:42)[6] that Jesus is the Christ when the Jewish council abused them, so also these believers exude the same qualities.[7] Although the prior scene describes what readers may perceive as the church at its lowest point, this brief statement affirms that neither murder nor persecution can stop these believers in their gospel proclamation.[8] The mention of that proclamation, which the narrative presents earlier as indicative of God's blessing and presence, suggests that the reader should also perceive similar indications of divine activity among them here. This subtle connection between the scattered believers and the earlier descriptions of the Jerusalem believers also will potentially create in readers the anticipation that the growth and success mentioned before may occur again in those new settings. The narrative account of Philip's ministry subsequently fulfills that anticipation (cf. 8:10–12);[9] Philip functions as a

---

6. The verb εὐαγγελίζομαι has only one prior occurrence in Acts (5:42) and refers to the apostles' activities following their arrest, interrogation, and beating by the Jewish council. The use here suggests an allusion to the earlier image. See Haenchen, *The Acts of the Apostles*, 301, who suggests that the term may be substituted for the verb λαλέω, which Luke also uses in reference to the gospel proclamation (cf., e.g., 4:29). See also Hans Conzelmann, *The Theology of St. Luke*, trans. Geoffrey Buswell (Philadelphia: Fortress, 1961), 221–22; Williams, *Acts*, 153–54; and Gerhard Friedrich, "εὐαγγελίζομαι ...," in *TDNT*, 2:707–37. Cf. Gerhard Krodel, *Acts*, ACNT (Minneapolis: Augsburg, 1986), 160–61, who observes that this same verb characterizes the activity of the scattered Christians (8:4), of Philip (8:12), and of the apostles (8:25).

7. Luke frequently uses the term ὁ λόγος in Acts 1:1–8:3 to describe the gospel message that the believers proclaim (cf. 2:22, 40, 41; 4:4, 29, 31; 6:2, 4, 7).

8. See I. Howard Marshall, *The Acts of the Apostles*, TNTC (Leicester: InterVarsity, 1980), 154, who states that Luke does not attribute this activity to the Holy Spirit. However, Luke *does* attribute such activity to the Spirit in earlier parts. Cf. Robert L. Brawley, *Centering on God: Method and Message in Luke-Act*, LCBI (Louisville: Westminster/John Knox, 1990), 95.

9. The narrator positively describes Philip's audience as "united together" (ὁμοθυμαδόν; 8:6) in their attention to that message, the same term used previously in the positive portrayal of the believers (cf. 1:14; 2:46; 4:24; 5:12). Cf. Haenchen, *The Acts of the Apostles*, 302; and

specific example of the believers' activity described generally in Acts
8:4.[10]

An Assessment of the Characterization of the Church or Group of Believers in Acts 8:4

The brief statement about the believers' activity after the Jewish perse-
cutors have run the believers out of town does not contribute to the
characterization of the Christian community by offering new images to
the developing portrait in Acts. Rather, this statement links the activities of the scattered believers to previous images and concepts related to
the believers in Jerusalem. Without the portrait of that church clearly in
the mind of the reader, this concise assertion has little effect. However,
the identification of the believers' activity here with the characteristics
of the Jerusalem believers suggests that nothing has changed. Therefore,
the description of scattered believers in this single assertion relies on the
paradigmatic nature of the portrait of the Christian community found in
Acts 1:1–8:3, ironically affirming that the *scattering* of those believers
could not destroy their *togetherness* of purpose and divine presence.[11]

THE EARLY BELIEVERS IN DAMASCUS (ACTS 9:19B–25)

The Literary Context (Acts 8:5–9:19a)

After the concise statement describing the continuation of the positive
characteristics of the believers despite the radical change in setting and
atmosphere, the Acts narrative focuses the reader's attention on events
surrounding two specific individuals: the Christian Philip and the persecutor Saul. In many ways Philip functions in the narrative as an example

---

Luke T. Johnson, *The Acts of the Apostles*, SP 5 (Collegeville, MN: Liturgical Press, 1992),
145–46.

10. The description of Philip "proclaiming the good news" (τῷ Φιλίππῳ εὐαγγελιζομένῳ;
Acts 8:12; cf. 8:35, 40), like other believers scattered from Jerusalem (cf. 8:4), suggests that he
functions as a specific example of the believers. Other descriptions of Philip's actions, such as τὰ
σημεῖα (8:6; cf. 8:7) and τε σημεῖα καὶ δυνάμεις μεγάλας (8:13), reflect similar imagery used to
describe the apostles and Stephen (cf. 5:12; 6:8). Cf. Krodel, *Acts*, 159; William S. Kurz, *Reading Luke-Acts: Dynamics of Biblical Narrative* (Louisville: Westminster/John Knox, 1993), 84;
Gerhard Schneider, *Die Apostelgeschichte*, 2 vols., HTKNT 5 (Freiburg: Herder, 1980–82),
1:487; William H. Shepherd Jr., *The Narrative Function of the Holy Spirit as a Character in
Luke-Acts*, SBLDS 147 (Atlanta: Scholars Press, 1994), 179–80; and Robert C. Tannehill, *The
Narrative Unity of Luke-Acts: A Literary Interpretation*, 2 vols. (Philadelphia/Minneapolis:
Fortress, 1986–90), 2:103–5.

11. Cf. Krodel, *Acts*, 159; and Tannehill, *The Narrative Unity of Luke-Acts*, 2:103.

of the believers' activity following the hostilities against them by the Jewish leaders and, in particular, Saul. Luke describes Philip as doing τὰ σημεῖα (Acts 8:6) and as actively proclaiming the good news, just as the apostles have done in earlier narrative scenes. The major difference in this initial scene is that Philip's ministry takes place in Samaria rather than Jerusalem. Nonetheless, the narrated results of Philip's ministry compare favorably to earlier positive descriptions of acceptance in Jerusalem, as Luke describes persons who believe, are baptized (8:12), accept "the word of God" (8:14), and receive the Holy Spirit (8:17).[12] The subsequent scene involving Philip reinforces the positive image already present in the narrative, as Luke directly describes Philip continuing to proclaim the gospel message under divine guidance.[13] These two narrative scenes, therefore, present Philip as a character consistent with the positive depiction of the activities and traits observed in the Jewish Christians of Jerusalem, as he proclaims the gospel message to those outside the exclusive circle of Jewish ethnicity and identity.[14]

The second individual on whom the narrative focuses is Saul, the one introduced earlier as maliciously pursuing the Christian believers (cf. Acts 8:3). At the beginning of chapter 9, the narrator vividly presents Saul as "still breathing threats and murder against the Lord's disciples" (9:1), an image consistent with earlier pictures of Saul and the Jewish leaders in Jerusalem.[15] The narrative also grammatically con-

---

12. All three descriptions of what the Samaritans experience are similar to what the Jewish people of Jerusalem have experienced: (1) the same verb most frequently used to characterize the Christians, πιστεύω, describes the Samaritans' response to Philip (8:12); (2) the baptism of these believers compares with Peter's call for baptism and the response by 3,000 persons at Pentecost (cf. 2:38, 41); (3) the acceptance of "the word of God" (τὸν λόγον τοῦ θεοῦ) is similar to the response in Jerusalem (cf., e.g., 6:7). Cf. Conzelmann, *Acts of the Apostles*, 65; Johnson, *The Acts of the Apostles*, 148; and Marshall, *The Acts of the Apostles*, 154–56.

13. Luke explicitly describes God as directing Philip's ministry by (1) inserting statements from "an angel of the Lord" (ἄγγελος κυρίου; 8:26) and "the Spirit" (τὸ πνεῦμα; 8:29) that instruct Philip, and (2) mentioning Philip's disappearance as activity of "the Spirit of the Lord" (πνεῦμα κυρίου; 8:39). Cf., e.g., Haenchen, *The Acts of the Apostles*, 310; Johnson, *The Acts of the Apostles*, 154–55, 160; and Marshall, *The Acts of the Apostles*, 161.

14. Cf., e.g., Brawley, *Centering on God*, 55; Haenchen, *The Acts of the Apostles*, 306–7; Johnson, *The Acts of the Apostles*, 150–51; and Tyson, *Images of Judaism in Luke-Acts*, 116.

15. The verb ἐμπνέω reveals one's inner character with connotations of pouring out one's inner self toward another. See LSJ, 546; and Eduard Schweizer, "πνέω, ἐμπνέω," in *TDNT*, 6:452. The two terms describing what Saul breathes out contribute to the negative portrait of Saul: (1) ἀπειλῆς (threats) is derived from the same root as the terms that described the Jewish council's earlier threats (cf. 4:17, 29); (2) φόνου (murder) alludes to what has been done to Stephen. See Johnson, *The Acts of the Apostles*, 162, who sees ἔτι forming a connection with

nects (δέ; 9:1) this narrative scene to the previous stories about Philip, making even more explicit for readers the ironic picture of the continuing persecution of the Christians, resulting in the spread of the gospel message to other areas.[16] The narrator explicitly states the purpose of Saul's trip to the synagogues of Damascus: to arrest any believers, "those who belonged to the Way" (9:2),[17] and to bring them to Jerusalem.[18] The dramatic scene of Saul's confrontation by the resurrected Jesus and the following scenes involving the disciple Ananias function as a surprising narrative reversal.[19] The one who opposed and persecuted the Christians is now *himself* ironically characterized as an identifiable part of the Christians through Ananias's stated purpose in coming to Saul: that Saul might be "filled with the Holy Spirit" (9:17).[20] Saul's baptism subtly suggests that the filling with the Holy Spirit indeed takes place, as Peter's response to the people on the day of Pentecost has stated (cf. 2:38).[21] Thus, the narrator dramatically and

---

Saul's earlier actions (8:1–3). Cf. Beverly Roberts Gaventa, *From Darkness to Light: Aspects of Conversion in the New Testament*, OBT 20 (Philadelphia: Fortress, 1986), 55.

16. Cf. Conzelmann, *Acts of the Apostles*, 71; and Kurz, *Reading Luke-Acts*, 86.

17. See Haenchen, *The Acts of the Apostles*, 319n2, who points out the variety of designations for the Christians in this chapter: μαθηταί (9:1, 19, 25, 38), τῆς ὁδοῦ ὄντας (9:2), μαθητής (9:10), ἅγιοι (9:13, 32, 41), ἐπικαλούμενοι τὸ ὄνομα κυρίου (9:14), ἀδελφός (9:17), ἀδελφοί (9:30), and μαθήτρια (9:36).

18. The narrator assumes that believers are in Damascus but does not provide further details (cf. Johnson, *The Acts of the Apostles*, 162). Apparently, they are part of the synagogues there. However, a major historical difficulty is that the high priest in Jerusalem probably has no authority over the Damascus synagogues; see F. F. Bruce, *The Book of the Acts*, rev. ed., NICNT (Grand Rapids: Eerdmans, 1988), 180–81; Haenchen, *The Acts of the Apostles*, 320–21; Johnson, *The Acts of the Apostles*, 162; Krodel, *Acts*, 174–75; Marshall, *The Acts of the Apostles*, 167–69; and Williams, *Acts*, 167–68.

19. For studies on the account of Saul's conversion or call, see, e.g., Gaventa, *From Darkness to Light*, 52–95; Charles W. Hedrick, "Paul's Conversion/Call: A Comparative Analysis of the Three Reports in Acts," *JBL* 100 (September 1981): 415–32; Rudolf Pesch, *Die Apostelgeschichte*, 2 vols., EKKNT 5 (Zurich: Neukirchener Verlag, 1986), 1:296–316; and Schneider, *Die Apostelgeschichte*, 2:18–45.

20. The narrative seems to contrast the description of the confrontation event and the narrative character of Ananias: (1) Ananias questions the divine instructions (cf. 9:10–11) and states that he has heard "how much evil [Saul] has done to your saints in Jerusalem" (9:13). Such reluctance is understandable, but also can be overcome by a divine command (cf. Johnson, *The Acts of the Apostles*, 164). Ananias not only goes obediently to Saul but also states that he is sent so that Saul might be "filled with the Holy Spirit" (πλησθῆς πνεύματος ἁγίου; 9:17), the description used for the Jerusalem believers (cf. 2:4; 4:8, 31). Cf. Krodel, *Acts*, 177; Marshall, *The Acts of the Apostles*, 172; and Shepherd, *The Narrative Function of the Holy Spirit*, 191–92.

21. Ananias's stated purpose for his visit — that Saul be "filled with the Holy Spirit" — is anticipated by the mention of Saul's praying in the Lord's message to Ananias (9:11), since

implicitly presents the persecutor as one joining the ranks of the persecuted (9:18; cf. 9:16) and being called by God to proclaim the gospel
message.[22]

The Characterization of the Church or Group of Believers in Acts 9:19b–25

The narrated conversion or call of Saul depicts a radical transformation
of that character. The narrator now characterizes the one who has despised the Jewish believers as a believer himself. The one who seemingly
was filled with rage is now filled with the Holy Spirit. After the initial meeting with Ananias, Luke briefly describes what happens to Saul
in Damascus. Two references to the believers of Damascus, however,
frame the narrated activity of Saul and their response to him, and these
references provide a narrative context for the description of this activity
and response.

The first picture of the disciples in Damascus (τῶν ἐν Δαμασκῷ
μαθητῶν) includes Saul's presence among them (Acts 9:19b). Luke provides no details concerning what happens; he only states that they are
together for several days (ἡμέρας τινάς). Considering the probability that
these believers fear Saul, which Luke has already indicated in Ananias's
objections to the Lord (cf. 9:13–14),[23] this seemingly insignificant detail
implies the acceptance of Saul by the Christian community.[24] Moreover,
the conjunction καί grammatically links this glimpse of the group of
disciples in Damascus to the activity described next: immediately Saul
begins to preach (ἐκήρυσσεν) about Jesus in the synagogues (9:20).[25]
The scarcity of details requires readers to contribute to the narrative
experience by making their own conclusions about the depicted scene.
Up to this point the proclamation of the gospel message has always
arisen out of the group of believers who demonstrably reflects two re-

---

Luke typically associates prayer with the coming of the Holy Spirit (see Acts 4). Cf. Brawley,
Centering on God, 153; Johnson, *The Acts of the Apostles*, 164; and Williams, *Acts*, 172.

22. Cf. Brawley, *Centering on God*, 151–52; and Johnson, *The Acts of the Apostles*,
165–66.

23. Since Luke describes Ananias as "a disciple in Damascus" (τις μαθητὴς ἐν Δαμασκῷ;
9:10), Ananias's objections may indicate similar responses of other disciples in Damascus.

24. See Brawley, *Centering on God*, 153, who suggests that Saul in taking food (9:19)
"signals his integration" into the church.

25. See Johnson, *The Acts of the Apostles*, 170; and Schneider, *Die Apostelgeschichte*,
2:35, who state that the verb's imperfect tense indicates that Paul's preaching is a repeated
practice.

lated characteristics: a sense of unanimity and community among them, and the evidence of divine blessing and presence. Saul's proclamation and the resultant effects (cf. 9:21–22) not only implicitly confirm that Saul has indeed been filled with the Holy Spirit; they also imply that the disciples have accepted him as part of their κοινωνία, thus providing him with communal support for that task.[26] Just as the apostles' proclamation arose from the communal context of unanimity and caring for one another's needs (cf. 2:42–47; 4:32–35; 6:7), so also the implicit picture here is of the church as the context from which Saul proclaims that Jesus is the Son of God (9:20).[27]

The narrator also describes the results of Saul's proclamation in Damascus — results that contrast with a final picture of the church there. The believers are not the only ones surprised by the puzzling turn of events; the astonished reply that Luke ascribes to "all who heard" (πάντες οἱ ἀκούοντες; 9:21) articulates what the readers probably think.[28] Nonetheless, the twofold description of Saul seems to reflect the ambiguity in the Jewish response to the Christian message in the latter stages of the narrative centering in Jerusalem.[29] On the one hand, the narrator describes Saul as becoming "more powerful" (μᾶλλον ἐνεδυναμοῦτο; 9:22),[30] which alludes to the same quality found in earlier glimpses of the believers and implies some degree of acceptance among those who hear what he has to say (cf. 4:7, 33; 6:8; 8:13). On the other hand, Luke also describes Saul as confounding "the Jews who lived in Damascus" (συνέχυννεν [τοὺς] Ἰουδαίους τοὺς κατοικοῦντας ἐν Δαμασκῷ; 9:22),[31] the Jewish people's same reaction to the initial hearing of the gospel

---

26. Cf. Brawley, *Centering on God*, 95.

27. See Philip Francis Esler, *Community and Gospel in Luke-Acts: The Social and Political Motivations of Lucan Theology*, SNTSMS 57 (Cambridge, UK: Cambridge University Press, 1987), 57, who sees this as a sign of separation from the synagogue.

28. See Schmithals, *Die Apostelgeschichte des Lukas*, 95, who observes that only here and in Gal 1 does one find Paul described in this way.

29. See Krodel, *Acts*, 178; Schmithals, *Die Apostelgeschichte des Lukas*, 95; and Tyson, *Images of Judaism in Luke-Acts*, 118, who recognize that Luke portrays this first event in Paul's ministry as to the Jews.

30. Cf. Johnson, *The Acts of the Apostles*, 171; and Schneider, *Die Apostelgeschichte*, 2:36.

31. This is the first reference in Luke-Acts to οἱ Ἰουδαῖοι, a general description of opponents to Jesus or his followers. See Zingg, *Das Wachsen der Kirche*, 203, who states that this designation refers to Diaspora Jews. Cf. Tyson, *Images of Judaism in Luke-Acts*, 119, who observes that earlier descriptions of opponents have always been individuals or *specific* groups of Jews.

message during Pentecost (cf. 2:6).[32] The narrated means that evoked both responses — one of implicit acceptance and joining together with the believers, and other of being joined together in confusion — was Saul's "proving" (συμβιβάζων) that Jesus is the Christ (9:22).[33] The narrator imaginatively assists the reader in creating an image in which Saul's argument, which "brings together" evidence to convince Jews in Damascus about Jesus, implicitly "brings together" people either in acceptance or in confusion.

The mixed response to Saul's ministry, which is of an unspecified duration (ὡς δὲ ἐπληροῦντο ἡμέραι ἱκαναί; Acts 9:23), includes οἱ Ἰουδαῖοι who ironically join together (συνεβουλεύσαντο) in a plan to kill Saul.[34] The narrative irony is twofold. On the one hand, the message that arises from the united community and brings together evidence about Jesus also brings together opponents from the Jews who act divisively. On the other hand, the former persecutor of the Jewish believers is now the believer whom the Jews target with their murderous plans — a negative response that alludes to earlier responses of jealousy and hatred by the Jewish leaders in Jerusalem.[35] Now the opposition is "the Jews" and not only the Jewish leaders, fulfilling the insinuations in chapter 6, when *some* of the Jewish people deceptively accuse Stephen of false charges. In the midst of such hostile opposition, Luke returns the reader's attention to the Christian community. With Saul's life in danger, οἱ μαθηταὶ αὐτοῦ[36] respond to ensure his safety and smuggle him out of the city. The Jews have reacted negatively to the gospel message — a reaction that is

---

32. See Tyson, *Images of Judaism in Luke-Acts*, 119, who stresses that the verb συγχέω means "to confuse" and connotes conflict.

33. The verb συμβιβάζω connotes bringing or uniting together. See Gerhard Delling, "συμβιβάζω," in *TDNT*, 7:763–66; BDAG, 956–57; LSJ, 1675.

34. The verb συμβουλεύω connotes planning *together*. The narrator's use of a compound verb with the prefix σύν ironically describes the unified action of division against the believers.

35. The verb ἀναιρέω (to murder; 9:23–24) corresponds with other forms of this verb in describing the reactions of the Jewish council (5:33, 36) and the Jewish people to the prophets and Jesus (cf. 2:23; 7:21, 28). Cf. Sanders, *The Jews in Luke-Acts*, 254; and Tyson, *Images of Judaism in Luke-Acts*, 118. See Charles H. Talbert, *Reading Acts: A Literary and Theological Commentary on the Acts of the Apostles*, Reading the New Testament (New York: Crossroad, 1997), 102, who sees these plans as the counterpoint to Paul's earlier plans against the believers.

36. The possessive pronoun αὐτοῦ modifying οἱ μαθηταί is an unusual construction in Acts since only here are disciples seemingly affiliated with a specific teacher. This may refer to the results of Paul's preaching (9:20). See Bruce M. Metzger, *A Textual Commentary on the Greek New Testament* (New York: United Bible Societies, 1971), 366; and Haenchen, *The Acts of the Apostles*, 332. Cf. C. K. Barrett, *A Critical and Exegetical Commentary on the Acts of the Apostles*, 2 vols., ICC (Edinburgh: T&T Clark, 1994–98), 466–67; Bruce, *The Book of the*

consistent with the characterization of the Jewish leaders and some of the Jewish people to this point in Acts.[37] However, in the midst of this negative scene of opposition and murderous plans, Luke also presents the contrasting picture of the believers, as he describes these disciples in ways that will remind readers of the positive, cumulative description of the church in earlier parts of the Acts narrative. Implicitly, the Lukan narrator describes the disciples as receiving the message of salvation from Saul, and they reciprocate by saving his life and providing for his needs (cf. 2:45; 4:34).

An Assessment of the Characterization of the Church or Group of Believers in Acts 9:19b–25

The characterization of the Christian community in Acts 9:19b–25 relies largely on intratextual allusions to earlier images of the church. The narrative seems to encourage the reader to make judgments about the Damascus believers based on their narrated actions as inserted at this particular point in the narrative sequence. For these who are called disciples, the narrator provides no direct statements or judgments but only brief accounts of their actions, which function as indirect presentations of that group. Such brief, implicit descriptions of the believers in Damascus who have not appeared beforehand in the narrative are somewhat surprising. However, those indirect intratextual connections with previous pictures of the Jerusalem Christians suggest that the believers in both places shared the same positive characteristics. Thus, readers are left to identify several similarities between the believers in Jerusalem and in Damascus: both groups are probably Jewish, both demonstrate a sense of unanimity and community as indicative of their belief in the gospel message, and both provide the context from which the proclamation of that message is accomplished. With these observed similarities, the reader may associate other positive characteristics of the Jerusalem believers with their Damascus counterparts: the presence and blessing of God within the church, and the unstoppable declaration of God's fulfilled promise through Jesus.

Acts, 192; Conzelmann, *Acts of the Apostles*, 74; Johnson, *The Acts of the Apostles*, 172; and Schneider, *Die Apostelgeschichte*, 2:37.

37. In 2 Cor 11:32–33, Paul gives a different account of what takes place. For discussions of this problem, see, e.g., Bruce, *The Book of the Acts*, 191–92; Haenchen, *The Acts of the Apostles*, 333–36; Krodel, *Acts*, 179–80; and Pesch, *Die Apostelgeschichte*, 1:311–15.

The Jerusalem Church Meets
the Believing Saul (Acts 9:26–30)

The Literary Context

In the literary context leading up to the scene of Acts 9:26–30, Luke describes Saul's dramatic transformation, from one who persecutes the believers to a believer himself, whose life is endangered by the Jews' hostile opposition. The reversal in Saul's narrative role results in him being smuggled out of Damascus by those who have become disciples because of his proclamation of the gospel—protective action necessitated by the murderous plot against him. Thus, Luke returns the narrative action to Jerusalem, as he depicts Saul's return from Damascus to Jerusalem in a different manner from what anyone would imagine (cf. 9:1–2).[38]

The Characterization of the Church or Group of Believers in Acts 9:26–30

The narrative scene in Jerusalem has many of the same characteristics as the previous scene in Damascus.[39] Descriptions of the believers frame this narrative scene as they respond to the former persecutor. However, the first statement functions somewhat ambiguously: it explicitly describes the Jerusalem believers' less-than-enthusiastic reception of Saul. Luke states that Saul "tried to join the disciples" (ἐπείραζεν κολλᾶσθαι τοῖς μαθηταῖς), but the believers are fearful of him (πάντες ἐφοβοῦντο αὐτόν 9:26) because they doubt his motives (μὴ πιστεύοντες ὅτι ἐστὶν μαθητής).[40] The narrative provides no details about the identity of these disciples, which leaves questions about them unanswered in the reader's mind since, when the narrative action left Jerusalem, all believers but the apostles scattered to Judea and Samaria (8:1b).[41] Nonetheless, this description of the Christian reception of Saul contrasts with other responses

---

38. See Richard I. Pervo, *Profit with Delight: The Literary Genre of the Acts of the Apostles* (Philadelphia: Fortress, 1987), 30, who observes that Saul's return to Jerusalem is improbable, for this would be like jumping "from frying pan to fire."

39. See Tyson, *Images of Judaism in Luke-Acts*, 118, who identifies a common literary pattern between these two narrative accounts. See also Pervo, *Profit with Delight*, 31, who states that "Luke inverted one incident to make it reflect credit upon his hero and then invented another."

40. See James D. G. Dunn, *The Acts of the Apostles*, Narrative Commentaries (Valley Forge, PA: Trinity Press International, 1996), 126, who states that these suspicions "would have been entirely understandable given his record and reputation as a prosecutor."

41. Cf. Haenchen, *The Acts of the Apostles*, 332.

to believers in the two previous narrative sections. In one earlier narrative section, the implicit reception of Saul by the Damascus believers was more positive and accepting than what one finds in Jerusalem. Although the narrator's "inside information" into Ananias's conversation with the Lord may indicate some hesitation (cf. 9:13–14, 19b–20), he mentions no active resistance or continuing hesitancy.[42] In that section, Luke also portrays the Jewish audience in the Damascus synagogue as questioning what has happened to Saul (9:21), whereas the Jewish believers of Jerusalem now reflect similar doubts. In another narrative section, the response to the believers after the Ananias and Sapphira incident stands in contrast with this reception of Saul by the Jerusalem believers. In that earlier section, the narrator summarizes that "none of the rest dared to join [κολλᾶσθαι] them" (5:13). The refusal to associate with the believers in the earlier description was the response of the nonbelieving part of the Jewish people toward the believers, but ironically the Jewish Christians now respond in the same manner toward Saul.[43] The emphatic position of πάντες suggests that this response is not simply a minority opinion; fear grips the *entire* group. This fear, which the narrator mentions as a direct description of the inner thoughts and motives of the Jerusalem believers, potentially creates an atmosphere of isolation from Saul. Such a picture, however, contrasts with earlier descriptions of fear that resulted in an atmosphere in which others accepted the Christian message (cf. 2:42–47; 5:11–16).

This ambiguous picture of the Jerusalem believers' reception of Saul leads to a second account of the interaction between the Jerusalem church and Saul. The character of Barnabas functions here as a mediator between the apostles and Saul (Acts 9:27).[44] Thus, Barnabas's narrative role implicitly suggests that the narrator includes the apostles in the larger group of the Jerusalem disciples who resist Saul's efforts to associate with them. The narrator does not recount everything Barnabas says to the apostles; the statement of verse 27 merely summarizes what

---

42. Although Ananias questions the Lord's message (cf. 9:13–14), the imperfect tense of ἐπείραζεν and ἐφοβοῦντο suggests that the disciples continue to resist Saul's attempts (9:26). Cf. Brawley, *Centering on God*, 151, who describes the disciples' suspicions as a "chorus" echoing Ananias's suspicions; and Tannehill, *The Narrative Unity of Luke-Acts*, 2:123.

43. Cf. Barrett, *The Acts of the Apostles*, 1:468.

44. Cf. Conzelmann, *Acts of the Apostles*, 75; Gaventa, *The Acts of the Apostles*, 154; Lüdemann, *Early Christianity according to the Traditions in Acts*, 117; Pesch, *Die Apostelgeschichte*, 1:313; and Tannehill, *The Narrative Unity of Luke-Acts*, 2:123–24.

has already been described in greater detail in chapter 9.[45] However, the concluding description of what Barnabas tells the apostles also prepares the reader for what follows: Saul speaking boldly "in the name of Jesus" (9:27).[46] The verb ἐπαρρησιάσατο clearly describes Saul's previous actions in Damascus in a way similar to the earlier affirmative descriptions of the apostles or believers (cf. 4:13, 29, 31). The participial phrase in the next verse, παρρησιαζόμενος ἐν τῷ ὀνόματι τοῦ κυρίου (9:28), has a grammatical structure similar to this summary of Saul's actions in 9:27, indicating that Saul does "more of the same" in Jerusalem.[47] This latter phrase, however, modifies the first part of the sentence: καὶ ἦν μετ' αὐτῶν εἰσπορευόμενος καὶ ἐκπορευόμενος εἰς Ἰερουσαλήμ (9:28). This periphrastic construction places the emphasis on Saul's continuous activity among or with the apostles (μετ' αὐτῶν),[48] so the implication is that they accept the transformed Saul into the Christian community.[49] Thus, the narrator describes Saul's repeated activity of bold proclamation (9:28; cf. 9:27) as occurring within the larger context of Saul's acceptance and inclusion by the apostles and, more generally, the Jerusalem believers.[50] The Christian community, once again, functions as the center or context from which the proclamation of the Christian message occurs.[51]

---

45. This summary does not agree entirely with Acts 9:1–25. For instance, the narrator states that Barnabas describes how Saul has seen the Lord (9:27), which is not mentioned in 9:3–9.

46. See Haenchen, *The Acts of the Apostles*, 332; Gottfried Schille, *Die Apostelgeschichte des Lukas*, THKNT 5 (Berlin: Evangelische Verlagsanstalt, 1983), 227; and Williams, *Acts*, 176, who observe that Luke does not state how Barnabas has gained access to such information about Saul. But see Joseph A. Fitzmyer, *The Acts of the Apostles: A New Translation with Introduction and Commentary*, AB (New York: Doubleday, 1998), 439; and Pesch, *Die Apostelgeschichte*, 1:313, who see Saul as the one disclosing the information.

47. Cf. Brawley, *Centering on God*, 151; and Johnson, *The Acts of the Apostles*, 172, who report that later Paul is also portrayed as speaking boldly (e.g., 13:46; 14:3; 18:26; 19:8; 26:26; 28:31).

48. Cf. Barrett, *The Acts of the Apostles*, 1:470; Johnson, *The Acts of the Apostles*, 172, 175; and Schneider, *Die Apostelgeschichte*, 2:39.

49. The imperfect tense suggests that Saul's inclusion into the church and his gospel proclamation are ongoing. Cf. Brawley, *Centering on God*, 158, who suggests that the apostles legitimate Saul here; Marshall, *The Acts of the Apostles*, 175; Pesch, *Die Apostelgeschichte*, 1:313; and Schmithals, *Die Apostelgeschichte des Lukas*, 96.

50. If the narrative implies that the apostles have questions about Saul like other believers do (9:27), then the apostles' acceptance of Saul implies that the other believers have accepted him, especially since Luke has always described the apostles and the believers as acting in unanimity.

51. Cf. Krodel, *Acts*, 181; and Alfons Weiser, *Die Apostelgeschichte*, 2 vols., ÖTNT (Würzburg: Echter, 1986), 1:234.

The narrator concludes this scene by describing the response to Saul's message and the continuing role of the believers in relation to Saul. That Luke describes Saul as engaged in the ongoing practice of speaking and arguing (ἐλάλει τε καὶ συνεζήτει; 9:29)[52] with the Greek-speaking Jews (πρὸς τοὺς Ἑλληνιστάς)[53] implies that the response is similar to the negative response Stephen has experienced in Acts 6.[54] A final description that is grammatically connected to this initial reaction accentuates the similarity in those negative responses: οἱ δὲ ἐπεχείρουν ἀνελεῖν αὐτόν (but they were trying to kill him; 9:29).[55] Luke does not state precisely what these Hellenistic Jews are trying to do, but what is important here is that murderous intents and attempts accompany the Jewish response to the gospel message. These negative responses contrast with the unanimity and concern for others in the church.[56] The believers, οἱ ἀδελφοί, provide the united means by which to secure Saul's safety in the face of the mounting opposition against him.[57] Luke does not clearly state whether οἱ ἀδελφοί refers specifically to the apostles or more generally to the believers. However, the narrated intervention by the Christian community (at least part if not the whole group) leaves the reader to ponder another image of believers who save the life of the one who has earlier sought to take the lives of believers. These Jewish believers in Jerusalem deliver what Saul needs when others threaten his life. Although the Jerusalem believers had serious doubts about Saul's motives upon his return to the city (cf. 9:26–27), their actions for his benefit implicitly suggest that the church has accepted him as one of them.

---

52. The verb συζητέω is the same term used to describe the negative reaction of some Jews in the initial stages of the Stephen narrative (cf. 6:9). Cf. Schille, *Die Apostelgeschichte des Lukas*, 227–28; Schneider, *Die Apostelgeschichte*, 2:39; and Williams, *Acts*, 177.

53. Cf. Krodel, *Acts*, 181; Pesch, *Die Apostelgeschichte*, 1:313; Tyson, *Images of Judaism in Luke-Acts*, 118; and Weiser, *Die Apostelgeschichte*, 1:235. See Johnson, *The Acts of the Apostles*, 172, who sees this as an example of narrative reversal, as Saul is fighting the same group he has formerly represented against Stephen (cf. 6:9–14).

54. Cf., e.g., Lüdemann, *Early Christianity according to the Traditions in Acts*, 117–18; Marshall, *The Acts of the Apostles*, 175–76; Schille, *Die Apostelgeschichte des Lukas*, 227–28; and Schmithals, *Die Apostelgeschichte des Lukas*, 96–97.

55. Once again, the action here is described with the imperfect tense (ἐπεχείρουν), indicating that these Greek-speaking Jews are repeatedly trying to "get rid" of Saul. Cf. Fitzmyer, *The Acts of the Apostles*, 440.

56. The verb ἀναιρέω is again used to describe the negative response by these Jewish persons — the same term that described the reaction of the Jewish council (5:33, 36) and of the Jews in Damascus (9:23-24). Cf. Sanders, *The Jews in Luke-Acts*, 255; Schneider, *Die Apostelgeschichte*, 2:39–40; and Tyson, *Images of Judaism in Luke-Acts*, 119.

57. Cf. Williams, *Acts*, 177.

An Assessment of the Characterization of the Church or Group of Believers in Acts 9:26–30

The narrative glimpses of the Jerusalem church included here in 9:26–30 provide a multifaceted portrait of that group. Their initial resistance and fear of Saul are both understandable and unacceptable, as their previous experiences of the persecutor Saul cause them to misunderstand the motives and actions of the persecuted believer Saul.[58] Continuing to resist Saul would create a sense of separation and division similar to what some of the Jewish people have created earlier (cf. 5:13). This ambiguous picture, however, quickly develops into a distinctive portrait of a community of believers that accepts its former opponent as one of that group, provides the communal basis from which proclamation occurs, and provides for needs as they arise. As this narrative scene rapidly progresses, the reader finds that the Christian community continues to function similarly in this section as in other previous narrative sections, as the believers overcome their initial questions and concerns.

THE CHURCH IN JUDEA, GALILEE, AND SAMARIA (ACTS 9:31)

The Literary Context

The narrative sequence of Acts 9:1–30 describes Saul's transformation from the persecutor of Christians to the persecuted Christian. His acceptance by the believers in both Damascus and Jerusalem provides the general context from which the narrative depicts his powerful proclamation of the gospel message. Accompanying the narrated description of the Jews' negative reaction against Saul is the presumed sense that others responded favorably to that message.[59] Nonetheless, the general impression left by these narrative scenes is that the major individual opponent of the Christian community and its message now is a part of that community. Such an impression will potentially create in readers a sense of anticipation that the fledgling Christian movement will continue to prosper as it spreads the gospel message.

---

58. Cf. Krodel, *Acts*, 180–81; Schneider, *Die Apostelgeschichte*, 2:38; and Weiser, *Die Apostelgeschichte*, 1:234.

59. The presumption of a favorable response arises from the earlier literary pattern found in Acts 3–7, when the gospel message received both a positive response of acceptance and a negative response of rejection. See Gaventa, "Toward a Theology of Acts," 156; and Joseph B. Tyson, "The Jewish Public in Luke-Acts," *NTS* 30 (October 1984): 580.

The Characterization of the Church or Group of Believers in Acts 9:31

The statement of Acts 9:31 is another narrative summary, a common literary feature of the Acts narrative. This statement, while a distinct section within the narrative, is also linked to the preceding events, as the use of μὲν οὖν suggests.[60] The subject of the statement is the church, ἡ ἐκκλησία. As used here, this term does not refer to a local assembly or group of believers, however, as previous appearances of the term suggest (cf. 5:11; 8:1b, 3).[61] Here, ἡ ἐκκλησία refers to the believers throughout the regions of Judea, Galilee, and Samaria, with more of a general connotation rather than a localized one.[62] Nonetheless, that change in focus is not inconsistent with the narrative sequence, as the narrator describes the spread of the believers and their proclaimed message to various geographical regions.

This narrative summary statement and its depiction of the church are constructed with two indicatives, which describe the general situation; each is modified by an adverbial participle, which provides additional information regarding the inner dynamics of the church from an omniscient narrator's perspective.[63] The first indicative with its direct object, εἶχεν εἰρήνην, implies that Saul's transformation has eliminated the hostilities against the believers.[64] The participle οἰκοδομουμένη explicitly describes what accompanies that peace. The passive voice of the participle indicates that the church does not accomplish this "building up" but receives that action. Although the reader is not told who does this work, the passive voice potentially leads the reader to conclude that God does

---

60. Cf., e.g., Barrett, *The Acts of the Apostles*, 1:472–73; Haenchen, *The Acts of the Apostles*, 333; Kurz, *Reading Luke-Acts*, 87; Lüdemann, *Early Christianity according to the Traditions in Acts*, 119; and Schneider, *Die Apostelgeschichte*, 2:40–41.

61. Cf., e.g., Bruce, *The Book of the Acts*, 196; Conzelmann, *Acts of the Apostles*, 75; Krodel, *Acts*, 182; Pesch, *Die Apostelgeschichte*, 1:313–14; Jürgen Roloff, *Die Apostelgeschichte*, NTD 5 (Göttingen: Vandenhoeck & Ruprecht, 1981), 157; Weiser, *Die Apostelgeschichte*, 1:235; and Ben Witherington III, *The Acts of the Apostles: A Socio-Rhetorical Commentary* (Grand Rapids: Eerdmans, 1998), 326.

62. This shift in the connotation of ἐκκλησία may be the reason for the textual variants here, particularly in the use of the plural ἐκκλησίαι. See Metzger, *A Textual Commentary on the Greek New Testament*, 367; and Fitzmyer, *The Acts of the Apostles*, 440–41.

63. Cf. William J. Larkin Jr., *Acts*, IVPNTC (Downers Grove, IL: InterVarsity, 1995), 148; and Weiser, *Die Apostelgeschichte*, 1:235.

64. Cf. Johnson, *The Acts of the Apostles*, 176; and Tannehill, *The Narrative Unity of Luke-Acts*, 2:124. That the time of peace occurs *after* Saul leaves the scene, however, may be a hint of some underlying problem. See Johnson, *The Acts of the Apostles*, 176; and Shepherd, *The Narrative Function of the Holy Spirit*, 195n134.

it since God's active presence has been a dominant characteristic of the Lukan descriptions of the church.[65] The second indicative, ἐπληθύνετο, stresses the continual increase in the number of believers, alluding to earlier images of the divine role in the success of the Christian message among the Jewish people in Jerusalem (cf. Acts 2:41, 47; 6:1, 7).[66] The growth of the Christian community, however, correlates to the nature of that community's existence, as the participial phrase describes. On the one hand, the increase continues to occur as they live in "the fear of the Lord" (πορευομένη τῷ φόβῳ τοῦ κυρίου). This narrative description alludes to the sense of religious awe or fear that captivates the believers both after the Pentecost events (cf. 2:43) and during the incident involving Ananias and Sapphira (cf. 5:5, 11). Thus, this summary reiterates the continuing work and presence of God within the ever-spreading Christian community that has moved beyond the walls of Jerusalem. On the other hand, they also live in "the comfort of the Holy Spirit" (πορευομένη ... τῇ παρακλήσει τοῦ ἁγίου πνεύματος), another direct description of divine presence found in the growing Christian community.[67] Just as Luke describes the believers of Jerusalem and their growth in relation to the Holy Spirit's coming and work, he reminds the reader that the same essential characteristic of the church continues to apply, even as the believers are found in the surrounding regions.[68]

An Assessment of the Characterization of the Church or Group of Believers in Acts 9:31

The narrative summary of Acts 9:31 provides a brief statement regarding the church in the regions of Judea, Samaria, and Galilee. The narrator provides direct descriptions and judgments of the believers that the reader may not necessarily conclude from the observation of their actions. The dominant image of the Christian community in this

65. The verb οἰκοδομέω may refer to constructing a building or "building up" individuals. See Otto Michel, "οἰκοδομέω," in TDNT, 5:136–44. Cf. Barrett, The Acts of the Apostles, 1:473; Johnson, The Acts of the Apostles, 176–77; and Krodel, Acts, 183.

66. The verb πληθύνω also described the growing number of believers in Jerusalem in Acts 6:1, 7. The imperfect tense emphasizes the continual aspect of this increase, and the passive voice implicitly suggests that God again is the source of this growth.

67. See Shepherd, The Narrative Function of the Holy Spirit, 194–95, who insists that the dative τῇ παρακλήσει is instrumental, to be taken with ἐπληθύνετο rather than πορευομένη (9:31). See also Otto Schmitz and Gustav Stählin, "παρακαλέω...," in TDNT, 5:773–99. Cf. Johnson, The Acts of the Apostles, 177; Larkin, Acts, 248; and Schneider, Die Apostelgeschichte, 2:41.

68. Cf. Roloff, Die Apostelgeschichte, 157; and Zingg, Das Wachsen der Kirche, 33.

verse, however, reinforces what the Acts narrative has already presented: the Christian community is identifiable as the people in whom God is working and blessing. That divine presence has enabled the believers to proclaim the word of God in the midst of the growing opposition in Jerusalem (cf. Acts 3–8), has transformed their *opponent* into their *proponent*, and is found in the Christian community in the aftermath of persecution. Although the geographical setting in the narrative is widening, the same images of divine presence and blessing with their earlier implicit connections to unanimity and communal care for one another in the Jerusalem church now characterize the ἐκκλησία, the assembly of God's people, as *one* church that extends beyond the city walls of Jerusalem.

PETER, CORNELIUS, AND THE FIRST GROUP OF GENTILE BELIEVERS (ACTS 10:44–48)

The Literary Context (9:32–10:43)

After the narrative events related to and resultant from Saul's conversion in Acts 9, Luke turns the reader's attention to selected events in the ministry of the apostle Peter. The narrator includes accounts of three events with Peter as the central character. The first two scenes depict Peter as a healer among believers in Lydda and Joppa, two towns about forty miles northwest of Jerusalem and near the Mediterranean Sea. Several important features of these two narrative accounts are strikingly similar. In both events, the narrator places Peter's ministry in the context of "the saints" (τοὺς ἁγίους; 9:32, 41) or "the disciples" (οἱ μαθηταί; 9:38).[69] Also, the narrator emphasizes that the populace of each town either observes the healed person or receives news of the healing (cf. 9:35, 41–42). Finally, the narrator states that an overwhelmingly positive response among these Jewish people results as persons come to believe ἐπὶ τὸν κύριον (9:35, 42).[70] These narrated events remind the reader of

---

69. See Johnson, *The Acts of the Apostles*, 177, who observes that Luke assumes the founding of the church and does not narrate that action. Cf. Haenchen, *The Acts of the Apostles*, 338.

70. After the first healing, in which Peter heals a paralyzed man (9:33–34), the Lukan narrator states that "all the residents of Lydda and Sharon saw him and turned to the Lord" (9:35), which creates in the reader's imagination the image of the entire population of two towns responding to the obvious sign of divine power and blessing. After the second healing, when Peter raises Tabitha (or Dorcas) from the dead (9:36–41), the narrator states that "this

earlier healing scenes (cf. 3:1–9; 5:12–16) and affirm the divine presence among the believers.[71]

The Lukan narration of the Peter and Cornelius story (Acts 10:1–48) dominates this section of the book of Acts and stands as a pivotal event in the narrative sequence.[72] Up to this point in the narrative, the believers have proclaimed the gospel message mainly to Jewish people or "peripheral" people, including Samaritans and Diaspora Jews.[73] The centurion Cornelius, however, is a Gentile,[74] so that Peter's proclamation of the gospel message at Cornelius's house crosses religious and ethnic barriers that separate Jews from non-Jews.[75] The Lukan narrator legitimizes what happens by emphasizing through repetition three specific matters about both Cornelius and Peter.[76] One particular emphasis is the character of

---

became known throughout Joppa, and many believed in the Lord" (9:42), creating another image of positive response. Cf. Haenchen, *The Acts of the Apostles*, 338, who sees the response as "hyperbolical"; and Marshall, *The Acts of the Apostles*, 178.

71. See Marshall, *The Acts of the Apostles*, 178, who states that Peter did what Jesus has done.

72. See Pesch, *Die Apostelgeschichte*, 1:330, who observes that this narrative section, the longest in Acts, is a "crucial epoch in the story of the early church." Cf. Stephen G. Wilson, *The Gentiles and the Gentile Mission in Luke-Acts*, SNTSMS 23 (Cambridge: Cambridge University Press, 1973), 177. For studies on the Cornelius episode, see, e.g., Roland Barthes, "L'analyse structurale du récit: A propos d'Actes X–XI," *RSR* 58 (1970): 17–37; Jouette M. Bassler, "Luke and Paul on Impartiality," *Bib* 66 (1985): 546–52; François Bovon, "Tradition et rédaction en Actes 10,1–11,18," *TZ* 26 (January–February 1970): 22–45; Martin Dibelius, "The Conversion of Cornelius," in *Studies in the Acts of the Apostles*, trans. Mary Ling (London: SCM, 1956), 109–22; Haenchen, *The Acts of the Apostles*, 343–63; Edgar Haulotte, "Fondation d'une communauté de type universel: Actes 10:1–11:18; Étude critique sur la rédaction, la 'structure' et la 'tradition' du récit," *RSR* 58 (1970): 63–100; Louis Marin, "Essai d'analyse structurale d'Actes 10:1–11:18," *RSR* 58 (1970): 39–61; J. Julius Scott Jr., "The Cornelius Incident in the Light of Its Jewish Setting," *JETS* 34 (December 1991): 475–84; Tannehill, *The Narrative Unity of Luke-Acts*, 2:128–45; and Ronald D. Witherup, "Cornelius Over and Over and Over Again: 'Functional Redundancy' in the Acts of the Apostles," *JSNT* 49 (1993): 67–86.

73. Tyson (*Images of Judaism in Luke-Acts*, 116–18) uses "peripheral people" to describe those the Jewish people (particularly in Jerusalem) considered as "marginal."

74. Since Cornelius is a centurion (ἑκατοντάρχης), he is not Jewish. Cf. Conzelmann, *Acts of the Apostles*, 81; Johnson, *The Acts of the Apostles*, 181–82; and Marshall, *The Acts of the Apostles*, 183–84.

75. See Jerome H. Neyrey, "Ceremonies in Luke-Acts: The Case of Meals and Table-Fellowship," in *The Social World of Luke-Acts: Models for Interpretation*, ed. Jerome H. Neyrey (Peabody, MA: Hendrickson, 1991), 380–81, who notices that the themes of food and people are "carefully woven together" in this account.

76. On the Lukan use of repetition in Acts, see Barthes, "L'analyse structurale du récit," 33–36; Haenchen, *The Acts of the Apostles*, 357–59; Kurz, *Reading Luke-Acts*, 88–89; and Witherup, "Cornelius Over and Over and Over Again," 45–66.

Cornelius, whom the narrator describes directly in verse 2: a devout man (εὐσεβής), one who fears God (φοβούμενος τὸν θεόν),[77] a giver of much alms (ποιῶν ἐλεημοσύνας πολλάς), and one who prays to God always (δεόμενος τοῦ θεοῦ διὰ παντός).[78] The repetition of both the direct description of Cornelius as one who fears God (10:2, 22) and the indirect presentation of Cornelius's practice of prayer (10:2, 3, 4, 30, 31) present this individual much like the Jewish believers in earlier scenes.[79] A second matter legitimizes what happens: Cornelius's obedience to the instructions given by an angel of God as he prays (ἄγγελον τοῦ θεοῦ; 10:3; cf. 10:22, 30).[80] Luke stresses a third matter through repetition: Peter also receives divine instructions when he is praying, both in his vision of the sheet with the animals (10:9–16, 28) and in the Spirit's instructions to travel with Cornelius's messengers (10:19–20).[81] Thus, through the narrator's direct description, the provided "conversations" between these characters and divine messengers, and the characters' own words, readers are encouraged to view both Cornelius and Peter positively and to perceive their actions as divinely ordained and legitimate.

The Lukan narrator depicts an ironic scene as Peter arrives at the house of Cornelius. When Peter and some believers from Joppa (τινες τῶν ἀδελφῶν τῶν ἀπὸ Ἰόππης; 10:23) go to Caesarea, they arrive at Cornelius's house to find it filled with "relatives and close friends" (τοὺς συγγενεῖς αὐτοῦ καὶ τοὺς ἀναγκαίους φίλους; 10:24), whom he has called

---

77. For studies on "God-fearers" as Gentiles who practice Jewish customs but do not convert to Judaism, see Shaye J. D. Cohen, "Respect for Judaism by Gentiles according to Josephus," *HTR* 80 (1987): 409–30; Jacob Jervell, "The Church of Jews and Godfearers," in *Luke-Acts and the Jewish People: Eight Critical Perspectives*, ed. Joseph B. Tyson (Minneapolis: Augsburg, 1988), 11–20; Kirsopp Lake, "Proselytes and God-Fearers," in *The Beginnings of Christianity*, ed. F. J. Foakes-Jackson and Kirsopp Lake, 5 vols. (London: Macmillan, 1933), 5:74–96; Joseph B. Tyson, "Jews and Judaism in Luke-Acts: Reading as a Godfearer," *NTS* 41 (1995): 19–38; and Max Wilcox, "The 'God-Fearers' in Acts — A Reconsideration," *JSNT* 13 (1981): 102–22.

78. See Tannehill, *The Narrative Unity of Luke-Acts*, 2:133, who stresses that Cornelius is described like a good Jew and, finally, like Jewish believers.

79. For "fear" that characterizes the believers in Acts, see 2:43; 5:11. For "prayer" and the believers, see 1:12–14; 2:42; 3:1; 4:24–31; 6:4, 6.

80. Cf. Lüdemann, *Early Christianity according to the Traditions in Acts*, 127–28; Marshall, *The Acts of the Apostles*, 184; and Tannehill, *The Narrative Unity of Luke-Acts*, 2:129.

81. See Schmithals, *Die Apostelgeschichte des Lukas*, 103, who observes that God must still overcome Peter's questioning. Cf. Brawley, *Centering on God*, 96; Pervo, *Profit with Delight*, 73; Pesch, *Die Apostelgeschichte*, 1:331–32; Tannehill, *The Narrative Unity of Luke-Acts*, 2:129; and Tyson, *Images of Judaism in Luke-Acts*, 121.

together.[82] The narrative directs the reader's attention to the meeting between these Jewish believers and the Gentiles gathered together at Cornelius's house to hear from Peter (cf. 10:33). Luke indirectly underscores the unlikely nature of this meeting through what Peter expresses to the gathered people: "It is unlawful for a Jew to associate with or to visit a Gentile" (ἀθέμιτόν ἐστιν ἀνδρὶ Ἰουδαίῳ κολλᾶσθαι ἢ προσέρχεσθαι ἀλλοφύλῳ; 10:28).[83] The same term used earlier to connote intimate, personal association, which some in Jerusalem avoided (5:13a) and which Saul sought with the Jerusalem believers who were fearful of him (9:26), is employed here and emphasizes that such a communal bond between Jews and non-Jews is *not* appropriate according to Jewish custom.[84] The Jewish self-understanding includes strict distinctions between non-Jews and themselves, so that Jewish purity as the people of God may be maintained.[85] The improbability of this meeting, however, is ironically presented along with the narrated picture of the conversation between Peter and Cornelius, in which Luke depicts the two persons as associating or joining together in conversation.[86] Peter, as the reliable spokesperson for the narrator, implicitly links his vision with the developing events at Cornelius's house, recognizing that God through that vision has shown him the invalidity of such religious and ethnic distinctions (10:28).[87]

The narrated events at Cornelius's house focus significantly on Peter's preaching to this group of Gentiles.[88] Luke depicts both Cornelius and

---

82. The aorist participle συγκαλεσάμενος describes a group that has joined *together* to hear Peter (10:24). In 10:27, the narrator states that Peter finds "many who had assembled there" (εὑρίσκει συνεληλυθότας πολλούς), with the perfect participle συνεληλυθότας stressing this sense of gathering together. Both participles, with the prefix σύν, depict a group that had united together in expectation. Cf. Bovon, "Tradition et rédaction en Actes 10,1–11,18," 27; Gaventa, *From Darkness to Light*, 116, 128; Witherup, "Cornelius Over and Over and Over Again," 52.

83. See Conzelmann, *Acts of the Apostles*, 82, who suggests that Jewish practice does not always coincide with the Jewish theory of separation (cf. Josephus, *Jewish Antiquities* 20.34–53).

84. See Larkin, *Acts*, 161, who gives several references to rabbinic law that proscribes social contact with non-Jews; Johnson, *The Acts of the Apostles*, 190; and Krodel, *Acts*, 191.

85. See Jerome H. Neyrey, "The Symbolic Universe of Luke-Acts: 'They Turn the World Upside Down,'" in Neyrey, *The Social World of Luke-Acts*, 271–304.

86. The verb συνομιλέω (10:27) has the general meaning of "conversing with." However, the root verb ὁμιλέω connotes not only conversation (see BDAG, 705) but also joining together in company (see LSJ, 1222). See Marshall, *The Acts of the Apostles*, 188, who notices that Luke has these men "talking together as equals."

87. Cf. Tyson, *Images of Judaism in Luke-Acts*, 120–21.

88. See Dibelius, "The Conversion of Cornelius," 118, who identifies Peter as the main character, not Cornelius.

the people gathered at his house in a positive manner, affirming through Cornelius's words that everyone has gathered "in the presence of God" (πάντες ἡμεῖς ἐνώπιον τοῦ θεοῦ; 10:33). Peter's proclamation affirms that the message of God's promise is not confined to an exclusive group (οὐκ ἔστιν προσωπολήμπτης ὁ θεός; 10:34) but is inclusive of those from various ethnic backgrounds (ἐν παντὶ ἔθνει; 10:35).[89] This beginning statement concerning the divine acceptance of those who fear God (ὁ φοβούμενος αὐτόν; 10:35) implicitly includes the Gentile Cornelius, whom the narrator characterizes as one who fears God (cf. 10:2, 22).[90] Central to Peter's proclamation is the divine nature of Jesus' ministry, whom Peter describes with imagery similar to what the Acts narrative has previously employed in describing the ministry of the Christian community.[91] Although many aspects of Peter's sermon resemble his earlier speeches in Acts 1–5,[92] the last part of the sermon emphasizes the inclusive offer of forgiveness through Jesus' name to all who believe in him.[93] Given the Gentile audience to which Peter is speaking, the clear indication is that these non-Jews receive the offer of forgiveness and salvation.[94]

The Characterization of the Church or Group of Believers in Acts 10:44–48

The Lukan account of the events at Cornelius's house concludes with an abbreviated description of the Gentiles' response to Peter's message. The specific details of that description, however, correlate with those found

---

89. Cf. Krodel, *Acts*, 195–96; and Larkin, *Acts*, 163.

90. Cf. Haenchen, *The Acts of the Apostles*, 351; and Krodel, *Acts*, 195–96.

91. The characterization of Jesus as anointed by God "with the Holy Spirit and with power" (πνεύματι ἁγίῳ καὶ δυνάμει; 10:38) is similar to the description of the believers as "filled with the Holy Spirit" (cf., e.g., 2:4; 4:31) and demonstrating power (cf., e.g., 3:12; 4:7, 33), just as Jesus' healing corresponds with other healings (3:1–10; 5:15–16; 9:32–43). This description of Jesus (10:36–41) is explicitly tied to God's presence (ὅτι ὁ θεὸς ἦν μετ' αὐτοῦ; 10:38), a key aspect of descriptions of the church in Jerusalem and the surrounding regions.

92. Cf. Conzelmann, *Acts of the Apostles*, 82; Dibelius, "The Conversion of Cornelius," 111; and Schmithals, *Die Apostelgeschichte des Lukas*, 106.

93. See Krodel, *Acts*, 100, who observes that Acts 10:43 returns to the theme of the universality of the gospel found in 10:34–35 and forms an *inclusio*. See also Tannehill, *The Narrative Unity of Luke-Acts*, 2:141, who identifies "everyone who believes" as in the emphatic position in 10:43.

94. This account is probably the second scene depicting the conversion of a Gentile, with the first scene being the conversion of the Ethiopian eunuch in chapter 8 (cf. Tannehill, *The Narrative Unity of Luke-Acts*, 2:109–11). However, this scene probably receives greater attention in Acts due to the apostolic role of Peter and to the *group* of Gentiles here.

in the earlier account of the Pentecost events. The narrator begins this section by explicitly stating that, while Peter is still speaking to his audience, "the Holy Spirit fell upon all who heard the message" (10:44), a description using terminology similar to 8:16 and alluding to the Holy Spirit's coming at Pentecost.[95] This direct statement, explicitly describing something about those who are listening to Peter, asserts that these Gentiles experience what the Jewish believers themselves have experienced.[96] However, the narrative depicts the circumcised believers (οἱ ἐκ περιτομῆς πιστοί; 10:45)[97] who accompany Peter as amazed (ἐξέστησαν) at what has occurred,[98] which is described explicitly as the "gift of the Holy Spirit" that has been "poured out" (ἐκκέχυται) on these Gentiles.[99] An explanation (γάρ) is provided to account for the circumcised believers' conclusions and reaction.[100] This explanation states that the Jewish believers who have come with Peter hear the Gentiles speaking in γλώσσαις and glorifying God (10:46), something that has occurred only after the extraordinary coming of the Holy Spirit in Jerusalem (2:1–4).[101] The

---

95. In both Acts 8:16 and 10:44, the verb ἐπιπίπτω describes the coming or "falling" of the Holy Spirit, thereby emphasizing the Holy Spirit's coming (contra Krodel, *Acts*, 200, who sees this description in contrast to Pentecost). Cf. William S. Kurz, "Effects of Variant Narrators in Acts 10–11," *NTS* 43 (October 1997): 583, who recognizes the narrator's advantage, unlike one of the characters, of referring "backward or forward to any part in the plot from beginning to end."

96. Cf. Larkin, *Acts*, 168; William Neil, *Acts*, NCB (Grand Rapids: Eerdmans, 1973), 140; and Williams, *Acts*, 195.

97. See Dunn, *The Acts of the Apostles*, 145; and Fitzmyer, *The Acts of the Apostles*, 467, who translate this description as "the faithful from circumcision."

98. See Tannehill, *The Narrative Unity of Luke-Acts*, 2:129, who stresses that these Jewish believers are amazed. Cf. Krodel, *Acts*, 200; Schmithals, *Die Apostelgeschichte des Lukas*, 104; and M. A. Seifrid, "Jesus and the Law in Acts," *JSNT* 30 (1987): 42.

99. The designation "gift of the Holy Spirit" (ἡ δωρεὰ τοῦ ἁγίου πνεύματος; 10:45) was used by Peter in his response to the Pentecost audience (cf. 2:38). The verb ἐκχέω (10:45) presents an image alluding to the prophetic promises that Peter quoted in his Pentecost speech (cf. 2:17–18) and that he declared to be fulfilled by God through Jesus (cf. 2:33). Cf. Tannehill, *The Narrative Unity of Luke-Acts*, 2:142–43; and Dunn, *The Acts of the Apostles*, 146.

100. See Johnson, *The Acts of the Apostles*, 194, who identifies Luke's adoption of the "spectator's perspective" rather than providing a direct description of the Spirit's effects. Cf. Matthias Klinghardt, *Gesetz und Volk Gottes: Das lukanische Verständnis des Gesetzes nach Herkunft, Funktion und seinem Ort in der Geschichte des Urchristentums*, WUNT (Tübingen: J. C. B. Mohr, 1988), 210–11, who sees Gentile impurity as irrelevant here.

101. The expression λαλούντων γλώσσαις (10:46) alludes to the description found in 2:4. Cf. Shepherd, *The Narrative Function of the Holy Spirit*, 201n150. Contra Haenchen, *The Acts of the Apostles*, 354; Krodel, *Acts*, 201; and Williams, *Acts*, 196. Cf. also Pesch, *Die Apostelgeschichte*, 1:332; and Schmithals, *Die Apostelgeschichte des Lukas*, 105–6: both suggest that, with this description, Luke sees this event as a "second Pentecost."

narrator's direct statement and his observations of the circumcised believers' reaction depict a scene in which the reader will recognize the
acceptance of the gospel message by these Gentiles and their reception
of the Holy Spirit. This group of Gentiles at Cornelius's house (cf. 10:24,
27) reflects the same characteristics as the Jewish believers have depicted in the preceding chapters.[102] Thus, the narrator both implicitly
and explicitly indicates that the reader should characterize these *Gentiles* as believers like the *Jewish* believers, although the Gentiles have
been historically, religiously, and socially excluded from the sphere of
God's presence and blessing.

This radical characterization of a group of Gentiles as believers and
as recipients of the Holy Spirit does not depend solely on the narrator's observations and direct statements. The narrator utilizes another
literary tool by which to convey convincingly what has just occurred,
inserting a question from Peter to substantiate what the narrative already describes. Because of Peter's earlier activities in Jerusalem, Lydda,
and Joppa, as well as his obedience in going to Cornelius's house, he
functions as a reliable character through whom Luke the narrator may
implicitly articulate his perspective and conclusions.[103] The Petrine question to his Jewish associates at the end of this section serves to legitimize
the conclusions found in the prior three verses.[104] On the one hand,
Peter's suggestion — that these Gentiles should be baptized because of
their reception of the Holy Spirit — validates what others have concluded and likens this occurrence to the Pentecost events (cf. Acts 2:38).
On the other hand, his comments also identify what has happened with
what the Jewish believers have themselves experienced.[105] The character of Peter, therefore, confirms what the reader may well conclude and
observe from the reaction of the Jewish believers: this group of Gentiles
is a group of believers who, despite their different social customs, enjoy
divine presence and activity among them.

The Lukan narrator concludes this narrative section with a lasting
portrait of the believers in Caesarea. After the coming of the Holy Spirit

---

102. Cf. Lüdemann, *Early Christianity according to the Traditions in Acts,* 128–29.

103. Cf. Shepherd, *The Narrative Function of the Holy Spirit,* 201.

104. See Haenchen, *The Acts of the Apostles,* 354, 359, who observes that only at this
point can baptism be mentioned, if the narrative is to have its potential effect.

105. Peter's last words (ὡς καὶ ἡμεῖς; 10:47) function as an implicit presentation of the
narrator's view by using a reliable character to articulate and validate what the reader has
encountered. Cf. Brawley, *Centering on God,* 141.

to the Gentiles at Cornelius's house, Peter orders (προσέταξεν; 10:48)[106] these new believers (αὐτούς) to be baptized. Following these instructions and probable fulfillment, the Gentile believers ask Peter to stay with them for a few days (10:48).[107] Two important images contribute to this particular narrative account. On the one hand, one image subtly conveyed by the narrative description involves the person or persons whom the Gentile Christians ask to stay. The text does not mention Peter's Jewish-Christian associates at all; those at Cornelius's house invite only Peter (αὐτόν) to stay.[108] The Jewish believers who accompany Peter and are amazed that Gentiles receive the same gift from God that they have received (cf. 10:45) now drop out of the picture.[109] The absence of these believers may provide a narrative hint for readers about some problem relating to Jewish-Gentile distinctions (cf. 10:9–16, 28) within the Christian community, to assist them in anticipating later narrative events and scenes.[110] Such an image will reflect a tension between the characterized unanimity of the Christian community in earlier chapters and the reality of religious and social barriers that can jeopardize such communal qualities. On the other hand, the picture also includes the dominant image of the Jewish Peter as he associates (cf. 10:28) and stays (ἐπιμεῖναι) with these Gentile believers for a brief time, although Jewish customs consider such close interaction unlawful (cf. 10:28).[111] This image implicitly refers to the transformation that has occurred in the

---

106. The verb προστάσσω (10:48) denotes the command to do something. Cf. Conzelmann, *Acts of the Apostles*, 84. See Gerhard Delling, "προστάσσω," in *TDNT*, 8:37–39.

107. See Pesch, *Die Apostelgeschichte*, 1:332, who compares this with Peter's stay in Joppa (9:43). Cf. Kurz, *Reading Luke-Acts*, 89, who sees the necessity of this stay to allow enough time for these events to become known.

108. Contra Witherington, *The Acts of the Apostles*, 360.

109. Cf. Johannes Munck, *The Acts of the Apostles*, AB 31 (Garden City, NY: Doubleday, 1967), 95.

110. The appearance of the "circumcised believers" (10:45), their implied absence (10:48), and then reappearance (11:2) may lead one to conclude that these Jewish Christians object to such interaction and leave. The Jewish believers then inform those in Judea about Peter's activities. This subtle, underlying tension hints about what will occur when Peter returns to Jerusalem.

111. The mention of Peter's invitation in Caesarea implies that he also accepts it (cf. Williams, *Acts*, 196). The verb ἐπιμένω connotes that Peter both "lodges" and eats with them. Therefore, Peter's vision in Joppa prepares him for overcoming the obstacles of entering a Gentile's house and breaking food regulations. For studies that consider the role of Jewish food regulations in Acts (esp. Acts 10–15), see Joseph B. Tyson, "Acts 6:1–7 and Dietary Regulations in Early Christianity," *PerRS* 10 (Spring 1983): 145–61.

social interaction between these believers through the gospel, resulting in an intimate association and communal bond between them that religious and social distinctions should not negate.[112] In this concluding picture, the narrator depicts the social bond that the gospel creates between a Jewish believer and a group of Gentile believers. This picture, alluding to the unanimity that characterizes the churches in the preceding chapters of the Acts narrative, presents a group of people characterized not by social and ethnic distinctions but by a common faith and response to the gospel.[113]

An Assessment of the Characterization of the Church or Group of Believers in Acts 10:44–48

The characterization of the Christian community in Acts 10:44–48, like most other narrative glimpses into groups of believers in this larger narrative unit of Acts 8:4–12:25, depends on the positive intratextual imagery depicting the Jerusalem believers. The narrator explicitly presents the believers in Caesarea as embodying many of the same characteristics as the Jerusalem church. What is significant about this depiction, however, is that the new believers in Caesarea are not Jewish, as they are in Jerusalem and Damascus. Thus, while Luke has earlier presented the Jewish believers as maintaining continuity with Jewish practices, now the portrayal of the church broadens to include non-Jewish persons. This broadening sense of inclusiveness now incorporates different social and ethnic groups into the Christian community along with their respective practices and customs.[114] While the Lukan portrayal of the believers in Caesarea does not ignore the problems associated with such inclusiveness, the image of the *Jewish* Peter with the *Gentile* believers suggests that the characteristics of unanimity and divine blessing that have earlier described the Jewish believers now also describe the communal bond between these Gentile believers and this Jewish believer. Luke thus characterizes the Christian community as that group in which God is found to be working — a group so united together because of God's presence that social and ethnic distinctions do not divide them.

---

112. See Gaventa, *From Darkness to Light*, 136: "By means of the issue of *hospitality*, Luke demonstrates that the conversion of the first Gentile required the conversion of the church as well."

113. Cf. Neyrey, "The Symbolic Universe of Luke-Acts," 293.

114. Cf. Gaventa, *The Acts of the Apostles*, 172.

THE JERUSALEM CHURCH QUESTIONS PETER
ABOUT HIS ACTIONS (ACTS 11:1–18)

The Literary Context

The previous narrative events involving Peter, Cornelius, and the proclamation of the gospel message provide the context for the next scene, depicting a church as a character group in Acts. The scattering of the believers not only results in the spread of the gospel to peripheral people in relation to the Jews, but now Gentiles have responded favorably to the believers' proclamation and have been incorporated into the Christian church by baptism (10:47–48). Consequently, such a radical turn of events will unsurprisingly provoke questions, as the believers are forced to wrestle with issues concerning the role of social and ethnic customs in relation to their understanding of God and their relationship with one another.

The Characterization of the Church or Group of Believers in Acts 11:1–18

Luke prepares the reader for this narrative scene by stating that the news about the Gentiles' acceptance of the gospel message (τὸν λόγον τοῦ θεοῦ; 11:1) has reached the Jewish Christians in Judea. This information results in Peter being confronted by "the circumcised believers" (οἱ ἐκ περιτομῆς; 11:2) in Jerusalem, the latter being a Lukan designation for the whole Jerusalem church that also contrasts them with the uncircumcised Gentile believers from whom Peter has just returned.[115] The narrator describes that confrontation by using an imperfect form of διακρίνω, the same word that earlier denotes how Peter is *not* to react regarding the Gentiles (cf. 10:20).[116] Thus, the narrator subtly suggests to the reader that the Jerusalem believers' initial response and continuing activity toward Peter are precisely that attitude and separation that

---

115. Cf. Haenchen, *The Acts of the Apostles*, 354, 359; and Marshall, *The Acts of the Apostles*, 195. Contra Bruce, *The Book of the Acts*, 220; and Johnson, *The Acts of the Apostles*, 197.

116. The verb διακρίνω is found in 10:20; 11:2, 12; and 15:9. The verb has the connotation of separation, differentiation, or dispute (cf. BDAG, 231; and LSJ, 399). See Friedrich Büchsel, "διακρίνω," in *TDNT*, 3:946–49. Cf. Gaventa, *The Acts of the Apostles*, 172; Johnson, *The Acts of the Apostles*, 197; and Robert W. Wall, "The Acts of the Apostles: Introduction, Commentary, and Reflections," in *NIB*, ed. Leander Keck, 12 vols. (Nashville: Abingdon, 2002), 10:168.

God has shown Peter to be *invalid* toward the Gentiles.[117] The specific question that the Jerusalem believers ask (11:2) confirms that attitude toward Peter, as they focus on the social and ethnic distinctions that would maintain separation between Jews and Gentiles.[118] However, in chapter 10 the reader has already encountered the answer to the question concerning Peter's reasons for going to "uncircumcised men" (πρὸς ἄνδρας ἀκροβυστίαν) and eating with them (συνέφαγες αὐτοῖς; 11:3).[119] Thus, although the believers in Jerusalem may not have had access to the information that the Lukan narrator provides for the reader, the narrative presentation of the Jerusalem believers does not depict them favorably, as they create an atmosphere of contention and confrontation.[120]

Peter's response to the questions of the Jerusalem believers provides a perspective on the events of Acts 10 from one who is both that chapter's main character and a reliable character in earlier scenes.[121] Thus, this view of the narrated events already described in the previous chapter allows the narrator to reaffirm implicitly through repetition three aspects of those events that are significant in understanding what Peter has done and how he has responded to those Gentile believers.[122] One aspect of those events that the narrator reiterates through Peter's response is the

117. See Schmithals, *Die Apostelgeschichte des Lukas*, 103, who points out that the questioning by the Jewish Christians is much like Peter's questioning of the vision.

118. Cf. Thomas Wieser, "Community — Its Unity, Diversity and Universality," *Semeia* 54 (1985): 89, who states that "the breakdown of the distinction between Jews and Gentiles predictably leads to a crisis in the Jewish community." Sanders, *The Jews in Luke-Acts*, 257, speculates that this reflects a later shunning of Christians by the synagogues.

119. The verb συνεσθίω (11:3) is another compound word emphasizing togetherness and social interaction along with eating. Cf. Bruce, *The Book of the Acts*, 220; and Tannehill, *The Narrative Unity of Luke-Acts*, 2:136.

120. Peter's mention of "these six brothers" (οἱ ἓξ ἀδελφοὶ οὗτοι; 11:12) suggests that the six believers have witnessed the event and can validate Peter's account. That the believers still respond to Peter in this way suggests that they have ignored indications of divine guidance. Cf. Brian Rapske, "Opposition to the Plan of God and Persecution," in *Witness to the Gospel: The Theology of Acts*, ed. I. Howard Marshall and David Peterson (Grand Rapids: Eerdmans, 1998), 240–41.

121. Cf. Dibelius, "The Conversion of Cornelius," 118; Schille, *Die Apostelgeschichte des Lukas*, 252; and Tannehill, *The Narrative Unity of Luke-Acts*, 2:143. See Kurz, "Effects of Variant Narrators in Acts 10–11," 579, who observes that the narrative character Peter uses a *telling* point of view, "expressing only what he knows from his perspective as an actor in the scene."

122. Cf. Jacques Dupont, "Les discours de Pierre," in *Nouvelles études sur les Actes des Apôtres*, LD 118 (Paris: Éditions du Cerf, 1984), 102; Dunn, *The Acts of the Apostles*, 150; Marshall, *The Acts of the Apostles*, 196; Schneider, *Die Apostelgeschichte*, 2:83; and Talbert, *Reading Acts*, 112. See Kurz, "Effects of Variant Narrators in Acts 10–11," 579–80, who identifies differences between the narrator's point of view and Peter's point of view.

divine guidance that has led Peter to Cornelius's house. Peter's explanation emphasizes again the divine source of that vision and the subsequent instructions (11:4–12).[123] The second aspect repeated here is the divine instruction also given to Cornelius. However, Peter's narration of what has happened includes the additional promise to Cornelius that Peter will deliver a message by which Cornelius and his entire household can receive salvation (σωθήσῃ; 11:14) from God.[124] The third aspect repeated from the previous narrated events is the identification of the coming of the Holy Spirit (ἐπέπεσεν τὸ πνεῦμα τὸ ἅγιον; 11:15) to the Gentiles "just as upon us at the beginning" (ὥσπερ καὶ ἐφ' ἡμᾶς ἐν ἀρχῇ; 11:15), an obvious reference to the events of Pentecost (cf. 10:47).[125] The narrator's description of the coming of the Holy Spirit as the fulfillment of Jesus' words (cf. 1:5; 2:1–4)[126] is affirmed again in Peter's response to his questioners (11:16; cf. Luke 3:16).[127] What has occurred is emphatically reiterated as "the same gift" (τὴν ἴσην δωρεάν; 11:17; cf. 2:38; 10:45) that God has given to the Jewish believers, and Peter accentuates the similarities of God's activity and presence in *both* the Jewish believers *and* the Gentile believers.[128] From Peter's perspective as narrated by Luke, his activity merely recognizes God's intentions and working. According to Peter, his actions affirm what God is doing and do not hinder (κωλῦσαι; 11:17) that divine work at all. Thus, through the character of Peter, the Lukan narrator indirectly affirms the divine work among the Gentiles at Cornelius's house and depicts these Gentile believers similarly to the

---

123. Peter's account stresses the divine role in the events in four ways: (1) the sheet came "from heaven" (ἐκ τοῦ οὐρανοῦ; 11:5, cf. 10:11), (2) the voice responding to Peter's refusal to eat anything "common or unclean" came from heaven (ἐκ τοῦ οὐρανοῦ; 11:9), (3) the sheet was taken back up to heaven (εἰς τὸν οὐρανόν; 11:10; cf. 10:16), and (4) the Spirit instructed him to go with the Caesarean men (11:11–12; cf. 10:19–20).

124. See Johnson, *The Acts of the Apostles*, 198; and Tannehill, *The Narrative Unity of Luke-Acts*, 2:144.

125. Cf. Dupont, "Les discours de Pierre," 102, who observes that some details are omitted, since the point of significance is that the Spirit has been given. Cf. also Bruce, *The Book of the Acts*, 222; Fitzmyer, *The Acts of the Apostles*, 472; and Marshall, *The Acts of the Apostles*, 197–98.

126. Cf. John A. Darr, *On Character Building: The Reader and the Rhetoric of Characterization in Luke-Acts*, LCBI (Louisville: Westminster/John Knox, 1992), 82.

127. See Shepherd, *The Narrative Function of the Holy Spirit*, 204, who identifies the Spirit's function as "a sign of reliability both for the reader and the characters in the story."

128. In the two phrases in the first part of 11:17, the emphatic positions of τὴν ἴσην δωρεάν in the first phrase and ἡμῖν in the second phrase indicate the similarities between "the same gift" received by the Gentiles and that which was received by the Jewish believers.

Jewish ones.[129] The implication of that picture is that the church now includes both Jewish *and* non-Jewish believers, since God has clearly demonstrated God's work and presence among both ethnic groups.

The Petrine explanation of what has occurred in Caesarea dominates the narrative section of Acts 11:1–18, but the narrated response of the believers in Jerusalem concludes that section. The narrator describes that response in two contrasting ways. On the one hand, the Jerusalem believers are silent (ἡσύχασαν; 11:18) after hearing what Peter has to say. While the persistent questions of the Jewish believers in Jerusalem have forced Peter to explain what has happened in Caesarea, his response acknowledging the divine role both in guidance and in the salvation of those who hear his message convinces Peter's critics that they too should not "hinder" God (cf. 11:17). On the other hand, the believers break the silence by praising God (ἐδόξασαν τὸν θεόν), a common response in earlier narrative sections to God's blessing and activity within Jerusalem.[130] This praise is accompanied by the affirmation of what God has done: Ἄρα καὶ τοῖς ἔθνεσιν ὁ θεὸς τὴν μετάνοιαν εἰς ζωὴν ἔδωκεν (then even to the Gentiles God has given the repentance to life; 11:18). The emphatic position of τοῖς ἔθνεσιν, however, accentuates what is significant: God's surprising activity in offering salvation and divine presence *also* to *non-Jews*.[131] Such an acknowledgment confirms the news mentioned in verse 1.

Although such a conclusion acknowledges that what God has done among the believing Gentiles in Caesarea is identical to what has occurred among the believing Jews in Jerusalem, the original question concerning the social interaction between Jews and non-Jews apparently remains unresolved. The Jewish Christians recognize some of the *theological* implications in the events that have happened in Caesarea, but apparently the *social* implications are left pending.[132] The narrative scene thereby concludes with an ambiguous image of the Christian church. The narrator depicts the Jewish believers of Jerusalem as recognizing the same

---

129. See Edith M. Humphrey, "Collision of Modes? — Vision and Determining Argument in Acts 10:1–11:18," *Semeia* 71 (1995): 77–78, who sees this speech as an "eccentric defense."

130. Cf. the use of a form of δοξάζω in 4:21, and the use of forms of αἰνέω in 2:47; 3:8–9.

131. Cf. Brawley, *Centering on God*, 202; and Haenchen, *The Acts of the Apostles*, 359–60.

132. Though the Jewish Christians recognize that their distinctions between themselves and the Gentiles are invalid in terms of salvation, the specific question concerning the social customs remains unanswered. Cf. Krodel, *Acts*, 204–5; and Marshall, *The Acts of the Apostles*, 198. See Neyrey, "The Symbolic Universe of Luke-Acts," 294.

characteristics in the Gentile believers of Caesarea that have characterized themselves as the Christian community and as a people blessed by
God's blessing and presence. However, the unanswered question that has
created the problem in the first place — the question concerning the social
interaction between Jewish and Gentile believers — suggests that these
social and ethnic distinctions may have further narrative implications in
the book of Acts.[133]

An Assessment of the Characterization of the Church or Group of Believers in Acts 11:1–18

The difficult problems of crossing social and ethnic boundaries in
Caesarea are magnified in the larger arena of the Jewish believers in
Jerusalem. The possible offense of a few Jewish believers in Caesarea is
minute compared to the concern that the Jerusalem church raises when
Peter returns to the city. Thus, the narrative scene presents the Jewish
Christians in Jerusalem as critical of Peter's transgression of Jewish cus-
toms concerning the association and eating with non-Jewish persons.
The narrated problem is not the Gentile mission or the proclamation
of the gospel to those of non-Jewish descent; rather, the problem is the
social interaction (table fellowship) with Gentiles that has occurred in
Caesarea (cf. Acts 10:24–29, 48).[134]

The narrated discussion between Peter and the Jewish Christians in
Jerusalem adds new and important material to the ongoing development
of the Christian church as a narrative character in Acts. Luke describes
little action that implicitly characterizes the believers; he provides readers with no direct description or judgments about either character. The
prominent means by which the narrator depicts the Christian community is through the dialogue of these two characters. On the one hand,
the character Peter functions as the implicit spokesperson for Luke, as he
explains about God's activity among the Gentiles gathered in Cornelius's
house. On the other hand, the Jerusalem believers function ambiguously
both as those who recognize God's work among the Gentiles and also

---

133. See Bruce, *The Book of the Acts*, 223, who suggests that some of the "zealous rank
and file" may not have been as enthusiastic as the apostles were. See also Luke T. Johnson,
Decision Making in the Church: A Biblical Model (Philadelphia: Fortress, 1983), 17, who states
that the relations issue is not solved. Cf. Klinghardt, *Gesetz und Volk Gottes*, 222–23.

134. Cf. Dibelius, "The Conversion of Cornelius," 118; Jacob Jervell, "The Law in
Luke-Acts," *HTR* 64 (1971): 26; Johnson, *The Acts of the Apostles*, 200; Pesch, *Die Apostel-
geschichte*, 1:335; Schneider, *Die Apostelgeschichte*, 2:82; and Tyson, *Images of Judaism in
Luke-Acts*, 122.

as those who question any intimate social interaction (such as table fellowship) with these same Gentiles. Thus, while the description of the believers in this passage affirms what the book of Acts has presented thus far about the church, the narrative also describes more obviously the social problems that arise within the Jerusalem church when the gospel message crosses traditional, social boundaries.[135] That these problems threaten one of the characteristic traits of the Christian community — the unanimity of the believers — may encourage readers to identify this unresolved issue as a significant factor in the unfolding plot of the Acts narrative.[136]

THE FIRST CHRISTIANS IN ANTIOCH
(ACTS 11:19–30)

The Literary Context

The previous narrative scenes present the Christian community as the obstacles of social and ethnic distinctions confront and challenge the unanimity that the group of Jewish believers has enjoyed. According to the Acts narrative, the Gentile acceptance of the gospel message apparently is not an issue of contention. The meeting of the Jerusalem church with Peter confirms that God has done God's salvific work even among the Gentiles. This confirmation provides the context, along with the larger context of the entire narrative unit starting with Acts 8:4, in which readers may understand the next section dealing with the first Christians in Antioch.

The Characterization of the Christian Church or Group of Believers in Acts 11:19–30

The narrator begins this section by linking the initial activity with the positive descriptions of earlier parts of the narrative. The first characters mentioned here are the believers scattered by the persecution that followed Stephen's so-called trial (11:19). These persons, οἱ διασπαρέντες, are some of the same Christians whom the narrator has earlier described

---

135. See Jacob Jervell, "The Acts of the Apostles and the History of Early Christianity," *ST* 37 (1983): 25, who observes that this narrative is rather peculiar since it is about "a church which is meant to be an ideal." Cf. Neyrey, "Ceremonies in Luke-Acts," 381.

136. See Pervo, *Profit with Delight*, 40; and Wilson, *The Gentiles and the Gentile Mission in Luke-Acts*, 173–74, who sees this section expressing a principle developed more fully in Acts 15.

as scattering to Judea and Samaria (8:1) and proclaiming the gospel message wherever they go (8:4).[137] Now, however, the geographical stage has expanded: the scattered Christians travel to Phoenicia, Cyprus, and Antioch (11:19). Nonetheless, these portraits of believers are consistent with earlier pictures of the early Christians, as the narrator describes only one action: they are "speaking the word" (11:19).[138] That activity is confined only to the Jews (μηδενὶ ... εἰ μὴ μόνον 'Ιουδαίοις; 11:19).[139] The reader of Acts will probably not find this limitation surprising, even after the last two chapters. The text mentions nothing of success or opposition, however, leaving the reader to draw conclusions about such responses described earlier in the narrative.[140] Again, the narrator presents the Christian community, even in its dispersion, as the bearer of the gospel message.

The next part of the narrative description of these scattered believers, however, takes a different turn. A part of these scattered believers include some Jewish men from Cyprus and Cyrene (ἦσαν δέ τινες ἐξ αὐτῶν ἄνδρες Κύπριοι καὶ Κυρηναῖοι; 11:20): they thus are not originally from Judea but are part of the Diaspora and can be designated as Hellenistic Jews.[141] These Jewish men arrive in Antioch and proclaim the gospel message (εὐαγγελιζόμενοι τὸν κύριον 'Ιησοῦν) to the "Hellenists" (πρὸς τοὺς 'Ελληνιστάς).[142] The contrast between this activity and the previous activity of speaking only to Jews (11:19) implies that this latter proclamation in Acts is directed also (καί) to the Gentiles.[143] As for earlier

---

137. Cf., e.g., Fitzmyer, *The Acts of the Apostles*, 475; Johnson, *The Acts of the Apostles*, 202; Kurz, *Reading Luke-Acts*, 89; Pesch, *Die Apostelgeschichte*, 1:351; Schneider, *Die Apostelgeschichte*, 2:87–89; and Christoph Zettner, *Amt, Gemeinde und kirchliche Einheit in der Apostelgeschichte des Lukas* (New York: Peter Lang, 1991), 268.

138. Cf. Zingg, *Das Wachsen der Kirche*, 202–3.

139. See ibid., 204, who sees an implicit reference to the synagogue as the starting point of this proclamation.

140. See Pesch, *Die Apostelgeschichte*, 1:351; Weiser, *Die Apostelgeschichte*, 275; and Zettner, *Amt, Gemeinde und kirchliche Einheit*, 269, who do not see this as Lukan material because of no negative Jewish behavior.

141. Cf., e.g., Marie-Émile Boismard and Arnaud Lamouille, *Les Actes des deux Apôtres*, 3 vols. ÉBib (Paris: J. Gabalda, 1990), 2:67; Bruce, *The Book of the Acts*, 225; Johnson, *The Acts of the Apostles*, 203; and Zingg, *Das Wachsen der Kirche*, 204.

142. Other Greek manuscripts have "Ελληνας (Greeks) rather than 'Ελληνιστάς (11:20). See Metzger, *A Textual Commentary on the Greek New Testament*, 386–89. See also Barrett, *The Acts of the Apostles*, 1:550–51; Fitzmyer, *The Acts of the Apostles*, 476; Haenchen, *The Acts of the Apostles*, 365n5; and Zingg, *Das Wachsen der Kirche*, 205–6.

143. Cf., e.g., Bruce, *The Book of the Acts*, 225–26; Pesch, *Die Apostelgeschichte*, 1:351–52; Sanders, *The Jews in Luke-Acts*, 257; and Schneider, *Die Apostelgeschichte*, 2:89.

scenes in Jerusalem and Caesarea, Luke describes a favorable response to what the scattered believers proclaim as the "hand of the Lord" (ἦν χεὶρ κυρίου; 11:21) being found among the believers (μετ᾽ αὐτῶν) who have traveled to these new areas.[144] The success of this proclamation, which Luke describes as πολύς τε ἀριθμὸς ὁ πιστεύσας ἐπέστρεψεν ἐπὶ τὸν κύριον (11:21), along with the explicit mention of the role of the divine presence, alludes to earlier intratextual images of positive responses to the gospel (cf. 2:41, 47; 4:4; 6:7; 9:31).[145] However, what is different about this specific scene is that this acceptance of the gospel message implicitly includes both Jews and non-Jews.[146] For the first time in the Acts narrative, the large numbers of new believers include non-Jews, suggesting that the Christian community in Antioch joins Jews and non-Jews together as part of the church.[147]

Reports concerning what has happened in Antioch reach the Jerusalem church.[148] The sending of Barnabas by the Jerusalem church to Antioch functions within the narrative as a confirmation of what the narrator has just briefly described.[149] The narrator describes what Barnabas sees as the "grace of God" (τὴν χάριν τοῦ θεοῦ; 11:23), which correlates with the earlier statement that "the hand of God" is with the proclaiming

---

144. The pronoun αὐτῶν (11:21) probably refers to the scattered believers in general, with the expression τινες ἐξ αὐτῶν (11:20) referring specifically to those scattered believers who proclaimed the gospel message to the Hellenists. Cf. Zingg, *Das Wachsen der Kirche*, 191, 198. Contra Williams, *Acts*, 203–4.

145. Cf. Haenchen, *The Acts of the Apostles*, 366; Johnson, *The Acts of the Apostles*, 203; and Schille, *Die Apostelgeschichte des Lukas*, 263.

146. Cf. Krodel, *Acts*, 207; Larkin, *Acts*, 176–77; and Weiser, *Die Apostelgeschichte*, 277. Contra Boismard and Lamouille, *Les Actes des deux Apôtres*, 2:67–68, who see this as a description of the conversion only of Gentiles; and Schneider, *Die Apostelgeschichte*, 2:85, 90.

147. The fact that these Jewish believers are part of the Diaspora and are more accustomed to social interaction with non-Jews may explain no mention of discord or disagreement between Jewish and non-Jewish believers in Antioch. Cf. Brawley, *Centering on God*, 40; and Marshall, *The Acts of the Apostles*, 201.

148. See Zingg, *Das Wachsen der Kirche*, 185, 208, who suggests that Barnabas possibly is sent because of rumors that have reached Jerusalem.

149. Although many have interpreted Jerusalem's action as a Lukan affirmation of the authority of the Jerusalem church, nothing in this scene suggests that the church functions in that manner. Although the Jerusalem church sent Peter and John to Samaria, leading to the reception of the Holy Spirit through them (8:17), they now send Barnabas to Antioch, who simply encourages in a manner consistent with the narrator's explicit characterization of him in 4:36. Cf. Haenchen, *The Acts of the Apostles*, 367; Johnson, *The Acts of the Apostles*, 207–8; and Tannehill, *The Narrative Unity of Luke-Acts*, 2:147. Contra Boismard and Lamouille, *Les Actes des deux Apôtres*, 2:68, 196; Bruce, *The Book of the Acts*, 226–27; and Pervo, *Profit with Delight*, 54.

believers (11:21; cf. 4:33; 6:8).[150] Barnabas responds to these Antioch believers by rejoicing (ἐχάρη)[151] and encouraging them to "remain faithful to the Lord" (παρεκάλει πάντας τῇ προθέσει τῆς καρδίας προσμένειν τῷ κυρίῳ; 11:23).[152] Such a response is consistent with the earlier characterization of Barnabas (4:36), and the narrator bolsters this developing picture by grammatically linking (ὅτι) to it an explicit description of Barnabas as a good man (ἀνὴρ ἀγαθός), who was "full of the Holy Spirit and faith" (πλήρης πνεύματος ἁγίου καὶ πίστεως; 11:24).[153] Therefore, Barnabas functions in this narrative as a reliable eyewitness, who indirectly confirms the narrator's description of the fledgling Christian community in Antioch. The mention of continuing success in conjunction with Barnabas's observations and actions (11:24),[154] as "a large crowd of people was added" (προσετέθη ὄχλος ἱκανός), insinuates to the reader that the same divine activity may be discovered in this group of believers in Antioch as in the Jerusalem believers (cf. 2:41, 47; 5:14).[155] Thus, the Lukan description of the church in Antioch reflects similar imagery to that found in the descriptions of the Jerusalem believers, but now the believers are not merely from a Jewish heritage but also include Gentiles.

The narrator concludes this aspect of the characterization of the Antioch church by reintroducing Saul into the narrative. After Barnabas departs to find Saul in Tarsus, they return to the church in Antioch. Luke reports that these two Jewish men stay in the city for an entire year, during which time they meet with the church (συναχθῆναι ἐν τῇ ἐκκλησίᾳ; 11:26; cf. 4:31) and teach a large crowd of people (διδάξαι ὄχλον ἱκανόν; 11:26; cf. 11:24).[156] Such a description implies that both

150. Cf. Zingg, *Das Wachsen der Kirche*, 210.

151. See Barrett, *The Acts of the Apostles*, 1:552, who observes the play on words with χάριν and ἐχάρη (11:23).

152. See Larkin, *Acts*, 178; and Williams, *Acts*, 204, who both correctly identify the imperfect tense of the indicative παρεκάλει, which suggests that this is Barnabas's customary practice (11:23).

153. The characterization of Barnabas (11:24) corresponds to the description of Stephen (6:5). Cf., e.g., Bruce, *The Book of the Acts*, 227; Fitzmyer, *The Acts of the Apostles*, 477; Weiser, *Die Apostelgeschichte*, 277–78; and Zingg, *Das Wachsen der Kirche*, 210–13.

154. The conjunction καί functions to connect this success to Barnabas's actions (11:24). Cf. Williams, *Acts*, 205.

155. Cf. Dunn, *The Acts of the Apostles*, 155–56; Tannehill, *The Narrative Unity of Luke-Acts*, 2:147–48; and Zingg, *Das Wachsen der Kirche*, 213.

156. Luke again uses a form of συνάγω to describe the believers' togetherness (cf. 4:31). Cf. Zettner, *Amt, Gemeinde und kirchliche Einheit*, 273, who sees their teaching task as given by the Jerusalem church.

Barnabas and Saul actively join together with this "mixed" group of Jewish and Gentile believers.[157] The narrative depiction of what happens there among the Antioch believers, however, includes a third aorist infinitival phrase: χρηματίσαι τε πρώτως ἐν Ἀντιοχείᾳ τοὺς μαθητὰς Χριστιανούς (and it was in Antioch that the disciples were first called "Christians"; 11:26).[158] The phrase suggests that the designation comes from those outside the group of believers and that others perceive the Christians as a group that is separate from the synagogue, or at least from other forms of Judaism.[159] The reader should not be surprised that this is the first time that such a distinction has been made in the book of Acts, since the Lukan narrator depicts the Christian community in Antioch as the first local church that includes persons from both Jewish and Gentile backgrounds.

Although the narrator briefly describes the Antioch church with images that allude to earlier affirmative depictions of the Jerusalem church, the last part of Acts 11:19–30 highlights a specific example of action by the Antioch believers that reflects the nature of that Christian community.[160] Luke tells of prophets who arrive in Antioch from Jerusalem. One of those prophets predicts a worldwide famine that will occur during the rule of Claudius — a prediction given credibility by the narrator's explicit description that the source of that prediction is the Spirit (διὰ τοῦ πνεύματος; 11:28).[161] In response to that prediction, Luke narrates in 11:29 that everyone (ἕκαστος αὐτῶν) of the Antioch believers

---

157. Contra Zettner, ibid., 277, who suggests that they taught only Gentile believers.

158. The aorist indicative ἐγένετο (11:26) is followed by three aorist infinitives that describe what happens. However, the third infinitive is distinguished from the first two infinitives, which are linked by καί.

159. Cf., e.g., Barrett, *The Acts of the Apostles*, 1:556–57; Fitzmyer, *The Acts of the Apostles*, 477–78; Haenchen, *The Acts of the Apostles*, 363–64; Johnson, *The Acts of the Apostles*, 204–5; and Weiser, *Die Apostelgeschichte*, 274, 278–79. See Martin Hengel, *Acts and the History of Earliest Christianity*, trans. John Bowden (Philadelphia: Fortress, 1979), 103, who suggests that Roman authorities in Antioch use the designation to distinguish between the Jewish synagogue and the church.

160. See Fitzmyer, *The Acts of the Apostles*, 481; Schneider, *Die Apostelgeschichte*, 2:94–95; and Zettner, *Amt, Gemeinde und kirchliche Einheit*, 276–77, who stress that this example is linked to the previous narrative materials by the phrase ἐν ταύταις δὲ ταῖς ἡμέραις (11:27).

161. For studies that deal with the historical difficulties of this prediction, see, e.g., Fitzmyer, *The Acts of the Apostles*, 481–82; Haenchen, *The Acts of the Apostles*, 376–78; Johnson, *The Acts of the Apostles*, 205–6; Schneider, *Die Apostelgeschichte*, 2:95–96; and Bruce W. Winter, "Acts and Food Shortages," in *The Book of Acts in Its Graeco-Roman Setting*, ed. David W. J. Gill and Conrad Gempf, BAFCS (Grand Rapids: Eerdmans, 1994), 59–78.

decides (ὥρισαν)[162] to send whatever one was able to give to the believers living in Judea (τοῖς κατοικοῦσιν ἐν τῇ Ἰουδαίᾳ ἀδελφοῖς). The Antioch Christians thus give financial resources as ministry (εἰς διακονίαν) or assistance to those in Judea.[163] Luke provides no other reason for such benevolence, except that the believers respond to the prediction of the famine.[164] Some scholars suggest that this response by the Antioch believers is an act of reciprocity for what Jerusalem has provided in terms of the gospel and the prophetic message.[165] While this interpretation has merit, the narrative accentuates the action of this Christian community of both Jewish and Gentile believers toward the Jewish believers of Jerusalem.[166] Though the previous scene depicting the Jerusalem church tells about believers who wrestle with the issue of associating with Gentile believers, this mixed group seeks to provide for the needs of the Jewish believers in Judea. This glimpse of the church in Antioch will remind readers of earlier narrative descriptions of the Jerusalem church, characterizing the believers as providing for all who have need (cf. 2:44–45; 4:34).[167] Luke's narration of such action on the part of the Antioch believers creates a particularly striking image of that Christian community, given the fact that the predicted famine will be felt not only in Judea but also "over the whole world" (ἐφ᾽ ὅλην τὴν οἰκουμένην; 11:28), including Antioch.[168] The initial narrative portrait of the church in Antioch, therefore, depicts that group as one concerned about providing for others'

---

162. The four other appearances of ὁρίζω in Acts (2:23; 10:42; 17:26, 31) refer to God's activity. This Lukan usage suggests that the Antioch Christians are to be seen in a positive light, as the believers make decisions and act in ways similar to God's action. Cf. Karl Ludwig Schmidt, "ὁρίζω," in *TDNT*, 5:452–53.

163. The Lukan use of διακονία includes both gospel proclamation (1:17, 25; 6:4) and assistance of the needy (6:1). Cf. Haenchen, *The Acts of the Apostles*, 375; Tannehill, *The Narrative Unity of Luke-Acts*, 2:148; and Williams, *Acts*, 206–7.

164. Cf. Bruce, *The Book of the Acts*, 230; Haenchen, *The Acts of the Apostles*, 379; and Schneider, *Die Apostelgeschichte*, 2:94. Contra Jacques Dupont, "La communauté des biens aux premiers jours de l'Eglise (Actes 2,42.44–45; 4,32.34–35)," in *Études sur les Actes des Apôtres*, LD 45 (Paris: Éditions du Cerf, 1967), 511–12.

165. See, e.g., Haenchen, *The Acts of the Apostles*, 375; Johnson, *The Acts of the Apostles*, 208–9; Krodel, *Acts*, 209–10; and Zingg, *Das Wachsen der Kirche*, 186.

166. Since the narrative suggests that the cause of the gospel being taken to Antioch is the scattering of the believers and not the initiative of the Jerusalem church, a view of this collection as an act of reciprocity to the Judean believers is unwarranted. Cf. Bruce, *The Book of the Acts*, 230–31; Larkin, *Acts*, 180; and Schmithals, *Die Apostelgeschichte des Lukas*, 113.

167. Cf. Pesch, *Die Apostelgeschichte*, 1:357; and Tannehill, *The Narrative Unity of Luke-Acts*, 2:148–49, both of whom compare this action to Barnabas's act (4:36–37).

168. Cf. Barrett, *The Acts of the Apostles*, 1:561; and Dunn, *The Acts of the Apostles*, 157.

needs — even the needs of those outside of their immediate group and in another region.

An Assessment of the Characterization of the Church or Group of Believers in Acts 11:19–30

The accumulation of imagery in the ancient narrative is a significant factor in the reading process and experience. The characterization of the Christian community in Acts 11:19–30 is an excellent illustration of the accumulation of various descriptions that will potentially affect the reader in moving progressively through an ancient narrative. The description of the church in Antioch stands significantly in the Acts narrative as it both compares and contrasts with images of the Jerusalem church. The narrator portrays the Antioch church with images of the ideal community, images used earlier to describe the Jerusalem believers.[169] In particular, the depiction of the believers in Antioch presents them as demonstrating communal concerns of benevolence toward the Jerusalem believers that are similar to those that characterized the Jerusalem believers in the initial stages of the Acts narrative (cf. 11:29–30; 2:44–45; 4:34). Also, the description of the Antioch church connects these communal bonds with divine presence and blessing (cf. 11:21, 23–24), reflecting similar emphases found in the narrative summaries in Acts 2–5 (2:42–47; 4:32–37; 5:12–16). Clearly, the Lukan narrator describes the Antioch believers as a Christian community similar to the Jerusalem church. Here in the Acts narrative we see the first time-extended description of a Christian community that consists of *both* Jews *and* Gentiles; hence, the comparison is all the more significant for two reasons.[170] On the one hand, while the previous narrative scene presents the difficulties for the Jewish believers in accepting Gentiles as "fellow" believers in terms of social interaction, no such problem is mentioned for the Antioch believers.[171] For the first time in the Acts narrative, Luke characterizes the Christian community as a group of believers in which the gospel message transcends the social and ethnic distinctions between Jews and

---

169. Cf. Pesch, *Die Apostelgeschichte*, 1:357–58; Schneider, *Die Apostelgeschichte*, 2:94; and Zettner, *Amt, Gemeinde und kirchliche Einheit*, 277.

170. While the events in Caesarea concluded with a description of Christian community (10:44–48), the problem of Jewish association with non-Jews remained. Also, that depiction of a group of believers includes a smaller group of Gentiles and one Jew, Peter. Thus, while Peter chose to stay with this group of Gentile believers, the description of the Antioch church includes a larger number of persons, more Jewish believers, and a longer period of time.

171. Cf. Bruce, *The Book of the Acts*, 228; and Conzelmann, *Acts of the Apostles*, 87–88.

Gentiles — a group of believers distinguished primarily by the presence and grace of God and by the communal bonds that join it together.[172] On the other hand, the inclusiveness that characterizes the church in Antioch also relates to the label of "Christians," given to the church there, to identify the group of believers distinguished from other Jewish or religious groups. Thus, the positive characteristics that Luke has reserved for Jewish believers in earlier narrative scenes now apply to a group of believers not restricted to those of Jewish heritage.

ANOTHER LOOK AT THE CHURCH IN JERUSALEM
(ACTS 12:1–19)

The Literary Context

The positive portrayal of the Antioch Christians in the previous narrative section includes their notable response of benevolence toward the Judean Christians. Though the famine will include the Antiochans, and though the social barriers between the Jews and Gentiles often prevent such hospitable action, the narrator affirmatively describes the church in Antioch, which is characterized by both divine presence and communal bonds that imply a unanimous attitude. The narrated collection for the believers in Judea, therefore, returns the reader's focus to Jerusalem.

The Characterization of the Church or Group of Believers in Acts 12:1–19

Luke begins this narrative section by stating briefly that King Herod has responded violently against some who belong to the church (12:1). Although Luke offers no explanation for such action,[173] the execution of the apostle James implicitly reflects negatively on the ruler, since the reader will find nothing in the first eleven chapters to warrant such hostile action against any Christian (12:2).[174] However, the narrator states that the Jews favorably endorse (ἀρεστόν) Herod's actions, so that the presented scene is again one of general opposition and hostility toward the believers in Jerusalem (12:3).[175] Peter's arrest (12:3–4)

---

172. Cf. Pesch, *Die Apostelgeschichte*, 1:354–55.

173. See Schille, *Die Apostelgeschichte des Lukas*, 261, who finds such scarce information surprising.

174. This implicitly negative picture of Herod compares with Jewish actions against Stephen in Acts 6–7; the believers are never described as doing anything deserving such opposition.

175. This scene of opposition both compares and contrasts with earlier depictions of opposition in Jerusalem. On the one hand, while initial descriptions of opposition have been

suggests that these hostile reactions might have something to do with what has occurred in Caesarea.[176] Nonetheless, Luke describes the Jerusalem Christians consistently with earlier depictions of them. While Peter is kept in prison, the church prays earnestly (ἐκτενῶς; 12:5), which is typical action for the Jerusalem believers in the first several chapters of Acts (cf. 1:14, 24–25; 2:42; 3:1; 4:24–31).[177] Such narrated activity also will potentially stimulate in the reader a sense of anticipation of what God may do, since these prior descriptions of prayer by the believers invariably resulted in a divine response.[178] This description of the church praying for Peter (περὶ αὐτοῦ) assists the audience in anticipating his divine rescue, which is a common occurrence in the book of Acts (cf. 5:17–21; 16:23–29).[179] The narration of Peter's divine rescue from prison confirms what the story anticipates, as Luke highlights an angel's role in saving Peter's life.[180] This rescue from prison implicitly suggests that God is on the side of the Christians, not on the side of Herod or the Jews.

The narration of the subsequent events after Peter's rescue presents an ambiguous image of the church in Jerusalem. Luke states in verse 12 that many have gathered (συνηθροισμένοι)[181] at the house of Mary (the mother of John Mark) and are praying (προσευχόμενοι), thereby linking the activity with that mentioned in verse 5.[182] The narrator states that

---

limited to the Sadducees and temple officials (Acts 4–5), opposition expanded beyond the Jewish leaders to include the Jewish people (6:12; cf. 9:29). On the other hand, no opposition from political officials has been included in Acts 1–11. Cf. Zettner, *Amt, Gemeinde und kirchliche Einheit*, 278, who identifies these opponents as θεομάχοι (cf. 5:39). Cf. also Krodel, *Acts*, 214; Tannehill, *The Narrative Unity of Luke-Acts*, 2:151; and Sanders, *The Jews in Luke-Acts*, 258.

176. Cf. Bruce, *The Book of the Acts*, 233–34, 240; and Zettner, *Amt, Gemeinde und kirchliche Einheit*, 278.

177. The emphatic position of προσευχή places the focus on what the church is doing (12:5). See Larkin, *Acts*, 183, who observes that the verbal construction indicates duration. Cf. Bruce, *The Book of the Acts*, 235; Fitzmyer, *The Acts of the Apostles*, 487; Haenchen, *The Acts of the Apostles*, 208; and Williams, *Acts*, 212.

178. Cf. Johnson, *The Acts of the Apostles*, 211.

179. Cf. ibid., 217; Pervo, *Profit with Delight*, 21; and Weiser, *Die Apostelgeschichte*, 1:290.

180. In the narration of Peter's rescue, an "angel of the Lord" (ἄγγελος κυρίου; 12:7) functions as a major character. Peter passively does what the angel tells him to do (cf. 12:9, 11). Cf. Marshall, *The Acts of the Apostles*, 209; and Williams, *Acts*, 212–13.

181. The verb συναθροίζω, which appears in the NT only here (12:12) and in 19:25, connotes a collection or gathering together. The prefix σύν accentuates this sense of being together.

182. Cf. Haenchen, *The Acts of the Apostles*, 385; Johnson, *The Acts of the Apostles*, 213; and Fitzmyer, *The Acts of the Apostles*, 488.

Peter goes to Mary's house after realizing that God has indeed rescued him but does not explain why Peter would go there. Nonetheless, his arrival precipitates a comedy of responses.[183] First, the one who goes to open the gate where Peter is knocking leaves him standing there as she joyfully (ἀπὸ τῆς χαρᾶς; 12:14) returns to tell the others the good news.[184] Then, the ones praying for Peter think the maid is "out of her mind" (Μαίνῃ; 12:15) and only discover Peter when they finally open the gate due to his incessant knocking (12:16). The narrative scene has an ironic character, as these Jewish believers praying for Peter do not immediately recognize the answer to their own prayers.[185] The believers have prayed but apparently expect Peter's death (cf. 12:15) rather than his deliverance.[186] Luke concludes this section by having Peter explain how "the Lord" (ὁ κύριος; 12:17) has delivered him, and then Peter departs, presumably to a safer place (12:17). Although the believers misunderstood, the clear picture is one of divine power and intervention, over against a political power that cannot stop the gospel.[187]

An Assessment of the Characterization of the Church or Group of Believers in Acts 12:1–19

The brief descriptions of the Jerusalem believers in Acts 12 ambiguously present that group in relation to Peter's arrest and rescue. For the first time in the Acts narrative, the civil authorities responded with hostility toward the Jerusalem church, actions that correspond with an increasingly widening gap between the Jews and the Christians.[188] The positive picture of the believers as those who persistently pray on Peter's behalf carries consistently throughout this narrative section — an image that alludes to the earlier instances of the prayerful activity among the

---

183. Cf. Johnson, *The Acts of the Apostles*, 218; and Pervo, *Profit with Delight*, 62–63.

184. See Johnson, *The Acts of the Apostles*, 213, who compares this response to those found in Hellenistic romances, in which characters' emotions prevent them from acting appropriately.

185. See Pervo, *Profit with Delight*, 63: "Peter is rescued at the last minute, in response to a praying community somewhat skeptical about the power of prayer."

186. Cf. Witherington, *The Acts of the Apostles*, 385.

187. See Tannehill, *The Narrative Unity of Luke-Acts*, 2:156: "This ironic perspective on central characters is a way of celebrating God's power. It also serves to remind humans, including the insiders favored by the narrator, of the continuing gap between human understanding and the wonder of God's ways. The church, too, experiences God ironically. New discoveries of the wonder of God are also discoveries of its own myopia."

188. See Sanders, *The Jews in Luke-Acts*, 258; and Tannehill, *The Narrative Unity of Luke-Acts*, 2:157, who both state that Peter's thanksgiving to God (12:11) reiterates the opposition by the Jewish people.

Jerusalem believers. However, the surprising initial response of the praying church to Peter's divine rescue presents an ironic picture, as Luke
describes their confusion rather than their expectant recognition. The
Jerusalem church prayed but had difficulties recognizing what God had
done. This peculiar story presents another scene that clearly indicates the
church's unstoppable mission, due to God's direct involvement. However, the puzzling reaction of the praying believers leaves an ambiguous
picture of the Jerusalem church in the mind of the reader.

THE CHARACTERIZATION OF THE CHRISTIAN CHURCHES OR GROUPS OF BELIEVERS IN JERUSALEM AND BEYOND (ACTS 8:4–12:25)

The previous narrative unit of Acts 1:1–8:3 focuses on the events involving the Jewish believers in Jerusalem. The characterization of the
church in Jerusalem accentuates the unanimity, κοινωνία, proclamation
of the gospel message, and divine presence and blessing that readers may
observe in the group's actions and in the dynamics among members of
that group. The hostile opposition of the Jewish leaders and, finally, the
Jewish people result in the scattering of these believers to other surrounding regions (cf. 8:1b). However, the Lukan description of the scattered
church ironically depicts continuing success as the gospel message is proclaimed to persons in these other regions (cf. 8:4; 11:19–21). As a result,
the narrative describes groups of believers not only in Jerusalem, but also
in Damascus, Caesarea, and Antioch of Syria. Although the spread of the
gospel as narrated by Luke results in a widening geographical area, much
of the Lukan depiction of the believers in this larger area remains consistent with the depiction of the Jerusalem believers in the first narrative
unit. Thus, the narrator depicts the believers in these cities as groups
blessed by God's presence and power (cf. 9:22, 31; 10:44–48; 11:21),
as proclaimers of the gospel (cf. 9:20, 28; 10:34–43; 11:19–20), and as
communities that meet the needs of one another (cf. 9:23–25, 29–30;
11:27–30). In this narrative unit the depictions of the various Christian communities are not detailed, nor are they similar to the narrative
summaries that the narrator has employed frequently in the previous
unit. Rather, these descriptions implicitly reflect much of the affirmative
images of the Christian community presented in the first seven chapters
of Acts. The narrator, then, alludes to those intratextual images as he
utilizes two different means of implicit characterization in describing the

Christian believers in this narrative unit: through the observation of reliable characters (e.g., Peter and Barnabas), and through the narrator's observation of the believers' actions and of their interaction with opponents.[189] The narrator's allusion to the earlier images of the Jerusalem believers clearly depicts these various groups as people who also belong to God.

The expanding geographical context of the Acts narrative, however, also reflects the broadening diversity in the location of groups of believers. The focus in the narrative unit of Acts 8:4–12:25 is no longer confined to the church in Jerusalem. As the gospel message is proclaimed, the narrative describes new groups of believers that naturally form. However, the Lukan description of these groups does not directly focus on the formal relationship between these local groups and the Jerusalem church. To be sure, the Jerusalem church functions as the body that confirms what God has done in other areas. When one considers the paradigmatic depiction of that group in the previous narrative unit, such a function will accentuate the similarities between these new groups and the Jerusalem church. However, since Luke employs the term ἐκκλησία in specific reference to the Jerusalem believers in the previous narrative unit (5:11; 8:1b, 3), one might ask whether each new group is also an ἐκκλησία (an assembly of people belonging to God) or a part of one ἐκκλησία. The narrative nature of Acts does not explicate this matter, but the term's use in this unit to describe both the local group (cf. 11:22, 26; 12:1, 5) and the Christians in general (cf. 9:31) suggests that *both* the local group of believers *and* these groups together are rightly to be called the ἐκκλησία, the assembly of God's people, demonstrated by κοινωνία (cf. 9:23–25, 29–30; 11:27–30) and divine blessing (cf. 12:17). The Lukan narrative focuses the reader's attention on the identification of these groups of believers as those belonging to God, as those who also are the recipients of the blessing and promise of God, like the believers in Jerusalem.

The growing diversity that accompanies the broadening geographical area leads to the proclamation of the gospel message both to peripheral people and to Gentiles, thus making these similarities in characterization all the more striking. Luke has shown that God ordains such

---

189. A basic feature of the characterization of the opponents, particularly the Jews, is that these persons not only oppose the Christians but also God, whom the reader will observe as present among the believers.

proclamation even to the Gentiles, from whom the Jews have distinguished themselves. The narrator's description of Gentile acceptance of the gospel both in Caesarea and in Antioch highlights that the narrator understood these Gentile believers to be included among those who belong to God. With such obvious indications in the narrative, two pictures of Christian communities — one in Jerusalem, and one in Antioch — in chapter 11 present differing responses to what God has done. On the one hand, while the Jerusalem church affirms that Gentiles may be offered the gospel, the social and ethnic distinctions between Jews and Gentiles are a point of contention and remain unresolved. Unanimity characterizes the Jerusalem believers, without the complications from Jewish–Gentile tensions. Thus, unanimity between Jews and non-Jews is another matter, and these Jewish believers have serious problems with such an idea — problems that hint at opposition against God (cf. Acts 11:17). On the other hand, the Antioch believers apparently include both Jews and Gentiles, with no narrated indications of tension or difficulties. The characterization of this Christian community is one that affirms the presence and blessing of God, as well as an attitude of communal sharing that extends even to the Jerusalem believers.

The contrast between these pictures of two churches underscores the struggles and differences between the two groups, both of which are identified by the narrator as believers. One Christian community apparently focuses on social and ethnic distinctions in identifying themselves as people belonging to God; the other Christian community apparently focuses on the blessing and activity of God in persons without regard for such traditional distinctions. The Lukan characterization of the Jerusalem church, therefore, accentuates the division potentially created by a focus on traditional categories that identifies the people of God. The depiction of the church in Antioch, however, emphasizes the blessing of God and the κοινωνία among the believers — a group in which such divisive distinctions do not play a decisive narrative role.[190] Thus, the narrator subtly employs the contrasting images of division and unanimity once again, but now those images appear in the characterization of these two churches.[191]

---

190. The designation "Christian" (11:26) also emphasizes this point, distinguishing the Christian community from the synagogue.

191. Cf. Hubert Cancik, "The History of Culture, Religion, and Institutions in Ancient Historiography: Philological Observations concerning Luke's History," *JBL* 116 (Winter 1997): 679–80.

As the narrative depicts two groups that might be called "people of God" in Acts 1:1–8:3 by contrasting the divisive behavior of the Jewish leaders and, ultimately, the Jewish people with the unanimous behavior of the believers, here in Acts 8:4–12:25 readers find similar imagery that contrasts the Jerusalem church and the Antioch church. Although the Jerusalem believers have not rejected the gospel, their challenges against Peter and the unresolved issue *potentially* threaten to divide the Christian community and to destroy the characteristic of unanimity that Luke has linked in the Acts narrative with the presence and blessing of God. The observed unanimity among the believers in Antioch, however, affirms the blessing of God upon them. Therefore, the Lukan narrative's utilization of the contrasting images of division and unanimity in Acts 8:4–12:25 creates two differing examples of those who claim to be God's people, two examples among those characterized as Christian believers, as those who belong to God, as those who together are ἡ ἐκκλησία. However, readers may only discover these different examples when they keep each portrait of a different local church (in a specific location) in its respective place within the narrative action and cast of characters. That the potential contrasts between these two pictures of Christian communities have only begun to become apparent in this narrative unit suggests the possibility that these pictures may be developed further in the next narrative unit of the book of Acts.

FOUR

THE CHURCHES
IN THE ROMAN EMPIRE
AS NARRATIVE CHARACTERS
(ACTS 13:1–28:31)

The first twelve chapters of Acts describe the Christian community within a widening geographical circle. The beginning narrative unit (Acts 1:1–8:3) focuses on the Christian community as a group of Jewish believers within the city of Jerusalem; the next narrative unit (8:4–12:25) describes the Christian church that has evolved as a result of the persecution following the Stephen incident. The scattering of these Jewish believers to the surrounding regions does not destroy the Christian community and its gospel proclamation. Rather, these believers continue to "speak the word" (cf. 11:19) in new locations to various groups of people. Thus, the Christians proclaim the gospel message to "peripheral" people in relation to the Jews and even address that message to Gentiles. With the broadening geographical area in which the believers are found also comes an enlarging circle of increasingly diverse people who hear and accept the message of salvation, a phenomenon that the guidance, power, and blessing of God legitimizes. The narrative of the first twelve chapters depicts these diverse people — both those who have historically been identified as God's people and those who have not been so identified — as part of the Christian community or the church in which the presence of God is found as a result of their belief and acceptance of the gospel message.

The divine role in what has occurred, however, does not eliminate the possibility of confusion and questions. If the social and ethnic distinctions that have given the Jewish people their identity as the people of

God continue to separate Jews and non-Jews, the Lukan presentation implies that the result will not only be the thwarting of God's saving activity among the non-Jews but also distinctions among the believers and their division. However, the narrator depicts the people of the church as those who belong to God, are blessed by God's presence, proclaim the gospel message, and enjoy genuine κοινωνία that makes no distinction between them. The pictures of the churches in Jerusalem and in Antioch, juxtaposed in Acts 11, vividly contrast the potential ramifications of two differing Christian perspectives of what it means to be the church, a Christian community, a people of God. On the one hand, a perspective that emphasizes social and ethnic distinctions creates the potential for division and exclusion. On the other hand, a perspective that emphasizes obedience and recognition of God's sometimes surprising activity creates the potential for unanimity and inclusion.

The third narrative unit of the book of Acts, 13:1–28:31, continues to describe churches or groups of believers as significant characters in that literary work. Given the earlier depictions of Christians proclaiming the gospel message and of diverse people accepting that message as the result of divine guidance and activity, the narrative will potentially create a sense of anticipation in the reader of what may occur as the word of God continues to spread. The differing perspectives concerning what it means to be the Christian community or ἡ ἐκκλησία during the early years of the Christian movement will be important issues in shaping the developing identity and nature of the Christian church.

The Church in Antioch Sends
Barnabas and Saul (Acts 13:1–3)

The Literary Context

The previous narrative unit of Acts 8:4–12:25 describes the activities of different churches in a context of growing geographical, ethnic, and social implications. The contrast between the two pictures of the Jerusalem church and the Antioch church in Acts 11 reflects the potential implications of the narrative events, which are explicitly portrayed by the narrator's descriptions and by reliable characters within those events as ordained and instigated by God. However, the Lukan depiction of the inclusive character of the Antioch believers presents them as an ideal Christian community, embodying not only the positive features of the

Jerusalem believers (cf. 1:1–8:3; 11:21–30) but also the κοινωνία of the gospel, and transcending social obstacles that typically separate persons rather than uniting them. The expanding geographical and ethnic setting of the believers' activities implicitly suggests that the Antioch church, not the Jerusalem church, will take the initiative in spreading the Christian message to other parts of the Roman Empire.[1]

The Characterization of the Church or Group of Believers in Acts 13:1–3

The narrator begins the third narrative unit (Acts 13:1–28:31) by focusing on the church in Antioch.[2] The scarcity of details in describing that group indicates that Luke is relying on the earlier positive depiction of that church (cf. 11:19–30). Thus, what the narrative includes here contributes to the characterization of the Antioch church developed earlier. The naming of five persons who are "prophets and teachers" (13:1)[3] confirms what the reader has already seen in the Antioch believers (cf. 11:26–27).[4] Both the previous description and this brief statement in 13:1 allude to earlier positive pictures of the Jerusalem church (cf. 2:42).[5]

---

1. Cf. Paul Zingg, *Das Wachsen der Kirche: Beiträge zur Frage der lukanischen Redaktion und Theologie*, OBO (Göttingen: Vandenhoeck & Ruprecht, 1974), 152.

2. See Luke T. Johnson, *The Acts of the Apostles*, SP 5 (Collegeville, MN: Liturgical Press, 1992), 220, who briefly considers two different meanings for the expression κατὰ τὴν οὖσαν ἐκκλησίαν (13:1).

3. Forms of προφήτης and προφητεύω appear 34 times in Acts; all but six refer to the OT prophets. The six remaining uses (11:27; 13:1; 15:32; 19:6; 21:9, 10) refer to persons in the church. Given the Joel quotation's emphasis on prophecy after the coming of the promised Spirit (2:17–21), these references suggest that the reader is to link these prophetic actions to that promise's fulfillment. See C. K. Barrett, *Critical and Exegetical Commentary on the Acts of the Apostles*, 2 vols., ICC (Edinburgh: T&T Clark, 1994–98), 1:601–2; and Ernst Haenchen, *The Acts of the Apostles: A Commentary*, trans. Bernard Noble and Gerald Shinn (Philadelphia: Westminster, 1971), 395n2.

4. Cf. Rudolf Pesch, *Die Apostelgeschichte*, 2 vols., EKKNT 5 (Zurich: Neukirchener Verlag, 1986), 2:16; Jürgen Roloff, *Die Apostelgeschichte*, NTD 5 (Göttingen: Vandenhoeck & Ruprecht, 1981), 193; and William H. Shepherd Jr., *The Narrative Function of the Holy Spirit as a Character in Luke-Acts*, SBLDS 147 (Atlanta: Scholars Press, 1994), 209. See also Gerhard Schneider, *Die Apostelgeschichte*, 2 vols., HTKNT 5 (Freiburg: Herder, 1980–82), 2:112–13, who sees the imperfect indicative ἦσαν (13:1) as suggesting that these prophets and teachers are continually present and characterizing that church.

5. Cf. Gerhard Krodel, *Acts*, ACNT (Minneapolis: Augsburg, 1986), 226; and Robert C. Tannehill, *The Narrative Unity of Luke-Acts: A Literary Interpretation*, 2 vols. (Philadelphia/Minneapolis: Fortress, 1986–90), 2:148. Forms of διδάσκαλος and διδάσκω appear 17 times in Acts, with all referring to Jesus' or the believers' activity. In Acts 1–12, the terms are used seven times, both in the narrator's description of believers' activity (4:2; 5:21, 42; 11:26) and in their opponents' accusations about them (4:18; 5:25, 28). In Acts 13–28, the

Given this general impression of the Antioch believers, the narrative then turns the reader's attention to a specific incident. The narrator describes the church worshipping the Lord and fasting (λειτουργούντων δὲ αὐτῶν τῷ κυρίῳ καὶ νηστευόντων; 13:2).[6] While these two verbs appear only here in the Acts narrative,[7] the described activity and scene show earnest reflection on God or serving God, activity not dissimilar to earlier depictions of the believers in Jerusalem (cf. 2:42–47). This corporate worship of the Lord provides the context for what happens next: the Holy Spirit speaks to the believers (εἶπεν τὸ πνεῦμα τὸ ἅγιον; 13:2).[8] The narrator does not state precisely how the Holy Spirit speaks,[9] but the clear picture is that the divine presence that has blessed the believers throughout the Acts narrative is manifest among the Antioch believers, who are worshipping together.[10] Again, divine instructions guide the believers, just as in the earlier narrative units. However, this divine guidance differs from other instances: it comes not to Jewish believers alone but to the Antioch church in worship, a mixed Christian audience of Jews and non-Jews.[11]

The narrator inserts the divine instructions that come to the worshipping church in Antioch. Luke mentions only one statement, which carries

---

narrator regularly describes Paul as teaching (e.g., 15:35; 18:11; 20:20; 28:31) but never as prophesying.

6. Although the referent is unclear, this corporate activity (whether five persons or the entire church) provides the context for what follows. Cf. Krodel, *Acts*, 228; I. Howard Marshall, *The Acts of the Apostles*, TNTC (Leicester: InterVarsity, 1980), 215; Pesch, *Die Apostelgeschichte*, 2:15, 17; and Roloff, *Die Apostelgeschichte*, 193.

7. The verbs λειτουργέω and νηστεύω only appear here in Acts, but the noun νηστεία is linked with "prayer" in 14:23 (cf. Luke 5:33–35). Cf. Hans Conzelmann, *Acts of the Apostles*, trans. James Limburg, A. Thomas Kraabel, and Donald H. Juel, Hermeneia (Philadelphia: Fortress, 1987), 99; Johnson, *The Acts of the Apostles*, 221; Ben Witherington III, *The Acts of the Apostles: A Socio-Rhetorical Commentary* (Grand Rapids: Eerdmans, 1998), 393; and Christoph Zettner, *Amt, Gemeinde und kirchliche Einheit in der Apostelgeschichte des Lukas* (New York: Peter Lang, 1991), 283. See Gottfried Schille, *Die Apostelgeschichte des Lukas*, THKNT 5 (Berlin: Evangelische Verlagsanstalt, 1983), 282, who associates the description here with *Didache* 15.1.

8. Cf. Alfons Weiser, *Die Apostelgeschichte*, 2 vols., ÖTNT (Würzburg: Echter, 1986), 2:306; and Zingg, *Das Wachsen der Kirche*, 191–92.

9. See, e.g., Barrett, *The Acts of the Apostles*, 1:605; F. F. Bruce, *The Book of the Acts*, rev. ed., NICNT (Grand Rapids: Eerdmans, 1988), 245; and Shepherd, *The Narrative Function of the Holy Spirit*, 210n177, who propose that a prophet served as the Spirit's spokesperson.

10. Cf. Marshall, *The Acts of the Apostles*, 216; and Zettner, *Amt, Gemeinde und kirchliche Einheit*, 282–83.

11. Cf. Alfons Weiser, "Das 'Apostelkonzil' (Apg 15,1–35): Ereignis, Überlieferung, lukanische Deutung," *BZ* 28 (1984): 159, who sees this passage suggesting the possibility of a church comprised of both Jews and Gentiles.

a sense of urgency (δή).[12] The imperative in the Spirit's instructions to the church, ἀφορίσατε (13:2), which refers to setting apart Barnabas and Saul, in the Septuagint denotes a sense of making holy or separating for divine service.[13] The Spirit also states the purpose for the church's sacred action: εἰς τὸ ἔργον ὃ προσκέκλημαι αὐτούς (13:2).[14] This narrated divine statement alludes to Gamaliel's warning to the Jewish council about opposing τὸ ἔργον that comes from God (ἐκ θεοῦ; 5:38–39). On the one hand, the inclusion of this statement subtly tells the reader that any opposition to "the work" of Barnabas and Saul will be opposition to God.[15] On the other hand, the statement also implies that this work, described later in the narrative (cf. 13:5), will be as unstoppable as the believers' proclamation in the first twelve chapters of Acts. The narrative description of the church's response to the Spirit's instructions suggests an attitude of obedience, as they release (ἀπέλυσαν; 13:3) them.[16] Three aorist participles modify and precede the main verb (ἀπέλυσαν; 13:3): νηστεύσαντες καὶ προσευξάμενοι καὶ ἐπιθέντες τὰς χεῖρας αὐτοῖς; they all describe the action of the worshipping church that precedes the actual sending of Barnabas and Saul to fulfill their divine mission.[17] Even in the following scene of the initial stages of Barnabas and Saul's mission, the narrator comments explicitly that the two men have been "sent out by the Holy Spirit" (ἐκπεμφθέντες ὑπὸ τοῦ ἁγίου πνεύματος; 13:4), a brief comment that closely aligns the Spirit's call with the church's obedient response.[18] Thus, this scene depicts the Antioch church with

---

12. See Johnson, *The Acts of the Apostles*, 221.

13. For examples of the LXX use of ἀφορίζω, see Exod 19:12; 29:26–27; Lev 13:4; Num 12:14; 2 Sm 8:1; and Isa 52:11. See also Schmidt, "ὁρίζω...," in *TDNT*, 5:454–55.

14. See William J. Larkin Jr., *Acts*, IVPNTC (Downers Grove, IL: InterVarsity, 1995), 191, who states that the perfect tense of προσκέκλημαι suggests that the call of Barnabas and Saul still needed to be fulfilled.

15. Cf. Gerhard Lohfink, *Die Sammlung Israels: Eine Untersuchung zur lukanischen Ekklesiologie*, SANT (Munich: Kösel, 1975), 87–88.

16. Cf. Zingg, *Das Wachsen der Kirche*, 246. See James D. G. Dunn, *The Acts of the Apostles*, Narrative Commentaries (Valley Forge, PA: Trinity Press International, 1996), 173, who suggests that the leaders do not obey the Spirit's instructions immediately.

17. Cf. Barrett, *The Acts of the Apostles*, 1:606; Roloff, *Die Apostelgeschichte*, 194; Schneider, *Die Apostelgeschichte*, 2:115; and David John Williams, *Acts*, NIBC 5 (Peabody, MA: Hendrickson, 1990), 222.

18. This close alignment of the church and the Spirit corresponds to Peter's declaration that Ananias has not lied merely to the church but also to God (5:4; cf. 5:9). Cf. Johnson, *The Acts of the Apostles*, 221; William S. Kurz, *Reading Luke-Acts: Dynamics of Biblical Narrative* (Louisville: Westminster/John Knox, 1993), 90; Tannehill, *The Narrative Unity of Luke-Acts*, 2:159–61; and Zettner, *Amt, Gemeinde und kirchliche Einheit*, 282–83.

characteristics similar to those found in earlier positive descriptions of the Jerusalem church: a community of prayer (cf. 1:14; 2:42; 4:24–31), worship (cf. 2:42–47), and a divinely ordained mission to proclaim the gospel (cf. 4:29–31, 33; 5:27–29). Luke presents the church in Antioch, a group of believers that includes both Jews and non-Jews, with the same ideal imagery that has characterized the early days of the Jewish believers in Jerusalem.

An Assessment of the Characterization of the Church or Group of Believers in Acts 13:1–3

The characterization of the Christian community in Antioch, as described in Acts 13:1–3, relies significantly on the positive, intratextual depictions both of that church in Acts 11 and of the Jerusalem church in the first narrative unit. The similar images in the characterization of these two churches will assist the reader in making judgments regarding the Antioch believers.[19] However, the Lukan narrative implicitly makes such comparisons by subtly directing the reader's attention to the narrated actions of these believers. Luke provides no direct judgments concerning these Christians. Rather, he narrates the episode briefly and thereby provides an indirect presentation of that group. That narrated scene — in which the church of Antioch is depicted as worshipping, fasting, and praying — provides the context that reveals divine presence and guidance. The narrative assimilates the believers' response and the Spirit's guidance and thereby intertwines the activities of the church and the Spirit.[20]

This portrait of the Christian believers in Antioch clearly identifies their action and mission through Barnabas and Saul as the result of divine initiative.[21] Again, the Christian community is the center for the proclamation of the gospel message.[22] That the narrator depicts the Antioch church in this manner rather than the Jerusalem church, however, is not surprising in light of the narrative progression of the book. Now the believers in Antioch rather than in Jerusalem are the ones described in terms of divine presence, unanimity, and proclamation.[23] On the one

---

19. See Tannehill, *The Narrative Unity of Luke-Acts*, 2:161, who recognizes the similarities between this scene and the beginning of Jesus' mission in Luke 3–4.

20. Cf. Pesch, *Die Apostelgeschichte*, 2:18–19.

21. Cf. Marshall, *The Acts of the Apostles*, 214; and Zettner, *Amt, Gemeinde und kirchliche Einheit*, 283.

22. Cf. Bruce, *The Book of the Acts*, 246; and Weiser, *Die Apostelgeschichte*, 2:305.

23. Cf. Zettner, *Amt, Gemeinde und kirchliche Einheit*, 268.

hand, the Jerusalem believers have demonstrated potentially divisive attitudes in their concerns over the Jewish laws and the social interaction with non-Jews (cf. Acts 11:1–18). On the other hand, the actions of the Antioch church — comprised of both Jewish and Gentile believers — demonstrate that among them is the presence of God, which leads to the gospel-proclaiming mission of Barnabas and Saul.[24] Given the narrative portraits of the two churches in Acts 11, the reader may compare the Antioch church more favorably to the paradigm for the Christian community in Acts 1:1–8:3. Thus, the church in Antioch now functions in the narrative as the Christian community that proclaims the gospel, due to the narrated signs of unanimity and divine presence.[25]

THE CHRISTIAN BELIEVERS IN ANTIOCH OF PISIDIA (ACTS 13:44–52)

The Literary Context (Acts 13:4–43)

The commissioning scene of Barnabas and Saul by the Antioch church leads the reader to an extended section that focuses on their mission (Acts 13–14). The reiteration of the Holy Spirit's role in sending them out (13:4) and in their initial activities (13:9) explicitly affirms what the reader has already encountered.[26] The narrative presents Barnabas and Saul as proclaiming the "word of God" (κατήγγελλον τὸν λόγον τοῦ θεοῦ; 13:5)[27] due to the initiative and continuing enablement of the Holy Spirit, which alludes to previous positive depictions of the believers.[28] The narrative setting of that initial proclamation in Salamis is in the "synagogues of the Jews" (13:5). Although the narrative states nothing more than this, the similarities to Saul's experiences and activity in

---

24. Contra Larkin, *Acts*, 189: "Through Paul it [the Jerusalem church] will embark on fulfilling the 'to the ends of the earth' phase of the Great Commission (9:15–16; 13:2)."

25. Cf. Philip H. Towner, "Mission Practice and Theology under Construction (Acts 18–20)," in *Witness to the Gospel: The Theology of Acts*, ed. I. Howard Marshall and David Peterson (Grand Rapids: Eerdmans, 1998), 422–23; and Zingg, *Das Wachsen der Kirche*, 194.

26. The Holy Spirit not only guides the Antioch church (13:1–3) but also is reaffirmed as the one who calls them (13:4). Cf. Haenchen, *The Acts of the Apostles*, 396; and Gerd Lüdemann, *Early Christianity according to the Traditions in Acts: A Commentary*, trans. John Bowden (Philadelphia: Fortress, 1989), 148.

27. Larkin, *Acts*, 193, writes that the imperfect tense suggests the beginning of the proclamation.

28. E.g., the same description of Saul before the opponent Elymas, πλησθεὶς πνεύματος ἁγίου (13:9), also characterizes Peter before the Jewish council (4:8) and the believers (4:31). Cf. Johnson, *The Acts of the Apostles*, 223–24; and Krodel, *Acts*, 229.

Damascus may create for the reader an allusion to both success and opposition.[29] The brief narration of the interactions between the characters — between Saul (now Paul) and a Jewish man who opposes him (13:8–11),[30] and between Paul and a Gentile official who believes the gospel (13:7, 12) — functions implicitly to confirm the Spirit's role in the mission of Barnabas and Paul.

The rest of Acts 13 focuses on events in another city called Antioch, this one in the region of Pisidia. That the author gives such considerable attention to this account in Pisidian Antioch suggests how significant this section is to the narrative.[31] The first activity about which the narrative informs the reader is the arrival of both Paul and Barnabas at the synagogue on the Sabbath. Throughout the last section of the book, the narrator mentions this practice repeatedly, emphasizing both Paul's faithfulness to Judaism and his priority of mission to the Jews (cf. 9:20; 13:5; 14:1; 17:1–2, 10, 17; 18:4; 19:8).[32] The invitation for Paul to speak provides the narrative setting in which the reader encounters an extended speech or sermon.[33] This Pauline speech has multiple functions in the Acts narrative: it repeats important themes found in previous speeches, it provides an example of what Paul speaks when he addresses the various synagogue audiences in the following chapters, and it implicitly advances the Lukan point of view in the narrative.[34]

The narrator carefully presents the speech as appropriate and persuasive, by a Jewish orator speaking to an audience consisting of Jewish

---

29. In the account of Saul's proclamation in Damascus (9:19b–25), both success (cf. 9:25) and opposition (cf. 9:23–24) accompany his activity in the synagogues (cf. 9:20). Also, the designation of the synagogues in Salamis as being "of the Jews" may be not redundant but a narrative hint of opposition. See Joseph B. Tyson, *Images of Judaism in Luke-Acts* (Columbia: University of South Carolina Press, 1992), 132, who underscores no mention of a positive Jewish response and the mention of a negative one in Elymas.

30. The characterization of Elymas or Bar-Jesus as both "a certain magician" and "a Jewish false prophet" (13:6) reveals his identity as one who serves Satan and who is completely opposite Barnabas and Saul, who are part of the "prophets and teachers" of the Antioch church. See Shepherd, *The Narrative Function of the Holy Spirit*, 209–12, who compares and contrasts the characterizations of Paul and Elymas.

31. Cf. Tannehill, *The Narrative Unity of Luke-Acts*, 2:175; and Tyson, *Images of Judaism in Luke-Acts*, 133–34.

32. The repetition suggests that the Pauline mission in Acts is not a mission to the *Gentiles* but to the *Jews*. Cf. Marie-Émile Boismard and Arnaud Lamouille, *Les Actes des deux Apôtres*, 3 vols., ÉBib (Paris: J. Gabalda, 1990), 1:26.

33. See Tannehill, *The Narrative Unity of Luke-Acts*, 2:164–75.

34. Cf. Johnson, *The Acts of the Apostles*, 237–39; Marshall, *The Acts of the Apostles*, 221; Tannehill, *The Narrative Unity of Luke-Acts*, 2:164, 174; and Williams, *Acts*, 229–30.

listeners and some Gentile synagogue worshippers.[35] The speech affirms the divine election of Israel (13:17) and the divine promise of a Savior from David's descendants (13:22–23).[36] However, alongside these affirmations is the recognition that "those who lived in Jerusalem and their leaders" (οἱ κατοικοῦντες ἐν Ἰερουσαλὴμ καὶ οἱ ἄρχοντες αὐτῶν; 13:27) ironically fulfill Scripture and God's plan through their ignorance and condemnation of Jesus (cf. 2:23; 3:17–18; 4:27–28).[37] Thus, the Lukan Paul does not blame the Jews of Paul's synagogue audience for Jesus' death.[38] Conversely, Paul proclaims the good news (εὐαγγελιζόμεθα; 13:32) that God has fulfilled God's promise to the Jews by raising Jesus from the dead (13:30–37).[39] The speech concludes with an offer of forgiveness and a warning. On the one hand, Paul offers the forgiveness of sins (13:38) to the audience through the resurrected Jesus, a forgiveness that is for *everyone* who believes (πᾶς ὁ πιστεύων; 13:39) and that he associates with "being set free" or justification (δικαιωθῆναι, 13:38; δικαιοῦται, 13:39).[40] On the other hand, the warning to avoid the fate described by Habakkuk (1:5) concludes the speech, thereby urging the audience not to be "scoffers" who refuse to believe the ἔργον (13:41) that God is doing among both Jews and Gentiles.[41] The Pauline

---

35. The latter part of Paul's initial address of the synagogue audience, Ἄνδρες Ἰσραηλῖται καὶ οἱ φοβούμενοι τὸν θεόν (13:6), reflects Cornelius's characterization (10:2). Cf. Tannehill, *The Narrative Unity of Luke-Acts*, 2:165–66; and Tyson, *Images of Judaism in Luke-Acts*, 133.

36. See Tyson, *Images of Judaism in Luke-Acts*, 136–37, who suggests that the historical summary in the Pauline speech supports the theme of promise and fulfillment. Cf. Robert L. Brawley, *Centering on God: Method and Message in Luke-Acts*, LCBI (Louisville: Westminster/John Knox, 1990), 115; Krodel, *Acts*, 233–35; and Marshall, *The Acts of the Apostles*, 224.

37. Cf. Krodel, *Acts*, 237; and Tannehill, *The Narrative Unity of Luke-Acts*, 2:165–66.

38. Cf. Jack T. Sanders, *The Jews in Luke-Acts* (Philadelphia: Fortress, 1987), 260; and Tyson, *Images of Judaism in Luke-Acts*, 139.

39. The pronoun ὑμῖν (13:34, 38) refers to the Jews, with whom Paul also identifies by calling them ἄνδρες ἀδελφοί (13:26, 38). Cf. Bruce, *The Book of the Acts*, 260; and Marshall, *The Acts of the Apostles*, 227.

40. These forms of the verb δικαιόω, a typical Pauline term, are surprising here. Cf. Haenchen, *The Acts of the Apostles*, 412–13; Johnson, *The Acts of the Apostles*, 235–36; and Tyson, *Images of Judaism in Luke-Acts*, 137–38. Contra Bruce, *The Book of the Acts*, 262.

41. Thus far in Acts, God's work (ἔργον; 13:41) includes the salvation of all who believe in what God has done through the resurrected Jesus, regardless of religious or social distinctions. This work also includes the ἔργον to which Paul and Barnabas are called (13:2). Cf., e.g., Brawley, *Centering on God*, 122; Haenchen, *The Acts of the Apostles*, 413; Johnson, *The Acts of the Apostles*, 236; and Lohfink, *Die Sammlung Israels*, 87–88.

speech to those at the synagogue in Pisidian Antioch concludes with the anticipation of possible Jewish rejection.

The narrative events during that Sabbath in Pisidian Antioch conclude in typical Lukan fashion with a sketchy picture of the audience's response to what they have heard. On the one hand, Luke states that, as the Christian duo is leaving, the synagogue audience encourages (παρεκάλουν)[42] them to speak (λαληθῆναι)[43] again about such matters on the next Sabbath (εἰς τὸ μεταξὺ σάββατον; 13:42). Thus, this sentence indicates that, at the very least, the audience has not rejected the gospel message but are perhaps "intrigued" by what Paul has said.[44] On the other hand, Luke also tells the reader of "many Jews and devout converts" (πολλοὶ τῶν Ἰουδαίων καὶ τῶν σεβομένων προσηλύτων; 13:43)[45] who follow Paul and Barnabas after the meeting has ended.[46] Although Luke typically uses the verb ἀκολουθέω in Acts to describe the act of physically following someone or something (cf. 12:8, 9; 21:36), this reference clearly depicts a positive response.[47] The narrative further describes Paul and Barnabas as "speaking to them"[48] and "persuading them to remain in the grace of God" (13:43), which indirectly alludes to earlier scenes of gospel acceptance and divine blessing among the believers (cf. 4:33; 11:23).[49] Thus, the narrated gospel acceptance in this scene at the Pisidian Antioch

---

42. In a wordplay, Paul and Barnabas (the latter meaning "son of encouragement") are the *recipients* of encouragement, as the audience "encourages" them to return and teach the gospel.

43. Once again, Luke uses the verb λαλέω to refer to the Christians' speaking activity. In the first two narrative units of Acts, the verb appears 33 times, all referring either to the speech of a divine speaker, Moses, David, the prophets, or believers. All but three of the remaining 26 appearances in the last unit (20:30; 23:18; 26:31) have similar connotations.

44. Cf. Krodel, *Acts*, 245.

45. On the issue of converts to Judaism, see, e.g., Shaye J. D. Cohen, "Crossing the Boundary and Becoming a Jew," *HTR* 82 (1989): 13–33.

46. See Tyson, *Images of Judaism in Luke-Acts*, 134, who suggests that this describes the positive response from a combination of Jews and another group. See also Johnson, *The Acts of the Apostles*, 240: "Luke obviously wants the reader to perceive, in the environs of the synagogue, a fringe element of interested Gentiles among whom the messianic message will find its most eager listeners."

47. See Sanders, *The Jews in Luke-Acts*, 261–62, who sees Luke in a "jam" because he wants to show *some* positive Jewish response but not *too* positive a response.

48. The verb προσλαλέω (13:43) is formed by the prefix πρός and the verb λαλέω, which is a favorite Lukan expression for believers "telling" or "speaking" the gospel.

49. To this point in Acts, the only explicit reference to the "grace of God" has described Barnabas as seeing such grace in the new believers in Antioch (11:23). Thus, this description suggests similar positive connotations: that these persons enjoy God's blessing and presence. Cf. Krodel, *Acts*, 245; and Williams, *Acts*, 237.

synagogue is the first description of substantial success in the mission of Paul and Barnabas.

The Characterization of the Church or Group of Believers in Acts 13:44–52

The narrative that begins with verse 44 picks up where the last two verses (13:42–43) have ended. Luke is completely silent about what transpires during the next week. The invitation to return to speak at the synagogue, however, provides the narrative context for what follows. The narrative picks up with the next Sabbath, when Luke simply states that almost the entire city gathers (σχεδὸν πᾶσα ἡ πόλις συνήχθη)[50] to hear "the word of the Lord" (τὸν λόγον τοῦ κυρίου; 13:44), a general image of *every-one* from the city coming together, presumably at the synagogue.[51] Luke does not state where they put all of the people; surely the synagogue cannot hold them all, since the undisclosed number of Gentiles would overrun the Jewish synagogue![52] The narrator, however, does describe in both explicit and implicit terms the reaction of "the Jews" (οἱ Ἰουδαῖοι) when they see the crowds (τοὺς ὄχλους; 13:45).[53] Explicitly, Luke states that the Jews are "filled with jealousy" (ἐπλήσθησαν ζήλου; 13:45),[54] the same negative description of the Jewish leaders in Jerusalem when

---

50. See Haenchen, *The Acts of the Apostles*, 414, who states that "Luke abandons all realism of presentation for the sake of depicting Paul as a great orator and successful missionary."

51. Cf. Krodel, *Acts*, 247, who observes that the exact location of this gathering is not indicated.

52. Cf. Barrett, *The Acts of the Apostles*, 1:655; Bruce, *The Book of the Acts*, 265; and Tannehill, *The Narrative Unity of Luke-Acts*, 2:172.

53. The text does not clarify whether οἱ Ἰουδαῖοι refers here to *all* of the Jews, *most* of them, or only *some* of them (13:45). More specifically, do those who are included in the πολλοὶ τῶν Ἰουδαίων (13:43) now react negatively? Or is the Lukan narrator simply trying to paint a picture of the Jews *in general* who react so negatively? Since the Lukan tendency is to present scenes in generalities, the latter scenario seems more likely, especially given the similarity of the events in Iconium (cf. 14:1–7) to what occurs in Pisidian Antioch. The mention of Gentiles believing (13:48) suggests that the initial Jewish acceptance and success results in the positive Gentile response, as the "entire city" response (13:44) reflects the obviously positive one of the Jews. Cf. Dixon Slingerland, " 'The Jews' in the Pauline Portion of Acts," *JAAR* 54 (1986): 314–17; Charles H. Talbert, *Reading Acts: A Literary and Theological Commentary on the Acts of the Apostles*, Reading the New Testament (New York: Crossroad, 1997), 132–33; and Tyson, *Images of Judaism in Luke-Acts*, 144.

54. Although the narrator provides a view into the thoughts of the Jews not otherwise accessible to the reader, nothing is stated explicitly on *why* the Jews are so jealous. Cf. Dunn, *The Acts of the Apostles*, 183, who suggests that the Jews are surprised by the appeal of Paul's message; Haenchen, *The Acts of the Apostles*, 414, who proposes that the Christians may have attracted non-Jews who are sympathetic toward Judaism; Larkin, *Acts*, 205, who sees this

the number of believers grew rapidly (cf. 5:17).[55] Implicitly, Luke states what actions reflect this negative attitude of the Jews: "blaspheming, they opposed what was spoken by Paul" (13:45).[56] Three aspects of this description of the Jews' actions suggest that the reader should perceive this action negatively. First, the verb ἀντιλέγω denotes opposition, which here is against Paul and the Christians, whom the narrative has already presented positively.[57] Second, the opposition reacts against what is said by Paul (τοῖς ὑπὸ Παύλου λαλουμένοις). Since the substantive participle is derived from λαλέω, a typical Lukan term that describes the believers' activity of telling the gospel message to others, the reader will perceive such opposition as the attempt to negate that message. Third, the adverbial participle βλασφημοῦντες further describes the negative nature of the opposition against what Paul is saying, implicitly suggesting that speaking against *Paul* is also speaking against *God*.[58] Consequently, both the precise wording of this description and the Jews' opposition to Paul and Barnabas coax the reader to view these actions negatively, in contrast to the positive portrayal of the Christian messengers. The narrative account of this opposition suggests that jealousy creates this negative reaction, as the whole city presumably of mostly Gentile backgrounds join together to hear the gospel.[59]

The response of Paul and Barnabas to the Jewish opposition, as narrated by Luke, stands in sharp contrast to the depiction of that negative Jewish response. Luke states that the two Christians speak boldly (παρρησιασάμενοι ... εἶπαν; 13:46) to their Jewish opponents. This description alludes to the boldness (παρρησία) of the believers in Jerusalem as they have proclaimed the gospel message before the Jewish leaders

---

jealousy due to Paul's willingness to receive the Gentiles directly into the church; and Williams, *Acts*, 238, who suggests that they are jealous of "their own privileged position."

55. Cf. Johnson, *The Acts of the Apostles*, 240; and Tyson, *Images of Judaism in Luke-Acts*, 134, who observes that Luke never narrates a positive response by an exclusively Jewish group.

56. The conjunction καί grammatically connects the explicit description of the Jews' inner motives and the implicit description of their actions, thereby relating these two descriptions (13:45).

57. The imperfect tense of ἀντέλεγον suggests ongoing opposition against what Paul has said, opposition that begins when the Jews see the crowds (13:45).

58. The verb βλασφημέω (13:45) negatively denotes one's speaking against God, but the narrator never tells what is said against Paul's message. See Hermann Wolfgang Beyer, "βλασφημέω...," in *TDNT*, 1:621–25. Cf. Johnson, *The Acts of the Apostles*, 240–41; Krodel, *Acts*, 248; Sanders, *The Jews in Luke-Acts*, 262; and Williams, *Acts*, 238.

59. Cf. Haenchen, *The Acts of the Apostles*, 417.

(cf. 4:13, 31).⁶⁰ Paul and Barnabas explain to their Jewish opponents the necessity to speak (ἦν ἀναγκαῖον ... λαληθῆναι) the "word of God" (τὸν λόγον τοῦ θεοῦ) first to the Jews (13:46), presumably because of their divine election and promise as asserted in the Pauline synagogue speech.⁶¹ The narrator uses these two Christian characters to voice implicitly his conclusions about the Jewish response, which they identify as the rejection of the divine message (13:46).⁶² The reader will recall that Paul has already warned his synagogue audience about rejecting what God has offered to them (13:40–41).⁶³ Thus, the two believers declare that this Jewish rejection of the gospel will result in their turning (στρεφόμεθα; 13:46) to the Gentiles.⁶⁴ The negative Jewish response places them outside that sphere or context in which the believers proclaim the gospel message and in which divine blessing and salvation will be demonstrably apparent.

The narrative scene that contrasts pictures of the two Christian proclaimers with the rejecting, opposing Jews provides the context into which a group of believers enters briefly as a character. Whereas the Jews respond with jealousy, opposition, and rejection of the "word of God" (τὸν λόγον τοῦ θεοῦ; 13:46), the narrator briefly states that the Gentiles respond with joy (ἔχαιρον),⁶⁵ praise of the "word of the Lord" (ἐδόξαζον τὸν λόγον τοῦ κυρίου),⁶⁶ and belief (ἐπίστευσαν; 13:48).⁶⁷ On the one hand, the narrator indirectly depicts the Jews through Paul's and Barnabas's words as rejecting the gospel message by judging themselves "unworthy of eternal life" (οὐκ ἀξίους κρίνετε ἑαυτοὺς τῆς αἰωνίου ζωῆς;

---

60. Cf. Johnson, *The Acts of the Apostles*, 241.

61. The emphatic position of the pronoun ὑμῖν, which refers specifically to the Jews opposing Paul and Barnabas, stresses that *to the Jews* the gospel is first presented (13:46).

62. While this response (13:46) may seem harsh after the initial gospel acceptance one week earlier, the Lukan portrait is one of *general* rejection. Cf. Tyson, *Images of Judaism in Luke-Acts*, 140.

63. Cf. Krodel, *Acts*, 248.

64. See Robert C. Tannehill, "Rejection by Jews and Turning to Gentiles: The Pattern of Paul's Mission in Acts," in *Luke-Acts and the Jewish People: Eight Critical Perspectives*, ed. Joseph B. Tyson (Minneapolis: Augsburg, 1988), 89: "Turning to the Gentiles means the end of such preaching in the Antioch synagogue."

65. Descriptions of "rejoicing," with forms of the verb χαίρω, have been positive ones only of believers (cf. 5:41; 8:39; 11:23). Cf. Johnson, *The Acts of the Apostles*, 242.

66. See Haenchen, *The Acts of the Apostles*, 414, who stresses that this rejoicing "epitomizes the joyful acceptance of the gospel by the Gentile world at large."

67. The imperfect tense of both ἔχαιρον and ἐδόξαζον contrasts the ongoing Gentile activity of rejoicing and praise (13:48) with the ongoing Jewish activity of contradiction and opposition.

13:46).[68] On the other hand, the narrator directly depicts the Gentiles' positive response as indicative of their being "destined for eternal life" (ὅσοι ἦσαν τεταγμένοι εἰς ζωὴν αἰώνιον; 13:48).[69] The believers in Pisidian Antioch, therefore, consist mostly of Gentiles. The narrative picture implies that, since the entire city has come to the synagogue to hear the gospel, much of the city has become believers.[70] Along with the positive effect of the gospel on the city, the narrator briefly states that "the word of the Lord" (ὁ λόγος τοῦ κυρίου) was continually spread (διεφέρετο) throughout the whole region (δι᾽ ὅλης τῆς χώρας; 13:49), presumably by the believers.[71] This success in the spread of that message implicitly alludes to earlier positive descriptions of the growth and multiplication of the gospel in connection with divine blessing and enablement (cf. 4:31; 6:7; 8:4).

The Lukan description of these Gentile believers contrasts with the continuing Jewish activity against Paul and Barnabas, activity that the narrator summarizes for readers by showing it in direct fashion. The narrator blames the Jews for creating trouble (παρώτρυναν) among the city's devout women of high standing and leading men (13:50) against Paul and Barnabas.[72] These Jews create division among the inhabitants of the city through their continuing attempts to undermine the Christian mission. The narrator also negatively presents these Jews as arousing persecution (ἐπήγειραν διωγμόν; 13:50) specifically against Paul and Barnabas.[73] The action of the Jews finally results in violent steps taken against Paul and Barnabas, as they are thrown out beyond the boundaries of their region (13:50). As the narrator describes the departure of Paul and Barnabas to the city of Iconium, he also leaves a brief picture of the Christians in Pisidian Antioch in the reader's mind.[74] In the

---

68. Cf. Joseph B. Tyson, "The Jewish Public in Luke-Acts," *NTS* 30 (October 1984): 574–83.

69. On the participle τεταγμένοι (13:48), see Bruce, *The Book of the Acts*, 267–68n111; Johnson, *The Acts of the Apostles*, 242; Conzelmann, *Acts of the Apostles*, 106; and Williams, *Acts*, 239.

70. Cf. Bruce, *The Book of the Acts*, 266.

71. The imperfect tense of διεφέρετο suggests that the "word of the Lord" was continually spread (13:49). Cf. Haenchen, *The Acts of the Apostles*, 414.

72. Cf. Lawrence M. Wills, "The Depiction of the Jews in Acts," *JBL* 110 (December 1991): 636.

73. The persecution (13:50) is apparently directed at Paul and Barnabas because they state that salvation will be taken to the Gentiles (13:46).

74. Cf. Bruce, *The Book of the Acts*, 269; Joseph A. Fitzmyer, *The Acts of the Apostles: A New Translation with Introduction and Commentary*, AB (New York: Doubleday, 1998), 522;

midst of all the trouble created by the Jews, the narrator directly describes these disciples (οἱ μαθηταί), whom readers will identify as both Jewish and Gentile believers (cf. 13:43, 48),[75] as "filled with joy and with the Holy Spirit" (ἐπληροῦντο χαρᾶς καὶ πνεύματος ἁγίου; 13:52). This description reaffirms the believers' initial joyful response (cf. 13:48)[76] and alludes to early positive images of the divine presence and blessing among the Christians (cf. 2:4; 4:8, 31; 13:9).[77] Just as in earlier scenes of opposition, Luke presents the gospel message and the Christian community that proclaims it as unstoppable.[78]

An Assessment of the Characterization of the Church or Group of Believers in Acts 13:44–52

The Lukan characterization of the Christian community in 13:44–52 is consistent with earlier depictions of the church in the book of Acts. Once again, the narrator uses both implicit and explicit means by which to depict the believers in Pisidian Antioch as those who enjoy divine blessing and proclaim the gospel. The importance of this particular example of Lukan characterization, however, lies in the vivid contrasts between this group and the Jews of that city. By portraying this group of believers as comprised of both Gentiles and Jews (cf. 11:19–26), the narrator does not imply that the Christian church and its mission are reserved only for Gentiles. Rather, the depiction of the believers in Pisidian Antioch is consistent with the message of the Pauline synagogue speech, which offers the gospel to everyone (cf. 13:38–39). Therefore, the Lukan narrator depicts the church in Pisidian Antioch as those who believe together in the salvific work God has done, who are characterized by joy, and who proclaim the gospel message. In sharp contrast, the narrator depicts the Jews as those who reject what God has done and who respond divisively against others. Thus, the narrator presents

---

Marshall, *The Acts of the Apostles*, 231; and Williams, *Acts*, 240–41. Contra Shepherd, *The Narrative Function of the Holy Spirit*, 214, who identifies the disciples as Paul and Barnabas.

75. Contra Dunn, *The Acts of the Apostles*, 185, who states that the Jewish community "closed ranks against Paul's message" so that the group of believers is comprised only of Gentiles.

76. For previous images of joy, see 5:41 and 11:23. Cf. Johnson, *The Acts of the Apostles*, 243; and Shepherd, *The Narrative Function of the Holy Spirit*, 214.

77. Although πίμπλημι is the typical Lukan term describing the Holy Spirit as "filling" a person, πληρόω as used here presents similar imagery. Cf. Johnson, *The Acts of the Apostles*, 243.

78. Cf. Kurz, *Reading Luke-Acts*, 92.

a vivid contrast between two groups of people who are in some way identified with God, yet the ones who demonstrate God's presence and blessing are the Christians or believers of Pisidian Antioch, not the Jews.

THE CHRISTIAN BELIEVERS IN LYSTRA AND OTHER CITIES (ACTS 14:19–28)

The Literary Context (Acts 14:1–18)

The next city to which Paul and Barnabas travel in this Lukan account of their ministry journey is Iconium. The Lukan narrator states directly in verse 1 that what has happened in Pisidian Antioch is repeated similarly in Iconium (κατὰ τὸ αὐτό). Thus, after entering the synagogue, the two men proclaim the gospel (λαλῆσαι), with the result that "a great number of both Jews and Greeks believe" (ὥστε πιστεῦσαι Ἰουδαίων τε καὶ Ἑλλήνων πολὺ πλῆθος; 14:1).[79] As what the narrative has already described in Pisidian Antioch, opposition by "unbelieving Jews" (οἱ ἀπειθήσαντες Ἰουδαῖοι)[80] follows the initial acceptance and success, as the narrator tells of their negative activity among the Gentiles "against the brothers" (κατὰ τῶν ἀδελφῶν; 14:2) or, more precisely, Paul and Barnabas.[81] Despite the unfavorable atmosphere, Paul and Barnabas are described as "speaking boldly for the Lord" (παρρησιαζόμενοι ἐπὶ τῷ κυρίῳ; 14:3), a picture that alludes to the positive descriptions of both the Jerusalem believers (cf. 4:13, 31) and these two men in Pisidian Antioch (cf. 13:46).[82] The narrator also tells about Paul and Barnabas doing "signs and wonders" (σημεῖα καὶ τέρατα; 14:3). This description implicitly compares Paul and Barnabas to the apostles and Stephen in

---

79. Cf. E. Nellessen, "Die Presbyter der Gemeinden in Lykaonien und Pisidien (Apg 14,23)," in *Les Actes des Apôtres: Traditions, rédaction, théologie,* ed. Jacob Kremer, BETL 48 (Leuven: Leuven University Press, 1979), 496; and Tannehill, *The Narrative Unity of Luke-Acts,* 2:176. See Haenchen, *The Acts of the Apostles,* 423, who sees this as certifying God's power (14:1).

80. See Johnson, *The Acts of the Apostles,* 246, who states that the verb ἀπειθέω denotes disobedience and rebellion against God in the LXX (Lev 26:15; Num 11:20; Deut 1:26; 9:7, 23, 24; 32:51; Isa 30:12).

81. Two verbs describe the unpersuaded Jews' despicable activity (14:2), which is not explicated further: (1) ἐπεγείρω, the term that describes the Jews' actions in Pisidian Antioch; and (2) κακόω, which depicts harmful action. See Walter Grundmann, "κακός...," in *TDNT,* 3:484.

82. Cf. Tannehill, *The Narrative Unity of Luke-Acts,* 2:177; and Williams, *Acts,* 244–45.

Jerusalem (cf. 5:12; 6:8), as the narrator explicitly credits the Lord with giving these abilities and thus confirming their message of God's grace (τῷ μαρτυροῦντι [ἐπὶ] τῷ λόγῳ τῆς χάριτος αὐτοῦ; 14:3).[83] The resultant division within the city (ἐσχίσθη δὲ τὸ πλῆθος τῆς πόλεως; 14:4) between those who side with the Jews (σὺν τοῖς ᾿Ιουδαίοις) and those who side with the apostles (σὺν τοῖς ἀποστόλοις)[84] is not limited merely to the Jews who reject the gospel.[85] The description of an attempt (ὁρμή)[86] by those who side with the Jews against Paul and Barnabas[87] to "mistreat and stone them" (ὑβρίσαι καὶ λιθοβολῆσαι αὐτούς; 14:5) reflects negatively on these opponents, since such action is typically perceived as uncivilized and disdainful.[88] That threatening action results in the two men escaping to the cities of Lystra and Derbe.[89]

The narrative description of what occurs in Lystra is a story of a city's mistaken identification of Paul and Barnabas.[90] Luke has already stated that the two men have been continually proclaiming the gospel message (14:7).[91] However, the action that dominates the narrative scene is the healing of a crippled man, which will remind readers of another crippled man whom Peter (accompanied by John) healed.[92] Readers will also recognize that Paul's healing activity is from God (cf. 14:3), but the

---

83. Cf. Bruce, *The Book of the Acts*, 271; Johnson, *The Acts of the Apostles*, 246; Marshall, *The Acts of the Apostles*, 233; and Tannehill, *The Narrative Unity of Luke-Acts*, 2:177.

84. On the only two designations of Paul and Barnabas as "apostles" in Acts (14:4, 14), see Bruce, *The Book of the Acts*, 271n7; and Krodel, *Acts*, 253.

85. Cf. Haenchen, *The Acts of the Apostles*, 420; and Kurz, *Reading Luke-Acts*, 92.

86. The noun ὁρμή (14:5) suggests impulsiveness not controlled by reason. See Haenchen, *The Acts of the Apostles*, 420–421; Tannehill, *The Narrative Unity of Luke-Acts*, 2:177n3; and Georg Bertram, "ὁρμή..." in *TDNT*, 5:467–72.

87. Those who have sided against Paul and Barnabas are "both Gentiles and Jews with their rulers" (τῶν ἐθνῶν τε καὶ ᾿Ιουδαίων σὺν τοῖς ἄρχουσιν αὐτῶν; 14:5).

88. The noun ὕβρις and the verb ὑβρίζω describe outrageous and violent action toward others (14:5). For examples of these terms in Herodotus's work, see *Histories*, 1.106, 189; 3.118; and 6.87. See also Georg Bertram, "ὕβρις...," in *TDNT*, 8:295–307; and Williams, *Acts*, 245.

89. See Pervo, *Profit with Delight*, 26, who sees this as a foreshadow of what will come.

90. Contra Johnson, *The Acts of the Apostles*, 251, who considers the people's response as "overwhelmingly, almost embarrassingly, positive."

91. The imperfect periphrastic construction in 14:7, εὐαγγελιζόμενοι ἦσαν, denotes the ongoing activity of Paul and Barnabas in proclaiming the gospel.

92. Although the details of the scenes are different, both men are crippled from birth (τις ἀνὴρ χωλὸς ἐκ κοιλίας μητρὸς αὐτοῦ; 3:2; 14:8). Cf., e.g., Haenchen, *The Acts of the Apostles*, 430; Johnson, *The Acts of the Apostles*, 247; Krodel, *Acts*, 256; Tannehill, *The Narrative Unity of Luke-Acts*, 2:177; and Williams, *Acts*, 247.

crowds who witness the event think that Paul and Barnabas are the gods Hermes and Zeus and want to offer sacrifices to them (14:11–13).[93] The narrator describes Paul's attempt to persuade the audience that he and Barnabas have come to proclaim the good news (εὐαγγελιζόμενοι) of the "living God" (θεὸν ζῶντα; 14:15), who has created all things. However, the narrator mentions nothing directly about the response of those Lystran crowds, and the statement about Paul and Barnabas experiencing difficulties (μόλις; 14:18) in convincing the crowds not to offer such sacrifices suggests little success.[94] Nonetheless, the final portion of Paul's brief speech to the Lystran people subtly hints at some acceptance by stating that God fills their hearts with joy (εὐφροσύνης; 14:17), the specific term appearing only here and in 2:28 to describe what one experiences in the presence of God.

The Characterization of the Church or Group of Believers in Acts 14:19–28

The last ten verses of Acts 14 describe the Christian community in a variety of ways. In most instances, the groups of believers are depicted either as passive recipients of others' actions or as those who form the communal context from which Paul and Barnabas proclaim the gospel. One finds the first description at the end of the narrative events in Lystra. The narrator states that the Jews from Pisidian Antioch and Iconium who have opposed Paul and Barnabas arrive in Lystra, persuade the crowds (πείσαντες τοὺς ὄχλους; 14:19) against Paul,[95] stone (λιθάσαντες) him,[96] and drag his seemingly lifeless body out of the city. Only now do the believers enter onto the narrative stage, but they do so only momentarily.[97] The narrative paints a scene in which the disciples surround Paul (κυκλωσάντων τῶν μαθητῶν αὐτόν; 14:20), using the same term that elsewhere describes the Israelites' encircling of the city of Jericho (Heb

---

93. See Sanders, *The Jews in Luke-Acts*, 265, who states that the crowds' reaction indicates that they are not Jews. However, the Jewish opposition still follows Paul to this city.
94. See Nellessen, "Die Presbyter der Gemeinden in Lykaonien und Pisidien," 496, who suggests that this rules out the conversion of Jews.
95. In an apparent wordplay, the Jews described earlier as "unpersuaded" (ἀπειθήσαντες; 14:2) now succeed in "persuading" (πείσαντες; 14:19) the confused crowds against Paul (and possibly Barnabas).
96. See Sanders, *The Jews in Luke-Acts*, 265, who points out the similarities between Paul, Stephen, and Jesus, as seen in this account of Paul's stoning. Cf. Pervo, *Profit with Delight*, 65.
97. Cf. Krodel, *Acts*, 256, 260.

11:30; cf. Josh 6:20, for the encircling wall).[98] Luke provides little information concerning this scene: he describes no other actions, he provides no explicit information, and one knows nothing about any disciples in Lystra until now.[99] However, Paul arises (ἀναστάς) from his apparently deceased condition.[100] Although the description of this episode includes rather limited information, the reader is left to make conclusions about what takes place as that scene falls within the progression of the narrative.[101] Among other things, the reader sees in this scene that even death is no match for the church.[102] Given the typical Lukan depiction of the church or Christian community as the people in whom God's presence is found, this implicit picture suggests that *nothing*, including opposition, can stop the proclamation of the gospel message. In the context of the Christian believers in Lystra, one sees implicitly the hand of God in the survival of Paul (cf. 9:36–43).[103]

The narrated return trip through Lystra, Iconium, and Antioch also includes another depiction of the groups of believers in those cities. Although the previous narrative sections imply that such a trip will have potential dangers,[104] the Christians are the recipients of Paul and Barnabas's activity of strengthening their souls (ἐπιστηρίζοντες τὰς ψυχάς; 14:22) and encouraging them to remain in the faith (παρακαλοῦντες ἐμμένειν τῇ πίστει).[105] The two men also appoint elders in every church (χειροτονήσαντες δὲ αὐτοῖς κατ' ἐκκλησίαν πρεσβυτέρους; 14:23), with the brevity of the description suggesting nothing more than that these persons will function as spiritual leaders within those groups.[106] The

---

98. BDAG, 574, stresses that κυκλόω usually refers to encircling with hostile intent. However, the LXX use implies God's presence and blessing. Cf. Johnson, *The Acts of the Apostles*, 253.

99. Cf. Dunn, *The Acts of the Apostles*, 192.

100. Although the verb ἀνίστημι often describes Jesus' resurrection in Acts (e.g., 2:24, 32; 10:41; 13:33, 34), often it does not (e.g., 5:17, 34; 9:18, 39), as is the case here.

101. See Pervo, *Profit with Delight*, 26, who counts this story as the recovery of an unstoppable "typical superhero."

102. See Johnson, *The Acts of the Apostles*, 256; and Witherington, *The Acts of the Apostles*, 428.

103. Cf. Williams, *Acts*, 252.

104. Cf. Tannehill, *The Narrative Unity of Luke-Acts*, 2:180; and Weiser, *Die Apostelgeschichte*, 2:355.

105. The reader will identify the encouragement by Paul and Barnabas as consistent with earlier descriptions of Barnabas (cf. 4:36; 11:23–24). Cf. Tannehill, *The Narrative Unity of Luke-Acts*, 2:180–81.

106. See Nellessen, "Die Presbyter der Gemeinden in Lykaonien und Pisidien," 495, who contends that the "elders" do not have a prominent role in Acts.

"praying with fasting" (προσευξάμενοι μετὰ νηστειῶν; 14:23) that accompanies those selections reflects positively on these believers, as the activities of Paul and Barnabas in their midst reflect similar positive activities among the church in Jerusalem and Antioch of Syria (cf. 1:14; 2:42; 4:23–31; 13:1–3).[107] As they leave each church (κατ᾽ ἐκκλησίαν), the narrator states that Paul and Barnabas "entrusted them to the Lord" (παρέθεντο αὐτοὺς τῷ κυρίῳ; 14:23), emphasizing again the integral relationship between the church and God. The relative clause that modifies "the Lord," ὃν πεπιστεύκεισαν (in whom they had come to believe), describes what identifies these groups as Christian churches or communities.[108] Thus, the narrative explicitly depicts these churches not only in terms of their past faith in God (cf. 14:23) but also their continuing faith in the present (cf. 14:22). Ethnic distinctions or social practices are not the distinguishing traits of these Christians. Rather, the Lukan narrator presents the church as those persons whose belief in the Lord has resulted in their identification together as an ἐκκλησία.

The final depiction of the churches in these verses is provided in the context of Paul's and Barnabas's return to the church in Antioch of Syria, the same church that has sent the two men to accomplish the work (τὸ ἔργον) that has now been completed (cf. 14:26).[109] The narrator describes the two returning men as gathering the church together (συναγαγόντες τὴν ἐκκλησίαν) so that they might report about what God has done (14:27).[110] Included in their report is the specific reference to a "door of faith" (θύραν πίστεως; 14:27) that God has opened to the Gentiles.[111] However, what also seems important to the narrative is that Paul and Barnabas return to the same church that has obediently sent

---

107. Cf. Johnson, *The Acts of the Apostles*, 255; Krodel, *Acts*, 262; Marshall, *The Acts of the Apostles*, 241; and Nellessen, "Die Presbyter der Gemeinden in Lykaonien und Pisidien," 494.

108. The pluperfect tense of πεπιστεύκεισαν denotes the past state of a past action. Cf. Haenchen, *The Acts of the Apostles*, 436.

109. Cf. Johnson, *The Acts of the Apostles*, 255; and Witherington, *The Acts of the Apostles*, 429.

110. See Williams, *Acts*, 255, who states that the imperfect tense of ἀνήγγελλον (14:27) may indicate that Paul and Barnabas repeat the report as they meet with different groups of believers scattered throughout Antioch. Cf. Udo Borse, "Kompositionsgeschichtliche Beobachtungen zum Apostelkonzil," in *Begegnung mit dem Wort: Festschrift für Heinrich Zimmermann*, ed. Josef Zmijewski, BBB 53 (Bonn: Peter Hanstein, 1980), 200.

111. The emphatic position of τοῖς ἔθνεσιν (14:27) highlights the significance of this point. Cf. Weiser, *Die Apostelgeschichte*, 2:360; and Krodel, *Acts*, 262.

them to fulfill God's calling.[112] Their report of what has happened signifies that the proclamation of the gospel has occurred because this group
of believing Christians has sent them.[113] The implicit picture, therefore,
is one of the Christian church as the source of the good news that is proclaimed through its representatives. In this light, the depiction of Paul
and Barnabas functions indirectly to characterize them as representatives
of the community of believers in Antioch in spreading the gospel.

An Assessment of the Characterization of the Church or Group of Believers in Acts 14:19–28

The brief depictions of the groups of believers in Acts 14:19–28 describe these Christians consistently with the earlier images in the Acts
narrative. However, the Lukan narrator presents these believers in two
distinct ways: as passive narrative characters, and as active ones. The
narrator thus describes these groups of believers both through the reception of others' actions and through their own actions. In both kinds of
descriptions, nonetheless, one finds intratextual connections with previous affirmative pictures of churches — in Jerusalem and in Antioch
of Syria. The Christian community is described as a group of those who
are identified by faith, the same trait that has characterized the Jerusalem
Christians in contrast to others. Although these narrative depictions of
the churches now regularly include the acceptance of the gospel by Gentiles as well as Jews, one finds similar connections with God's presence
and the proclamation of the gospel. Luke presents the narrative events
and the descriptions of these churches, therefore, within an *inclusio* of
two brief descriptions of the Syrian Antioch church in Acts 13–14. The
Christian community there is responsible for sending Paul and Barnabas
on their journey, which results in the success of the gospel among both
Jews and Gentiles; the same church is depicted positively in comparison with the Jerusalem church. Thus, the narrative places the successful
spread of the gospel within the context of the Antioch church, implying
a relation between that proclamation and the positive dynamics of unanimity and divine presence within that "mixed" church of both Jewish
and non-Jewish believers.

---

112. Cf. Kurz, *Reading Luke-Acts*, 92; Schneider, *Die Apostelgeschichte*, 2:167; Weiser,
Die Apostelgeschichte, 2:360; and Zingg, *Das Wachsen der Kirche*, 192.
113. Cf. Borse, "Kompositionsgeschichtliche Beobachtungen zum Apostelkonzil," 196; and
Tannehill, *The Narrative Unity of Luke-Acts*, 2:182.

The Controversy in Antioch and the Jerusalem Council (Acts 15:1–35)

The Literary Context

The success of Paul and Barnabas's mission, presented in Acts 13–14 and sponsored by the church in Antioch of Syria, results in both Jews and non-Jews accepting the gospel message. That narrated journey clearly presents the church in terms of a "mixed" response from a "mixed" group of respondents. On the one hand, the response toward the gospel message proclaimed by the church is mixed, as the Lukan narrative describes both acceptance and rejection. On the other hand, those who respond, either negatively or positively, are not confined to either Jews or Gentiles: both groups are represented in the narrative accounts of that mission.[114] The narrated success among both groups mirrors the positive response to the gospel in Antioch, which results in an affirmative description of the fledgling church there. However, as mentioned previously, the association of Jews and Gentiles because of the gospel has created problems for the Jerusalem church (cf. 11:1–18). The narrative regularity of the inclusion of Gentiles among those who respond favorably to the gospel and the increasing Gentile presence in the various groups of believers can create in the reader the anticipation of a possible "crisis of identity" for the early church.[115]

The Characterization of the Church or Group of Believers in Acts 15:1–35

The narrated events of 15:1–35 focus on the two dominant churches mentioned thus far in the narrative: the Jerusalem church and the Antioch church.[116] The structure of this literary section reflects these two settings.[117] On the one hand, the section begins and ends with scenes in the Antioch church (15:1–5, 30–35).[118] On the other hand, the section's central part (15:6–29) includes the discussions and decisions of

---

114. The narrated success, as seen in the acceptance of the gospel by both Jews and Gentiles, is accompanied by the narrated opposition, as seen in the rejection of the gospel. Although this rejection is largely depicted as coming from Jews, the accounts of events in Pisidian Antioch (13:50), Iconium (14:4–6), and Lystra (14:19) all include Gentile involvement in that rejection and opposition.

115. M. A. Seifrid, "Jesus and the Law in Acts," *JSNT* 30 (1987): 45.

116. See Weiser, "Das 'Apostelkonzil,'" 158, who sees the Antioch church as representing Gentile Christianity and the Jerusalem church as representing Jewish Christianity.

117. Cf. Krodel, *Acts*, 271–72; and Weiser, "Das 'Apostelkonzil,'" 146.

118. Cf. Pesch, *Die Apostelgeschichte*, 2:74; and Weiser, *Die Apostelgeschichte*, 2:365–66.

the Jerusalem church, as Paul, Barnabas, and others from Antioch travel to Jerusalem and meet with the Jerusalem Christian leaders — a meeting frequently called the Apostolic Council or the Jerusalem Council.[119] Thus, both churches function as significant characters in this narrative section,[120] and the interaction between them, depicted typically as representatives from one group interact with the other church, is a potentially significant aspect of the characterization of the Christian churches in the book of Acts.

The initial narrated event, which provides the reason for the Jerusalem meeting, occurs within the church in Antioch. The narrative reports that some individuals from Judea arrive (τινες κατελθόντες ἀπὸ τῆς Ἰουδαίας)[121] and begin to teach (ἐδίδασκον)[122] the believers (τοὺς ἀδελφούς)[123] of the "mixed" Antioch church that Jewish circumcision is necessary for their salvation (σωθῆναι; 15:1).[124] Since earlier narrative sections presenting the mission of Paul and Barnabas do not mention the

---

119. For studies on the Jerusalem Council of Acts 15, see, e.g., Paul J. Achtemeier, "An Elusive Unity: Paul, Acts, and the Early Church," *CBQ* 48 (1986): 1–26; Marie-Émile Boismard, "Le 'concile' de Jérusalem (Act 15,1–33)," *ETL* 64 (1988): 433–40; Borse, "Kompositionsgeschichtliche Beobachtungen zum Apostelkonzil," 195–211; Martin Dibelius, "The Apostolic Council," in *Studies in the Acts of the Apostles*, trans. Mary Ling (London: SCM, 1956), 93–101; Haenchen, *The Acts of the Apostles*, 455–72; Jacob Jervell, *Luke and the People of God: A New Look at Luke-Acts* (Minneapolis: Augsburg, 1972), 185–207; Luke T. Johnson, *Decision Making in the Church: A Biblical Model* (Philadelphia: Fortress, 1983), 46–58, 67–87; Kirsopp Lake, "The Apostolic Council of Jerusalem," in *The Beginnings of Christianity*, ed. F. J. Foakes-Jackson and Kirsopp Lake, 5 vols. (London: Macmillan, 1933), 5:195–212; Earl Richard, "The Divine Purpose: The Jews and the Gentile Mission (Acts 15)," in *Luke-Acts: New Perspectives from the Society of Biblical Literature Seminar*, ed. Charles H. Talbert (New York: Crossroad, 1984), 188–209; Justin Taylor, "Ancient Texts and Modern Critics: Acts 15, 1–34," *RB* 89 (1992): 373–78; Huub van de Sandt, "An Explanation of Acts 15.6–21 in the Light of Deuteronomy 4.29–35 (LXX)," *JSNT* 46 (1992): 73–97; and Weiser, "Das 'Apostelkonzil,'" 145–67. For studies on the historical difficulties presented by the Lukan account in Acts 15 as compared with the Pauline material in Gal 2, see also John Knox, *Chapters in a Life of Paul*, rev. ed. (Macon, GA: Mercer University Press, 1987), 43–52; Lüdemann, *Early Christianity according to the Traditions in Acts*, 1–18; and Stephen G. Wilson, *The Gentiles and the Gentile Mission in Luke-Acts*, SNTSMS 23 (Cambridge: Cambridge University Press, 1973), 178–89.

120. Cf. Weiser, "Das 'Apostelkonzil,'" 147.

121. See Zingg, *Das Wachsen der Kirche*, 187, who observes that the whole Jerusalem church is not involved; and Weiser, "Das 'Apostelkonzil,'" 158, who thinks only a minority is involved.

122. The imperfect tense of ἐδίδασκον is taken here as inceptive, referring to the beginning of a repeated activity. Cf. Barrett, *The Acts of the Apostles*, 2:698.

123. This is the first reference in Acts to a group that including Gentiles as "brothers."

124. Cf. Barrett, *The Acts of the Apostles*, 2:697; and Weiser, "Das 'Apostelkonzil,'" 146, who sees this teaching as a clear indication that the Antioch church is already a "mixed" church

practice of circumcision, the reader will probably infer that they have not required this practice among the Gentile believers.[125] To the reader, this specific teaching by the Judean believers will contradict what has already been encountered in the variety of episodes along the narrated journey of Paul and Barnabas.[126] Such teaching also conflicts with earlier descriptions and statements regarding salvation, including statements by both Peter and Paul that have linked the salvation of Gentiles to God's will and guidance rather than to Jewish customs.[127] Luke, then, directly and negatively summarizes what this teaching causes as "no small dissension and debate" (στάσεως καὶ ζητήσεως οὐκ ὀλίγης; 15:2)[128] between these Judean Christians[129] and Paul and Barnabas, the representatives of the believers in Antioch.[130] Although Luke does not explicitly describe the thoughts or motives of these Judean believers, the selection of wording and the concise statement about the results of their teaching clearly depicts a negative scene of disruptive behavior that has intruded into the Antioch setting.[131]

This negative and disruptive behavior of those Judean believers, who insist on adherence to the Mosaic law for salvation, results in the Antioch church sending a party of representatives including Paul, Barnabas, and others to the Jerusalem church (15:2–3).[132] Obviously, the dispute is not

---

of both Jews and Gentiles. See Marshall, *The Acts of the Apostles*, 248, who states that the issue is not Gentile salvation but the necessity of their circumcision.

125. See Tyson, *Images of Judaism in Luke-Acts*, 146.

126. Cf. Pesch, *Die Apostelgeschichte*, 2:75.

127. Both the verb σῴζω and the noun σωτηρία appear in earlier sections of Acts and refer to the "requirements" of salvation. See, e.g., 2:21; 11:14; 13:26, 47. Cf. Krodel, *Acts*, 273.

128. The noun στάσις has a negative connotation of rebellion, civil strife, and division. Ancient historians used the term to depict destructive behavior by political leaders (see, e.g., Herodotus, *Histories* 1.59, 60; 5.28; Thucydides, *History of the Peloponnesian War* 2.20; 4.71). Plato uses the term to describe hostility between two parties who are not enemies (see *Republic* 5.470b). See LSJ, 1634; and Gerhard Delling, "στάσις," in *TDNT*, 7:568–71. However, the noun ζήτησις is a neutral term describing the investigation and discussion of important matters. See LSJ, 756; and Heinrich Greeven, "ζητέω...," in *TDNT*, 2:893–94.

129. Cf. Wills, "The Depiction of the Jews in Acts," 638, who concludes that the *Jewish* believers create the division.

130. Although 15:1–2 does not explicitly state that those who have come from Judea are Jewish believers, the general context suggests that this the identity of these characters.

131. Cf. Brian Rapske, "Opposition to the Plan of God and Persecution," in Marshall and Peterson, *Witness to the Gospel*, 242; Krodel, *Acts*, 273; and Williams, *Acts*, 261. See Weiser, "Das 'Apostelkonzil,'" 146, who observes that the narrator carefully links these events with those in Antioch at the end of chapter 14 (cf. 14:26–28).

132. The grammatical construction of 15:2 links the "dissension and debate" to the appointment of these representatives to go to Jerusalem, since those who have created the problem came from that region.

settled in Antioch. While the brief description of the trip in verse 3 does not contribute directly to the resolution of the conflict, it does prepare the reader for what happens in Jerusalem. The report of the conversion of the Gentiles (τὴν ἐπιστροφὴν τῶν ἐθνῶν) to believers in the regions of Phoenicia and Samaria created "great joy" (χαρὰν μεγάλην) among all the believers (πᾶσιν τοῖς ἀδελφοῖς; 15:3), a picture reflecting earlier positive images of the believers (cf. 5:41; 11:23).[133] In contrast, after the entire Jerusalem church has welcomed the Antioch church representatives, the narrator mentions nothing about *any* positive response by the Jerusalem believers to a report concerning "what God has done with them" (ὅσα ὁ θεὸς ἐποίησεν μετ' αὐτῶν; 15:4).[134] Rather, what Luke does mention is the response of some believers (τινες … πεπιστευκότες) from the "sect of the Pharisees" (ἀπὸ τῆς αἱρέσεως τῶν Φαρισαίων) who insist that Gentile converts, to whom the report refers, must (δεῖ) be circumcised and keep the Mosaic law (15:5).[135] Although this scene is the first time that Luke includes Pharisees among the believers, their narrated response still reflects negatively on them, since they appear as opponents to all the narrated activity in the last five chapters of Acts that Luke has linked directly to the will and guidance of God.[136] In the progression of the Acts narrative, these negative responses occur *after* the increasing presence of Gentiles among those who are believers. The question, therefore, focuses not on the legitimacy of the Christian mission to the Gentiles but on the

---

133. Cf. Walter Schmithals, *Die Apostelgeschichte des Lukas*, ZB (Zurich: Theologischer Verlag, 1982), 137.

134. Cf. Pesch, *Die Apostelgeschichte*, 2:76; and Schneider, *Die Apostelgeschichte*, 2:178.

135. The focus of the two opposing statements (cf. 15:1, 5) has changed. The first statement (15:1) indicates that circumcision is necessary for salvation; cf. Stephen G. Wilson, *Luke and the Law*, SNTSMS 50 (Cambridge: Cambridge University Press, 1983), 72. However, the second statement (15:5) suggests that circumcision is necessary for the Gentiles to be included in the people of God; cf. Jervell, *Luke and the People of God*, 66. Contra Barrett, *The Acts of the Apostles*, 2:705; Matthias Klinghardt, *Gesetz und Volk Gottes: Das lukanische Verständnis des Gesetzes nach Herkunft, Funktion und seinem Ort in der Geschichte des Urchristentums*, WUNT 2:32 (Tübingen: J. C. B. Mohr, 1988), 207; and Zingg, *Das Wachsen der Kirche*, 187, who identify the two statements as parallel.

136. Cf. John A. Darr, *On Character Building: The Reader and the Rhetoric of Characterization in Luke-Acts*, LCBI (Louisville: Westminster/John Knox, 1992), 120–21; Jack T. Sanders, "The Pharisees in Luke-Acts," in *The Living Text: Essays in Honor of Ernest W. Saunders*, ed. Dennis E. Groh and Robert Jewett (Lanham, MD: University Press of America, 1985), 183–84; Tyson, *Images of Judaism in Luke-Acts*, 146; and J. A. Ziesler, "Luke and the Pharisees," *NTS* 25 (January 1979): 147. Cf. also François Bovon, "Israel, die Kirche und die Völker im lukanischen Doppelwerk," *TL* 108 (1983): 404, who suggests that the Pharisees are fighting for the purity of the Jewish people.

issue of Gentile partnership in the Christian community. The problem concerning circumcision seems to be a problem of Jewish identity and self-understanding, since this is a primary issue of distinction and identity that the Gentile presence is perceived to threaten.[137] The higher level of inclusiveness within the Christian community, which the Jerusalem believers seemingly recognized earlier (cf. 11:18), now is contrasted with the demand for circumcision, a condition for entry or membership that would maintain the exclusive nature of the Jewish Christian community.[138]

The central portion of the Lukan account of the Jerusalem Council (Acts 15:6–29) recounts the deliberations among the Jerusalem believers regarding the issues of the salvation of Gentiles and, more generally, the nature of the Christian church or community.[139] The narrative account includes the description of two meetings: one of the apostles and elders (τε οἱ ἀπόστολοι καὶ οἱ πρεσβύτεροι; 15:6), and another of the "whole assembly" (πᾶν τὸ πλῆθος; 15:12).[140] The first part relates the apostles and elders meeting together (συνήχθησαν) to discuss the matter before them (15:6–7). The Petrine speech functions as an implicit articulation of the narrator's perspective.[141] The speech reminds both the Jerusalem audience and the reader of the Cornelius situation, when God selected Peter to deliver the gospel message to the Gentiles so that they might believe (πιστεῦσαι; 15:7).[142] Through Peter's lips the narrator

---

137. See James D. G. Dunn, *The Partings of the Ways: Between Christianity and Judaism and Their Significance for the Character of Christianity* (Philadelphia: Trinity Press International, 1991), 127; Seifrid, "Jesus and the Law in Acts," 45; and Weiser, "Das 'Apostelkonzil,' " 158.

138. See Johnson, *The Acts of the Apostles*, 260–61, who compares this situation to two incidents described by Josephus (cf. *Life* 113; *Jewish Antiquities* 13.258).

139. Cf. Weiser, "Das 'Apostelkonzil,' " 146.

140. The different designations of those involved suggest that two different meetings took place. Cf. Frederick W. Danker, "Reciprocity in the Ancient World and in Acts 15:23–29," in *Political Issues in Luke-Acts*, ed. Richard J. Cassidy and Philip J. Scharper (New York: Orbis, 1983), 54–55; and Barrett, *The Acts of the Apostles*, 2:712, 721. See F. F. Bruce, "The Apostolic Decree of Acts 15," in *Studien zum Text und zur Ethik des Neuen Testaments: Festschrift zum 80. Geburtstag von Heinrich Greeven*, ed. Wolfgang Schrage (Berlin: Walter de Gruyter, 1986), 121–22, who refers to two meetings; and idem, *The Book of the Acts*, 289, who refers only to *one* meeting.

141. Cf. Klinghardt, *Gesetz und Volk Gottes*, 209. See also Weiser, "Das 'Apostelkonzil,' " 154, who observes that this Petrine speech has obvious Lukan characteristics; and William S. Kurz, "Effects of Variant Narrators in Acts 10–11," *NTS* 43 (October 1997): 580–81, who states that Peter's speech here has a different perspective than his speech in Acts 11.

142. Cf. Borse, "Kompositionsgeschichtliche Beobachtungen zum Apostelkonzil," 201–2; Jacques Dupont, "Les discours de Pierre," in *Nouvelles études sur les Actes des Apôtres*, LD 118 (Paris: Éditions du Cerf, 1984), 104; and Johnson, *The Acts of the Apostles*, 262.

emphasizes that God has worked similarly among the Gentiles at Cornelius's house as he has among the Jewish believers at Pentecost (15:8–9; cf. 10:47; 11:15–17). Thus, the Jewish Christians cannot claim that God has worked exclusively among them.[143] The Jewish law obviously makes no difference in this matter, since both Jews and Gentiles have experienced the same divine blessing of salvation.[144] Peter presents the Jewish law as powerless to save both Jews and Gentiles.[145] Thus, Peter concludes that requirements on the Gentiles would be a negative, unreasonable response (15:10).[146] The narrator ends the Petrine speech by affirming the basic requirement for membership in the Christian community: the salvation (σωθῆναι) of both Jewish and Gentile believers "through the grace of the Lord Jesus" (διὰ τῆς χάριτος τοῦ κυρίου Ἰησοῦ; 15:11).[147] The narrated speech emphasizes that the inclusiveness of grace, not the exclusiveness of Jewish customs and laws, characterizes the Christian church.[148]

---

143. Cf. F. F. Bruce, "The Holy Spirit in the Acts of the Apostles," *Int* 27 (April 1973): 171–72; Dupont, "Les discours de Pierre," 104; Pesch, *Die Apostelgeschichte*, 2:77–78; van de Sandt, "An Explanation of Acts 15.6–21," 88; and Weiser, *Die Apostelgeschichte*, 2:373–74.

144. Cf. Jervell, *Luke and the People of God*, 65: "As a substitute for Jewish membership in the people of God, God accepts as valid the cleansing that has come upon them by faith (v. 9b)." Cf. also Jacques Dupont, "Un peuple d'entre les nations (Actes 15.14)," *NTS* 31 (July 1985): 323; Pesch, *Die Apostelgeschichte*, 2:86–87; and Seifrid, "Jesus and the Law in Acts," 46.

145. Cf. Marshall, *The Acts of the Apostles*, 250; Schneider, *Die Apostelgeschichte*, 2:179–80; and Joseph B. Tyson, "Jews and Judaism in Luke-Acts: Reading as a Godfearer," *NTS* 41 (1995): 32.

146. The Lukan Peter describes requirements suggested by the Pharisaic Christians as a "yoke" (ζυγόν) that the Jews have been unable to bear (βαστάσαι; 15:10). The noun ζυγόν is often used positively to refer to obedience to the law in Hellenistic Jewish writings (cf. Haenchen, *The Acts of the Apostles*, 446n3; Johnson, *The Acts of the Apostles*, 262–63; and Krodel, *Acts*, 277). In addition, the verb βαστάζω also is used predominantly in a positive sense in these writings; cf. John Nolland, "A Fresh Look at Acts 15.10," *NTS* 27 (October 1980): 113–14. However, the narrative context suggests that the reader should perceive the Jewish law as a *requirement* for membership in the church negatively. Cf. Dunn, *The Acts of the Apostles*, 201; Dupont, "Les discours de Pierre," 105; Fitzmyer, *The Acts of the Apostles*, 547–48; and Sanders, "The Pharisees in Luke-Acts," 173. Contra Nolland, "A Fresh Look at Acts 15.10," 105–15.

147. The phrase διὰ τῆς χάριτος τοῦ κυρίου Ἰησοῦ stands in the emphatic position in the sentence (15:11). However, the change in wording is interesting. Earlier comparisons state that the Gentile experience of salvation is like that of the Jewish believers. Here the order is reversed: *Jewish* believers will be saved just as the *Gentiles*. See Dupont, "Les discours de Pierre," 105.

148. See Karl Löning, "Das Verhältnis zum Judentum als Identitätsproblem der Kirche nach der Apostelgeschichte," in *"Ihr alle aber seid Brüder": Festschrift für A. Th. Khoury zum 60. Geburtstag*, ed. Ludwig Hagemann and Ernst Pulsfort (Würzburg: Echter, 1990), 315–17,

The second part of the Lukan account of the Jerusalem Council recounts what happens in a second meeting. The narrator includes two parties as speakers at this second meeting among πᾶν τὸ πλῆθος (15:12).[149] Barnabas and Paul are mentioned as the first ones to speak. Luke does not include the direct speech of these men but merely summarizes what they say to the gathering. Thus, the narrator reports that Barnabas and Paul tell of the "signs and wonders" (σημεῖα καὶ τέρατα; 15:12) that God has done through them among the Gentiles. This description corresponds to earlier sections of the Acts narrative in two ways. On the one hand, this report reminds the reader of the earlier positive depictions of God at work through Jesus and among the believers.[150] On the other hand, this brief summary implicitly refers the reader back to the narrative accounts of the last two chapters rather than repeating them.[151] Thus, the limited narrative account of the activities of Barnabas and Paul does not minimize their role in the meeting, as they report how God has worked among the Gentiles.[152]

The second part of the Lukan account of the Jerusalem Council recounts not only what Barnabas and Paul have said in the second meeting among πᾶν τὸ πλῆθος (15:12) but also a speech by James (15:13–21).[153] The narrator states nothing explicitly about James the brother of Jesus (Gal 1:19); the only previous reference to him (cf. 12:17) merely mentions him in passing.[154] This silence, along with the prominence of his speech in this account of the Jerusalem Council, suggests to the reader that James may be an undisputed authority, so that a statement delineating his credentials is unnecessary.[155] His speech, which occupies the center of this narrative section, functions as another implicit declaration

---

who suggests that Peter's speech covers soteriological issues, whereas James's speech covers ecclesiological issues.

149. Johnson, *The Acts of the Apostles*, 268, states that the description depicts the believers as a deliberative body, a typical literary device providing an opportunity to review the story.

150. Cf. 2:22, 43; 4:16, 22, 30; 5:12; 6:8; 14:3. Cf. Roloff, *Die Apostelgeschichte*, 231; and Shepherd, *The Narrative Function of the Holy Spirit*, 217–18.

151. Cf. Dibelius, "The Apostolic Council," 96; Krodel, *Acts*, 279; Weiser, *Die Apostelgeschichte*, 2:374, 381–82; and Barrett, *The Acts of the Apostles*, 2:721.

152. One must try to account for the composition of Acts, rather than merely try to reconstruct its historical situation. Contra Achtemeier, "An Elusive Unity," 6; Boismard, "Le 'concile' de Jérusalem," 435; and Taylor, "Ancient Texts and Modern Critics," 375.

153. See Jervell, *Luke and the People of God*, 185–207.

154. Cf. ibid., 185; and Barrett, *The Acts of the Apostles*, 2:722–23.

155. See Jervell, *Luke and the People of God*, 187; and Joseph B. Tyson, "The Emerging Church and the Problem of Authority in Acts," *Int* 42 (1988): 139–42, who sees authority moving away from the apostles.

of the Lukan narrator's perspective through one of the characters.[156] A significant aspect of this speech is its explanation of several themes regarding the nature of the Christian church.[157] In the Lukan account of that speech, James reaffirms what God has done among the Gentiles, stating that God has taken from them (ἐξ ἐθνῶν) a "people for God's name" (λαὸν τῷ ὀνόματι αὐτοῦ; 15:14).[158] The term λαός, which Luke typically reserves only for the Jewish people as the people of God, is used here with reference to the Gentiles.[159] According to the Lukan James, God had made it possible for Gentiles to be identified with God. This inclusion of non-Jewish persons within the λαός or people of God is related to a quotation from Amos 9:11–12. In that passage, all others (οἱ κατάλοιποι τῶν ἀνθρώπων) and "all of the Gentiles" (πάντα τὰ ἔθνη; Acts 15:17) who will become identified with God will do so as a result of the restoration of Israel (cf. 15:16).[160] The picture here is one of God's fulfillment of God's promises to Israel, resulting in the *inclusion* of the Gentiles among God's people.[161] The narrative, then, does not depict one λαός of the Jews and a different λαός of the Gentiles, but one λαός consisting of both Jews and Gentiles.[162] The insertion of this quotation validates what Luke has described in Acts 1–14: God has fulfilled God's promise among God's people, as the first narrative unit (1:1–8:3) clearly indicates; and as a result God has also offered the Gentiles the opportunity to join God's people.[163] Through the inserted speech by James, Luke implicitly

---

156. See Klinghardt, *Gesetz und Volk Gottes*, 209; and Richard, "The Divine Purpose," 191. Cf. Weiser, "Das 'Apostelkonzil,'" 155.

157. Cf. Löning, "Das Verhältnis zum Judentum," 315–17; Lüdemann, *Early Christianity according to the Traditions in Acts*, 168; and Weiser, "Das 'Apostelkonzil,'" 153.

158. Cf. Zingg, *Das Wachsen der Kirche*, 188, who points out that this is the third speech or report affirming what God had done among the Gentiles. Cf. also Dupont, "Un peuple d'entre les nations," 329; Johnson, *The Acts of the Apostles*, 264; and Krodel, *Acts*, 280, who observes that λαός and Gentiles are a deliberate contradiction of terms.

159. Cf. Bruce, *The Book of the Acts*, 293; Dupont, "Un peuple d'entre les nations," 322, 324–25; Lohfink, *Die Sammlung Israels*, 58–59; and Zingg, *Das Wachsen der Kirche*, 159.

160. Cf. Jervell, *Luke and the People of God*, 52–54; Krodel, *Acts*, 282; Tyson, *Images of Judaism in Luke-Acts*, 152; and Weiser, "Das 'Apostelkonzil,'" 161. Contra Marshall, *The Acts of the Apostles*, 252, who interprets 15:16 as referring to the church.

161. See Dupont, "Un peuple d'entre les nations," 329, who stresses that the believing Gentiles still do not belong to Israel, but that does not minimize their belonging to God.

162. Cf. Dupont, ibid., who downplays the idea of two different peoples of God. See Lohfink, *Die Sammlung Israels*, 59–60, who contends that Luke depicts the true Israel coming out of the "old people of God," followed by the conversion of Gentiles.

163. See Jacob Jervell, "The Law in Luke-Acts," *HTR* 64 (1971): 32, who suggests that the idea of a people joining Israel (15:14) differentiates between a people of God and an "associate" people of God.

characterizes the λαός that is identified with God as a people that includes both Jews and Gentiles, a λαός created by the divine fulfillment of God's promises to Israel.[164]

The conclusion of James's speech makes a dual suggestion to the church in Jerusalem and prepares the reader for what follows in the narrative.[165] On the one hand, the Lukan James determines that the Jewish Christians should not create difficulties (παρενοχλεῖν)[166] for the Gentile believers (τοῖς ἀπὸ τῶν ἐθνῶν ἐπιστρέφουσιν ἐπὶ τὸν θεόν; 15:19), a decision that reaffirms what Peter has stated earlier (cf. 15:10). On the other hand, James suggests that they write a letter to the Gentile believers and provide a list of four matters from which they should abstain. The recommendation, however, mentions nothing of the circumcision issue, implicitly agreeing with Peter's statement (cf. 15:10) that the Jewish law would be an unnecessary hindrance to the Gentile believers. This statement does not substitute those four matters for Jewish law observance.[167] However, such a concession will positively facilitate the social contact and community building among both Jewish and Gentile Christians by protecting Jewish concerns about defilement by Gentiles.[168] Thus, the recommendation to the Gentile believers clearly recognizes both what God has done among them and acknowledges their inclusion as part of the λαός of God, which the Lukan narrator implicitly identifies as the church.

The Lukan narrator further characterizes the church in Jerusalem through his narration of their actions that James's speech prompts. The narrative depiction of the joint decision between the Jerusalem Christian leaders and "the whole church" (σὺν ὅλῃ τῇ ἐκκλησίᾳ; 15:22) presents

---

164. While Luke depicts the people of God through James's speech as now including both Jews and Gentiles, he does not describe the church as the *new* Israel. The designation of "Israel" is never given to the Christian community which, if Luke perceives the church to be the new Israel, one would expect to find it stated in this crucial passage. Cf. Roloff, *Die Apostelgeschichte*, 232.

165. The two parts (15:19–20) are grammatically linked and must be considered together.

166. See Johnson, *The Acts of the Apostles*, 266, who points out that the verb παρενοχλέω (15:19) has the connotation of creating an annoyance for someone else. Cf. Aristotle, *Rhetoric* 2.4.21.

167. Cf. Conzelmann, *Acts of the Apostles*, 118; and Tyson, "Jews and Judaism in Luke-Acts," 33.

168. Cf. Boismard, "Le 'concile' de Jérusalem," 435; Bruce, *The Book of the Acts*, 295–96; Seifrid, "Jesus and the Law in Acts," 47–48; and Weiser, "Das 'Apostelkonzil,' " 162. See Krodel, *Acts*, 280, who stresses that this is an "apostolic interpretation of Luke 16:17 with respect to the social function of the Torah in interracial communities."

the Jerusalem believers as similar to earlier positive images of the same group (cf. 1:15–26; 6:1–6) and the Antioch church (cf. 13:1–3).[169] The Jerusalem church decides that they will send two representatives, Judas Barsabbas and Silas, with the letter to Antioch along with Paul and Barnabas (15:22). The letter's contents repeat much of what Luke has already narrated. However, the letter confirms the narrator's observations by functioning as an explicit description of the Jerusalem believers from their perspective.[170] The letter, as Luke presents it, emphasizes two important points in relation to the characterization of the Christian community. First, the letter stresses the identification of the Jewish believers in Jerusalem with the Gentile believers in Antioch (cf. 15:8–9, 11). On the one hand, the letter addressed the Gentile believers as "brothers" (τοῖς ... ἀδελφοῖς τοῖς ἐξ ἐθνῶν; 15:23), the first time non-Jewish persons are described in that manner by *Jewish* characters in Acts.[171] Thus, this address suggests that a similar bond exists between the Jewish believers in Jerusalem and the Gentile believers in Antioch as between Jewish persons.[172] On the other hand, the letter depicts the Jerusalem believers as distancing themselves from those who have caused the original trouble among the Gentile believers in Antioch.[173] Thus, the letter from the Jerusalem believers both affirms their identification and bond with the Gentile believers in Antioch and characterizes the church in terms of the bonds of a common faith and grace (cf. 15:8–11), not in terms of ethnic bonds.

Second, the letter from the Jerusalem believers to the Gentile believers in Antioch stresses their resolution of a controversial issue. That resolution, which affirms James's recommendation and which the letter

---

169. Cf. Weiser, "Das 'Apostelkonzil,'" 155, 163–64. See Williams, *Acts*, 269, who states that outside the council "there remained a significant number of Jewish Christians who wished to take a much harder line with the Gentiles."

170. Cf. Kurz, *Reading Luke-Acts*, 93.

171. Cf. 15:1, where the narrator identifies the Antioch believers as "brothers," and 15:23, where the Jewish believers in Jerusalem also identify the Gentile believers in Antioch as "brothers." Cf. Krodel, *Acts*, 288; and Williams, *Acts*, 269.

172. The letter is addressed only to the Gentile believers in Antioch, suggesting that (1) the Antioch church is predominantly Gentile and that the success of the gospel (11:21) is confined largely to the Gentiles, (2) the issue has nothing to do with the Jewish believers in Antioch, or (3) Luke is not consistent at this point.

173. The letter's depiction of the actions of those who have gone to Antioch (15:24) is most negative, as the verbs ταράσσω (to trouble/disturb) and ἀνασκευάζω (to upset/unsettle) suggest along with them teaching "that which we have not ordered." Cf. Johnson, *The Acts of the Apostles*, 276.

presents, is introduced affirmatively in two ways.[174] The letter states that the Jerusalem believers make the decision "unanimously" (ὁμοθυμαδόν; 15:25), which reflects the positive characteristic that the reader will have seen earlier in the Jerusalem believers (cf. 1:14; 2:46; 4:24; 5:12).[175] Although those who hold a different position have created this controversy, Luke mentions nothing about their opposition here. Also, the letter states that the decision is not merely a human one; rather, the Holy Spirit is linked favorably to their decision-making process (15:28).[176] The actions of the believers in Jerusalem again present them as the group in which one finds the activity of the Holy Spirit, which will positively dispose both the Antioch believers and the readers toward the decision.[177]

The stated decision, commonly referred to as the Apostolic Decree,[178] does not represent the imposition of Jewish law or a substitution for the Torah, for such a response would contradict what Peter and James have said and would not evoke a joyful response from the Gentile believers in Antioch (cf. 15:31).[179] The decree also does not imply that the Jewish

---

174. On the repetition of the decree after the report of James's recommendation, see Kurz, *Reading Luke-Acts*, 93; and Tannehill, *The Narrative Unity of Luke-Acts*, 2:192–93. On the issues of the differing versions of the decree (cf. 15:20, 29; 21:25) and variant readings, see Bruce M. Metzger, *A Textual Commentary on the Greek New Testament* (New York: United Bible Societies, 1971), 429–34.

175. The unanimous spirit is implied in the apparent agreement between the partners of Paul and Barnabas and the partners of Judas and Silas (cf. 15:25–27). Cf. Bovon, "Israel, die Kirche und die Völker im lukanischen Doppelwerk," 411; Eckhard Plümacher, *Lukas als hellenistischer Schriftsteller: Studien zur Apostelgeschichte*, SUNT (Göttingen: Vandenhoeck & Ruprecht, 1972), 69–70; Weiser, *Die Apostelgeschichte*, 2:374–75.

176. Cf., e.g., Haenchen, *The Acts of the Apostles*, 453; Johnson, *The Acts of the Apostles*, 277; Schneider, *Die Apostelgeschichte*, 2:186–87; and Weiser, *Die Apostelgeschichte*, 2:385–86.

177. Cf. Achtemeier, "An Elusive Unity," 15; Martin Hengel, *Acts and the History of Earliest Christianity*, trans. John Bowden (Philadelphia: Fortress, 1979), 115; Krodel, *Acts*, 290; and Weiser, "Das 'Apostelkonzil,'" 164–65.

178. For studies on the decree, see Peder Borgen, "Catalogues of Vices, the Apostolic Decree, and the Jerusalem Meeting," in *The Social World of Formative Christianity and Judaism*, ed. Ernest S. Frerichs, Jacob Neusner, Peder Borgen, and Richard Horsley (Philadelphia: Fortress, 1982), 126–41; Bruce, "The Apostolic Decree of Acts 15," 115–24; Klinghardt, *Gesetz und Volk Gottes*, 207–24; Charles Perrot, "Les décisions de l'assemblée de Jérusalem," *RSR* 69 (1981): 195–208; Sanders, *The Jews in Luke-Acts*, 115–23; and Wilson, *Luke and the Law*, 73–102.

179. Cf., e.g., Borgen, "Catalogues of Vices," 136; Dibelius, "The Apostolic Council," 97; Haenchen, *The Acts of the Apostles*, 449n3; J. L. Houlden, "The Purpose of Luke," *JSNT* 21 (1984): 60; and Seifrid, "Jesus and the Law in Acts," 47–48. Contra Jervell, "The Law in Luke-Acts," 33; and Donald Juel, *Luke-Acts: The Promise of History* (Atlanta: John Knox, 1983), 105–6.

and Gentile believers have reached a compromise, for they have soundly rejected the original arguments of the Pharisaic Christians.[180] Rather, these four abstentions facilitate the social interaction or fellowship between the Jewish and non-Jewish Christians.[181] This decree implies that the gospel cannot be tied to a specific culture, thus resulting in a greater sense of inclusiveness.[182] Hence, the Lukan narrator does not depict the Jerusalem church as an authority over the Antioch church but as a mediating party that offers a solution to a controversial question. This picture further accentuates the sense of unity between the churches as the letter states (cf. 15:23), although some within the Jerusalem church have acted differently.

The concluding part of this narrative section returns the action to the Antioch church. Luke states that the letter from the Jerusalem church is delivered to the Antioch believers after they gather together (συναγαγόντες τὸ πλῆθος; 15:30).[183] The narrator describes the letter's contents as "encouragement" (τῇ παρακλήσει; 15:31) and the reaction as joyful (ἐχάρησαν), suggesting that the Antioch believers accept the decree as a positive response from the Jerusalem church.[184] These believers also receive the affirming ministry of Judas and Silas, whom the narrator describes positively as prophets who encourage and strengthen

---

180. See, e.g., Marshall, *The Acts of the Apostles*, 254; Sanders, *The Jews in Luke-Acts*, 117–19; and Tyson, *Images of Judaism in Luke-Acts*, 149. See also Boismard, "Le 'concile' de Jérusalem," 435; and Bruce, "The Apostolic Decree of Acts 15," 116, who both write that the decree does not *state* that circumcision is not required. Contra Marshall, *The Acts of the Apostles*, 243; and Schneider, *Die Apostelgeschichte*, 2:183–84.

181. Cf., e.g., Craig L. Blomberg, "The Law in Luke-Acts," *JSNT* 22 (1984): 66; Robert L. Brawley, *Luke-Acts and the Jews: Conflict, Apology, and Conciliation*, SBLMS 33 (Atlanta: Scholars Press, 1987), 152; Danker, "Reciprocity in the Ancient World and in Acts 15:23–29," 51–54; Edvin Larsson, "Paul: Law and Salvation," *NTS* 31 (July 1985): 430; and Weiser, "Das 'Apostelkonzil,'" 159. Contra Sanders, *The Jews in Luke-Acts*, 119–21.

The question concerning the relation of the Apostolic Decree to Lev 17–18, which governs the behavior of Gentiles living among the Israelites, focuses ultimately on the issue of social interaction between Jews and non-Jews. Cf., e.g., Barrett, *The Acts of the Apostles*, 2:733–35; Boismard and Lamouille, *Les Actes des deux Apôtres*, 2:65–66; Fitzmyer, *The Acts of the Apostles*, 557–58; Sanders, *The Jews in Luke-Acts*, 115–16, 267–68; and Witherington, *The Acts of the Apostles*, 464–66.

182. Cf. Weiser, "Das 'Apostelkonzil,'" 166; and Thomas Wieser, "Community — Its Unity, Diversity and Universality," *Semeia* 54 (1985): 90.

183. See Haenchen, *The Acts of the Apostles*, 454, who states that Luke does not say whether the representatives from Jerusalem or Paul and Barnabas call the meeting of the believers.

184. Cf. Krodel, *Acts*, 290; Roloff, *Die Apostelgeschichte*, 234; Schmithals, *Die Apostelgeschichte des Lukas*, 142; and Weiser, *Die Apostelgeschichte*, 2:375.

the "brothers" (τοὺς ἀδελφούς; 15:32).[185] In turn, the Antioch believers send off the two men in peace (ἀπελύθησαν μετ᾽ εἰρήνης), an indication of the mutual and harmonious support between the churches (15:33).[186] In contrast to the narrative scene of dissension and strife at the chapter's beginning, Luke shapes this concluding narrative scene as one characterized by unanimity.[187] The final picture of this section presents the Antioch church as the center from which Paul and Barnabas, along with many others (μετὰ καὶ ἑτέρων πολλῶν; 15:35), continue to teach and proclaim (διδάσκοντες καὶ εὐαγγελιζόμενοι) the word of the Lord, an image consistent with earlier positive descriptions of the believers' activities.[188] The mention of teaching and proclamation, within the scope of the church and its ministry, implies to the reader both that a period of growth follows the reception of the message from the Jerusalem church and that the divine presence is at work within the church. Although the narrative section begins with a controversy created by believers from Judea, the section ends with the affirmation that the Jerusalem church has responded appropriately to the problem, resulting in signs of divine blessing.

An Assessment of the Characterization of the Church or Group of Believers in Acts 15:1–35

The Lukan account of the Jerusalem Council stands at a strategic point in the Acts narrative. Some scholars have suggested that this narrative section includes the most important events and decisions of the early Christian movement.[189] Within the narrative itself, these events and associated deliberations function to provide the reader with both a retrospective and prospective examination of the Christian community and the divine activity among the believers.[190] Therefore, the narrator

---

185. The two verbs describing Judas's and Silas's activity (15:32), παρακαλέω and ἐπιστηρίζω, have previously described Paul and Barnabas's activity on their return trip through Lystra, Iconium, and Pisidian Antioch (cf. 14:21–22). Cf. Pesch, *Die Apostelgeschichte*, 2:84.

186. The verb ἀπολύω describes the Antioch church's response of sending Barnabas and Saul (cf. 13:3). Cf. Johnson, *The Acts of the Apostles*, 278; and Tannehill, *The Narrative Unity of Luke-Acts*, 2:192–93.

187. See Weiser, *Die Apostelgeschichte*, 2:386. Cf. Krodel, *Acts*, 291.

188. For references focusing on teaching among the believers, see, e.g., 2:42; 4:2, 18; 5:21, 25, 28, 42; 11:26; and 13:1–3. For references focusing on proclamation, see, e.g., 5:42; 10:36; 11:20; 14:7, 21.

189. See, e.g., Johnson, *Decision Making in the Church*, 68; Pesch, *Die Apostelgeschichte*, 2:85; Roloff, *Die Apostelgeschichte*, 222; and Schneider, *Die Apostelgeschichte*, 2:168.

190. See Krodel, *Acts*, 263.

invites the reader to evaluate what has happened and what the Christian community might be like from the vantage point of this narrative section. Although the narrator does not explicitly characterize those who create the tension and turmoil among the believers (cf. Acts 15:1–5), their activities in the previous two chapters implicitly present them as opponents of God's activities among the Gentiles. Thus, within the Jerusalem church are those who resist the work of God and the inclusion of Gentiles into the Christian church.[191] One cannot ignore the fact that some within the church of Jerusalem have acted divisively against the mixed group of believers in Antioch. However, Luke does present implicit judgments through the characters of Peter (cf. 15:7–11) and James (cf. 15:13–21) concerning what has occurred among both the Jews and Gentiles, so that these reported deliberations also contribute to the developing Lukan characterization of the churches.

The Lukan emphases on the unanimity of the Christian community and on the divine presence among the believers are apparent once again in this narrative section.[192] The narrator, through the speeches and the response by the Jerusalem church to the question concerning the need for Gentile Christians to become Jewish Christians, identifies the church as the people of God. The Lukan presentation of what occurs claims that the identity of the people of God is founded not on ethnic practices (the Jewish law) but on their common salvation through grace (cf. 15:8–11). Although the actions of those believers who identify God's people by Torah observance have created turmoil and threatened the church's unity, the affirmation of the Christian community, characterized by faith in God's salvific activity, results in unanimity and a benevolent spirit among the believers (cf. 15:31–32).[193] Thus, the four requirements of the so-called Apostolic Decree do not substitute for Torah observance but are perceived as divine provision (cf. 15:28) for the social and communal interaction between Jewish and Gentile believers (cf. 15:20, 29). The narrative characterization of the Christian community, which initially has included only Jewish persons, now unequivocally affirms the

---

191. Cf. Joseph B. Tyson, "The Problem of Jewish Rejection in Acts," in Tyson, *Luke-Acts and the Jewish People*, 135.

192. See Johnson, *The Acts of the Apostles*, 279, who states that Luke's version of what happens when Paul and Barnabas meet with the Jerusalem church is "indeed idealized."

193. See Tyson, "The Problem of Jewish Rejection in Acts," 135, who observes that those who insist on the Gentile Christians becoming Jewish do not gain the "upper hand."

Gentile believers as part of the church; Jewish believers and Gentile believers constitute those who are together united and identified as God's
people.[194] Nevertheless, while Luke characterizes the Christian community in this manner, the divisive actions in Antioch by some Jerusalem
believers suggest to the reader that the church still has difficulties to
overcome if it is truly the people of God.

The Churches in Antioch and Asia
after the Jerusalem Council (Acts 15:36–16:5)

The Literary Context

The prior scenes of the Jerusalem Council and the delivery of the letter sent by the Jerusalem church arise out of a larger literary context,
in which Paul and Barnabas take the gospel to new regions, resulting
in both Jews and Gentiles accepting that message and joining the ranks
of the believers. Although one should not characterize that mission as a
Gentile mission since Paul and Barnabas typically go to the synagogue
first and proclaim the gospel there (cf. 13:5, 14–15; 14:1), the Lukan
narrator does mention that Gentiles as well as Jews respond favorably to
their message (cf. 13:43–44; 14:1). That Gentile response, in particular,
has induced the questions raised by some of the Jewish believers in Acts
15. Since the questions have been raised in Antioch because of the increasing presence of Gentiles among the Christians in that city and others
(cf. 8:4–14:28), the positive conclusion as articulated in the letter and
the message to the Gentile believers in Antioch seem to anticipate what
is to follow in other cities, as presented in subsequent sections of Acts.

The Characterization of the Church or Group of Believers
in Acts 15:36–16:5

The section begins by mentioning Paul's suggestion to Barnabas that they
return to visit the cities and churches (τοὺς ἀδελφούς) where they have
"proclaimed the word of the Lord" (κατηγγείλαμεν τὸν λόγον τοῦ κυρίου;
15:36).[195] These churches certainly consist of both Jewish and Gentile

---

194. Brian S. Rosner, "The Progress of the Word," in Marshall and Peterson, *Witness to
the Gospel*, 227, who suggests that "only geographical boundaries need to be crossed" after
Acts 15, misses crucial elements of the narrative.

195. See Schneider, *Die Apostelgeschichte*, 2:195; and Weiser, *Die Apostelgeschichte*,
2:395, who see 15:36–40 as a continuation of 14:28 in the source used by Luke.

believers. Thus, Paul's suggestion means that the implications of the decisions made in Jerusalem now extend beyond Antioch to the areas where Paul and Barnabas have ministered on their first journey. A dispute arises between Paul and Barnabas, however, over whether they should allow John Mark to accompany them.[196] The narrative briefly explains Barnabas's side of the dispute: he wishes to take Mark with them (ἐβούλετο συμπαραλαβεῖν; 15:37). However, the narrative provides a more complete explanation about why Paul thinks Mark should *not* go with them (ἠξίου . . . μὴ συμπαραλαμβάνειν τοῦτον; 15:38):[197] Earlier Mark deserted them (τὸν ἀποστάντα ἀπ' αὐτῶν)[198] in Pamphylia and did not go with them (μὴ συνελθόντα αὐτοῖς) in the work (τὸ ἔργον; 15:38) that the Antioch church sent them to do.[199] The reason for Mark's desertion may have been that Mark disapproved of a ministry that includes preaching also to Gentiles, so that Paul's objections may reflect differences over that same issue, even *after* the Jerusalem Council.[200] The disagreement results in the astonishing parting of the ways between Paul and Barnabas. The reader would see this turn of events as rather startling, considering the unanimity among believers and the positive, almost idealistic portraits of both

---

196. See Haenchen, *The Acts of the Apostles*, 474, who suggests that the expression of 15:39 blames neither party. For a study of the portrayal of John Mark in Acts, see C. Clifton Black, *Mark: Images of an Apostolic Interpreter* (Columbia: University of South Carolina Press, 1994), 25–49, which first appeared as "The Presentation of John Mark in the Acts of the Apostles," *PerRS* 20 (1993): 235–54, and was subsequently revised as "John Mark in the Acts of the Apostles," in *Literary Studies in Luke-Acts: Essays in Honor of Joseph B. Tyson*, ed. Richard P. Thompson and Thomas E. Phillips (Macon, GA: Mercer University Press, 1998), 101–20.

197. See Black, *Mark*, 38; and Barrett, *The Acts of the Apostles*, 2:754, who observe that the different tenses of the infinitives συμπαραλαβεῖν (15:37) and συμπαραλαμβάνειν (15:38) suggest that Barnabas decides, at the last moment, that Mark should join them, whereas Paul does not want Mark with them "day in and day out." See Johnson, *The Acts of the Apostles*, 282, who observes that the same term describes Mark's earlier recruitment (cf. 12:25).

198. The verb ἀφίστημι (15:38) has the negative connotation of apostasy or defection. See BDAG, 157–58; LSJ, 289–90; Rudolf Bultmann, "ἀφίημι . . . ," in *TDNT*, 1:509–12; and Black, *Mark*, 47n43.

199. The expression τὸ ἔργον apparently refers to "the work" to which Paul and Barnabas have been divinely called (cf. 13:2; 14:26). Cf. Haenchen, *The Acts of the Apostles*, 474; Larkin, *Acts*, 231; and Weiser, *Die Apostelgeschichte*, 2:394.

200. See Black, *Mark*, 40–41. See also Roloff, *Die Apostelgeschichte*, 236–37, who suggests that Paul sees Mark's desertion as giving up on the Christian mission to Gentiles. However, since Acts 13–14 describes a mission to *Jews* resulting in Gentile acceptance of the gospel, this conclusion should be amended. Thus, the *inclusion* of Gentiles into the community of believers (the church) may be Mark's problem, which reflects the reaction of some in the Jerusalem church and is therefore unsurprising since he is from Jerusalem.

men in Acts.[201] For only the second time in the narrative, Luke presents an unresolved problem relating to the unanimity of the believers (cf. 5:1–11). Nonetheless, the Lukan account of the difficulties suggests that their ministry continues, albeit in separate and different directions,[202] as Barnabas goes with Mark to Cyprus (15:39) and Paul chooses Silas to accompany him on his trip as planned (15:40).[203]

In spite of the ambiguities in the narrated disintegration of the ministry partnership of Paul and Barnabas, Luke affirmatively describes the activity of the Antioch believers. They figuratively hand Silas over "to the grace of the Lord" (παραδοθεὶς τῇ χάριτι τοῦ κυρίου ὑπὸ τῶν ἀδελφῶν; 15:40) as Paul's new ministry partner, a description similar to the earlier picture of their corporate activity in sending out Paul and Barnabas (cf. 14:26).[204] Thus, the Antioch church again provides the communal context from which the ministry of the gospel is launched, even though Silas has come from the Jerusalem church (cf. 15:22, 36).[205] As a result, Luke reports that Paul and Silas visit the churches in Syria and Cilicia and strengthen them (ἐπιστηρίζων τὰς ἐκκλησίας; 15:41); this description alludes to similar positive pictures of the ministry of the churches in Antioch and Jerusalem (cf. 14:22; 15:32).[206] The subsequent narrative scenes in Derbe and Lystra imply similar images (16:1–3). However, the Lukan narrator provides more information about what Paul, Silas, and now Timothy do in the towns and churches they visit: they present what

---

201. See Richard J. Cassidy, *Society and Politics in the Acts of the Apostles* (Maryknoll, NY: Orbis, 1987), 66–67. See also Black, *Mark*, 41, who suggests the possibility that Barnabas may be caught "on the horns of a dilemma on which he cannot help but be impaled." If he sides with either Paul or Mark, the Christian movement will be internally fractured.

202. See Kurz, *Reading Luke-Acts*, 94, who interprets the separation as having positive results by doubling the size of the missionary force. However, that interpretation does not appreciate the ambiguity here. See also Marshall, *The Acts of the Apostles*, 257; and Tannehill, *The Narrative Unity of Luke-Acts*, 2:194, who point out that there is no mention of the Spirit's guidance.

203. It is unclear how Silas is available for Paul's selection in Antioch, since the Antioch believers have sent him back to Jerusalem (cf. 15:33). Cf. Borse, "Kompositionsgeschichtliche Beobachtungen zum Apostelkonzil," 196; and Conzelmann, *Acts of the Apostles*, 124. See Tannehill, *The Narrative Unity of Luke-Acts*, 2:196, who interprets the partnership between Paul and Silas as representing the unity of purpose between the Jerusalem and Antioch churches.

204. The verb παραδίδωμι is used to refer to the Antioch believers' action of committing the men for the work to which God has called them (14:26). See Johnson, *The Acts of the Apostles*, 283; and Tannehill, *The Narrative Unity of Luke-Acts*, 2:194.

205. Cf. Bruce, *The Book of the Acts*, 302; Marshall, *The Acts of the Apostles*, 258; Roloff, *Die Apostelgeschichte*, 237; and Tannehill, *The Narrative Unity of Luke-Acts*, 2:195–96.

206. Cf. Fitzmyer, *The Acts of the Apostles*, 574.

the Jerusalem church has decided (τὰ δόγματα τὰ κεκριμένα; 16:4) in the meetings recounted in the previous chapter. Luke concludes this narrative section by positively characterizing these churches as continually being "strengthened in the faith" (ἐστερεοῦντο τῇ πίστει) and increasing daily in the number of believers (ἐπερίσσευον τῷ ἀριθμῷ καθ᾽ ἡμέραν; 16:5).[207] Although the terminology is different, the reader is encouraged to link these scenes with similar positive images of groups of believers depicted earlier in the narrative, as Luke continues to portray the churches in ways that imply the characteristics of unanimity and divine blessing.[208] The juxtaposition of the positive imagery in depicting the various churches and the description of the delivery of the Apostolic Decree to those churches suggests that the decree has positive effects on the various Christian groups, perhaps in assisting Jewish and Gentile believers to live together in oneness.[209] Consequently, the Acts narrative continues to present the Christian community as the people among whom the reader finds the presence of God.

An Assessment of the Characterization of the Christian Church or Group of Believers in Acts 15:36–16:5

The Lukan characterization of the churches in the narrative section of 15:36–16:5 corresponds to the positive images resulting from the decisions of the Jerusalem church in the previous section. Once again, the narrator employs indirect or implicit means of description, allowing the reader to make judgments about the believers based on the actions as presented. However, what the narrative includes also alludes to the positive qualities of unanimity and divine blessing that are repeatedly evident in earlier narrative sections. Although these qualities are not explicitly emphasized, the narrator focuses the reader's attention on the development of these churches, which he links affirmatively to the Apostolic Decree. Even the surprising dispute between Paul and Barnabas and the ensuing termination of their partnership do not detract from the Lukan

---

207. The verbs στερεόω and περισσεύω appear in the imperfect tense (16:5), suggesting that these are typical traits. The verb στερεόω only appears here and in 3:7, 16, where it refers to strengthening the healed lame man's legs. The verb περισσεύω appears only here in Acts and has the connotation of abundance. See Georg Bertram, "στερεός . . . ," in *TDNT*, 7:609–14; and Friedrich Hauck, "περισσεύω . . . ," in *TDNT*, 6:58–61.

208. E.g., 2:41, 47; 4:4; 5:14; 6:7; 9:31; and 12:24. Cf. Haenchen, *The Acts of the Apostles*, 479; Johnson, *The Acts of the Apostles*, 285; and Kurz, *Reading Luke-Acts*, 95.

209. Cf. Krodel, *Acts*, 299; Marshall, *The Acts of the Apostles*, 261; and Tannehill, *The Narrative Unity of Luke-Acts*, 2:196. Contra Conzelmann, *Acts of the Apostles*, 125.

portrayal of the ever-growing church. Thus, this narrative section seems to affirm the Apostolic Decree by describing its positive results among the "mixed" churches of both Jews and Gentiles, the same churches that Paul and Barnabas have started during their narrated ministry trip (cf. 13:4–14:26).

THE BELIEVERS IN THESSALONICA AND BEROEA (ACTS 17:1–15)

The Literary Context (Acts 16:6–40)

The Acts narrative takes a geographical turn after Paul and Silas visits the churches in Phrygia and Galatia (16:6). Luke directly states that divine intervention forbid them from entering the regions of Asia and Bithynia (16:6–7), culminating in a vision to go to Macedonia, which they *together* interpret (συμβιβάζοντες) as God's call to proclaim the gospel message there (16:9–10).[210] Their experiences in Philippi (16:1–40) results in imprisonment, the expected divine rescue (cf. 5:17–21; 12:6–11),[211] and some positive response to the gospel (cf. 16:14–15, 30–34, 40).[212]

The Characterization of the Church or Group of Believers in Acts 17:1–15

The narrative continues with the Pauline ministry party traveling through Amphipolis and Apollonia before arriving at Thessalonica. Luke presents Paul as going to the Jewish synagogue in the city, a practice in the Pauline portions of Acts that the narrator explicitly explains as Paul's custom (κατὰ τὸ εἰωθός; 17:2).[213] After going to the synagogue for three Sabbaths, which includes discussions with the people and Paul's proclamation of Jesus as the Messiah (17:2–3), the narrator reports that some

---

210. See Larkin, *Acts*, 233–34, who emphasizes the corporate discernment as God is leading them to Macedonia. Cf. Pervo, *Profit with Delight*, 72–73; Pesch, *Die Apostelgeschichte*, 2:91–103; Schneider, *Die Apostelgeschichte*, 1:193–208; and Williams, *Acts*, 278.

211. Cf. Pervo, *Profit with Delight*, 23–24; and Tannehill, *The Narrative Unity of Luke-Acts*, 2:198.

212. Acts 16:40 states that Paul and Silas encourage the "brothers" (τοὺς ἀδελφούς) before they leave Philippi. The narrative mentions little of believers except for the households of Lydia (16:14–15) and the jailer (16:30–33).

213. Cf. Kurz, *Reading Luke-Acts*, 95; Pesch, *Die Apostelgeschichte*, 2:122; Fitzmyer, *The Acts of the Apostles*, 594; and Witherington, *The Acts of the Apostles*, 504.

Jews (τινες ἐξ αὐτῶν), "a large number of the devout Greeks" (τῶν τε σεβομένων Ἑλλήνων πλῆθος πολύ), and "not a few of the leading women" (γυναικῶν τε τῶν πρώτων οὐκ ὀλίγαι; 17:4) respond favorably by joining the believers.[214]

The narrative account of the acceptance of the gospel message in Thessalonica also mentions the general response of "the Jews" (οἱ Ἰουδαῖοι), using three aorist participles followed by an imperfect indicative to depict an overwhelmingly negative response in verse 5.[215] The first participle, ζηλώσαντες, explicitly characterizes these Jews by giving the reader access to their thoughts and attitudes of jealousy, which is apparently due to the success of the Christian message.[216] The next two participles negatively describe what the Jews do: they join forces with some evil men (προσλαβόμενοι . . . ἄνδρας τινὰς πονηρούς)[217] and form a mob (ὀχλοποιήσαντες; 17:5). Thus, the actions of these Jews begin to create turmoil (ἐθορύβουν)[218] throughout the city, resulting in a futile search for Paul and his partner, Silas.[219] The mention of the mob's inability to find the two men implies that Paul and Silas must have gone into hiding as the riotlike situation was developing.[220] Consequently, that scene ends with the opponents' seizure of one named Jason and "some brothers" (τινας

---

214. See Sanders, *The Jews in Luke-Acts*, 272, who states that the narrative suggests that few if any Jews actually become believers. However, his understanding of αὐτῶν (17:4) as inconclusive fails to recognize that the pronoun αὐτοῖς (17:2) seems to refer to τῶν Ἰουδαίων (17:1).

215. See Tyson, *Images of Judaism in Luke-Acts*, 134, 144, who identifies a literary pattern describing the Pauline mission to the Jews and Gentiles, with a positive Jewish response typically qualified by a description of Jewish rejection. Cf. Conzelmann, *Acts of the Apostles*, 135, who suggests that οἱ Ἰουδαῖοι now connotes "disobedient Jews." Contra Sanders, *The Jews in Luke-Acts*, 272; and Williams, *Acts*, 295, who see the Lukan picture as one of a predominantly Gentile group of believers, with the Jews in opposition.

216. The depiction of the Jews as jealous (17:5) is similar to earlier negative images, which result in harsh reactions against the believers (cf. 5:17; 13:45). See Larkin, *Acts*, 246–47, who argues that "jealousy" refers to a misguided zeal; and similarly Talbert, *Reading Acts*, 157.

217. The verb προσλαμβάνω (17:5) has the connotation of accepting a person into one's circle of friends, or of forming an association with someone else. See LSJ, 1518–19.

218. The verb θορυβέω (17:5) has negative connotations of confusion and turmoil. See BDAG, 458; and LSJ, 803. For the term's use, see Herodotus, *Histories* 3.78; 4.130; Josephus, *Jewish Antiquities* 17.251; and Thucydides, *History of the Peloponnesian War* 4.129; 8.50.

219. See Lüdemann, *Early Christianity according to the Traditions in Acts*, 187, who suggests that the Jews cause the trouble, grammatically speaking, but also that the mob does it, contextually speaking. Either way, the narrative description implicates the Jews.

220. Cf. Bruce, *The Book of the Acts*, 324; and Pesch, *Die Apostelgeschichte*, 2:123.

ἀδελφούς; 17:6). The new believers in Thessalonica are the recipients of the uncivilized, divisive reaction of the opponents to the gospel.[221] The narrated depiction makes it clear to the reader that the Jews and their negative response are responsible for disturbing (ἐτάραξαν) the Thessalonians and their political officials (17:8). This picture also implies that the believers are innocent both of the charges brought against them (cf. 17:6–7) and of the troubles created in the city.[222]

The narrative context presents Paul and Silas, along with the new believers of Thessalonica, as facing serious danger due to the negative Jewish reaction. In the midst of the chaos, the narrative mentions affirmatively the role of the believers in protecting these two men. Although the narrative merely states that the "brothers" (οἱ ἀδελφοί) send Paul and Silas immediately (εὐθέως) to Beroea under the cover of darkness (διὰ νυκτός; 17:10),[223] the implication is that these believers respond to the situation by caring for their fellow brothers' needs.[224] The narrator inserts no other details, other than that the group of believers in Thessalonica provides for the safety of Paul and Silas. Thus, the reader is encouraged to associate this image of the church with those earlier intratextual depictions of the Christian community as providing for the needs of one another (cf. 2:42–47; 4:32–37; 11:27–30).

The narrated situation in Beroea describes a more receptive atmosphere than what they have found in Thessalonica, with only the initial mention of the positive response of faith among Beroeans from both the Jewish and non-Jewish populations (17:10–12).[225] However, Luke tells of the Thessalonian Jews having heard that Paul has proclaimed the "the word of God" (κατηγγέλη ὑπὸ τοῦ Παύλου ὁ λόγος τοῦ θεοῦ) in Beroea and reports that they arrive in town, creating similar upheaval to what

---

221. Cf. Tannehill, *The Narrative Unity of Luke-Acts*, 2:208–9.

222. Cf. Plümacher, *Lukas als hellenistischer Schriftsteller*, 25; Sanders, *The Jews in Luke-Acts*, 273; and Wills, "The Depiction of the Jews in Acts," 646–47. See Conzelmann, *Acts of the Apostles*, 135, who observes that those who create the riots complain that *believers* cause them.

223. See Johnson, *The Acts of the Apostles*, 307, who compares other night action in Acts (cf. 5:19; 9:25; 12:6; 16:33).

224. Cf. Haenchen, *The Acts of the Apostles*, 508; Kurz, *Reading Luke-Acts*, 95–96; and Marshall, *The Acts of the Apostles*, 280. Contra Larkin, *Acts*, 249; and Williams, *Acts*, 296, who suggest that the believers are compliant with the terms of the bond (cf. 17:9).

225. Luke states that the Beroean Jews "welcome the message with all zeal" (17:11) and "believe," along with many non-Jews (17:12). See Tannehill, *The Narrative Unity of Luke-Acts*, 2:207, who writes here that Luke "has not completely stereotyped Diaspora Jews."

has occurred in their own city (17:13).[226] Whereas many Beroeans have responded favorably to the gospel message and are now depicted in the narrative as believers, these Thessalonian Jews function as opponents both of the believers and of God.[227] The narrative scene resembles the previous one and implies that the threat to the lives of Paul and Silas has returned.[228] The narrator's brief description of the believers' response to this threat also resembles what he has mentioned of the Thessalonian believers: the "brothers" (οἱ ἀδελφοί) immediately (εὐθέως) escort Paul to Athens (17:14–15).[229] The narrated actions of the church or group of believers in Beroea, like those in Thessalonica, suggest that they respond to Paul's need, alluding to earlier images of the provision of need within the community of believers.

An Assessment of the Characterization of the Church or Group of Believers in Acts 17:1–15

In these descriptions of the Pauline mission in Thessalonica and Beroea, Luke provides a brief glimpse of the groups of persons in each city who become part of the Christian church. The lack of detailed information corresponds with the narrator's interest in following the travels and ministry of Paul and his companions into Macedonia and Greece. However, given the consistent opposition created by Jews who reject the gospel, the narrator depicts Paul as spending little time in any one city before he must escape. Thus, the believers, who have responded positively to the gospel and who have come from both Jewish and Gentile backgrounds, do not function as prominent characters in the narrative account. That Luke depicts the Christian community as the group that provides for Paul's safety, however, places these actions as significant for his ongoing ministry. Such action implicitly compares these fledgling Christian communities with the ideals of the beginning section of the Acts narrative,

---

226. Luke uses two participles to describe the opposing Jews after arriving in Beroea: σαλεύοντες καὶ ταράσσοντες τοὺς ὄχλους (17:13). The verb σαλεύω literally connotes shaking, such as the place where the believers are praying (cf. 4:31). However, the term may also figuratively describe the shaking or disturbing of another. The verb ταράσσω also has similar connotations, referring to political and social agitation (see LSJ, 1757–58).

227. Cf. Johnson, *The Acts of the Apostles*, 308; and Tannehill, *The Narrative Unity of Luke-Acts*, 2:209.

228. Cf. Tyson, *Images of Judaism in Luke-Acts*, 133.

229. Cf. Barrett, *The Acts of the Apostles*, 2:819; Larkin, *Acts*, 250; Pesch, *Die Apostelgeschichte*, 2:125.

suggesting that these churches are also characterized by unanimity and divine blessing.

THE CHURCH IN CORINTH (ACTS 18:1–17)

The Literary Context (Acts 17:16–34)

The Acts narrative continues with an account of Paul's ministry in Athens. What Luke describes as happening in Athens is similar to what he typically describes as Paul enters a city. In particular, the narrative again presents Paul as engaged in discussions with those in the Jewish synagogue and includes initial descriptions of the acceptance of the gospel message by those who hear him.[230] However, the narrator also tells about opposition that typically confronts Paul as he proclaims the gospel message.[231] This opposition arises as a number of *non-Jewish* persons ridicule Paul for his message and reject the idea of the resurrection of the dead (cf. 17:18–20, 32).[232] Thus, in the narrated events in Athens, both those who believe (ἐπίστευσαν; 17:34) the gospel message and those who oppose Paul are apparently not Jewish. Nonetheless, the Lukan narrator places the positive image of those who accept the gospel message as the final image of the episode.

The Characterization of the Church or Group of Believers in Acts 18:1–17

In several ways, the narrative account of the Pauline ministry in Corinth reflects what has already occurred in Athens and elsewhere. The narrator presents Paul as engaged in serious discussions every Sabbath at the synagogue (18:4; cf. 17:17). The word selection makes it clear

---

230. In the accounts of Paul's ministry in Athens and Corinth, Luke states that Paul "argues in the synagogue" (διελέγετο...ἐν τῇ συναγωγῇ; 17:17, 18:4) and mentions that some accept the gospel (cf. 17:34; 18:8). Cf. Tannehill, *The Narrative Unity of Luke-Acts*, 2:213.

231. The narrative positively characterizes Paul's activity in Athens in three ways: (1) It lets Epicurean and Stoic philosophers describe Paul as the "proclaimer of foreign divinities" (δαιμονίων...καταγγελεύς; 17:18), with the term καταγγελεύς having the same root as καταγγέλλω, a common Lukan term that refers to proclaiming the gospel (cf. 4:2; 13:5, 38; 15:36; 16:17, 21; 17:3, 13). (2) It explains that the Athenians say what they do because Paul "was telling the good news about Jesus and the resurrection" (τὸν Ἰησοῦν καὶ τὴν ἀνάστασιν εὐηγγελίζετο; 17:18), using another common Lukan term, εὐαγγελίζομαι, to describe the activity of proclamation. (3) It lets the Athenians ask about the new teaching that Paul has spoken (λαλουμένη), using a third common Lukan term, λαλέω (17:19), to describe this proclamation.

232. The Lukan account of Paul's stay in Athens (cf. 17:16–34) mentions neither Jewish opposition nor physical opposition. Cf. Sanders, *The Jews in Luke-Acts*, 274–75.

that Paul is actively proclaiming the gospel message, both in his attempts to "persuade both Jews and Greeks" (ἔπειθέν τε ᾽Ιουδαίους καὶ "Ellhna"; 18:4) and in his testimony to the Jews (διαμαρτυρόμενος τοῖς ᾽Ιουδαίοις; 18:5), that Jesus was the Christ.[233] However, Luke negatively describes the Jewish response to that message in terms of opposition (ἀντιτασσομένων) and slander (βλασφημούντων; 18:6).[234] That opposition leads both to Paul's declaration that he will go to the Gentiles (18:6) and to his dramatic departure from the synagogue (18:6–7), the first explicit description in Acts of Paul separating his ministry of proclamation from the synagogue context.[235] The scene concludes with additional pictures of Jewish opposition, presented as a "united attack" (κατεπέστησαν ὁμοθυμαδὸν οἱ ᾽Ιουδαῖοι) against Paul, their fellow Jew (18:12). The adverb ὁμοθυμαδόν invites the reader to make two different kinds of intratextual connections. On the one hand, the united Jewish opposition compares ironically to the *positive* characteristic among the believers in Jerusalem (cf. 1:14; 2:46; 4:24; 5:12; 15:25). On the other hand, the united Jewish opposition compares similarly to earlier hostilities against Stephen (cf. 7:57). However, the civil authorities refuse the opposing Jews' attempts to have Paul arrested.[236] The narrative episode concludes with an ugly mob scene in which πάντες,[237] apparently the

233. Cf. Conzelmann, *Acts of the Apostles*, 152; Johnson, *The Acts of the Apostles*, 323; and William Neil, *Acts*, NCB (Grand Rapids: Eerdmans, 1973), 195. See also Witherington, *The Acts of the Apostles*, 548, who observes that the imperfect indicative συνείχετο (18:5) refers to Paul devoting himself to that work.

234. These two participles describing the Jewish response have negative connotations: (1) ἀντιτάσσω, which often describes a battle between two opponents (cf. Herodotus, *Histories* 4.134; 5.110; 7.103; Thucydides, *History of the Peloponnesian War* 2.87; 3.83; 4.55); and (2) βλασφημέω, which describes Jewish opposition in Acts (cf. 13:45). Cf. Sanders, *The Jews in Luke-Acts*, 275; and Wills, "The Depiction of the Jews in Acts," 637.

235. See Brawley, *Centering on God*, 204, who sees this as an example of reversal in the Acts narrative; and Dunn, *The Acts of the Apostles*, 243, who states that Paul's ministry meeting next door to the synagogue gives the report "a peculiar piquancy."

236. The charges against Paul (that he is persuading or misleading people to worship God in ways contrary to the law; 18:13) appear groundless, unless they reflect the relocation of Paul's ministry from the synagogue to "next door." See Pervo, *Profit with Delight*, 45, who counts the legal issues now as central to the plot. See also Michael Pettem, "Luke's Great Omission and His View of the Law," *NTS* 42 (January 1996): 39, who states that the Lukan Paul as a law-observing Jew "has no chance or need to defend himself."

237. The identity of πάντες is unclear. Since only Gallio, Paul, and the Jews are mentioned, the antecedent seems to be the Jews, who turn on Sosthenes after Paul is not formally charged. Cf. Larkin, *Acts*, 266–67; and Witherington, *The Acts of the Apostles*, 555–56. Contra Conzelmann, *Acts of the Apostles*, 154; Haenchen, *The Acts of the Apostles*, 536–37; Johnson, *The Acts of the Apostles*, 329; and Weiser, *Die Apostelgeschichte*, 2:487.

Jewish opponents, seize and beat Sosthenes, the ruler of their synagogue (18:17).[238]

Within these two negative depictions of the Jews, Luke places a description of some Jews and "many of the Corinthians who hear Paul" (πολλοὶ τῶν Κορινθίων ἀκούοντες) who also believe and are baptized (ἐπίστευον καὶ ἐβαπτίζοντο; 18:8).[239] Immediately after the brief description of those who have become believers, Luke inserts an account of a vision, in which "the Lord" (ὁ κύριος; 18:9) speaks to Paul and reassures him that he has no reason to fear because many in the city are "my people" (λαός ἐστί μοι πολὺς ἐν τῇ πόλει ταύτῃ; 18:10).[240] This use of λαός is only the second time that it has referred to persons outside of the exclusive context of the Jewish people (cf. 15:14). The inference again is that these persons, both Jews and Gentiles, belong to God and are identified by God.[241] These distinct references to the incorporation of both Jews and non-Jews into the church as the people of God implicitly nudge the reader to conclude that these believers also enjoy a unanimous spirit and God's blessing. That communal context, along with the implied activity among the believers, provides for the confidence of Paul to remain and teach (διδάσκων ἐν αὐτοῖς τὸν λόγον τοῦ θεοῦ; 18:11) for an extended period of time.[242] This description will remind the reader of previous positive portrayals of teaching and proclamation that are inherent qualities of the Christian community.[243] This affirmative portrayal of the church in Corinth, however, stands as a direct contrast to the described hostile activities of οἱ Ἰουδαῖοι that frame the Lukan portrayal of the Christians. The striking contrast in this narrative section alludes to many incongruent depictions between the Jews and the believers throughout Acts 3–15, in which Luke presents the church as guided and blessed by God and the Jews as the opponents of God and the church.[244]

---

238. Cf. Pervo, *Profit with Delight*, 60, who states that Sosthenes seeks Paul's arraignment but instead receives the punishment he seeks for Paul.

239. See Williams, *Acts*, 315, who observes that the imperfect tense of the two verbs suggests that this positive acceptance of the gospel is an ongoing occurrence (18:8).

240. See Marshall, *The Acts of the Apostles*, 295; and Tannehill, *The Narrative Unity of Luke-Acts*, 2:223, who mention the abruptness of the introduction of this vision account.

241. Cf. Dupont, "Un peuple d'entre les nations," 322, 329; Beverly Roberts Gaventa, *The Acts of the Apostles*, ANTC (Nashville: Abingdon, 2003), 259; Krodel, *Acts*, 344; Sanders, *The Jews in Luke-Acts*, 276–77; Tannehill, *The Narrative Unity of Luke-Acts*, 2:224–25; and Zingg, *Das Wachsen der Kirche*, 159.

242. Cf. Marshall, *The Acts of the Apostles*, 296; and Williams, *Acts*, 317.

243. Cf. 2:42; 4:2, 18; 5:21, 25, 28, 42; 11:26; 15:35.

244. Cf. Johnson, *The Acts of the Apostles*, 326.

An Assessment of the Characterization of the Church or Group of Believers in Acts 18:1–17

The Lukan narrator does not depict the Christian community in Corinth by using direct statements or observations from reliable characters in the narrative. Luke does not even describe the Christians' actions, which is the most common means by which ancient historiography depicts characters in a narrative. Rather, the characterization of the believers relies largely on inference, thereby leaving the reader to make judgments about the Corinthian believers by recognizing the similarities between these scenes and earlier positive images of the Christian community. However, the dominant image in this depiction of the Corinthian believers is of the church as the communal context from which the gospel message is proclaimed and taught (cf. 18:11), which contrasts with the Jewish opposition to that same message. The narrative section of 18:1–17 presents the group of believers as similar to earlier Christian groups, as Paul receives the communal support necessary to proclaim the gospel, despite the obstacles created by the Jewish opponents. However, for the first time in the narrated accounts of the Pauline missions, the reader encounters the separation of the Christian community from the Jewish synagogue, suggesting that the Jewish rejection of the gospel message creates that scenario.

SOME BELIEVERS IN EPHESUS
(ACTS 18:24–28)

The Literary Context (Acts 18:18–23)

The Pauline ministry in the city of Corinth is the last major narrative scene in the Lukan account of Paul's second journey and is accompanied by both positive and negative responses to his message there. Luke presents the Christian "missionary," after remaining at Corinth for eighteen months (18:11), as traveling back to the same church from which he has started on this latest journey: the church in Antioch. Along the way, Paul stops in Ephesus, has a discussion with the Jews (διελέξατο τοῖς Ἰουδαίοις; 18:19; cf. 17:2, 17; 18:4) in the synagogue, and receives an invitation to stay longer (18:20). The precise wording and the invitation both suggest the possibility of an initial positive response by the Jews, but Luke offers nothing more to help the reader substantiate that suggestion.[245] Nonetheless, the similarity in description to earlier narrative scenes will potentially create in the reader an expectation that some form of both positive acceptance and rejection of the gospel message will follow. Nonetheless, the Lukan narrator keeps the narrative moving at this point, as it continues to build anticipation in the reader for what may happen later with the insertion of Paul's stated intention to return to Ephesus (cf. 18:21). The last part of the narrative section (18:22–23) is a brief summary that functions both as the conclusion to the second Pauline journey in Acts and as the inauguration of his third journey.[246] The mention of Paul's stops in Jerusalem and Antioch emphasizes both his constant allegiance to these believers and links his ministry to the church.[247]

The Characterization of the Church or Group of Believers in Acts 18:24–28

Before the Lukan account of the Pauline ministry in the city of Ephesus, Luke inserts a short narrative section that introduces a Jewish person named Apollos. The omission of several details creates difficulties for the reader in assessing this particular section. Luke directly and positively depicts Apollos as an eloquent man who "had been instructed in the Way of the Lord" (οὗτος ἦν κατηχημένος τὴν ὁδὸν τοῦ κυρίου), "spoke with burning enthusiasm" (ζέων τῷ πνεύματι ἐλάλει), and "accurately taught the things about Jesus" (ἐδίδασκεν ἀκριβῶς τὰ περὶ τοῦ Ἰησοῦ; 18:25).[248] However, the Lukan narrator never provides any details about Apollos's "conversion" yet does describe his activities, like Paul's, as taking place in the synagogue.[249] Thus, this sketchy picture

---

245. Cf. Krodel, *Acts*, 351; Larkin, *Acts*, 268; Sanders, *The Jews in Luke-Acts*, 277–78; and Tannehill, *The Narrative Unity of Luke-Acts*, 2:231.

246. E.g., Luke describes Paul as "strengthening all the disciples" throughout the region of Galatia and Phrygia (18:23), the same type of activity that has described the beginning of the second journey (cf. 15:41). In both cases, the Lukan narrator uses the same participle (ἐπιστηρίζων) to describe that activity (cf. 14:21–22).

247. Cf. Haenchen, *The Acts of the Apostles*, 547–48; Johnson, *The Acts of the Apostles*, 334–35; and Tannehill, *The Narrative Unity of Luke-Acts*, 2:230.

248. The description of Apollos in 18:25 uses three terms that the Lukan narrator has reserved for the believers' activities: (1) τὴν ὁδόν, which identifies Apollos with the "Way of the Lord" and the Christian movement as "the Way" (9:2); (2) ἐλάλει, a form of λαλέω, which Luke usually reserves for those who "speak" the gospel message; and (3) ἐδίδασκεν, a form of διδάσκω, which Luke consistently uses to describe the positive activity of the believers.

249. Thus, in Corinth, Paul has spoken to the Jews in the synagogue (18:19; cf. 19:8), and now the narrator describes Apollos as doing the same thing (18:25).

of Apollos is shaded with ambiguity. On the one hand, the reader may recognize similarities between this picture and earlier positive depictions of the Christian believers. On the other hand, the reader may also discover hints of some degree of incompleteness in Apollos's instruction and proclamation (cf. 18:25–26).[250]

The remaining part of this narrative section concisely focuses the reader's attention on Apollos's ministry within the larger context of the Christian church. When Apollos reveals his plans to go to Achaia, Luke states that the brothers encourage him (προτρεψάμενοι οἱ ἀδελφοί)[251] and write letters of recommendation for him to the disciples there (18:27).[252] What this narrative section does not provide is any explicit explanation about the origin of this group of believers.[253] From the narrative description, however, the reader may infer that these believers are still part of the synagogue, unlike the church that Paul has left behind in Corinth.[254] However, as in numerous narrative sections of the preceding chapters, the believers have a narrative function of providing the communal support for the ongoing proclamation of the gospel. Luke presents the believers in Ephesus as those who contribute what Apollos needs to

---

250. While Priscilla and Aquila "took him aside and explained the Way of God to him more accurately" (προσελάβοντο αὐτὸν καὶ ἀκριβέστερον αὐτῷ ἐξέθεντο τὴν ὁδὸν [τοῦ θεοῦ]), Luke has already stated that Apollos "began to speak boldly in the synagogue" (ἤρξατο παρρησιάζεσθαι ἐν τῇ συναγωγῇ; 18:26), which alludes to the earlier positive depictions of the believers (cf. Acts 4). Cf. Darr, *On Character Building*, 82–83; and Krodel, *Acts*, 353–54.

251. The aorist participle προτρεψάμενοι describes an action that precedes the action of the main verb (18:27). Cf. Johnson, *The Acts of the Apostles*, 332.

252. Literally, Luke states that the believers "wrote to the disciples to welcome him" (ἔγραψαν τοῖς μαθηταῖς ἀποδέξασθαι αὐτόν; 18:27).

253. There are several possibilities concerning the origin of these believers. One possibility may be found in the earlier reference to Paul's discussion in the synagogue and the invitation to stay a while longer (cf. 18:19–20), which may subtly indicate an initial positive response resulting in a group of believers that continue to meet at the synagogue. Another possibility may be that these are the results of the efforts of Priscilla and Aquila (cf. Neil, *Acts*, 201–2; and Williams, *Acts*, 323). A third possibility is that these believers are the results of Apollos's ministry (cf. Krodel, *Acts*, 355). A fourth possibility, explained by the Western text, is that these believers are from Corinth (cf. Metzger, *A Textual Commentary on the Greek New Testament*, 467–68; and Bruce, *The Book of the Acts*, 360). A fifth possibility is that all of the above possibilities contribute to the evolution of the Ephesian church (cf. Marshall, *The Acts of the Apostles*, 304). See Lüdemann, *Early Christianity according to the Traditions in Acts*, 208–9, who credits this reference to a pre-Pauline tradition.

254. Such a deduction is based on Apollos's proclamation in the synagogue (18:26) and on Priscilla and Aquila hearing Apollos in that context. Thus, the presence of Priscilla and Aquila suggests that the Christians, at this point in the narrative, had not separated from the synagogue.

fulfill his ministry in Achaia.[255] The brief summary of the positive results in Achaia, in which Luke describes Apollos's ministry among the believers (τοῖς πεπιστευκόσιν) as great help (συνεβάλετο πολύ)[256] by means of grace (διὰ τῆς χάριτος; 18:27),[257] explicitly confirms what Luke has just depicted.[258]

An Assessment of the Characterization of the Church or Group of Believers in Acts 18:24–28

The Lukan narrator places the focus of 18:24–28 on the character of Apollos. Thus, the character of the group of Christian believers in Ephesus is mentioned little in this narrative section. However, although Apollos takes center stage, the believers fulfill an important narrative function: the Christian community provides the context from which the proclamation and ministry of the gospel take place. The Christian community provides the communal support from which the ministry of Apollos extends to Achaia. Thus, the depicted picture here in 18:24–28 is consistent with the Lukan portraits of Christian community in the preceding chapters, as Luke identifies the church as the communal source of the proclamation of the gospel message.

MORE BELIEVERS IN EPHESUS
(ACTS 19:1–41)

The Literary Context

The two previous narrative sections provide the context for the Lukan description of Paul's ministry in Ephesus. Both Paul's stated intentions to return to that city (cf. 18:19–21) and Apollos's ministry provide hints to the reader of what may be found in Acts 19. These sections depict some degree of acceptance of the gospel message and a developing group of believers. However, the partial and ambiguous descriptions leave some

---

255. Cf. Tannehill, *The Narrative Unity of Luke-Acts*, 2:232; and Williams, *Acts*, 325.

256. Two terms in 18:27 stand out as significant: (1) the verb συμβάλλω reflects the Lukan stylistic tendency to use verbs with the prefix σύν; and (2) the perfect participle τοῖς πεπιστευκόσιν denotes not only that those identified with the church are characterized by faith but also that they continue in the results of that faith.

257. Cf. Conzelmann, *Acts of the Apostles*, 158; and Williams, *Acts*, 325.

258. See Tannehill, *The Narrative Unity of Luke-Acts*, 2:232, who states: "The Christian community in Ephesus supported him [Apollos], and the Corinthian community benefited from him."

loose narrative ends for the reader and imply that the story about the Ephesian believers is not finished.

The Characterization of the Church or Group of Believers in Acts 19:1–41

In the extended narration of events related to the Pauline ministry in Ephesus, Luke includes the Christian believers as a significant character. The first glimpse of the believers is given as Paul comes to the city and finds "some disciples" (τινες μαθητάς; 19:1). In typical Lukan fashion, the narrator does not explicitly identify who these disciples are, although the reader may infer that they are Jewish believers.[259] However, the narrator's insertion of a Pauline question directed to these persons tends to smudge the beginning sketch marks of this picture (19:2).[260] On the one hand, the narrator uses the question, in which Paul seems to recognize them as believers (πιστεύσαντες), as an indirect means to characterize these persons. On the other hand, Paul's question about whether they have "received the Holy Spirit" (εἰ πνεῦμα ἅγιον ἐλάβετε; 19:2) and the associated reply of unawareness do not correlate with the Lukan combination of belief and the presence of the Holy Spirit in the portrayal of the Christian community. However, the reader may recognize that this ambiguous picture of these believers does not stand alone in this narrative scene but provides the narrative context for what follows.[261] Luke briefly describes the conversation between these believers and Paul about two baptisms: one baptism with regard to John (19:3), another with regard to Jesus (19:4). This conversation results in these believers being "baptized in the name of the Lord Jesus" (ἐβαπτίσθησαν εἰς τὸ ὄνομα τοῦ κυρίου Ἰησοῦ; 19:5), a sign of inclusion into the Christian church. Grammatically linked (καί) to this act of baptism are concise descriptions of three subsequent occurrences. Luke narrates actions both of Paul and of the believers: after Paul lays his hands on these same believers (ἐπιθέντος αὐτοῖς τοῦ Παύλου τὰς χεῖρας),[262] they begin both to "speak in tongues"

---

259. If these disciples are those mentioned with Apollos (18:27), then they can be either Jews or Gentiles sympathetic to Judaism. The conversation about John's baptism implies that they are of Jewish heritage. Cf. Lüdemann, *Early Christianity according to the Traditions in Acts*, 211; Williams, *Acts*, 337; and Witherington, *The Acts of the Apostles*, 570.

260. Cf. Bruce, *The Book of the Acts*, 363; Krodel, *Acts*, 357; and Pervo, *Profit with Delight*, 9.

261. Cf. Darr, *On Character Building*, 83. Contra Marshall, *The Acts of the Apostles*, 305.

262. Luke has used the imagery of "laying hands on persons" to describe the church's activity, in terms of the Holy Spirit's coming (cf. 8:17) or of blessing for ministry (cf. 6:6;

and prophesy (ἐλάλουν τε γλώσσαις καὶ ἐπροφήτευον; 19:6).²⁶³ Included within the narration of these actions, however, is a direct description of the believers that provides the reader with an explanation of what has happened: "the Holy Spirit came upon them" (ἦλθε τὸ πνεῦμα τὸ ἅγιον ἐπ᾽ αὐτούς; 19:6).²⁶⁴ This narrated description, which includes the baptism of the Ephesian believers and the subsequent happenings, alludes to numerous intratextual images that affirm the believers in the Acts narrative (e.g., at Pentecost, in Samaria, and in Caesarea).²⁶⁵ What Luke clearly depicts in this initial scene of Paul's Ephesian ministry is the establishment of the Christian community; the reader is encouraged to recognize the characterization of these believers in terms of the presence of the Holy Spirit among them and the resultant prophecy.

The continuation of the Lukan account of Paul's activities in Ephesus focuses on the Ephesians' responsiveness to the gospel message. The narrator presents Paul as entering the synagogue *after* some initial activities in the city, unlike previous instances in Paul's ministry when the first activity reported is his synagogue attendance (cf. 13:5, 14; 14:1; 17:1–2, 17; 18:4). Nonetheless, the synagogue functions as the location for Paul's ministry during a three-month span; Luke depicts that Paul speaks out boldly (ἐπαρρησιάζετο; 19:8), alluding to earlier pictures of the believers' boldness due to the Holy Spirit (cf. 4:29–31).²⁶⁶ Luke has described Paul in this manner only within the general context of the Christian believers (cf. 9:27–28; 13:46; 14:3). The narrator only describes Paul's activities in terms of boldness and the implied empowerment by the Holy Spirit as he is associated in the narrative with a local group of believers or

---

13:3). Cf. Conzelmann, *Acts of the Apostles*, 159–60; Johnson, *The Acts of the Apostles*, 338; Marshall, *The Acts of the Apostles*, 307–8; and Tannehill, *The Narrative Unity of Luke-Acts*, 2:236.

263. The expression "speaking in tongues" (ἐλάλουν τε γλώσσαις; 19:6) uses the same terminology to narrate the Holy Spirit's coming as found in 2:4 and 10:46. Although Luke does not provide any more details, he seems to allude to the Pentecost event, so that readers should see the similarities between this and what has occurred in Acts 2. Cf. Johnson, *The Acts of the Apostles*, 338; and Larkin, *Acts*, 274. Contra Krodel, *Acts*, 358; and Williams, *Acts*, 331.

264. The description of the Holy Spirit as "coming" (ἦλθε; 19:6) has not been used in Acts until now. However, Luke has already used a number of verbs to describe the way in which the Holy Spirit has been identified with the believers (e.g., πίμπλημι, πληρόω, and πίπτω).

265. Cf. Pervo, *Profit with Delight*, 9. For brief discussions that consider the possibility of the number "twelve" as symbolic in 19:7, see e.g., Haenchen, *The Acts of the Apostles*, 554; Johnson, *The Acts of the Apostles*, 338; Kurz, *Reading Luke-Acts*, 96–97; Marshall, *The Acts of the Apostles*, 308; and Schneider, *Die Apostelgeschichte*, 2:265.

266. Cf. Johnson, *The Acts of the Apostles*, 338; and Krodel, *Acts*, 360.

after some acceptance of the gospel in a particular city. Thus, the reader is again subtly coaxed to link the boldness of Paul's proclamation to the group of believers that surrounds him, a group implicitly characterized by the presence of the Holy Spirit. The two participles that further describe the activities of Paul, διαλεγόμενος (discussing) and πείθων (persuading; 19:8), also allude to earlier positive presentations and suggest that other Ephesians respond favorably to his message.[267]

In typical Lukan fashion, however, the narrator contrasts this positive response by describing a negative Jewish response in the next sentence. The narrative describes some who persistently are hardened and dissuaded (τινες ἐσκληρύνοντο καὶ ἠπείθουν; 19:9), which the reader may associate with similar intertextual images found in the Septuagint of those who oppose God.[268] The narration of Paul's failure to persuade such persons partly explains why they are speaking evil (κακολογοῦντες) against "the Way" (τὸν ὁδόν; 19:9), actions that create a picture contrary to the affirmative depiction of the Christian believers. Although Luke mentions no other negative response, the strong terminology used to describe the withdrawal of Paul and the believers from the synagogue (cf. 18:7) indicates that the Christians are forced to make a clean break from the synagogue (19:9).[269] Thus, as in the episode in Corinth, Luke depicts the developing Christian community as a distinctive entity apart from the Jewish synagogue.[270] However, that contextual distinction results in everyone in Ephesus and the surrounding region of Asia (πάντας τοὺς κατοικοῦντας τὴν Ἀσίαν) hearing "the word of the Lord" (τὸν λόγον τοῦ κυρίου), which includes "both Jews and Greeks" (Ἰουδαίους τε καὶ Ἕλληνας; 19:10). The Lukan portrayal of the Christian church

---

267. Cf. Johnson, *The Acts of the Apostles*, 338–39. Contra Sanders, *The Jews in Luke-Acts*, 279, who sees no positive response here but fails to recognize the narrative allusions to such.

268. The imperfect tense of the two indicatives ἐσκληρύνοντο and ἠπείθουν suggests that this negative response is a persistent reaction (19:9). For LXX references for σκληρύνω, see, e.g., Exod 4:21; 7:3; 8:15, 19 [15 LXX]; 9:35; 13:15; Deut 2:30; 10:16; Ps 95:8 [94:8]; Isa 63:17; Jer 7:26; 19:15. See also Karl Ludwig Schmidt and Martin Anton Schmidt, "παχύνω...," in *TDNT*, 5:1030–31.

269. The verbs ἀφίστημι and ἀφορίζω are strong terms that denote a radical separation. The verb ἀφίστημι has various meanings, ranging from withdrawal to revolt and apostasy (see BDAG, 157–58; and LSJ, 291). The verb ἀφορίζω refers to separation or to mark off by boundaries (see BDAG, 158; and LSJ, 292). See Schneider, "ὁρίζω...," 5:454–55. Cf. Johnson, *The Acts of the Apostles*, 339.

270. Cf., e.g., Brawley, *Centering on God*, 204, 163; Johnson, *The Acts of the Apostles*, 339; and Towner, "Mission Practice and Theology under Construction (Acts 18–20)," 424–32.

suggests that, because of the Christians' forced withdrawal from that distinctly Jewish setting, the gospel message spreads to the entire Asian populace and is not limited to those who go to the synagogue.

The subsequent narrative scene depicts the increasing influence of the gospel both *from* the context of the church depicted in the first eleven verses and *within* a cultural context marked by "superstition" and magic. The narrator indirectly presents Paul by observing the public response to him and the miracles (δυνάμεις τε οὐ τὰς τυχούσας; 19:11) that he works, with further elaboration depicting Paul like Peter (cf. 5:12–16) and Philip (cf. 8:4–13).[271] However, almost at the beginning of the sentence that begins this scene (19:11–12), Luke directly describes these extraordinary activities as God's work *through* Paul (ὁ θεὸς ἐποίει διὰ τῶν χειρῶν Παύλου).[272] In stark contrast, the disastrous failure of certain Jewish persons to practice exorcism by invoking "the name of the Lord Jesus" (τὸ ὄνομα τοῦ κυρίου Ἰησοῦ; 19:13) without any mentioned association with the Christian community implicitly demonstrates the presence of God among the believers. The narrated response includes both explicit and implicit statements by Luke. On the one hand, Luke provides direct access into the minds of the Ephesian residents by stating that "fear fell" (ἐπέπεσεν φόβος; 19:17) upon them all (πάντας αὐτούς),[273] an image that the reader would relate to similar responses in earlier chapters.[274] On the other hand, Luke simply observes that, along with φόβος,[275] "the name of the Lord Jesus was praised" (ἐμεγαλύνετο τὸ ὄνομα τοῦ κυρίου Ἰησοῦ; 19:17), both of which the reader would also

---

271. The noun δύναμις, which Luke uses to describe Paul's actions, occurs in earlier narrative sections to describe various believers and Jesus (cf. 3:12; 4:7, 33; 6:8; 8:13; 10:38). Cf. Bruce, *The Book of the Acts*, 367; Conzelmann, *Acts of the Apostles*, 163; Kurz, *Reading Luke-Acts*, 97; and Tannehill, *The Narrative Unity of Luke-Acts*, 2:236–37.

272. Although δυνάμεις τε οὐ τὰς τυχούσας is in the emphatic position, ὁ θεός is the subject, not Paul (19:11). See Williams, *Acts*, 332, who observes that the imperfect tense of ἐποίει emphasizes God's ongoing activity; and Haenchen, *The Acts of the Apostles*, 563, who states that Luke describes Paul as one "who so overflowed with divine power that even the clothes on his body are drenched with it."

273. The prepositional phrase ἐπὶ πάντας αὐτούς (19:17) refers to the people mentioned earlier in 19:17: πᾶσιν Ἰουδαίοις τε καὶ Ἕλλησιν τοῖς κατοικοῦσιν τὴν Ἔφεσον.

274. The description of φόβος as a positive response to what has occurred in the church context is mentioned previously four times in Acts (cf. 2:43; 5:5, 11; 9:31). However, the verb ἐπιπίπτω has been used (not in connection with φόβος) to describe the Spirit's coming (cf. 8:16; 10:44; 11:15). Cf. Tannehill, *The Narrative Unity of Luke-Acts*, 2:238; and Weiser, *Die Apostelgeschichte*, 2:525.

275. The conjunction καί (19:17) links the direct description of fear to the indirect description of praise.

recognize as alluding to earlier affirmative pictures of the believers (cf. 2:43; 10:46).[276] Luke also tells about many who have become believers (πολλοί ... τῶν πεπιστευκότων; 19:18) and have renounced their magical practices, as demonstrated in the collection and destruction of their valuable magic books (19:19).[277] In this context, where the superior power of God is overwhelmingly revealed, Luke concludes the narrative scene by reaffirming that "the might of the Lord" (κατὰ κράτος τοῦ κυρίου; 19:20)[278] causes continuing success and growth in the number of believers.[279]

The Lukan narrator provides one final glimpse of the Ephesian believers in Acts 19. The scene is much different from what Luke describes in the first half of the chapter.[280] Now the atmosphere is characterized negatively in terms of trouble and turmoil (τάραχος οὐκ ὀλίγος; 19:23) toward the believers, because a meeting of local craftsmen (τοῖς τεχνίταις; 19:24) identifies Paul and the gospel as a serious threat to the local economy and the city's religious practices (19:25–27).[281] The narrated situation quickly develops into an ugly mob scene, as the enraged craftsmen (πλήρεις θυμοῦ; 19:28)[282] so excite the Ephesian

---

276. Cf. Tannehill, *The Narrative Unity of Luke-Acts*, 2:238. See Williams, *Acts*, 334, who again identifies the imperfect tense of the indicative as referring to a continuing activity.

277. See Johnson, *The Acts of the Apostles*, 341–42, who reports (and provides references) that the burning of books was a typical way in the Greco-Roman world to control the spread of unacceptable ideas. The large value of these books reminds the reader that magical practices have provided financial gain for the ones believed to have such powers.

278. Although τοῦ κυρίου is usually understood to refer to ὁ λόγος (19:20), such a conclusion is not entirely convincing for two reasons: (1) the typical Lukan expression is ὁ λόγος τοῦ κυρίου (cf. 8:25; 13:44, 48, 49; 15:35, 36; 16:32; 19:10; 20:35), with no variations of this construction; and (2) the sentence of 19:20 begins and ends with imagery of strength, which Luke has already described as belonging to God (cf. 19:11). Thus, if τοῦ κυρίου modifies κράτος, the scene ends similarly as it begins: with an affirmation of divine power among the believers.

279. The imperfect tense of the indicatives ηὔξανεν and ἴσχυεν suggests that this growth continues (19:20). The verb αὐξάνω alludes to earlier images of growth (cf. 6:7; 12:24), which point to God as the source of that success.

280. Cf. Tannehill, *The Narrative Unity of Luke-Acts*, 2:241–42.

281. The term τάραχος or τάραχη has the negative connotation of disorder or confusion (19:23; see LSJ, 1758). See, e.g., Aristotle, *Politics* 2.5.8; Herodotus, *Histories* 3.126; Plato, *Republic* 10.602c; Thucydides, *History of the Peloponnesian War* 3.79; 5.25; Josephus, *The Jewish War* 1.216; *Jewish Antiquities* 14.273. See also the LXX use of this term in, e.g., Judg [B] 11:35; Isa 22:5; 24:19; Ezek 30:4, 9, 16; and 2 Macc 15:29.

282. The depiction of the craftsmen as "filled with rage" (πλήρεις θυμοῦ; Acts 19:28) both contrasts to references to believers as filled with the Holy Spirit, faith, and so on and compares with earlier portrayals of Jewish leaders who respond with rage (cf. 5:33; 7:54). Cf. Plümacher, *Lukas als hellenistischer Schriftsteller*, 98–100; Schneider, *Die Apostelgeschichte*, 2:275; and Tannehill, *The Narrative Unity of Luke-Acts*, 2:242. See Johnson, *The Acts of*

people that the city becomes "filled with the confusion" (ἐπλήσθη ἡ πόλις τῆς συγχύσεως; 19:29).[283] The mob ironically acts with unanimity (ὁμοθυμαδόν) and dragged two of Paul's companions to the theater (19:29).[284] At this point in the narrative, Luke mentions that Paul wishes "to go into the crowd" (εἰσελθεῖν εἰς τὸν δῆμον; 19:30), apparently so he could intervene for his two partners. Here the disciples (οἱ μαθηταί) briefly return to the narrative as those who refuse to allow Paul (οὐκ εἴων αὐτόν; 19:30)[285] to get directly involved because of the dangerous situation.[286] As has now become typical in the Lukan presentation of Paul's ministry, the Christian community is depicted as that which provides for his security and safety (cf. 9:25, 30; 17:10, 14–15).[287] While the scene negatively presents the entire city as unruly and desirous to lash out in anger against Paul because of its inhabitants' selfish concerns, the Christian believers respond by providing for his needs, although that means resisting his good intentions.[288]

An Assessment of the Characterization of the Church or Group of Believers in Acts 19:1–41

Although one may contend that in the narrative section of 19:1–41 is found a "complete lack of information about a community of believers,"[289] a close examination of this passage suggests otherwise. The Christian community in Ephesus does not stand out as a dominant character in this narrative section. Nevertheless, the evidence suggests that Luke utilizes allusions to previous portrayals of believers and contrasts

---

the Apostles, 348, 351–52, who reports that Hellenistic historiography typically includes such violent emotions.

283. The noun σύγχυσις (19:29) has the connotation of confusion, particularly among a city's citizens or inhabitants (see BDAG, 954; and LSJ, 1669). Cf. Josephus, The Jewish War 2.294; 4.129; Plato, Republic 2.379e; Thucydides, History of the Peloponnesian War 1.146; 5.26. For the LXX use of the term, see Gen 11:9 (verb form); 1 Sam 5:6, 11; and 14:20.

284. Although the adverb ὁμοθυμαδόν refers to the believers' unanimity (Acts 1:14; 2:46; 4:24; 5:12; 15:25), this is the third time that it ironically describes united opposition against them (7:57; 18:12; 19:29). Cf. Lüdemann, Early Christianity according to the Traditions in Acts, 216.

285. The imperfect tense of the indicative εἴων (19:30) suggests ongoing resistance to Paul's wishes. Cf. Fitzmyer, The Acts of the Apostles, 659.

286. Other φίλοι or "friends" of Paul, who are political officials, also warn him to stay out of the situation (19:31). Cf. Bruce, The Book of the Acts, 376; Krodel, Acts, 367; Marshall, The Acts of the Apostles, 319; and Pervo, Profit with Delight, 10.

287. Cf. Bruce, The Book of the Acts, 376; and Larkin, Acts, 284.

288. Cf. Haenchen, The Acts of the Apostles, 579; Krodel, Acts, 368; and Larkin, Acts, 284.

289. Pervo, Profit with Delight, 9.

those believers with Paul's opponents to present another affirmative image of the community of believers. The Lukan narrator offers little explicit characterization of those believers and provides little insight into the inner feelings and thoughts of those who constitute the Ephesian church. Nonetheless, several aspects of the Lukan characterization of the Christian church are duplicated or emphasized here: the presence of the Holy Spirit, the proclamation of the gospel message, and the unanimity among believers demonstrated by genuine concern for meeting one another's needs. Although the Lukan depiction of the believers in the context of the Pauline ministry now clearly distinguishes the Christian community from the Jewish synagogue because of Jewish opposition, the reader will recognize that the same positive qualities associated with the beginning pictures of Jewish believers now characterize the Christian community in Ephesus, which consists of Jewish and Gentile believers.

THE EPHESIAN CHURCH AND PAUL SAY FAREWELL (ACTS 20:17–38)

The Literary Context (Acts 20:1–16)

The Lukan account of the Pauline ministry in Ephesus concludes with Paul encouraging (παρακαλέσας) "the disciples" (τοὺς μαθητάς) after the upheaval has ceased (20:1).[290] The narrative includes only a brief summary of Paul's ministry of encouragement as he resumes his travels through Macedonia and Greece (20:2). However, as Paul is about to sail to Syria, the narrator mentions something that the reader will undoubtedly perceive as a typical response by οἱ Ἰουδαῖοι: they have devised a plot (ἐπιβουλῆς; 20:3) against him. Thus, Paul's itinerary is altered, which the reader will probably infer as providing safer travel back to the eastern Mediterranean region. The revised itinerary for his return trip takes him back through Macedonia and across the northeast portion of the Aegean Sea from Philippi to Troas (20:3–6). During a time when Paul has "gathered together to break bread" (συνηγμένων ἡμῶν κλάσαι ἄρτον; 20:7), presumably with some believers,[291] a lengthy

---

290. Encouragement is a favorite Lukan expression in describing believers (see 2:40; 11:23; 14:22; 15:32; 16:40; 20:1, 2, 12; 21:12; 27:33, 34; 28:14, 20). For occurrences of the noun παράκλησις referring to the believers, see 4:36; 9:31; 13:15; 15:31.

291. The Lukan account does not directly state who worships with Paul and his associates. Rather, it states that "*we* gathered together to break bread" (20:7, with emphasis added).

discussion[292] leads to a young man falling asleep and falling out of a third-story window, resulting in the young man's death (20:7–9).[293] The narrative omits most details but leaves the reader with the distinct impression that Paul raises the young man from the dead (20:10, 12).[294] Much like the narrative account of Peter's raising of Tabitha from the dead in chapter 9 (9:36–43), this extraordinary act apparently occurs in the context of believers (cf. 20:7, 11), reminding the reader of other "supernatural" deeds done both by Paul and by the apostles in earlier scenes.[295] From Troas, Paul travels southward by land and by sea along the western shore of Asia to Miletus, a large seaport south of Ephesus (20:13–16).

The Characterization of the Church or Group of Believers in Acts 20:17–38

Although Paul's schedule leaves no time for a personal visit to Ephesus, Luke inserts an account of one final meeting between Paul and the elders or leaders of the Ephesian church (τοὺς πρεσβυτέρους τῆς ἐκκλησίας; 20:17) in Miletus.[296] The major focus of this narrative section is on Paul's speech, the only one in the book of Acts addressed to a Christian audience.[297] The speech functions as an implicit articulation of the narrator's perspective through Paul, a reliable character.[298] The speech begins with Paul reviewing his ministry in Ephesus, contrasting his obedience and service to God with the opposition and plots of the

---

292. The verb διαλέγομαι (20:7) was used earlier to describe Paul's discussions with those in the synagogues (cf. 17:2, 17; 18:4, 19; 19:8, 9).

293. See Pervo, *Profit with Delight*, 65–66, who sees this episode revealing Luke's "cleverness and wit."

294. See Kurz, *Reading Luke-Acts*, 99; and Tannehill, *The Narrative Unity of Luke-Acts*, 2:248–49, who observe that the perspective here is that of a participant, since the narrator provides no additional information to suggest whether the young man is really dead.

295. Cf. Krodel, *Acts*, 377 who views the miracle as downplayed; Johnson, *The Acts of the Apostles*, 358; and Tannehill, *The Narrative Unity of Luke-Acts*, 2:247.

296. For other references to "elders" in the Jerusalem church, see 11:30; 15:2, 4, 6. Only here and in 14:23 does one find references to "elders" outside of the Jerusalem church.

297. All other *reported* Pauline speeches in Acts are directed to non-Christian audiences: the synagogue at Pisidian Antioch (13:16–41), the Areopagus in Athens (17:22–31), the Jewish crowd in Jerusalem (22:1–21), his defense before Felix (24:10–21), his hearing before King Agrippa (26:1–23), and the Roman Jewish leaders (28:17–22, 25–28). Cf. Bruce, *The Book of the Acts*, 387; Jacob Jervell, "Paulus in der Apostelgeschichte und die Geschichte des Urchristentums," *NTS* 32 (July 1986): 383; and Lohfink, *Die Sammlung Israels*, 89.

298. Cf. Jervell, "Paulus in der Apostelgeschichte und die Geschichte des Urchristentums," 383; and Johnson, *The Acts of the Apostles*, 366.

Jews in a manner that confirms to the reader what the narrator has already presented in previous narrative scenes (cf. 20:18–19).[299] As Paul continues to speak in this scene, emphasis is given to God's role, both in Paul's ministry of proclaiming the gospel to all the Ephesians (cf. 20:21, 24, 26–27)[300] and in his future endeavors in Jerusalem (cf. 20:22).[301] Thus, this indirect description of divine involvement functions to validate the narrative as Luke presents it.[302] In this narrated recollection from the lips of Paul, the speaker asserts that the product of his divinely ordained ministry, a group of Jews and Gentiles (cf. 20:21) who believe in "the good news of the grace of God" (τὸ εὐαγγέλιον τῆς χάριτος τοῦ θεοῦ; 20:24), is consistent with the "whole purpose of God" (πᾶσαν τὴν βουλὴν τοῦ θεοῦ; 20:27).[303]

The central part of Paul's speech to the Ephesian church leaders, however, progresses beyond divine validation of Paul's ministry and focuses on the divine character of the church.[304] Luke presents Paul as instructing the elders to serve "all the flock" (παντὶ τῷ ποιμνίῳ)[305] as "overseers" (ἐπισκόπους; 20:28)[306] because the Holy Spirit has appointed them (τὸ πνεῦμα τὸ ἅγιον ἔθετο; 20:28) to that ministry. This instruction implies

---

299. See Brawley, *Centering on God*, 28, 109, who observes that the passage focuses on God's activity *through* Paul.

300. Cf. Conzelmann, *Acts of the Apostles*, 174; Jervell, "Paulus in der Apostelgeschichte und die Geschichte des Urchristentums," 382; Johnson, *The Acts of the Apostles*, 361; Tannehill, *The Narrative Unity of Luke-Acts*, 2:256–57; and Weiser, *Die Apostelgeschichte*, 2:575–76.

301. Paul's reflected uncertainty (20:22–23) about his future in Jerusalem, including the statement about the Holy Spirit's testimony of what awaits him in every city, hints of what will occur. Cf. Brawley, *Centering on God*, 56, 98–99; Schneider, *Die Apostelgeschichte*, 2:295; and Tannehill, *The Narrative Unity of Luke-Acts*, 2:254.

302. Cf. Shepherd, *The Narrative Function of the Holy Spirit*, 233–34.

303. Cf. Weiser, *Die Apostelgeschichte*, 2:583–84. See Tyson, *Images of Judaism in Luke-Acts*, 152, who says the reader should assume that Gentiles are included in this group.

304. Cf. Weiser, *Die Apostelgeschichte*, 2:577. See Talbert, *Reading Acts*, 187, who states that "the pastoral care of the Ephesian church is central" to the speech.

305. The term ποίμνιον (20:28) or related imagery is frequently used in the LXX to refer to the people of God (cf., e.g., Ps 100:3 [99:3]; Isa 40:11; Jer 13:17; Ezek 34; Zech 10:3). See Tannehill, *The Narrative Unity of Luke-Acts*, 2:257, who suggests that παντὶ τῷ ποιμνίῳ (20:28) corresponds to πᾶσαν τὴν βουλὴν τοῦ θεοῦ (20:27) as "the inclusive church of Jews and Gentiles that results from announcing God's saving purpose for all."

306. See Fitzmyer, *The Acts of the Apostles*, 678–79; and Tannehill, *The Narrative Unity of Luke-Acts*, 2:258, who compares the term ἐπίσκοπος (20:28) to the LXX use of the verb ἐπισκέπτομαι, which connotes Israel's leaders as shepherds who are supposed to care for the people (cf. Jer 23:2; Ezek 34:11; Zech 10:3; 11:16). See also Hans Conzelmann, *The Theology of St. Luke*, trans. Geoffrey Buswell (Philadelphia: Fortress, 1961), 217–18, who warns that Luke is not attempting to describe "the constitution of the Church."

that the Holy Spirit is guiding the believers, a description consistent with the Lukan characterization of the church in terms of divine presence.[307] Also implicitly related to this description is Paul's later statement that he is entrusting these elders "to God and to the word of God's grace" (τῷ θεῷ καὶ τῷ λόγῳ τῆς χάριτος αὐτοῦ; 20:32), which recognizes the divine presence that is to characterize the Christian community.[308] Within that communal context blessed by God's presence, however, Paul directs his instructions to the elders about the ministry and care for others that he himself has modeled (cf. 20:28, 35).[309] However, Paul's legacy to the church is not his example but the proclaimed gospel of God's grace for all humanity.[310] Like earlier descriptions of the believers in the beginning sections of Acts, the depiction of the church is one of divine blessing through the gospel, which is reflected by the church's ministry and the communal dynamics among the believers.

As Luke recounts the Pauline instructions to these Christian leaders, he inserts an explicit description of the Christian community found only here in the Acts narrative. The Christian community is described uniquely here as τὴν ἐκκλησίαν τοῦ θεοῦ, ἣν περιεποιήσατο διὰ τοῦ αἵματος τοῦ ἰδίου, "the church of God, which he obtained with his own blood" (20:28).[311] The genitive τοῦ θεοῦ in the expression τὴν ἐκκλησίαν τοῦ θεοῦ may function in one of several ways in articulating the relation of the church and God: the church as the possession of God, the church that exists because of God, or the church that has its source in God. The relative clause following τὴν ἐκκλησίαν τοῦ θεοῦ clarifies why Luke, through the Pauline speech and throughout the Acts narrative, has identified the church with God: because *God* "obtained"

---

307. Cf. Brawley, *Centering on God*, 115; Lohfink, *Die Sammlung Israels*, 92; and Alfons Weiser, "Gemeinde und Amt nach dem Zeugnis der Apostelgeschichte," in *Mitverantwortung aller in der Kirche: Festschrift zum 150jährigen Bestehen der Gründung Vinzenz Pallottis*, ed. Franz Courth and Alfons Weiser (Limburg: Lahn-Verlag, 1985), 120.

308. See Tannehill, *The Narrative Unity of Luke-Acts*, 2:255, who observes that the security of the church will be found only in God, not in the elders.

309. Cf. Brawley, *Centering on God*, 28; Jervell, "Paulus in der Apostelgeschichte und die Geschichte des Urchristentums," 383; and Weiser, *Die Apostelgeschichte*, 2:578–79.

310. See Tannehill, *The Narrative Unity of Luke-Acts*, 2:257.

311. Cf. Dunn, *The Acts of the Apostles*, 272–73; Conzelmann, *Acts of the Apostles*, 175; and Lohfink, *Die Sammlung Israels*, 89. See Lüdemann, *Early Christianity according to the Traditions in Acts*, 228, who suggests that the Lukan redactor puts separate traditional statements together in this expression. For discussions concerning the two variant readings, τὴν ἐκκλησίαν τοῦ θεοῦ and τὴν ἐκκλησίαν τοῦ κυρίου (20:28), see Metzger, *A Textual Commentary on the Greek New Testament*, 480–81; Barrett, *The Acts of the Apostles*, 2:976–77; Fitzmyer, *The Acts of the Apostles*, 679–80; and Johnson, *The Acts of the Apostles*, 363.

(περιεποιήσατο) it.[312] By borrowing language from the Septuagint that refers to God obtaining a λαός (Israel) to depict God obtaining the ἐκκλησία that is comprised of Jews and Gentiles, here one finds "that God's relation to the mixed church ... is being understood after the pattern of God's relation to Israel in Scripture."[313] Much like the two statements attributed to James (15:14) and the Lord (18:10) that include Gentiles in the λαός of God, the Christian community of Jewish and non-Jewish believers again receives the designation that has been reserved historically for the Jews as the people of God.[314] Thus, the ongoing existence of the church is depicted as theocentric because its origin is traced to the work of God.[315] While the narrative includes no additional explanation about this activity of God, the clear emphasis is that, through the death of Jesus, God was at work in the establishment of the church, a group no longer limited to the Jews.[316] Thus, this Pauline statement functions within Acts both as an implicit description of the Christian community and as a confirmation from a reliable character of the divine presence and blessing among the Ephesian believers.

The Lukan characterization of the Christian community, as found in this Pauline speech to the leaders of the Ephesian church, does not focus exclusively on ideal imagery. Rather, along with this identification of the church as a people who belong to God and among whom God is working and blessing, Luke presents Paul as warning the church leaders about two types of persons who might threaten them as a united people belonging to God. One threat to the church is depicted metaphorically as "savage wolves" (λύκοι βαρεῖς)[317] having no concern for the well-being of "the flock" or, in other words, the church (μὴ φειδόμενοι τοῦ ποιμνίου; 20:29). This first threat seemingly compares to the various acts of jealous opposition endured by Paul throughout his travels. However,

---

312. Cf. Lohfink, *Die Sammlung Israels*, 90, who suggests that περιποιέω (20:28) has the same theological sense as in Isa 43:21 (LXX): λαόν μου, ὃν περιεποιησάμην (my people, whom I obtained). See C. F. D. Moule, "The Christology of Acts," in *Studies in Luke-Acts*, ed. Leander E. Keck and J. Louis Martyn (Philadelphia: Fortress, 1980), 171: "Paul ... is not evangelizing but recalling an already evangelized community to its deepest insights."

313. Tannehill, *The Narrative Unity of Luke-Acts*, 2:259.

314. Cf. Weiser, "Gemeinde und Amt nach dem Zeugnis der Apostelgeschichte," 121.

315. Cf. Brawley, *Centering on God*, 57; and Lohfink, *Die Sammlung Israels*, 86, 91.

316. See Weiser, *Die Apostelgeschichte*, 2:578–79, who states that the obtaining "with his own blood" defines both the responsibility and service of the elders toward the church.

317. See Barrett, *The Acts of the Apostles*, 2:978; Conzelmann, *Acts of the Apostles*, 175; Fitzmyer, *The Acts of the Apostles*, 680–81; and Johnson, *The Acts of the Apostles*, 363, who identify several references in which false teachers are designated as wolves.

another threat that is grammatically linked (καί) to the first destructive threat will not come from outside the church but from within (ἐξ ὑμῶν; 20:30).[318] The wording of verse 30, ἄνδρες λαλοῦντες διεστραμμένα, negatively describes the threat as coming from those teachings that might appear to be the gospel message but are, in reality, distortions or perversions that result in a division of the believers (τοῦ ἀποσπᾶν τοὺς μαθητὰς ὀπίσω αὐτῶν; 20:30).[319] This warning suggests that both the unanimity among the believers and a faithfulness to the proclamation of the gospel message, which is founded in God's gracious activity for all humanity, must be maintained if the Christian community is to be identified as τὴν ἐκκλησίαν τοῦ θεοῦ, the assembly of people belonging to God (20:28).[320]

Luke concludes this narrative section by describing an emotional scene as Paul prepares to leave,[321] and only now does Luke present the group of church leaders as active characters in this section.[322] As the narrator briefly observes that Paul prays with them (σὺν πᾶσιν αὐτοῖς; 20:36),[323] the reader will be reminded of earlier positive descriptions of believers who have gathered together in prayer (cf. 1:12–14, 24–25; 2:42; 4:24–31; 6:6; 13:1–3; 14:23). The Lukan observations in verse 36 of the leaders as they weep, embrace Paul (ἐπιπεσόντες ἐπὶ τὸν τράχηλον τοῦ Παύλου), and kiss him implicitly depict the intimate bonds of friendship

---

318. See Haenchen, *The Acts of the Apostles*, 593; Lüdemann, *Early Christianity according to the Traditions in Acts*, 227; and Weiser, *Die Apostelgeschichte*, 2:576, who see these warnings as reflecting problems in Luke's day. Contra Robert Maddox, *The Purpose of Luke-Acts*, FRLANT 126 (Göttingen: Vandenhoeck & Ruprecht, 1982), 69.

319. The description of these divisive teachings, λαλοῦντες διεστραμμένα, implies that these were intentional perversions that appeared consistent with the gospel (20:30). The use of λαλέω here is its first negative appearance in Acts; only here and in 26:31 is the term used to describe the speaking of someone other than a believer, a prophet, a divine figure, or a supernatural character. Thus, the subtle picture is one of distortion "dressed in gospel clothing." The verb διαστρέφω (20:30) connotes distortion and is used negatively to describe a person's actions (e.g., Aristotle, *Nicomachean Ethics* 2.9; 6.5; Epictetus, *Dissertations* 3.6.8; Deut 32:5).

320. See Tyson, *Images of Judaism in Luke-Acts*, 143, who states that "the opposition of non-Jewish groups cannot be compared with that of Jews in terms of covert intrigue, repeated occurrence, and sustained hostility." However, 20:30 suggests that this "inside" opposition may be just as dangerous as another example of those who divide or destroy community.

321. Cf. Pervo, *Profit with Delight*, 67: "By the conclusion all are in tears, and the scene dissolves in a general breakdown." Cf. also Kurz, *Reading Luke-Acts*, 99–100.

322. Up to this point, the group of leaders as Paul's audience in this section have been passive characters.

323. The prepositional phrase σὺν πᾶσιν αὐτοῖς (20:36) could modify either θεὶς τὰ γόνατα αὐτοῦ or προσηύξατο. If the phrase modifies the indicative, then it stands in the emphatic position and highlights this prayerful act in the context of this group of believers.

between the Ephesian leaders and Paul (20:37).[324] The parting scene depicts nothing but affection and grief over Paul's leaving, showing the intimate bonds created among a diverse group of Jews and Gentiles by the good news of God's grace for all humanity.

An Assessment of the Characterization of the Church or Group of Believers in Acts 20:17–38

A literary convention in ancient historiography is the use of speeches to convey the narrator's perspective implicitly through narrative characters. Such speeches function both to assist readers in the interpretation of previous narrative events and to provide them with useful information for interpreting subsequent events. The Pauline speech to the Ephesian elders or church leaders reflects such ancient literary conventions; the speech provides the narrative means by which Luke implicitly interprets previous events, scenes, and characters. As the narrator presents Paul, who is reminiscing about his past ministry in Ephesus, the subject of the speech is not Paul but God as the one who guides Paul to proclaim the good news of God's grace to all people (cf. 20:21, 24). Therefore, this understanding of God's involvement confirms what Acts 1–19 has already presented. The outcome of God's activity and the ministry through Paul is described as τὴν ἐκκλησίαν τοῦ θεοῦ, the assembly of people who are the possession of God because of what God has done (20:28). Because the proclamation of the gospel message does not distinguish between Jews and Gentiles, the Lukan Paul describes τὴν ἐκκλησίαν τοῦ θεοῦ as including both Jewish and non-Jewish believers, which also confirms what the narrative has depicted in Acts 10–19. Thus, the explicit characterization of the Christian church in Acts 20 highlights and reaffirms the significant images already presented in the Acts narrative: the presence and blessing of God, the belief in the good news of God's salvific work for all humanity, the unanimity of the believers, and the communal bonds of friendship and care among them. The Lukan narrator emphatically presents these characteristics, which he has directly described among the Jewish believers in the narrative summaries of Acts 1–5 (cf. 2:42–47; 4:32–37; 5:12–16), in the context of the Ephesian "mixed" congregation of Jewish and Gentile believers. This mixed group of believers, like the Jewish believers in earlier chapters, is explicitly identified as belonging to God.

---

324. Cf. Krodel, *Acts*, 393; and Witherington, *The Acts of the Apostles*, 627.

GROUPS OF BELIEVERS AS PAUL
APPROACHES JERUSALEM (ACTS 21:1–16)

The Literary Context

The previous chapter (Acts 20) has already presented Paul in what may be called his "farewell tour," as he visits those churches in Asia, Macedonia, and Greece with which he has associated in his ministry. The narrator has already stated that Paul plans to return to the eastern Mediterranean region after completing this journey, although those plans are modified because of the ever-present Jewish opposition against him (cf. 20:3). Thus, his revised itinerary takes Paul to Miletus, where he speaks to the Ephesian church leaders. The narrator provides a final opportunity for the reader to evaluate, through the perspective of the reliable character Paul, what God has done in gathering together τὴν ἐκκλησίαν τοῦ θεοῦ, a people who belong to God, an identification based not on Jewish heritage and practices but on belief in the gospel. Now that this understanding of the Christian church has been verified for the reader, the narrative returns to Paul's journey as he continues on his way to Jerusalem.

The Characterization of the Christian Church or Group of Believers in Acts 21:1–16

Once Paul and his entourage have landed at the city of Tyre, the narrator briefly describes a general scene in each of two cities where they stay with fellow believers.[325] While the traveling party stays in Tyre with τοὺς μαθητάς, these disciples or believers speak to Paul διὰ τοῦ πνεύματος (21:4), which the reader would identify as a positive description of those believers.[326] The narrator simply summarizes the essence of their message, which warns Paul not to go to Jerusalem. The inclusion of this warning contributes to the increasing suspense that Paul's own words to

---

325. The verb ἐπιμένω is used in both instances to describe Paul and his companions staying with believers: ἐπεμείναμεν (21:4) and ἐπιμενόντων (21:10). The term is used in Acts 1–20: in 10:48 when Peter stays with the new Gentile believers in Caesarea, and in 12:16, when Peter continues to knock on the door at Mary's house (the term appears in 15:34, but there are textual questions about this verse).

326. The prepositional phrase διὰ τοῦ πνεύματος (21:4) suggests that the believers warn Paul after they hear the Spirit's message. Thus, the Spirit's message gives rise to the occasion but is not the source of the warning, as the narrative balances the Spirit's presence with the caring concerns of the believers. Note how this conflicts with 20:22–23, where Paul attributes his compulsion to go to Jerusalem to the Spirit. Cf. Bruce, *The Book of the Acts*, 398; Marshall, *The Acts of the Apostles*, 338–39; and Tannehill, *The Narrative Unity of Luke-Acts*, 2:263.

the Ephesian elders have already created about what might happen in Jerusalem (cf. 20:22–24).[327] The narrator clearly presents the believers as concerned for Paul's well-being but mentions nothing else about Paul's stay with them. However, as Paul prepares to continue on his journey, Luke observes in concise fashion that all the believers with their families accompany the travelers outside the city, where they all pray together (21:5).[328] Although the narrative includes little of what transpires during that week in Tyre, the description of the believers relies on the positive images that have typified the Christians throughout Acts: the presence of the Holy Spirit, the care and concern for other believers (such as Paul), the communal sense of unanimity and togetherness, and the activity of prayer.

The second city where Luke describes Paul's visit with believers as he travels to Jerusalem is Caesarea. The narrator mentions that Paul stays with Philip the evangelist while in Caesarea, probably the same Philip as in Acts 8. However, what stands out in this narrative scene is the prominent role of prophets. The four daughters of Philip are described as prophesying (21:9),[329] and the arrival of Agabus the prophet[330] leads to his dramatic articulation[331] of a message that he attributes to the Holy Spirit (21:11).[332] All of the believers, including Paul's companions and the local believers (ἡμεῖς τε καὶ οἱ ἐντόπιοι), encourage (παρεκαλοῦμεν; 21:12)[333] Paul to abort his travel plans to Jerusalem after hearing this message from the Spirit. The narrator depicts the Christians who gather

---

327. Cf. Haenchen, *The Acts of the Apostles*, 603; Kurz, *Reading Luke-Acts*, 101; and Weiser, *Die Apostelgeschichte*, 2:589.

328. The text of 21:5 explains the actions of the Tyre believers and their families more fully than the actions of Paul and his associates. Cf. Haenchen, *The Acts of the Apostles*, 600; and Johnson, *The Acts of the Apostles*, 369.

329. The imperfect periphrastic construction ἦσαν ... προφητεύουσαι emphasizes the ongoing prophetic activity of these four daughters (21:9). See Krodel, *Acts*, 394; Schneider, *Die Apostelgeschichte*, 2:304; and Weiser, *Die Apostelgeschichte*, 2:591, who suggest that these prophetesses prepare the scene for Agabus's prophecy.

330. The reader should recognize Agabus as the same one who has earlier predicted the famine to the Antioch church (cf. 11:27–30). Cf. Dunn, *The Acts of the Apostles*, 282; Fitzmyer, *The Acts of the Apostles*, 689; and Witherington, *The Acts of the Apostles*, 633.

331. This dramatic presentation of a divine message resembles similar OT instances of prophets using symbolic actions to reinforce the message (cf., e.g., 1 Kgs 11:29–40; Isa 20:2–6; Jer 13:1–11; Ezek 4:1–17). Cf. Haenchen, *The Acts of the Apostles*, 601–2; Johnson, *The Acts of the Apostles*, 370; Krodel, *Acts*, 394; and Neil, *Acts*, 217.

332. See Roloff, *Die Apostelgeschichte*, 310, who observes that Agabus's message only describes what will happen to Paul in Jerusalem

333. The verb παρακαλέω (21:12), which describes the believers' response to Paul, is the same one used earlier to depict Paul's positive response in ministry to the believers (cf. 14:22;

together as unanimously demonstrating concern for Paul's safety and well-being.[334] The narrated Pauline reply further depicts their collective concern, as he questions them about their crying and breaking his heart (Τί ποιεῖτε κλαίοντες καὶ συνθρύπτοντές μου τὴν καρδίαν; 21:13).[335]

The depicted differences between the believers and Paul do not, however, present a negative situation when considered within the progression of the Acts narrative. The narrated scene thus does not depict the rest of the believers as opposing Paul, nor does it depict Paul as ignoring a group of believers that he would include in his description of the Christian community as τὴν ἐκκλησίαν τοῦ θεοῦ (cf. 20:28). Rather, while both the believers and Paul claim divine rationale for their proposals,[336] the overwhelmingly positive portrayal of Paul as a reliable character in Acts 13–20 suggests that Paul's understanding of the divine will is also reliable here.[337] While the response of the believers affirms Paul's reliability and his resolve to follow the divine will,[338] Luke positively represents the believers as those who respond together to protect Paul. Thus, Luke's description of the Caesarean Christians reflects similar portrayals of believers who have provided for Paul's safety (cf. 9:23–25, 30; 14:20; 17:10, 14–15; 19:30). This narrative scene concludes with another glimpse of the unanimity of the believers, as some of them join together with Paul and his associates in the final leg of his journey to Jerusalem.[339] Although the Caesarean believers already know what Paul will face when they reach their destination, their uniting together with

---

16:40; 20:1, 2, 12). The imperfect tense suggests that they are pleading for Paul to change his plans.

334. Cf. Tannehill, The Narrative Unity of Luke-Acts, 2:263.

335. The prefix σύν added to the verb θρύπτω (to break into pieces) suggests that the believers are collectively breaking Paul's heart (21:13). Cf. Johnson, The Acts of the Apostles, 370; and Roloff, Die Apostelgeschichte, 310–11.

336. The believers respond to Agabus's message from the Holy Spirit (21:11–12), whereas Paul states his willingness to face whatever might happen in Jerusalem ὑπὲρ τοῦ ὀνόματος τοῦ κυρίου Ἰησοῦ (21:13).

337. Cf. Tannehill, The Narrative Unity of Luke-Acts, 2:265.

338. The believers' response, after they do not persuade Paul to change his plans (τοῦ κυρίου τὸ θέλημα γινέσθω; 21:14), places τοῦ κυρίου in an emphatic position, stressing their wish for the Lord's will.

339. The first half of the sentence in 21:16 describes the response of the Caesarean believers in typical Lukan fashion by emphasizing their joining together with the Pauline party through the use of the prefix and preposition σύν: συνῆλθον δὲ καὶ τῶν μαθητῶν ἀπὸ Καισαρείας σὺν ἡμῖν. The verb συνέρχομαι connotes coming, traveling, assembling, or uniting together (see LSJ, 1712). For examples of authors using this term to affirm the joining together of persons, see, e.g., Herodotus, Histories 4.120; and Aristotle, Politics 3.4.3.

Paul suggests that this group of believers provides the corporate context of support and encouragement through which Paul can fulfill the divine will.

An Assessment of the Characterization of the Church or Group of Believers in Acts 21:1–16

As Paul approaches Jerusalem, the Lukan portrayal of two believer groups in 21:1–16 contributes to the growing suspense and anticipation associated with the plot. The Christian community provides the narrative context through which the Spirit informs the believers and the reader of what will happen in Jerusalem. However, the Lukan narrator also links that prophetic message to an overwhelming sense of affection and concern for Paul, resulting in ambiguous scenes of disagreement over what he should do. As Robert Tannehill states, "Paul finds himself in conflict with his own friends, who try to dissuade him from completing his trip. Both prophetic messages and human advice play important roles in this conflict, and the narrative reveals some of the difficulties in using either to determine God's will for human life."[340]

Regardless of the ambiguity, the narrator presents the Christian community in these scenes as the people in whom the Holy Spirit works and among whom a concern for one another's needs is demonstrated. In the concluding images of both narrative scenes, Luke presents the believers *together* with Paul, implying that their differences only arise out of their oneness as believers, as the church or the assembly of people who belong to God.

THE JERUSALEM CHURCH MEETS WITH PAUL (ACTS 21:17–36)

The Literary Context

Since the beginning of chapter 20, the narrative has presented Paul as traveling to the city of Jerusalem. The narrator has provided information along the way that builds suspense in the reader as Paul nears the city (cf. 20:22–24; 21:4, 11–12). Throughout the narrative of 20:1–21:16, Luke has depicted the Christians in terms of the Holy Spirit's presence and the believers' genuine affection for Paul. These pictures, along with the communal acts of support and encouragement in the conclusion of

---

340. Tannehill, *The Narrative Unity of Luke-Acts*, 2:262.

the last three scenes, positively present these believers in ways that reflect the ideal images of the beginning days of the Jerusalem church in Acts.

The Characterization of the Church or Group of Believers in Acts 21:17–36

The account of Paul's arrival in Jerusalem begins with a concise statement about him meeting "the brothers" (οἱ ἀδελφοί; 21:17) or the church.[341] The reception of Paul by the Jerusalem believers is presented favorably, as they enthusiastically welcome Paul and his companions (ἀσμένως ἀπεδέξαντο ἡμᾶς; 21:17). However, the narrator provides no further information. What the narrator *does* describe in more detail is a meeting the next day with James and "all the elders" (πάντες ... οἱ πρεσβύτεροι; 21:18). Luke begins his description of the meeting by presenting Paul as "greeting them" (ἀσπασάμενος αὐτούς)[342] and recounting all the good things that God has done among the Gentiles through his ministry (21:19), a description resembling the earlier Lukan description of Barnabas and Paul's report in chapter 15.[343] The initial narrated response to Paul's report is positive, as those listening to Paul begin to praise God (ἐδόξαζον τὸν θεόν; 21:20),[344] reminding the reader of earlier pictures of believers praising God (cf. 2:47; 4:21; 11:18; 13:48).[345] However, that Luke grammatically links (τε; 21:20) the raising of serious concerns about Paul's ministry to this praise appears to depict the subsequent response as most inappropriate.[346] The Lukan narration juxtaposes the raising of these complaints or "charges" with the believers'

---

341. See Lüdemann, *Early Christianity according to the Traditions in Acts*, 231, who does not see 21:17 as referring to welcome from the whole church. Cf. Haenchen, *The Acts of the Apostles*, 607, who sees this referring to the Hellenistic believers.

342. For other occurrences of the verb ἀσπάζομαι (21:19) in Acts, see 18:22; 20:1; 21:7 and 25:13.

343. Readers can see similarities between the three Pauline reports as Luke summarizes them in Acts 15:4, 12; and 21:19: ἀνήγγειλάν τε ὅσα ὁ θεὸς ἐποίησεν μετ᾿ αὐτῶν (15:4); ἐξηγουμένων ὅσα ἐποίησεν ὁ θεὸς ... ἐν τοῖς ἔθνεσιν δι᾿ αὐτῶν (15:12); and ἐξηγεῖτο ... ὧν ἐποίησεν ὁ θεὸς ἐν τοῖς ἔθνεσιν διὰ τῆς διακονίας αὐτοῦ (21:19). In all three cases, the main focus is on ὁ θεὸς ἐποίησεν. See Borse, "Kompositionsgeschichtliche Beobachtungen zum Apostelkonzil," 197–200.

344. The imperfect tense of ἐδόξαζον (21:20) denotes the beginning of an action (an inceptive imperfect). Cf. Barrett, *The Acts of the Apostles*, 2:1006, who sees the imperfect tense indicating continuing activity.

345. See Brawley, *Centering on God*, 121, who sees this praise as indicative of the leaders' "evaluative role for the Gentile mission as God's work."

346. This part of the account is similar to 15:4–5, when Paul and Barnabas's report about God's activity is followed immediately and inappropriately by those who insist on Gentile Christians becoming Jews. The one major difference in Acts 21 is that Luke briefly mentions

praise for what God has done, thereby quickly turning what begins as a hospitable meeting into a rather bewildering scene that may leave the reader wondering what the Jerusalem believers are thinking.

The narrated explanation by these Jewish-Christian leaders for the complaints about Paul contributes significantly to the Lukan depiction of the Jerusalem church, as the narrator gives the reader access to what the leaders have to say. The first statement out of the mouths of these leaders reminds Paul that thousands of Jews had become believers (πόσαι μυριάδες εἰσὶν ἐν τοῖς Ἰουδαίοις τῶν πεπιστευκότων)[347] and that they all are "zealous of the law" (πάντες ζηλωταὶ τοῦ νόμου ὑπάρχουσιν; 21:20).[348] These matters are important because certain rumors about Paul relate to the Jewish law. In particular, these rumors accuse Paul of teaching the Jews to rebel against Moses (ἀποστασίαν διδάσκεις ἀπὸ Μωϋσέως; 21:21) or to apostasize from the Jewish laws and customs.[349] These charges are apparently taken seriously for at least two reasons: (1) This kind of teaching is rumored to be Paul's regular practice, as the present tense indicative suggests. (2) Paul is said to be teaching *all* Jews living in the Diaspora, or among the Gentiles (τοὺς κατὰ τὰ ἔθνη πάντας Ἰουδαίους; 21:21).[350]

The reader will probably conclude that these serious charges against Paul are unwarranted, since the Lukan narrator has never included such teachings in his account of Paul's ministry.[351] However, the reader may not see these reports as *completely* unbelievable or fictitious, like the

---

a positive response to the report (21:20a), unlike Acts 15. Cf. Robert W. Wall, "The Acts of the Apostles: Introduction, Commentary, and Reflections," in *NIB*, ed. Leander Keck, 12 vols. (Nashville: Abingdon, 2002), 10:292. Contra Lüdemann, *Early Christianity according to the Traditions in Acts*, 232, who sees these similarities as a sign that Paul has a good relationship with the Jerusalem church to the end.

347. Cf. Lohfink, *Die Sammlung Israels*, 53–54, who suggests that the church is "huge," the Jewish law dominates the scene, and many of Israel are believers; and Jacob Jervell, *The Unknown Paul: Essays on Luke-Acts and Early Christian History* (Minneapolis: Augsburg, 1984), 26–51. For a different reading, see Michael J. Cook, "The Mission to the Jews in Acts: Unraveling Luke's 'Myth of the "Myriads"'" in Tyson, *Luke-Acts and the Jewish People*, 102–23.

348. See Weiser, "Das 'Apostelkonzil,'" 100, who sees the dominance of the Pharisaic believers. Cf. Bovon, "Israel, die Kirche und die Völker im lukanischen Doppelwerk," 409.

349. Cf. Barrett, *The Acts of the Apostles*, 2:1007–8; Dunn, *The Acts of the Apostles*, 286; and Talbert, *Reading Acts*, 192–93.

350. Cf. Gaventa, *The Acts of the Apostles*, 298, who notes that these are neither questions about Paul's ethical behavior nor demands that he alter his teaching or practices.

351. Cf. Barrett, *The Acts of the Apostles*, 2:1007; Fitzmyer, *The Acts of the Apostles*, 693; Talbert, *Reading Acts*, 194; and Dunn, *The Acts of the Apostles*, 286–87, who observes that 16:1–3 shows how unwarranted the rumor is.

charges against Stephen (cf. 6:13–14),[352] because they may reflect a different perspective or interpretation of Paul's ministry in the same two cities where he has separated from the synagogue, a perspective that the Acts narrative does not completely squelch.[353] In the Corinth episode (18:1–17), the narrative includes two perspectives of the Pauline character. From the perspective of the narrator, Paul is described as "teaching the word of God" (διδάσκων ἐν αὐτοῖς τὸν λόγον τοῦ θεοῦ; 18:11). Conversely, from the narrated perspective of the Jewish opponents, Paul is described in the charges raised against him as persuading or, perhaps as the verb ἀναπείθω may connote, *misleading* or *seducing* people to worship God in ways "contrary to the law" (18:13).[354] In the Ephesus episode, the narrative description of Paul's withdrawal from the synagogue, ἀποστὰς ἀπ' αὐτῶν (19:9), uses similar language as the rumors about Paul's teaching to describe Paul's actions in leaving the synagogue. Thus, the withdrawal from the synagogue by Jewish believers including Paul may be interpreted as a threat to the Jewish community and its identity.[355] However, given the narrator's perspective of Paul and his ministry, the reader of the Acts narrative is certainly encouraged to view the rumors unfavorably.[356]

---

352. Notice the similarities between the rumors about Paul and the charges against Stephen. Cf. Bruce, *The Book of the Acts*, 409–10; Johnson, *The Acts of the Apostles*, 375; Sanders, *The Jews in Luke-Acts*, 285; and Tannehill, *The Narrative Unity of Luke-Acts*, 2:273.

353. See Richard P. Thompson, "'Say It Ain't So, Paul!' The Accusations against Paul (Acts 21) in Light of His Ministry in Acts," *BR* 45 (2000): 34–50; and "'What Do You Think You Are Doing, Paul?' Synagogues, Ministry, and Ethics in Acts 16-21," in *Acts and Ethics*, ed. Thomas E. Phillips (Sheffield: Sheffield Phoenix, 2005), 64–78.

354. Παρὰ τὸν νόμον ἀναπείθει οὗτος τοὺς ἀνθρώπους σέβεσθαι τὸν θεόν (18:13). Cf. Jacob Jervell, *The Theology of the Acts of the Apostles* (Cambridge, MA: Cambridge University Press, 1996), 88: "According to the charges Paul is a false teacher in Israel. At issue is his teaching on the law and Israel, which concerns Jews throughout the world. The charges do not relate to the mission among the Gentiles.... But Paul has sinned against the people, Israel (21:28; 28:17): he is charged with apostasy; he is guilty of forsaking the law and is therefore no longer a member of the people of God."

355. See Johnson, *The Acts of the Apostles*, 379; and Tannehill, *The Narrative Unity of Luke-Acts*, 2:236, 269.

356. In the account of Paul's ministry in Ephesus, the reader will probably recognize two points affirmimg that these charges are unwarranted: (1) Paul only withdraws from the synagogue because of Jewish opposition (e.g., 19:8–9), and (2) Paul never is presented as having *taught* against the Jewish law but is always presented as a loyal, law-observing Jew. Cf., e.g., Robert L. Brawley, "Paul in Acts: Aspects of Structure and Characterization," in *SBLSP 1988*, ed. David Lull (Atlanta: Scholars Press, 1988), 90–105; Jervell, "Paulus in der Apostelgeschichte und die Geschichte des Urchristentums," 378–92; I. Howard Marshall, "Luke's View of Paul," *SwJT* 33 (Fall 1990): 48–49; Jürgen Roloff, "Die Paulus-Darstellung des

Although the rumors reflect an interpretation of the Pauline ministry that runs counter to the Lukan point of view, the majority of the Jewish believers apparently believe them (cf. 21:22).[357] The proposal that Paul *himself*, whom the reader is invited to view according to the narrator's perspective as the innocent party, provide the remedy to the controversy according to the leaders' specifications implies one of two things: (1) that the Christian leaders also believe the charges against him, or (2) that the law-zealous Jewish Christians are such a strong group within the Jerusalem church that the leaders can only attempt to pacify them.[358] In either case, the Lukan depiction of the Jerusalem church is anything but affirmative. Whereas Luke implicitly describes the Jerusalem church leaders as having done nothing to dispel the reports about Paul that he sees as unwarranted rumors, the narrator describes in contrast a conciliatory Paul, who fulfills the recommended solution (21:26).[359] Those believers, whom the Jerusalem church leaders characterize as zealous for the Jewish law, themselves seem to threaten the church by creating division over their insistence on matters of ethnic and religious customs.[360]

The narrative scene involving Paul and the Jews at the temple also contributes to the developing negative picture of the Jerusalem church. When "the Jews from Asia" see Paul in the temple (21:27),[361] they themselves accuse Paul of being the one who has taught "everyone everywhere" (πάντας πανταχῆ) against everything sacred to the Jews: the people (τοῦ λαοῦ), the law (τοῦ νόμου), and the temple (τοῦ τόπου τούτου; 21:28).[362]

Lukas," *EvT* 39 (1979): 510–31; and Slingerland, " 'The Jews' in the Pauline Portion of Acts," 305–12.

357. The similarity of the accusations by the church leaders (21:21) and the "Jews from Asia" (21:27–28) implies that *all* Jews believe the charges and oppose Paul. See Roloff, *Die Apostelgeschichte*, 313–14; and Weiser, *Die Apostelgeschichte*, 2:597, who wonder how welcome Paul *really* is (cf. 21:17).

358. Cf. Jervell, "Paulus in der Apostelgeschichte und die Geschichte des Urchristentums," 387; Sanders, *The Jews in Luke-Acts*, 284; and Tyson, "The Problem of Jewish Rejection in Acts," 136. Contra Richard Bauckham, "James and the Jerusalem Church," in *The Book of Acts in Its Palestinian Setting*, ed. Richard Bauckham, BAFCS (Grand Rapids: Eerdmans, 1995), 475, who sees no evidence for control by the conservative group.

359. See Tannehill, *The Narrative Unity of Luke-Acts*, 2:270–71, who states that "Paul is risking his life in order to make clear that he affirms the rights of Jewish Christians to live according to the law."

360. Cf. Johnson, *The Acts of the Apostles*, 379; and Zingg, *Das Wachsen der Kirche*, 176. Contra Pervo, *Profit with Delight*, 41–42.

361. The mention of "the Jews from Asia" (21:27) as Paul's accusers at the temple may help readers to see the relationship between the accusations and Paul's ministry in Ephesus.

362. Cf. Brawley, *Centering on God*, 104; Dunn, *The Acts of the Apostles*, 288–89; Roloff, *Die Apostelgeschichte*, 317; Weiser, *Die Apostelgeschichte*, 2:602.

Thus, they charge Paul with religious disloyalty, charges similar to the rumors reported by the church leaders.[363] The narration of what transpires presents what quickly turns into a mob scene created entirely by the Jews. The agitation of the entire crowd at the temple (συνέχεον πάντα τὸν ὄχλον; 21:27) spread to include the whole city (ὅλη συγχύννεται Ἰερουσαλήμ; 21:31).[364] The narrator intensifies this vivid picture of the entire city reacting against Paul by stating that the people rush together (ἐγένετο συνδρομὴ τοῦ λαοῦ), seize him, and drag him from the temple (21:30).[365] Only the intervention of the military prevent the Jewish mob from killing the innocent Paul (ζητούντων τε αὐτὸν ἀποκτεῖναι; 21:31–32).[366] Even then, the ugly scene of the confused uproar (τὸν θόρυβον; 21:34) and violence (τὴν βίαν; 21:35) that has led to Paul's arrest forces the soldiers to carry him away from the riotous throngs of the Jews (21:35).[367]

What is surprisingly silent in this narrative depiction of tumultuous noise and raging violence, however, is Luke's observation of the Jerusalem believers during the detestable scene. Where are the Jewish believers when Paul is attacked while doing what *they* have instructed him to do? Luke mentions nothing.[368] Why is Luke silent, not depicting the Jewish believers as actively concerned for the safety of their fellow Jewish believer, Paul? That would positively reflect similar concerns among other groups of believers (cf. 9:23–25; 17:10, 14–15; 19:30; 21:4, 12–13) and even among their own group in earlier days (cf. 9:30).[369] Does Luke's

---

363. See John T. Carroll, "Literary and Social Dimensions of Luke's Apology for Paul," in Lull, *SBLSP 1988*, 110–11.

364. In 21:27, 31, a form of συγχέω is used with either πᾶς or ὅλος. This verb, with the prefix σύν and these adjectives, ironically suggests unanimity among the Jerusalem populace in its agitation over Paul. Contra Haenchen, *The Acts of the Apostles*, 616, who interprets this as exaggerating what really happens.

365. See Tannehill, *The Narrative Unity of Luke-Acts*, 2:242, who compares this riotous scene and the earlier riotous scene in Ephesus (cf. 19:23–41).

366. The verb ἀποκτείνω appears only twice in Acts 1–20, referring to the Jews' killing of "the Author of Life" (3:15) and the prophets foretelling the coming of the "Righteous One" (7:52). Thus, the terminology reflects the Jewish attempt to do similarly to Paul.

367. See Roloff, *Die Apostelgeschichte*, 317–18, who compares this description (21:35) to Agabus's prophecy (cf. 21:11).

368. See Dunn, *The Acts of the Apostles*, 289, who asks: "Could it be that the Jerusalem Christians left Paul to stew in his own juice?" Contra Bauckham, "James and the Jerusalem Church," 478–79, who states that Luke does not record *everything* that happens, and so the actions of the Christian leaders are not important here.

369. Cf. Johnson, *The Acts of the Apostles*, 378; and Rapske, "Opposition to the Plan of God and Persecution," 245.

description of the *whole* populace of Jerusalem reacting violently together against Paul also include the Jewish *believers* ?[370] Although the narrator has presented the ideal, communal care for those in the Christian community (e.g., Paul) with increasing regularity, that specific image is conspicuously absent at this point in the Acts narrative, when the narrated events indicate that this trait is most needed. When Paul needs the Christian community, whose huge numbers (cf. 21:20) could provide ample protection and support, the Lukan narrator observes no Christian response. Consequently, this narrative silence is deafening in the midst of a narrative scene of commotion and bedlam, and that silence implicitly presents an overwhelmingly negative portrayal of the Christian community in Jerusalem.[371]

An Assessment of the Characterization of the Church or Group of Believers in Acts 21:17–36

The Lukan account of Paul's return to Jerusalem presents an ugly scene in the Jewish Holy City. The characterization of the Jerusalem church, however, does not fare any better than the Jerusalemites. The narrator does not make explicit statements or judgments either about the Jews or, more specifically, the Jewish believers. Rather, the narrator implicitly portrays various characters of this narrative section by observing their actions in ways that subtly reflect both positive and negative images presented in earlier portions of Acts. Thus, this negative portrayal of the Jerusalem church contrasts significantly with earlier images of the believers in that city. Earlier decisions involved the entire church and reflected both the unanimity of the believers and God's activity among them (cf. 6:1–7; 15:23–29). Conversely, Luke mentions nothing, either explicitly or implicitly, of an unanimous spirit but implicitly describes a situation of adversity.

Earlier activities of the Jerusalem believers are characterized by a sense of communal care and friendship that provides for one another's need

---

370. The narrated statement by the Jerusalem church leaders (21:22) provides a narrative hint that the law-zealous Jewish believers will react negatively to Paul's presence because of the rumors against him. When one considers the announcement of his presence in the temple and his so-called violations against everything sacred to the Jews (cf. 21:28), the reader may infer that these believers are included in the violent reaction against him. Cf. Sanders, *The Jews in Luke-Acts*, 286; and Rapske, "Opposition to the Plan of God and Persecution," 245.

371. This silence from the Christian community in Jerusalem (or their absence) continues throughout the rest of Acts. Cf. Tyson, "The Problem of Jewish Rejection in Acts," 136.

(cf. 2:42–47; 4:32–37). Conversely, the Lukan portrayal of the Jerusalem believers in Acts 21 describes nothing that reflects their concern for their fellow Jewish believer, Paul. The narrative account mentions nothing of divine blessing or presence, whereas earlier scenes have presented an inseparability between the believers and God. The ambiguity in describing the Jewish opposition and the narrative silence of the Jewish Christian community implies that these believers, like the numerous examples of other Jews found in the Acts narrative, may no longer be identified as people who belong to God.

The Roman Believers Meet Paul
(Acts 28:11–31)

The Literary Context (Acts 21:37–28:10)

The arrest of Paul in Jerusalem begins a series of narrative scenes in which Paul the accused defends himself before the Jewish people (21:37–22:21), the Jewish council (22:30–23:10), and Roman political officials (24:1–26:32). The narrator portrays Paul as one who endures the entangled webs of the Roman legal system alone, with no explicit mention of assistance from the believers. During those legal proceedings, Paul appeals his case to Caesar (25:10–12; cf. 25:21, 25; 26:32), which leads to Paul being transported by sea as a prisoner to Rome, with a shipwreck that nearly brings his death (27:1–44).

The Characterization of the Church or Group of Believers in Acts 28:11–31

The Lukan narrator concisely describes the final leg of the Pauline journey to Rome (28:11–13). Once the second ship on which Paul and his companions are traveling lands at the port of Puteoli (28:13), the rest of the trip is by land. While Luke presents the Pauline party along with his guards traveling to Rome, he provides a brief glimpse of the Roman believers. Even while the traveling party is over forty miles away from Rome, the narrator reports that the believers (οἱ ἀδελφοί) come to meet them (εἰς ἀπάντησιν ἡμῖν; 28:15). This description of these Roman believers, albeit quite simple and concise, stands in sharp contrast to the Lukan silence about the believers in the last six chapters.[372] However,

---

372. On the trip to Rome, Paul stays with believers in Puteoli (28:14), but the narrator mentions nothing more.

the narrated Pauline reaction to seeing (οὓς ἰδών) these fellow Christians contributes significantly to the Lukan portrayal of the church in Rome: ὁ Παῦλος εὐχαριστήσας τῷ θεῷ ἔλαβε θάρσος (28:15).[373] The presence of the Christian community in Rome gives Paul a renewed sense of determination and thanksgiving, as he faces all the challenges that are before him there.[374]

The narrated account of Paul's meetings at the place of his confinement with both the local Jewish leaders (28:17) and large numbers of Jews (28:23) results in a mixed response, much like the responses in earlier narrative episodes. Those meetings end with some who are persuaded by what Paul proclaims (οἱ μὲν ἐπείθοντο τοῖς λεγομένοις) and some who refuse to believe (οἱ δὲ ἠπίστουν; 28:24).[375] After Paul's statement that "this salvation of God has been sent to the Gentiles" (τοῖς ἔθνεσιν ἀπεστάλη τοῦτο τὸ σωτήριον τοῦ θεοῦ; 28:28),[376] Luke concludes the Acts narrative with a summary description of Paul's activities while under house arrest. Though some have interpreted this third statement by Paul in the Acts narrative about his turning to the Gentiles (cf. 13:46; 18:6; 28:28) to suggest that the Jewish mission has now been completed,[377] the summary states clearly that Paul welcomes *everyone* (πάντας; 28:30) during his confinement.[378] Hence, the narrator describes Paul as continuing to do the same things as he has done throughout this narrative unit: proclaim (κηρύσσων)[379] and teach (διδάσκων) the gospel message. Thus, the inference is that there will be new believers, consisting of both Jews and Gentiles. That Luke's final picture of Paul presents him proclaiming the gospel message "with all boldness" (μετὰ πάσης παρρησίας) and

---

373. See Krodel, *Acts*, 482, who interprets these actions of 28:15 as exhibiting the unity of the church.

374. Cf. Bruce, *The Book of the Acts*, 503; and Johnson, *The Acts of the Apostles*, 465.

375. The imperfect tense of both verbs suggests that this mixed response regularly occurs (28:24). Cf. Dunn, *The Acts of the Apostles*, 354; and Talbert, *Reading Acts*, 227.

376. In Paul's statement, τοῖς ἔθνεσιν is placed in the emphatic position, stressing that *to the Gentiles* God's salvation has been sent (28:28).

377. See, e.g., Lloyd Gaston, "Anti-Judaism and the Passion Narrative in Luke and Acts," in *Anti-Judaism in Early Christianity*, vol. 1, *Paul and the Gospels*, ed. Peter Richardson with David Granskou, Studies in Christianity and Judaism 2 (Waterloo, ON: Wilfrid Laurier University Press, 1986), 27–53; Haenchen, *The Acts of the Apostles*, 721–32; Robert Maddox, *The Purpose of Luke-Acts*, 31–65; and Wilson, *The Gentiles and the Gentile Mission in Luke-Acts*, 219–38.

378. Cf. Barrett, *The Acts of the Apostles*, 2:1252; Brawley, *Luke-Acts and the Jews*, 77–83; Fitzmyer, *The Acts of the Apostles*, 797; and Tannehill, *The Narrative Unity of Luke-Acts*, 2:350–51.

379. For other uses of κηρύσσω (28:31) in describing Paul, see 9:20; 19:13; 20:25.

"unhindered" (ἀκωλύτως; 28:31) also implicitly portrays the believers in Rome.[380] Since the Lukan narrator only describes the boldness of Paul's proclamation within the general context of his association with a group of believers,[381] the implicit image here is of a Christian community that enables Paul to spread the good news effectively again.

An Assessment of the Characterization of the Church or Group of Believers in Acts 28:11–31

In this final portrayal of Christian community in the book of Acts, the simplicity of the Lukan description refers the reader to earlier narrative episodes when the church has functioned as a narrative character. The significant gap between the last portrayal of believers, the Jerusalem church, and this one provides some time for the reader to evaluate and interpret with the Roman judicial officials what has happened in Jerusalem before hearing about one last group of believers. The plainness of description allows for the reader's retrospection on many of the positive images of Christian community as they have accumulated throughout the narrative. Although the Lukan narrator contributes little to that cumulative portrait of the church with these brief glimpses of the Roman believers, the inference is that this group of believers stands within a long line of churches that reflect the characteristics that identify them as people who belong to God. Although the lasting picture of the Jerusalem church is one of failure, this basic picture suggests that the gospel message will continue to be proclaimed as the Christian church continues to be identified as inclusive communities of faith that belong to the God who offers God's grace to all.

THE CHARACTERIZATION OF THE CHRISTIAN CHURCHES OR GROUPS OF BELIEVERS IN THE ROMAN EMPIRE (ACTS 13:1–28:31)

The Acts narrative in the first two units presents in a progressive fashion a view of the Christian community that is initially Jewish in its constituency and ministry but which also has begun to spread to people

---

380. Cf. Marshall, *The Acts of the Apostles*, 419–20; and Roloff, *Die Apostelgeschichte*, 375. Contra Krodel, *Acts*, 484.

381. The verb παρρησιάζομαι, not the noun παρρησία, is otherwise used to depict Pauline activity in Acts, which is typically linked to the presence of a group of believers (cf. 9:27, 28; 13:46; 14:3; 18:26; 19:8).

peripheral to the Jews. This broadening category includes the conversion of Cornelius because he is characterized as pious and has lived in many respects like a good Jew. However, although some Jewish believers raise questions concerning the validity of offering the gospel to the Gentiles and of Jewish association with them, most Christians are still Jewish. However, the Lukan depiction of the church in Antioch (11:19–30) presents a positive model of a mixed congregation of Jews and non-Jews united together and blessed by God's presence, a church that Luke portrays much like the early images of the church in Jerusalem. The differences between the ethnic and religious constituency of the two churches in Jerusalem and Antioch indicate that the salvific work of God transcends such barriers. The overcoming of such obstacles results in a group of believers characterized by God's presence as seen through their unanimity and concern for one another.

This third narrative unit of the book of Acts (13:1–28:31) presents the Christian community with a broadening geographical and ethnic context. As the narrator presents the story of the expansion of the Christian mission to other regions of the Roman Empire, the reader may observe three general developments of the expanding church that contribute significantly to the characterization of the church in Acts. The first general development is the success of the Christian mission among both Jews and Gentiles. The Jerusalem church does not initiate what Luke narrates as the ministry journey of Paul and Barnabas. Rather, the mixed congregation of Antioch sends Paul and Barnabas into ministry in other regions of the eastern Mediterranean area (13:1–3). The Lukan narrator describes their success among both Jews and Gentiles in regular fashion, which will not surprise the reader since the Antioch church also consists of both Jews and Gentiles. Thus, the various reports about the Pauline ministry that the narrator inserts into the Acts narrative highlight how God has worked specifically among the Gentiles (cf. 14:27; 15:4, 12; 21:19) and show that these local groups of believers are typically inclusive groups of both Jews and Gentiles.[382]

The various descriptions of a continuing Jewish opposition to the believers suggest that the narrator continues to juxtapose these portraits of the Jews and of the churches in order to contrast them. Whereas the narrator implicitly presents the Jews, the historical people of God,

---

382. These reports thus indicate an increasing Gentile presence in the early Christian movement.

as responding negatively to "the word of God" with divisiveness and rejection, those groups of both Jews and Gentiles who respond favorably to that same message are implicitly presented in contrasting terms: unanimity, the blessing of God, and the continuing proclamation of the gospel. These contrasting images function within the narrative to highlight for the reader different understandings of what it might mean for a group to be identified with God in some way. On the one hand, the Jewish people are identified historically as the people of God but function within the narrative as opponents of God. On the other hand, the Christian church of both Jewish and Gentile believers is presented as those among whom God's presence and blessing are found, as demonstrated by a unity among the believers that transcends the religious and ethnic boundaries that have created division in the past.

A second general development that the Lukan narrator presents about the expanding church that contributes significantly to the characterization of the church in Acts is the explicit identification of Jewish and Gentile believers together as the "people of God." Although the narrated controversy created by certain Jewish believers (cf. 15:1–5) presents a negative picture of "inside opposition" in Jerusalem to the inclusion of Gentiles as equal partners within the Christian community, the narrated proceedings provide an opportunity for the narrator to make clear yet implicit statements about this issue through the lips of Peter and James. The affirmation that believing Gentiles are included as part of the *one* people or λαός of God, because of God's saving work among both the Jewish and Gentile believers, has a dual narrative function (cf. 15:14). On the one hand, this statement explicitly interprets and confirms what readers will already have already "witnessed" themselves through the narrative events of chapters 13–14. On the other hand, the statement also provides an interpretive perspective from which to understand the subsequent narrative events, as the plot continues with additional scenes that depict the various local groups of believers in contrast to Jewish opposition (cf. 17:1–20:38).

The Lukan narrator reaffirms God's relation to the mixed church of both Jews and Gentiles within the narrated accounts of the continuing Pauline ministry throughout Asia, Macedonia, and Greece on two later occasions (cf. 18:10; 20:28). Thus he shows that this concept is central to the Lukan characterization of the church. Hence, an important development as presented in this cumulative portrayal of the Christian believers in the book of Acts is the identification of the people of God, not on the basis of historical, religious distinctions, but on the basis of God's blessing and presence as demonstrated by faith in the gospel message, by unanimity, and by genuine concern for one another that transcends traditional distinctions.

The third general development in the progression of the Acts narrative that the Lukan narrator presents about the expanding church that contributes to the Lukan characterization of the church is the increasing separation of the Christian community from Judaism. This development is integrally related to the identification of the church as the λαός or the people of God. Within the narrative progression, that idea of inclusiveness with the λαός of God may have contributed to the separation of believers from the synagogue. However, what is significant to recognize is the narrative place where Luke inserts the two latter statements that reaffirm the identity of the *Christian* community as the people who belong to God (cf. 18:10; 20:28). In both cases, this affirmation appears within the specific contexts of the only two groups that Luke narrates as becoming separated from the *Jewish* synagogue because of Jewish opposition: Corinth and Ephesus.[383] Given that these two episodes occur *after* the recognition of Gentiles as equal partners within the people of God by the Jerusalem Council, the reader may infer that the Jewish *nonbelievers* of the synagogue oppose the acceptance of Gentile believers by Jewish *believers* as equal partners within the reconstituted people of God.

However, this narrated separation of both Jewish and Gentile believers from the synagogue also means the separation of Jewish believers from the context that typically maintains Jewish *identity* within the Greco-Roman world.[384] This inclusion of Gentile believers in the Christian understanding of the people of God may result in Jewish believers being *excluded* from the institution that maintains their Jewish identity, heritage, and culture.[385] Consequently, these subsequent definitions of the *Christian* community or church as the people of God function

---

383. While one might contend that the designation of the believers in Antioch as "Christians" (11:26) also suggests either the distinction between them and the synagogue at large or the separation of this group from the synagogue, there is no indication of Jewish opposition in Antioch. However, in Acts 18–19 the scenes in Corinth and Ephesus both describe Jewish opposition that results in the separation of the Christians from the synagogue.

384. See Johnson, *The Acts of the Apostles,* 379; and Tannehill, *The Narrative Unity of Luke-Acts,* 2:236, 269.

385. Therefore, the Jewish opposition and not the believers will be the separating factor of the Christians from the synagogue. Thus, consistent with the image of the Jews throughout Acts, Luke depicts the Jews as creating division among *themselves.*

to affirm their true identity with God and to strengthen the communal bonds among the mixed group of believers.[386] The Lukan characterization of the Christian community thereby shifts the focus of the believers' identity as the people of God from issues of Jewishness to "typical" signs of divine blessing and possession.[387]

One perceives the intense difficulties in trying to understand the nature of Christian community as the people of God in the final scene with Paul and the Jerusalem believers. The charges against Paul are accusations of apostasy from Judaism. However, the obvious orientation of the Jerusalem church to the Jewish law (cf. 21:20) implies that *Jewish* identity takes precedence over *Christian* identity for that group of Jewish believers. The implicit Lukan picture of the failure of the Jerusalem church suggests that, when Paul is seized and attacked, the Jewish believers side with those who accuse him of violating their Jewishness. Hence, the narrated actions of the Jerusalem believers implicitly suggest that they define themselves as the people of God *primarily* by their Jewish identity rather than their Christian identity. Like the Jewish opponents as depicted from Acts 3 through the rest of the narrative, the Jerusalem believers' actions implicitly reveal their misunderstanding of the nature of Christian community. Their tacit refusal to protect Paul, this fellow believer whom God has led to their city (cf. 20:22; 21:13–14), compares them to the Jewish opponents of the Christians and God. Therefore, the Lukan characterization of the Jerusalem church, which has deteriorated from the initial ideal images, ultimately provides a powerful portrayal of the antithesis to what the narrative presents as the Christian community, an inclusive people identified together by faith in the God who has blessed them with God's grace and presence. However, the readers may only discover this developing portrait of the church when they keep the church, as a central figure among the cast of characters, in its rightful place in the various scenes and episodes of Acts.

---

386. Given the Lukan characterization of the church, one may tentatively conclude that the original or implied audience is also a mixture of Jewish and Gentile believers. Cf. Philip Francis Esler, *Community and Gospel in Luke-Acts: The Social and Political Motivations of Lucan Theology*, SNTSMS 57 (Cambridge, UK: Cambridge University Press, 1987); and Robert C. Tannehill, *Luke*, ANTC (Nashville: Abingdon, 1996), 24–27. Contra Löning, "Das Verhältnis zum Judentum," 304–5; and Roloff, "Die Paulus-Darstellung des Lukas," 527–31, who both stress that Luke is addressing problems of theological identity for a Gentile-Christian church.

387. That shift in focus meant that one's identification as a part of those who belong to God will not be *defined* by the Jewish law, although one's *ethnic* identity can be maintained by following the Jewish law.

CONCLUSION

A traditional, historical-critical approach to the study of the church or the Christian community would attempt either to extract theological statements or beliefs from the book of Acts or to glean information about the historical developments of the early Christian movement in the first century CE. However, such attempts would destroy the Acts narrative as a literary work, in which Lukan theology and historical information are inseparably intertwined with the narrative story itself.[1] To do justice to the Lukan characterization of the church, one must work with the book of Acts as a narrative text. More precisely, one must examine Acts as an ancient historical narrative, written by an author who employs the literary conventions of his era to create that narrative with potential effects for its listening audience. Thus, any attempt to understand the church in Acts must keep the church in its narrative place.

Although literary approaches to the book of Acts have largely ignored or downplayed the role of the church in the narrative,[2] the plot includes a variety of groups of believers or churches as significant characters. As this study has shown, the inclusion of these selected episodes and the role of these Christian churches or groups as characters in these episodes suggest that one must reassess such opinions. What this study has found is that the Christian community or church functions as a central character among the cast of characters in the Acts narrative, and through a variety of ways the characterization of the church throughout that narrative emphasizes certain features that compare and contrast significantly with other depicted characters.

The arrangement of the Acts narrative presents the dynamic movement and growth of the church and its proclaimed message from

---

1. Cf., e.g., Beverly Roberts Gaventa, "Toward a Theology of Acts," *Int* 42 (1988): 150–52; William H. Shepherd Jr., *The Narrative Function of the Holy Spirit as a Character in Luke-Acts*, SBLDS 147 (Atlanta: Scholars Press, 1994), 245; and Joseph B. Tyson, "The Emerging Church and the Problem of Authority in Acts," *Int* 42 (1988): 133.

2. See the introduction to this study (above).

Jerusalem to much of the Roman Empire.[3] Interwoven in the narrative progression are episodes that usually depict the Christian believers positively, whom the narrator often describes directly or explicitly. The first narrative unit (Acts 1:1–8:3) generally presents the believers in Jerusalem with ideal imagery, as Luke describes them as blessed by God, unanimous in spirit, caring toward one another, and earnest in proclaiming the gospel (cf. 2:42–47; 4:32–37). Initially, the huge numbers of those accepting the gospel and the excitement in Jerusalem among the Jewish people implicitly present a picture of oneness between Judaism and the Christian gospel (cf. 2:41, 47; 4:4; 5:14; 6:7). These positive images of the believers provide a literary paradigm or an ideal model that may assist the reader in the evaluation of the Christian community (and other characters) in subsequent portraits.

While these positive characteristics of the believers in the early chapters of the Acts narrative are apparent, the possible reasons for the Lukan emphasis on *these* characteristics and not others become visible in the context of this narrative unit. Alongside these positive descriptions of the believers, the reader discovers increasingly contrasting images of the Jewish leaders and some of the Jewish people in the narrative.[4] That these latter characters increasingly and contrastingly interact with the Jewish believers throughout that first unit, leading to the death of Stephen and the scattering of the believers from Jerusalem, reflects one of the ancient literary conventions used to present and emphasize important narrative elements vividly.[5] Considering that Luke also applies the term ἐκκλησία to the believers (5:11), a Septuagint term used with reference to Israel as the people or the assembly of God, it appears that these two contrasting groups present two opposing views or understandings of what one might

---

3. Cf. Tyson, "The Emerging Church and the Problem of Authority in Acts," 133, who highlights the narrative's dynamic character and some significant transitions: geographical, ethnic, cultic, and institutional.

4. Cf. Gaventa, "Toward a Theology of Acts," 154, who correlates the growth of hostility with the growth of the Christian community; and Daniel Marguerat, "La mort d'Ananias et Saphira (Ac 5.1–11) dans la stratégie narrative de Luc," *NTS* 39 (1993): 215.

5. See Dionysius, *On the Style of Demosthenes* 21: "He [Demosthenes] does not set out each separate pair of actions in finicky detail, old and new, and compare them, but carries the whole antithesis through the whole theme by arranging the items in two contrasting groups.... He has deployed more force and more powerful emphasis, and avoided the frigid and juvenile figures which adorn the other's style to excess" (LCL). Cf. Luke T. Johnson, *The Literary Function of Possessions in Luke-Acts*, SBLDS 39 (Missoula, MT: Scholars Press, 1977), 107–11, 115–17, who identifies the use of the division imagery in relation to the people in the Gospel of Luke.

call "the people of God." On the one hand, Luke presents the believers as those in whom God is at work and among whom is unanimity. On the other hand, Luke presents the Jews, the historical "people of God," as increasingly becoming God's *opponents* (cf. 5:39) and divisive in their actions against those believers. Therefore, Luke depicts the unbelieving Jews as the ones who reject God's fulfilled promise and whose divisive actions implicitly place *them* outside the realm of God's salvific activity.[6] These contrasting images in this first narrative unit invite readers to conclude that the church, the Jewish believers in Jerusalem, are the ones who are demonstrably those people who belong to God.[7]

The second narrative unit (Acts 8:4–12:25) presents various episodes in relation to the spread of the gospel to other regions surrounding Jerusalem. Intricately tied to the geographical movement in the narrative are the associated ethnic and cultic changes.[8] As the narrative progresses, the plot thickens to include another line of action. Along with the continuing

---

6. See especially Jacob Jervell, *Luke and the People of God A New Look at Luke-Acts* (Minneapolis: Augsburg, 1972), 41–74, who argues that Israel has become divided over the gospel (49); idem, "Retrospect and Prospect in Luke-Acts Interpretation," in *SBLSP 1991*, ed. Eugene H. Lovering Jr. (Atlanta: Scholars Press, 1991), 391; Johnson, *The Literary Function of Possessions in Luke-Acts*, 122; and Gerhard Lohfink, *Die Sammlung Israels: Eine Untersuchung zur lukanischen Ekklesiologie*, SANT (Munich: Kösel, 1975), 58.

7. If the Lukan narrative presents the Jewish people (the historical "people of God") as a picture antithetical to that of the believers as the true people of God, this assists the readers to sort out the complex issues in evaluating the portrayal of the Jews in Acts. In other words, the primary issue would not be the possible Lukan anti-Semitism or the presentation of a negative image of the Jews, which scholars do not typically reconcile with Luke's portrayals of Paul as a Jew and of the church as including Jewish believers. Rather, the negative portrayal of the Jewish people functions specifically in the narrative as the antithesis to the positive portrayal of the church and does not reflect a negative perspective of *all* Jews, when considered with other descriptions of Jews. Cf. Richard P. Thompson, "Believers and Religious Leaders in Jerusalem: Contrasting Portraits of Jews in Acts 1–7," in *Literary Studies in Luke-Acts: Essays in Honor of Joseph B. Tyson*, ed. Richard P. Thompson and Thomas E. Phillips (Macon, GA: Mercer University Press, 1998), 327–28, 343–44; and Hubert Cancik, "The History of Culture, Religion, and Institutions in Ancient Historiography: Philological Observations concerning Luke's History," *JBL* 116 (Winter 1997): 673–95. Contra, e.g., Jack T. Sanders, "Who Is a Jew and Who Is a Gentile in the Book of Acts?" *NTS* 37 (1991): 436–38; and Dixon Slingerland, "'The Jews' in the Pauline Portion of Acts," *JAAR* 54 (1986): 305–21. For two studies that examine the Lukan portrayal of Jews from a literary perspective, see Robert L. Brawley, *Luke-Acts and the Jews: Conflict, Apology, and Conciliation*, SBLMS 33 (Atlanta: Scholars Press, 1987); and Joseph B. Tyson, *Images of Judaism in Luke-Acts* (Columbia: University of South Carolina Press, 1992). For a collection of brief essays that address the Lukan portrayal of the Jews from a variety of perspectives, see Joseph B. Tyson, ed., *Luke-Acts and the Jewish People: Eight Critical Perspectives* (Minneapolis: Augsburg, 1988).

8. Cf. Tyson, "The Emerging Church and the Problem of Authority in Acts," 134–35.

Jewish opposition that becomes commonplace in the Acts narrative (cf. 9:23–25, 29),[9] Luke describes the tensions that arise when the gospel message is accepted by *Gentiles* as well as Jews. While unanimity is a characteristic among Jewish believers, such a quality is quite another matter among Jewish believers and Gentile believers combined (cf. 10:44–48; 11:1–18). Through selected narrative elements and episodes, Luke depicts explicitly that God, not the believers themselves, instigate the proclamation of the gospel to non-Jews. Thus, God is the one who is working salvifically among the Gentiles, which implies to the reader that they too are included as a part of the church, the people of God. The ideal description of the Antioch church (11:19–30), composed of both Jewish and Gentile believers, offers a similar and yet distinctive portrait of a third possible understanding of what is meant by the designation "the people of God."[10] The juxtaposition of two portraits in Acts 11 — the ideal portrait of the Antioch believers and the portrait of the Jerusalem believers with their mounting questions — suggests that the narrator implicitly identifies the unanimity that transcends ethnic and cultic boundaries as characteristic of the Christian church or those who belong to God.

The last narrative unit, Acts 13:1–28:31, focuses on the spread of the gospel to various parts of the Roman Empire, due to the obedience of the church in Antioch. Interspersed within the narrative account of the rapidly growing Christian "movement," which Luke describes as including both Jews and Gentiles who as believers respond to the gospel message, is a deteriorating picture of the Jewish believers in Jerusalem. Although the gospel message continues to gain acceptance from both Jews and non-Jews in Paul's travels, the Lukan portrait of the Jerusalem church becomes increasingly negative. On the one hand, this Jewish group of believers continues to focus on ethnic, social, and religious issues for their identity as a "people of God" (cf. 15:1–5; 21:17–26). On the other hand, the depictions of groups of believers other than the Jerusalem church allude to those ideal images that the reader finds in the early

---

9. Cf. Robert C. Tannehill, "Israel in Luke-Acts: A Tragic Story," *JBL* 104 (March 1985): 72.

10. The two possible understandings of what might be called the "people of God" in the first narrative unit — the historical understanding that includes all the Jewish people, and the understanding that includes all Jewish *believers* — are joined by a third understanding, which depicts both Jewish and Gentile believers as gathered together in unity, blessed by God, and functioning as the center of gospel proclamation.

narrative scenes with the Jerusalem church. In the midst of opposition and in the specific contexts where the Christian believers are separated from the Jewish synagogue, the Lukan narrator through a reliable character inserts the identification of the Christian church or community as God's λαός (18:10) or ἐκκλησία (20:28). However, the ugly scenes of Paul's visit to Jerusalem in Acts 21–22 stand in sharp contrast, as Luke implicitly presents the Jewish believers there in a negative way. These narrative episodes do not negate the positive, cumulative Lukan characterization of the church in the first twenty chapters; yet they do present the failure of one believing group to identify the nature of the church with divine activity and unanimity rather than historical Jewish distinctions.

The narrative progression of the book of Acts includes a distinctive arrangement of episodes and images of the Christian community. In this arrangement, the Lukan author in progressive fashion presents three different understandings of what one may designate "the people of God": Israel or the Jewish people as the historical people of God, repentant or believing Israel, and the Jewish *and* non-Jewish believers of the gospel. In the Lukan presentation of these differing views, readers will be invited to identify those who truly belong to God, not through traditional Jewish distinctions but through the working of God as demonstrated primarily by unanimity, the caring for one another's needs, and the proclamation of the gospel. In the initial episodes, the contrasting portraits — of the Jewish believers in Jerusalem and of the growing opposition by unbelieving Jewish leaders and others — function to present vividly that the believers *among* the Jewish people, not Israel itself or *all* the Jewish people, represent a valid understanding of the people of God. This juxtaposition of similarly contrasting pictures continues throughout the remainder of the Acts narrative, as Luke presents the Christian church, which evolves into a group consisting of both Jews and Gentiles, in sharp contrast to the general Jewish population.[11]

---

11. The Acts narrative does not present a Pauline mission to the Gentiles. Rather, the acceptance (and rejection) of the gospel occurs among *both* the Jews *and* the Gentiles. Cf. François Bovon, "Israel, die Kirche und die Völker im lukanischen Doppelwerk," *TL* 108 (1983): 405; and Jervell, *Luke and the People of God*, 41–48. Nonetheless, the picture of the Jews is not positive; cf. Karl Löning, "Das Verhältnis zum Judentum als Identitätsproblem der Kirche nach der Apostelgeschichte," in *"Ihr alle aber seid Brüder": Festschrift für A. Th. Khoury zum 60. Geburtstag*, ed. Ludwig Hagemann and Ernst Pulsfort (Würzburg: Echter, 1990), 304; and Lawrence M. Wills, "The Depiction of the Jews in Acts," *JBL* 110 (December 1991): 644–47.

The Lukan view of the church or the Christian believers as the people of God, however, must consider the place of non-Jewish believers. The question that readers may ask, when reading through the Acts narrative, is not whether the Gentile believers are Christians or part of the church as the "people of God." In the description of what transpires, the narrative makes it clear that both the proclamation of the gospel to the Gentiles and the acceptance of that message by some of them are part of God's plan and are evidence of God's blessing. Rather, the question before the readers (and the earliest Christians) is whether the *Jewish* believers will respond to the *Gentile* believers as equal partners in the church, with actions demonstrating unanimity or division. If the Jewish believers respond in ways that affirm what God is doing, they will also acknowledge their identity together with non-Jewish believers as those who belong to God. However, if the Jewish believers respond divisively against those in whom God has worked and whom God has blessed, they will deny that divine presence and activity as the basis of their identity as the people of God. More important, this latter possibility would identify the Jewish believers with the Jews in general, whom Luke depicts as God's opponents, rather than with those whom the narrator presents as the people of God, the ones in whom one finds the divine presence and blessing.[12] The contrasting images and the narrative interactions among the various groups of believers and the Jews in general all seem to invite the reader to identify the Christian church as the people of God that is not distinguished by traditional Jewish boundaries but by divine activity and a strong, communal bond among those who are believers in the gospel message.[13] Therefore, the reader discovers that these issues regarding the nature of the church or Christian community are not minor themes or insignificant elements in the book but stand as integral parts of the Acts narrative, when the church is kept in its rightful narrative place(s).[14]

---

12. This is a crucial issue seen in the depiction of the Jewish church in its response to Paul in Acts 21.

13. Contra I. Howard Marshall, *Luke: Historian and Theologian* (Grand Rapids: Zondervan, 1970), 212–15, who sees no Lukan concern for relational issues but only sees a concern for institutional issues.

14. Contra Gerhard Schneider, *Lukas, Theologe der Heilsgeschichte: Aufsätze zum lukanischen Doppelwerk*, BBB 59 (Königstein: Peter Hanstein, 1985), 207–8, who stresses that the increase of the word of God is the object of Luke-Acts, not the increase of the church itself.

One of the debates in contemporary scholarship has focused on the Lukan understanding of the church and Israel. For the majority of scholars, the Lukan understanding of the church is of the "new" Israel, which replaces the historical people of God. For others such as Jacob Jervell and Gerhard Lohfink, the church is the "true" Israel or the "restored" Israel, which represents the repentant ones among the historical people of God.[15] The Gentile Christians, in this latter understanding, may be included as an "associate" people of God, due to the acceptance of God's promises by repentant and faithful Israel.[16] However, while the Lukan narrative affirms the continuity of the church with the historical understanding of God's people, such interpretations do not adequately account for the dynamic quality of the church as a character in various episodes in the Acts narrative. On the one hand, these interpretations do not consider the rhetorical nature of the contrasting portrayals of the church and of the Jewish people. Narrative texts do not lend themselves to precision in definition but to the creation of potential effects and experiences in an audience or reader, who is invited to participate in the narrative world of the text.[17] On the other hand, the progressive nature of the Acts narrative indicates that the replacement of the Jewish people is *not* the critical issue. Rather, Luke assists the reader in wrestling with the issue of the identity of a church *in its own situations.*

The Acts narrative thus does not precisely define the relation between God and the Jewish people. However, what the narrative *does* present for the reader to ponder and evaluate is an understanding of the church, consisting of both Jewish and non-Jewish believers, as those who belong to God, as those who are God's λαός, as those who are God's ἐκκλησία. Thus, the Lukan narrative directs the reader's attention to the church as the group that belongs to God and in which God's blessing and activity are found.[18] This divine presence, which definitively identifies the people

---

15. See, e.g., Jervell, *Luke and the People of God*, 41–74. Cf., e.g., Donald Juel, "Hearing Peter's Speech in Acts 3: Meaning and Truth in Interpretation," *WW* 12 (1992): 47–48; David P. Moessner, "Paul in Acts: Preacher of Eschatological Repentance to Israel," *NTS* 34 (1988): 102–3; and David L. Tiede, " 'Glory to Thy People Israel': Luke-Acts and the Jews," in Tyson, *Luke-Acts and the Jewish People*, 21–34.

16. See Jacob Jervell, "The Law in Luke-Acts," *HTR* 64 (1971): 32; and idem, "The Acts of the Apostles and the History of Early Christianity," *ST* 37 (1983): 19.

17. Cf. Lohfink, *Die Sammlung Israels*, 97, who correctly recognizes that Luke does not provide a systematic concept or "ecclesiology," but does portray or tell about the church; and Johannes Panagopoulos, "Zur Theologie der Apostelgeschichte," *NovT* 14 (April 1972): 152.

18. Cf. Panagopoulos, "Zur Theologie der Apostelgeschichte," 152–53.

of God, is maintained and observed by the communal bond among the believers and by the continuing proclamation of the gospel message. The readers discover and contribute to such a characterization of the church, however, when they keep each church in its narrative place and evaluate each one as part of the larger cast of characters, action, and plot of the Acts narrative.

BIBLIOGRAPHY

❦

Achtemeier, Paul J. "An Elusive Unity: Paul, Acts, and the Early Church." *Catholic Biblical Quarterly* 48 (1986): 1–26.

———. *The Quest for Unity in the New Testament Church: A Study in Paul and Acts.* Philadelphia: Fortress, 1987.

Adams, Marilyn McCord. "Separation and Reversal in Luke-Acts." In *Philosophies and the Christian Faith*, edited by Thomas V. Morris, 92–117. Notre Dame, IN: University of Notre Dame Press, 1988.

Alexander, L. C. A. "Acts and Ancient Intellectual Biography." In *The Book of Acts in Its Ancient Literary Setting*, edited by Bruce W. Winter and Andrew D. Clarke, 31–64. The Book of Acts in Its First Century Setting. Grand Rapids: Eerdmans, 1993.

Alter, Robert. *The Art of Biblical Narrative.* New York: Basic Books, 1981.

Andersen, T. David. "The Meaning of *ECHONTES CHARIN PROS* in Acts 2.47." *New Testament Studies* 34 (1988): 604–10.

Anderson, Graham. *Lucian: Theme and Variation in the Second Sophistic.* Leiden: E. J. Brill, 1976.

Annas, Julia. "Plato and Aristotle on Friendship and Altruism." *Mind* 86 (October 1977): 532–52.

Aristotle. *The Athenian Constitution: The Eudemian Ethics; On Virtues and Vices.* Translated by H. Rackham. Loeb Classical Library. London: Heinemann, 1935.

———. *The Nicomachean Ethics.* Translated by H. Rackham. Loeb Classical Library. London: Heinemann, 1934.

———. *The Poetics.* Translated by W. Hamilton Fyfe. Loeb Classical Library. London: Heinemann, 1927.

———. *The Politics.* Translated by H. Rackham. Loeb Classical Library. London: Heinemann, 1950.

———. *The Art of Rhetoric.* Translated by John H. Freese. Loeb Classical Library. London: Heinemann, 1947.

Arrington, French L. *The Acts of the Apostles: An Introduction and Commentary.* Peabody, MA: Hendrickson, 1988.

Attridge, Harold W. *The Interpretation of Biblical History in the Antiquitates Judaicae of Flavius Josephus.* Harvard Dissertations in Religion 7. Missoula, MT: Scholars Press (for Harvard Theological Review), 1976.

Auerbach, E. *Mimesis: The Representation of Reality in Western Literature.* Princeton, NJ: Princeton University Press, 1953.

Aune, David E. *The New Testament in Its Literary Environment.* Library of Early
    Christianity 8. Philadelphia: Westminster, 1987.
Avery, Harry C. "The Resolution of Rhetorical Conflict in Greek Historians." In
    Conflict, Antithesis, and the Ancient Historian, edited by June W. Allison, 92–
    111. Columbus: Ohio State University Press, 1990.
Bachmann, Michael. *Jerusalem und der Tempel: Die geographisch-theologischen
    Elemente in der lukanischen Sicht des jüdischen Kultzentrums.* Beiträge zur
    Wissenschaft vom Alten und Neuen Testament. Stuttgart: W. Kohlhammer,
    1980.
Balch, David L. "Acts as Hellenistic Historiography." In *Society of Biblical Litera-
    ture 1985 Seminar Papers,* edited by Kent Harold Richards, 429–32. Atlanta:
    Scholars Press, 1985.
———. "Comments on the Genre and a Political Theme of Luke-Acts: A Preliminary
    Comparison of Two Hellenistic Historians." In *Society of Biblical Literature
    1989 Seminar Papers,* edited by David Lull, 343–61. Atlanta: Scholars Press,
    1989.
———. "The Genre of Luke-Acts: Individual Biography, Adventure Novel, or
    Political History?" *Southwestern Journal of Theology* 33 (Fall 1990): 5–19.
———, ed. *Social History of the Matthean Community: Cross-Disciplinary Ap-
    proaches.* Minneapolis: Fortress, 1991.
Baldwin, Barry. *Studies in Lucian.* Toronto: Hakkert, 1973.
Baldwin, Charles S. *Ancient Rhetoric and Poetic, Interpreted from Representative
    Works.* New York: Macmillan, 1924.
Banks, Robert. *Paul's Idea of Community.* Grand Rapids: Eerdmans, 1980.
Barrett, C. K. *A Critical and Exegetical Commentary on the Acts of the Apostles.* 2
    vols. International Critical Commentary. Edinburgh: T&T Clark, 1994–98.
Bartchy, S. Scott. "Community of Goods in Acts: Idealization or Social Reality?" In
    The Future of Early Christianity: Essays in Honor of Helmut Koester, edited by
    Birger A. Pearson, 309–18. Minneapolis: Fortress, 1991.
Barthes, Roland. "L'analyse structurale du récit: A propos d'Actes X–XI." *Recherches
    de science religieuse* 58 (1970): 17–37.
Bassler, Jouette M. "Luke and Paul on Impartiality." *Biblica* 66 (1985): 546–52.
Bauckham, Richard, ed. *The Book of Acts in Its Palestinian Setting.* The Book of
    Acts in Its First Century Setting. Grand Rapids: Eerdmans, 1995.
———. "James and the Jerusalem Church." In *The Book of Acts in Its Palestinian
    Setting,* edited by Richard Bauckham, 415–80. The Book of Acts in Its First
    Century Setting. Grand Rapids: Eerdmans, 1995.
Bauer, Walter. *A Greek-English Lexicon of the New Testament and Other Early
    Christian Literature.* 3rd ed. Translated and edited by William F. Arndt, F. Wilbur
    Gingrich, and Frederick W. Danker. Chicago: University of Chicago Press, 2000.
Behm, J. "νῆστις...." In *Theological Dictionary of the New Testament,* edited
    by Gerhard Kittel and Gerhard Friedrich, 10 vols., 4:924–35. Translated by
    Geoffrey W. Bromiley. Grand Rapids: Eerdmans, 1964-76.
Belfiore, Elizabeth. "Aristotle's Concept of *Praxis* in the *Poetics.*" *Classical Journal*
    79 (December–January 1983-84): 110–24.

————. "*Peripeteia* as Discontinuous Action: Aristotle *Poetics* 11.1452a22–29." *Classical Philology* 83 (July 1988): 183–94.

Benoit, Pierre. "Remarques sur les 'sommaires' de Actes 2. 42 à 5." In *Aux sources de la tradition chrétienne: Mélanges offerts à M. Maurice Goguel*, 1–10. Bibliothèque théologique. Neuchâtel: Delachaux & Niestlé, 1950.

Berlin, Adele. *Poetics and Interpretation of Biblical Narrative*. Sheffield: Almond, 1983.

Bertram, Georg. "ὁρμή. . . . " In *Theological Dictionary of the New Testament*, edited by Gerhard Kittel and Gerhard Friedrich, 10 vols., 5:467–74. Translated by Geoffrey W. Bromiley. Grand Rapids: Eerdmans, 1964–76.

————. "στερεός. . . . " In *Theological Dictionary of the New Testament*, edited by Gerhard Kittel and Gerhard Friedrich, 10 vols., 7:609–14. Translated by Geoffrey W. Bromiley. Grand Rapids: Eerdmans, 1964–76.

————. ὕβρις. . . . " In *Theological Dictionary of the New Testament*, edited by Gerhard Kittel and Gerhard Friedrich, 10 vols., 8:295–307. Translated by Geoffrey W. Bromiley. Grand Rapids: Eerdmans, 1964-76.

Betz, Otto, Klaus Haacker, and Martin Hengel, eds. *Josephus — Studien: Untersuchungen zu Josephus, dem antiken Judentum und dem Neuen Testament*. Göttingen: Vandenhoeck & Ruprecht, 1974.

Beydon, France. "Luc et 'ces dames de la haute société.' " *Études théologiques et religieuses* 61 (1986): 331–41.

Beye, Charles Rowan. *Ancient Greek Literature and Society*. 2d ed. Ithaca, NY: Cornell University Press, 1987.

Beyer, Hermann Wolfgang. "βλασφημέω. . . . " In *Theological Dictionary of the New Testament*, edited by Gerhard Kittel and Gerhard Friedrich, 10 vols., 1:621–25. Translated by Geoffrey W. Bromiley. Grand Rapids: Eerdmans, 1964-76.

Bilde, Per. *Flavius Josephus between Jerusalem and Rome: His Life, His Works, and Their Importance*. Journal for the Study of the Pseudepigrapha: Supplement Series 2. Sheffield: JSOT Press, 1988.

Black, C. Clifton. "John Mark in the Acts of the Apostles." In *Literary Studies in Luke-Acts: Essays in Honor of Joseph B. Tyson*, edited by Richard P. Thompson and Thomas E. Phillips, 101–20. Macon, GA: Mercer University Press, 1998.

————. *Mark: Images of an Apostolic Interpreter*. Columbia: University of South Carolina Press, 1994.

————. "The Presentation of John Mark in the Acts of the Apostles." *Perspectives in Religious Studies* 20 (1993): 235–54.

Blomberg, Craig L. "The Law in Luke-Acts." *Journal for the Study of the New Testament* 22 (1984): 53–80.

Blue, Bradley. "Acts and the House Church." In *The Book of Acts in Its Graeco-Roman Setting*, edited by David W. J. Gill and Conrad Gempf, 119–222. The Book of Acts in Its First Century Setting 2. Grand Rapids: Eerdmans, 1994.

Boismard, Marie-Émile. "Le 'concile' de Jérusalem (Act 15,1–33)." *Ephemerides theologicae lovaniense* 64 (1988): 433–40.

Boismard, Marie-Émile, and Arnaud Lamouille. *Les Actes des deux Apôtres*. 3 vols. Études bibliques. Paris: J. Gabalda, 1990.

————. *Le texte occidental des Actes des Apôtres: Reconstitution et réhabilitation.*
2 vols. Paris: Éditions recherche sur les civilisations, 1984.

Booth, Wayne C. *The Company We Keep: An Ethics of Fiction.* Berkeley: University
of California Press, 1988.

————. "Narrative Choices and Ethical Criticism." In *Reading Narrative: Form,
Ethics, Ideology,* edited by James Phelan, 57–78. Columbus: Ohio State
University Press, 1989.

————. *The Rhetoric of Fiction.* 2d ed. Chicago: University of Chicago Press, 1983.

————. *A Rhetoric of Irony.* Chicago: University of Chicago Press, 1974.

Borgen, Peder. "Catalogues of Vices, the Apostolic Decree, and the Jerusalem Meet-
ing." In *The Social World of Formative Christianity and Judaism,* edited by
Ernest S. Frerichs, Jacob Neusner, Peder Borgen, and Richard Horsley, 126–41.
Philadelphia: Fortress, 1982.

————. "From Paul to Luke: Observation toward Clarification of the Theology of
Luke-Acts." *Catholic Biblical Quarterly* 31 (April 1969): 168–82.

Borse, Udo. "Kompositionsgeschichtliche Beobachtungen zum Apostelkonzil." In
Begegnung mit dem Wort: Festschrift für Heinrich Zimmermann, edited by Josef
Zmijewski, 195–211. Bonner biblische Beiträge 53. Bonn: Peter Hanstein, 1980.

Bovon, François. "Israel, die Kirche und die Völker im lukanischen Doppelwerk."
Theologische Literaturzeitung 108 (1983): 403–14.

————. *Luke the Theologian: Thirty-Three Years of Research (1950–1983).* Princeton Theological Monograph Series 12. Allison Park, PA: Pickwick Publications,
1987.

————. "Tradition et rédaction en Actes 10,1–11,18." *Theologische Zeitschrift* 26
(January–February 1970): 22–45.

Brawley, Robert L. *Centering on God: Method and Message in Luke-Acts.* Literary
Currents in Biblical Interpretation. Louisville: Westminster/John Knox, 1990.

————. "The God of Promises and the Jews in Luke-Acts." In *Literary Studies in
Luke-Acts: Essays in Honor of Joseph B. Tyson,* edited by Richard P. Thompson
and Thomas E. Phillips, 279–96. Macon, GA: Mercer University Press, 1998.

————. *Luke-Acts and the Jews: Conflict, Apology, and Conciliation.* Society of
Biblical Literature Monograph Series 33. Atlanta: Scholars Press, 1987.

————. "Paul in Acts: Aspects of Structure and Characterization." In *Society of
Biblical Literature 1988 Seminar Papers,* edited by David Lull, 90–105. Atlanta:
Scholars Press, 1988.

Brehm, H. Alan. "The Significance of the Summaries for Interpreting Acts."
Southwestern Journal of Theology 33 (Fall 1990): 29–40.

Breisach, Ernst. *Historiography: Ancient, Medieval, and Modern.* Chicago: University of Chicago Press, 1983.

Brooks, Stephenson H. *Matthew's Community: The Evidence of His Special Material.* Journal for the Study of the New Testament Supplement Series 16. Sheffield:
JSOT Press, 1987.

Broshi, Magen. "The Credibility of Josephus." *Journal of Jewish Studies* 33 (Winter
1982): 379–84.

Brown, Raymond E. *The Community of the Beloved Disciple.* New York: Paulist
Press, 1979.

Bruce, F. F. "The Apostolic Decree of Acts 15." In *Studien zum Text und zur Ethik des Neuen Testaments: Festschrift zum 80. Geburtstag von Heinrich Greeven*, edited by Wolfgang Schrage, 115–24. Berlin: Walter de Gruyter, 1986.

———. *The Book of the Acts*. Rev. ed. New International Commentary on the New Testament. Grand Rapids: Eerdmans, 1988.

———. "The Holy Spirit in the Acts of the Apostles." *Interpretation* 27 (April 1973): 166–83.

———. "The Significance of the Speeches for Interpreting Acts." *Southwestern Journal of Theology* 33 (Fall 1990): 21–28.

Brunt, P. A. *Studies in Greek History and Thought*. Oxford: Clarendon, 1993.

Büchsel, Friedrich. "διακρίνω." In *Theological Dictionary of the New Testament*, edited by Gerhard Kittel and Gerhard Friedrich, 10 vols., 3:946–49. Translated by Geoffrey W. Bromiley. Grand Rapids: Eerdmans, 1964–76.

Bultmann, Rudolf. "ἀφίημι...." In *Theological Dictionary of the New Testament*, edited by Gerhard Kittel and Gerhard Friedrich, 10 vols., 1:509–12. Translated by Geoffrey W. Bromiley. Grand Rapids: Eerdmans, 1964-76.

Bury, J. B. *The Ancient Greek Historians*. London: Macmillan, 1909.

Cadbury, Henry J. *The Book of Acts in History*. New York: Harper & Brothers, 1955.

———. "Four Features of Lucan Style." In *Studies in Luke-Acts*, edited by Leander E. Keck and J. Louis Martyn, 87–102. Philadelphia: Fortress, 1980.

———. "The Hellenists." In *The Beginnings of Christianity*, edited by F. J. Foakes-Jackson and Kirsopp Lake, 5 vols., 5:59–74. London: Macmillan, 1933.

———. *The Making of Luke-Acts*. 2d ed. London: SPCK, 1958.

———. "The Speeches in Acts." In *The Beginnings of Christianity*, edited by F. J. Foakes-Jackson and Kirsopp Lake, 5 vols., 2:489–510. London: Macmillan, 1933.

———. "The Summaries in Acts." In *The Beginnings of Christianity*, edited by F. J. Foakes-Jackson and Kirsopp Lake, 5 vols., 5:392–402. London: Macmillan, 1933.

Cadbury, Henry J., F. J. Foakes-Jackson, and Kirsopp Lake. "The Greek Traditions of Writing History." In *The Beginnings of Christianity*, edited by F. J. Foakes-Jackson and Kirsopp Lake, 5 vols., 2:7–29. London: Macmillan, 1922.

Callan, Terrance. "The Preface of Luke-Acts and Historiography." *New Testament Studies* 31 (October 1985): 576–81.

Cameron, Averil, ed. *History as Text: The Writing of Ancient History*. Chapel Hill: University of North Carolina Press, 1989.

Cancik, Hubert. "The History of Culture, Religion, and Institutions in Ancient Historiography: Philological Observations concerning Luke's History." *Journal of Biblical Literature* 116 (Winter 1997): 673–95.

Capper, Brian. "The Palestinian Cultural Context of Earliest Christian Community of Goods." In *The Book of Acts in Its Palestinian Setting*, edited by Richard Bauckham, 323–56. The Book of Acts in Its First Century Setting. Grand Rapids: Eerdmans, 1995.

————. "Reciprocity and the Ethic of Acts." In *Witness to the Gospel: The Theology of Acts*, edited by I. Howard Marshall and David Peterson, 499–518. Grand Rapids: Eerdmans, 1998.

Carroll, John T. "Literary and Social Dimensions of Luke's Apology for Paul." In *Society of Biblical Literature 1988 Seminar Papers*, edited by David Lull, 106–18. Atlanta: Scholars Press, 1988.

Carroll, John T. "Luke's Portrayal of the Pharisees." *Catholic Biblical Quarterly* 50 (1988): 604–21.

Cassidy, Richard J. *Society and Politics in the Acts of the Apostles*. Maryknoll, NY: Orbis, 1987.

Cassidy, Richard J., and Philip J. Scharper, eds. *Political Issues in Luke-Acts*. Maryknoll, NY: Orbis, 1983.

Chance, J. Bradley. *Jerusalem, the Temple, and the New Age in Luke-Acts*. Macon, GA: Mercer University Press, 1988.

————. "The Jewish People and the Death of Jesus in Luke-Acts: Some Implications of an Inconsistent Narrative Role." In *Society of Biblical Literature 1991 Seminar Papers*, edited by Eugene H. Lovering Jr., 50–81. Atlanta: Scholars Press, 1991.

Cicero. *De Inventione*. Translated by H. M. Hubbell. Loeb Classical Library. London: Heinemann, 1976.

————. *De Oratore*. 2 vols. Translated by E. W. Sutton. Loeb Classical Library. Cambridge, MA: Harvard University Press, 1942.

Co, Maria Anicia. "The Major Summaries in Acts: Acts 2,42–47; 4,32–35; 5,12–16 Linguistic and Literary Relationship." *Ephemerides theologicae lovanienses* 68 (1992): 49–85.

Cobet, Justus. *Herodots Exkurse und die Frage der Einheit seines Werkes*. Historia Einzelschriften 17. Wiesbaden: Franz Steiner, 1971.

Cochrane, Charles N. *Thucydides and the Science of History*. New York: Russell & Russell, 1965.

Cohen, Shaye J. D. "Crossing the Boundary and Becoming a Jew." *Harvard Theological Review* 82 (1989): 13–33.

————. *Josephus in Galilee and Rome: His Vita and Development as a Historian*. Columbia Studies in the Classical Tradition 8. Leiden: E. J. Brill, 1979.

————. "Masada: Literary Tradition, Archaeological Remains, and the Credibility of Josephus." *Journal of Jewish Studies* 33 (Winter 1982): 385–405.

————. "Respect for Judaism by Gentiles according to Josephus." *Harvard Theological Review* 80 (1987): 409–30.

Combet-Galland, Corina. "Actes 4/32–5/11." *Études théologiques et religieuses* 52 (1977): 548–53.

Connor, W. Robert. "Narrative Discourse in Thucydides." In *The Greek Historians: Literature and History*, 1–17. Saratoga, CA: Anma Libri, 1985.

Conzelmann, Hans. *Acts of the Apostles*. Translated by James Limburg, A. Thomas Kraabel, and Donald H. Juel. Hermeneia. Philadelphia: Fortress, 1987.

————. *The Theology of St. Luke*. Translated by Geoffrey Buswell. Philadelphia: Fortress, 1961.

Cook, Michael J. "The Mission to the Jews in Acts: Unraveling Luke's 'Myth of the "Myriads."'" In *Luke-Acts and the Jewish People: Eight Critical Perspectives*, edited by Joseph B. Tyson, 102–23. Minneapolis: Augsburg, 1988.

Cooper, John M. "Aristotle on Friendship." In *Essays on Aristotle's Ethics*, edited by Amélie Oksenberg Rorty, 301–30. Berkeley: University of California Press, 1979.

Cornford, Francis MacDonald. *Thucydides Mythistoricus*. London: Edward Arnold, 1907.

Crane, R. S., ed. *Critics and Criticism: Ancient and Modern*. Chicago: University of Chicago Press, 1952.

Croke, Brian, and Alanna M. Emmett, eds. *History and Historians in Late Antiquity*. Sydney: Pergamon, 1983.

Danker, Frederick W. "The Endangered Benefactor in Luke-Acts." In *Society of Biblical Literature 1981 Seminar Papers*, edited by Kent Harold Richards, 39–48. Chico, CA: Scholars Press, 1981.

————. "Reciprocity in the Ancient World and in Acts 15:23–29." In *Political Issues in Luke-Acts*, edited by Richard J. Cassidy and Philip J. Scharper, 49–58. New York: Orbis, 1983.

Darr, John A. "Irenic or Ironic? Another Look at Gamaliel before the Sanhedrin (Acts 5:33–42)." In *Literary Studies in Luke-Acts: Essays in Honor of Joseph B. Tyson*, edited by Richard P. Thompson and Thomas E. Phillips, 121–40. Macon, GA: Mercer University Press, 1998.

————. "Narrator as Character: Mapping a Reader-Oriented Approach to Narration in Luke-Acts." *Semeia* 63 (1993): 43–60.

————. *On Character Building: The Reader and the Rhetoric of Characterization in Luke-Acts*. Literary Currents in Biblical Interpretation. Louisville: Westminster/John Knox, 1992.

Davidson, James. "The Gaze in Polybius' *Histories*." *Journal of Roman Studies* 81 (1991): 10–24.

Dawsey, James M. "Characteristics of Folk-Epic in Acts." In *Society of Biblical Literature 1989 Seminar Papers*, edited by David Lull, 317–25. Atlanta: Scholars Press, 1989.

————. *The Lukan Voice: Confusion and Irony in the Gospel of Luke*. Macon, GA: Mercer University Press, 1986.

De Foucault, Jules Albert. *Recherches sur la langue et le style de Polybe*. Collection d'études anciennes. Paris: Les Belles Lettres, 1972.

De Jonge, Marianus. "Josephus und die Zukunftserwartungen seines Volkes." In *Josephus-Studien: Untersuchungen zu Josephus, dem antiken Judentum und dem Neuen Testament*, edited by Otto Betz, Klaus Haacker, and Martin Hengel, 205–19. Göttingen: Vandenhoeck & Ruprecht, 1974.

De Romilly, Jacqueline. *Thucydides and Athenian Imperialism*. Translated by Philip Thody. New York: Barnes & Noble, 1963.

De Ste. Croix, G. E. M. "Aristotle on History and Poetry." In *Essays on Aristotle's Poetics*, edited by Amélie Oksenberg Rorty, 23–32. Princeton, NJ: Princeton University Press, 1992.

Degenhardt, Hans-Joachim. *Lukas, Evangelist der Armen: Besitz und Besitzverzicht in den lukanischen Schriften.* Stuttgart: Verlag Katholisches Bibelwerk, 1965.

Degenhardt, Johannes Joachim. "Die ersten Christen und der irdische Besitz." In *Die Freude an Gott — unsere Kraft,* edited by Johannes Joachim Degenhardt, 150–56. Stuttgart: Verlag Katholisches Bibelwerk, 1991.

Delebecque, Édouard. "L'hellénisme de la 'relative complexe' dans le Nouveau Testament et principalement chez saint Luc." *Biblica* 62 (1981): 229–38.

Delling, Gerhard. "προστάσσω." In *Theological Dictionary of the New Testament,* edited by Gerhard Kittel and Gerhard Friedrich, 10 vols., 8:37–39. Translated by Geoffrey W. Bromiley. Grand Rapids: Eerdmans, 1964–76.

———. "στάσις." In *Theological Dictionary of the New Testament,* edited by Gerhard Kittel and Gerhard Friedrich, 10 vols., 7:568–71. Translated by Geoffrey W. Bromiley. Grand Rapids: Eerdmans, 1964–76.

———. "συμβιβάζω." In *Theological Dictionary of the New Testament,* edited by Gerhard Kittel and Gerhard Friedrich, 10 vols., 7:763–66. Translated by Geoffrey W. Bromiley. Grand Rapids: Eerdmans, 1964-76.

Demetrius. *On Style.* Translated by W. Rhys Roberts. Loeb Classical Library. London: Heinemann, 1927.

Deslauriers, Marguerite. "Character and Explanation in Aristotle's *Ethics* and *Poetics.*" *Dialogue* 29 (1990): 79–94.

D'Huys, V. "Κρήσιμον καί τερπνόν in Polybios' Schlachtschilderungen: Einige literarische Topoi in seiner Darstellung der Schlacht bei Zama (XV 9–16)." In *Purposes of History: Studies in Greek Historiography from the 4th to the 2nd Centuries B.C.,* edited by Herman Verdin, Guido Schepens, and Eugénie de Keyser, 267–88. Studia hellenistica 30. Leuven: Lovanii, 1990.

Dibelius, Martin. "The Acts of the Apostles as an Historical Source." In *Studies in the Acts of the Apostles,* 102–8. Translated by Mary Ling. London: SCM, 1956.

———. "The Apostolic Council." In *Studies in the Acts of the Apostles,* 93–101. Translated by Mary Ling. London: SCM, 1956.

———. "The Conversion of Cornelius." In *Studies in the Acts of the Apostles,* 109–22. Translated by Mary Ling. London: SCM, 1956.

———. "The First Christian Historian." In *Studies in the Acts of the Apostles,* 123–37. Translated by Mary Ling. London: SCM, 1956.

———. *Die Reden der Apostelgeschichte und die antike Geschichtsschreibung.* Sitzungsberichte der Heidelberger Akademie der Wissenschaften, Philosophisch-Historische Klasse. Heidelberg: C. Winter, 1949.

———. "The Speeches in Acts and Ancient Historiography." In *Studies in the Acts of the Apostles,* 138–85. Translated by Mary Ling. London: SCM, 1956.

———. *Studies in the Acts of the Apostles.* Translated by Mary Ling. London: SCM, 1956.

Diodorus Siculus. *Library of History.* 12 vols. Translated by C. H. Oldfather et al. Loeb Classical Library. London: Heinemann, 1933-67.

Dionysius of Halicarnassus. *The Critical Essays.* 2 vols. Translated by Stephen Usher. Loeb Classical Library. London: Heinemann, 1974–85.

———. *Roman Antiquities.* 7 vols. Translated by Earnest Cary. Loeb Classical Library. London: Heinemann, 1937-50.

Downing, F. Gerald. "Freedom from the Law in Luke-Acts." *Journal for the Study of the New Testament* 26 (February 1986): 49–52.

———. "Law and Custom: Luke-Acts and Late Hellenism." In *Law and Religion: Essays on the Place of the Law in Israel and Early Christianity*, edited by Barnabas Lindars, 148–58. Cambridge, UK: James Clarke, 1988.

Dubuisson, M. "La vision polybienne de Rome." In *Purposes of History: Studies in Greek Historiography from the 4th to the 2nd Centuries B.C.*, edited by Herman Verdin, Guido Schepens, and Eugénie de Keyser, 233–44. Studia hellenistica 30. Leuven: Lovanii, 1990.

Dunn, James D. G. *The Acts of the Apostles*. Narrative Commentaries. Valley Forge, PA: Trinity Press International, 1996.

———. *The Partings of the Ways: Between Christianity and Judaism and Their Significance for the Character of Christianity*. Philadelphia: Trinity Press International, 1991.

Dupont, Jacques. "La communauté des biens aux premiers jours de l'Eglise (Actes 2,42.44–45; 4,32.34–35)." In *Études sur les Actes des Apôtres*, 503–19. Lectio divina 45. Paris: Éditions du Cerf, 1967.

———. "Les discours de Pierre." In *Nouvelles études sur les Actes des Apôtres*, 58–111. Lectio divina 118. Paris: Éditions du Cerf, 1984.

———. *Études sur les Actes des Apôtres*. Lectio divina 45. Paris: Éditions du Cerf, 1967.

———. *Nouvelles études sur les Actes des Apôtres*. Lectio divina 118. Paris: Éditions du Cerf, 1984.

———. "La prière des apôtres persécutés (Actes 4,23–31)." In *Études sur les Actes des Apôtres*, 521–22. Lectio divina 45. Paris: Éditions du Cerf, 1967.

———. "La question du plan des Actes des Apôtres à la lumière d'un texte de Lucien de Samosate." In *Nouvelles études sur les Actes des Apôtres*, 24–36. Lectio divina 118. Paris: Éditions du Cerf, 1984.

———. "Le salut des gentils et la signification théologique du Livre des Actes." *New Testament Studies* 6 (1959-60): 132–55.

———. *The Salvation of the Gentiles: Essays on the Acts of the Apostles*. Translated by John R. Keating. New York: Paulist Press, 1979.

———. "The Salvation of the Gentiles and the Theological Significance of Acts." In *The Salvation of the Gentiles: Essays on the Acts of the Apostles*, 11–34. Translated by John R. Keating. New York: Paulist Press, 1979.

———. "L'union entre les premiers chrétiens dans les Actes des Apôtres." In *Nouvelles études sur les Actes des Apôtres*, 296–318. Lectio divina 118. Paris: Éditions du Cerf, 1984.

———. "Un peuple d'entre les nations (Actes 15.14)." *New Testament Studies* 31 (July 1985): 321–35.

Easterling, P. E. "Constructing Character in Greek Tragedy." In *Characterization and Individuality in Greek Literature*, edited by Christopher Pelling, 83–99. Oxford: Clarendon, 1990.

———. "Presentation of Character in Aeschylus." *Greece and Rome* 20 (April 1973): 3–18.

Eckstein, A. M. "Josephus and Polybius: A Reconsideration." *Classical Antiquity* 9 (October 1990): 175–208.

———. "Polybius, the Achaeans, and the 'Freedom of the Greeks.' " *Greek, Roman, and Byzantine Studies* 31 (Spring 1990): 45–71.

Edwards, Douglas R. "Acts of the Apostles and the Graeco-Roman World: Narrative Communication in Social Context." In *Society of Biblical Literature 1989 Seminar Papers*, edited by David Lull, 362–77. Atlanta: Scholars Press, 1989.

Eisen, Karl F. *Polybiosinterpretationen: Beobachtungen zu Prinzipien griechischer römischer Historiographie bei Polybios.* Bibiothek der klassischen Altertumswissenschaften, Neue Folge 2. Heidelberg: Carl Winter, 1966.

Elliott, John H. "Temple versus Household in Luke-Acts: A Contrast in Social Institutions." In *The Social World of Luke-Acts: Models for Interpretation*, edited by Jerome H. Neyrey, 211–40. Peabody, MA: Hendrickson, 1991.

Else, Gerald F. *Plato and Aristotle on Poetry.* Chapel Hill: University of North Carolina Press, 1986.

Erickson, Keith V., ed. *Aristotle: The Classical Heritage of Rhetoric.* Metuchen, NJ: Scarecrow, 1974.

Esler, Philip Francis. *Community and Gospel in Luke-Acts: The Social and Political Motivations of Lucan Theology.* Society for New Testament Studies Monograph Series 57. Cambridge, UK: Cambridge University Press, 1987.

Evans, James A. S. *Herodotus.* Twayne's World Authors Series 645. Boston: Twayne, 1982.

———. *Herodotus, Explorer of the Past: Three Essays.* Princeton, NJ: Princeton University Press, 1991.

Fehling, Detlev. *Herodotus and His 'Sources': Citation, Invention, and Narrative Art.* Translated by J. G. Howie. ARCA Classical and Medieval Texts, Papers, and Monographs 21. Liverpool: Francis Cairns, 1989.

Feldman, Louis H. "Josephus as an Apologist of the Greco-Roman World: His Portrait of Solomon." In *Aspects of Religious Propaganda in Judaism and Early Christianity*, edited by Elisabeth Schüssler Fiorenza, 68–98. University of Notre Dame Center for the Study of Judaism and Christianity in Antiquity 2. Notre Dame, IN: University of Notre Dame Press, 1976.

Fiensy, David A. "The Composition of the Jerusalem Church." In *The Book of Acts in Its Palestinian Setting*, edited by Richard Bauckham, 213–36. The Book of Acts in Its First Century Setting. Grand Rapids: Eerdmans, 1995.

Finley, John H., Jr. *Three Essays on Thucydides.* Loeb Classical Monographs. Cambridge, MA: Harvard University Press, 1967.

Finley, M. I. *The Greek Historians: The Essence of Herodotus, Thucydides, Xenophon [and] Polybius.* New York: Viking, 1959.

———. *The Use and Abuse of History.* London: Chatto & Windus, 1975.

Fiorenza, Elisabeth Schüssler, ed. *Aspects of Religious Propaganda in Judaism and Early Christianity.* University of Notre Dame Center for the Study of Judaism and Christianity in Antiquity 2. Notre Dame, IN: University of Notre Dame Press, 1976.

Fitzmyer, Joseph A. *The Acts of the Apostles: A New Translation with Introduction and Commentary.* Anchor Bible. New York: Doubleday, 1998.

———. "Jewish Christianity in Acts in Light of the Qumran Scrolls." In *Studies in Luke-Acts,* edited by Leander E. Keck and J. Louis Martyn, 233–57. Philadelphia: Fortress, 1980.

———. *Luke the Theologian: Aspects of His Teaching.* New York: Paulist Press, 1989.

Fliess, Peter J. *Thucydides and the Politics of Bipolarity.* Baton Rouge: Louisiana State University Press, 1966.

Foakes-Jackson, F. J., and Kirsopp Lake, eds. *Beginnings of Christianity.* 5 vols. London: Macmillan, 1920-33.

Fornara, Charles W. *Herodotus: An Interpretative Essay.* Oxford: Clarendon, 1971.

———. "Human History and the Constraint of Fate in Herodotus." In *Conflict, Antithesis, and the Ancient Historian,* edited by June W. Allison, 25–45. Columbus: Ohio State University Press, 1990.

———. *The Nature of History in Ancient Greece and Rome.* Eidos: Studies in Classical Kinds. Berkeley: University of California Press, 1983.

Fortenbaugh, William W. "Aristotle's Analysis of Friendship." *Phronesis* 22 (1975): 51–62.

———. "Aristotle's *Rhetoric* on Emotions." In *Aristotle: The Classical Heritage of Rhetoric,* edited by Keith V. Erickson, 205–34. Metuchen, NJ: Scarecrow, 1974.

Fowler, Robert M. "Characterizing Character in Biblical Narrative." *Semeia* 63 (1993): 97–104.

———. *Let the Reader Understand: Reader-Response Criticism and the Gospel of Mark.* Minneapolis: Fortress, 1991.

Freeland, Cynthia A. "Plot Imitates Action: Aesthetic Evaluation and Moral Realism in Aristotle's *Poetics.*" In *Essays on Aristotle's Poetics,* edited by Amélie Oksenberg Rorty, 111–32. Princeton, NJ: Princeton University Press, 1992.

Friedrich, Gerhard. "εὐαγγελίζομαι...." In *Theological Dictionary of the New Testament,* edited by Gerhard Kittel and Gerhard Friedrich, 10 vols., 2:707-37. Translated by Geoffrey W. Bromiley. Grand Rapids: Eerdmans, 1964-76.

Funk, Robert. *The Poetics of Biblical Narrative.* Sonoma, CA: Polebridge, 1988.

Gabba, Emilio. *Dionysius and the History of Archaic Rome.* Sather Classical Lectures 56. Berkeley: University of California Press, 1991.

Gager, John G. "Jews, Gentiles, and Synagogues in the Book of Acts." In *Christians among Jews and Gentiles: Essays in Honor of Krister Stendahl on His Sixty-fifth Birthday,* edited by George W. E. Nickelsburg with George W. MacRae, 91–99. Philadelphia: Fortress, 1986.

Garton, C. "Characterisation in Greek Tragedy." *Journal of Hellenic Studies* 77 (1957): 247–54.

Gasque, W. W. "A Fruitful Field: Recent Study of the Acts of the Apostles." *Interpretation* 42 (1988): 117–31.

———. "The Historical Value of Acts." *Tyndale Bulletin* 40 (May 1989): 136–57.

———. "The Historical Value of the Book of Acts." *Theologische Zeitschrift* 28 (May–June 1972): 177–96.

———. *A History of the Interpretation of the Acts of the Apostles.* Peabody, MA: Hendrickson, 1989.

Gaston, Lloyd. "Anti-Judaism and the Passion Narrative in Luke and Acts." In *Anti-Judaism in Early Christianity,* vol. 1, *Paul and the Gospels,* edited by Peter Richardson with David Granskou, 127–53. Studies in Christianity and Judaism 2. Waterloo, ON: Wilfrid Laurier University Press, 1986.

Gauger, Jörg-Dieter. *Beiträge zur jüdischen Apologetik.* Bonner biblische Beiträge. Bonn: Peter Hanstein, 1977.

Gaventa, Beverly Roberts. *The Acts of the Apostles.* Abingdon New Testament Commentaries. Nashville: Abingdon, 2003.

———. *From Darkness to Light: Aspects of Conversion in the New Testament.* Overtures to Biblical Theology 20. Philadelphia: Fortress, 1986.

———. "The Overthrown Enemy: Luke's Portrait of Paul." In *Society of Biblical Literature 1985 Seminar Papers,* edited by Kent Harold Richards, 439–49. Atlanta: Scholars Press, 1985.

———. "Toward a Theology of Acts: Reading and Rereading." *Interpretation* 42 (1988): 146–57.

Gentili, Bruno. *Poetry and Its Public in Ancient Greece.* Translated by A. Thomas Cole. Baltimore: Johns Hopkins University Press, 1988.

Gill, Christopher. "The Character-Personality Distinction." In *Characterization and Individuality in Greek Literature,* edited by Christopher Pelling, 1–31. Oxford: Clarendon, 1990.

———. "The *Éthos/Pathos* Distinction in Rhetorical and Literary Criticism." *Classical Quarterly* 34 (1984): 149–66.

———. "The Question of Character and Personality in Greek Tragedy." *Poetics Today* 7 (1986): 251–73.

———. "The Question of Character-Development: Plutarch and Tacitus." *Classical Quarterly* 33 (1983): 469–87.

Gill, David W. J., and Conrad Gempf, eds. *The Book of Acts in Its Graeco-Roman Setting.* The Book of Acts in Its First Century Setting. Grand Rapids: Eerdmans, 1994.

Ginsberg, Warren. *The Cast of Character: The Representation of Personality in Ancient and Medieval Literature.* Toronto: University of Toronto Press, 1983.

Goldhill, Simon. "Character and Action, Representation and Reading: Greek Tragedy and Its Critics." In *Characterization and Individuality in Greek Literature,* edited by Christopher Pelling, 100–127. Oxford: Clarendon, 1990.

Goodenough, Erwin R. "The Perspective of Acts." In *Studies in Luke-Acts,* edited by Leander E. Keck and J. Louis Martyn, 51–59. Philadelphia: Fortress, 1980.

Gould, John. *Herodotus.* New York: St. Martin's, 1989.

Gowler, David B. *Host, Guest, Enemy, and Friend: Portraits of the Pharisees in Luke and Acts.* Emory Studies in Early Christianity 2. New York: Peter Lang, 1991.

Grant, Michael, ed. *Readings in the Classical Historians.* New York: Charles Scribner's Sons, 1992.

Green, Joel B., and Michael C. McKeever. *Luke-Acts and New Testament Historiography.* IBR Bibliographies 8. Grand Rapids: Baker, 1994.

Greeven, Heinrich. "ζητέω...." In *Theological Dictionary of the New Testament,* edited by Gerhard Kittel and Gerhard Friedrich, 10 vols., 2:892–96. Translated by Geoffrey W. Bromiley. Grand Rapids: Eerdmans, 1964–76.

Grube, G. M. A. *The Greek and Roman Critics.* London: Methuen, 1965.

Grundmann, Walter. "κακός...." In *Theological Dictionary of the New Testament,* edited by Gerhard Kittel and Gerhard Friedrich, 10 vols., 3:469–86. Translated by Geoffrey W. Bromiley. Grand Rapids: Eerdmans, 1964–76.

———. "προσκαρτερέω." In *Theological Dictionary of the New Testament,* edited by Gerhard Kittel and Gerhard Friedrich, 10 vols., 3:618–19. Translated by Geoffrey W. Bromiley. Grand Rapids: Eerdmans, 1964-76.

Haacker, Klaus. "Das Bekenntnis des Paulus zur Hoffnung Israels nach der Apostelgeschichte des Lukas." *New Testament Studies* 31 (July 1985): 437–51.

Haenchen, Ernst. *The Acts of the Apostles: A Commentary.* Translated by Bernard Noble and Gerald Shinn. Philadelphia: Westminster, 1971.

———. "The Book of Acts as Source Material for the History of Early Christianity." In *Studies in Luke-Acts,* edited by Leander E. Keck and J. Louis Martyn, 258–78. Philadelphia: Fortress, 1980.

Hägg, Tomas. *The Novel in Antiquity.* Berkeley: University of California Press, 1983.

Hainsworth, J. B. *The Idea of Epic.* Eidos: Studies in Classical Kinds. Berkeley: University of California Press, 1991.

Halliwell, Stephen. *Aristotle's Poetics.* Chapel Hill: University of North Carolina Press, 1986.

———. "Aristotle's Poetics." In *The Cambridge History of Literary Criticism,* vol. 1, *Classical Criticism,* edited by George A. Kennedy, 149–83. Cambridge, UK: Cambridge University Press, 1989.

———. "Pleasure, Understanding, and Emotion in Aristotle's *Poetics.*" In *Essays on Aristotle's Poetics,* edited by Amélie Oksenberg Rorty, 241–60. Princeton, NJ: Princeton University Press, 1992.

———. "Traditional Greek Conceptions of Character." In *Characterization and Individuality in Greek Literature,* edited by Christopher Pelling, 32–59. Oxford: Clarendon, 1990.

Hands, A. R. *Charities and Social Aid in Greece and Rome.* Ithaca, NY: Cornell University Press, 1968.

Hankinson, R. J. "Perception and Evaluation: Aristotle on the Moral Imagination." *Dialogue* 29 (1990): 41–63.

Hare, Douglas R. A. "The Rejection of the Jews in the Synoptic Gospels and Acts." In *Antisemitism and the Foundations of Christianity,* edited by Alan Davies, 27–47. New York: Paulist Press, 1979.

Harnack, Adolf. *The Acts of the Apostles.* Crown Theological Library. New York: G. P. Putnam's Sons, 1909.

Hart, John. *Herodotus and Greek History.* New York: St. Martin's, 1982.

Hartog, François. "Herodotus and the Historiographical Operation." *Diacritics* 22 (Summer 1992): 83–93.

———. *The Mirror of Herodotus: The Representation of the Other in the Writing of History.* Translated by Janet Lloyd. New Historicism 5. Berkeley: University of California Press, 1988.

Harvey, W. J. *Character and the Novel.* Ithaca, NY: Cornell University Press, 1965.

Hauck, Friedrich. "περισσεύω. . . ." In *Theological Dictionary of the New Testament,* edited by Gerhard Kittel and Gerhard Friedrich, 10 vols., 6:58–63. Translated by Geoffrey W. Bromiley. Grand Rapids: Eerdmans, 1964–76.

Haulotte, Edgar. "Fondation d'une communauté de type universel: Actes 10:1–11:18; Étude critique sur la rédaction, la 'structure' et la 'tradition' du récit." *Recherches de science religieuse* 58 (1970): 63–100.

Havelaar, Henriette. "Hellenistic Parallels to Acts 5.1–11 and the Problem of Conflicting Interpretations." *Journal for the Study of the New Testament* 67 (Summer 1997): 63–82.

Heath, Malcolm. "The Universality of Poetry in Aristotle's *Poetics.*" *Classical Quarterly* 41 (1991): 389–402.

Hedrick, Charles W. "Paul's Conversion/Call: A Comparative Analysis of the Three Reports in Acts." *Journal of Biblical Literature* 100 (September 1981): 415–32.

Heidland, Hans Wolfgang. "ὁμοθυμαδόν." In *Theological Dictionary of the New Testament,* edited by Gerhard Kittel and Gerhard Friedrich, 10 vols., 5:185–86. Translated by Geoffrey W. Bromiley. Grand Rapids: Eerdmans, 1964-76.

Hemer, Colin J. *The Book of Acts in the Setting of Hellenistic History.* Winona Lake, IN: Eisenbrauns, 1990.

Hengel, Martin. *Acts and the History of Earliest Christianity.* Translated by John Bowden. Philadelphia: Fortress, 1979.

———. *Property and Riches in the Early Church: Aspects of a Social History of Christianity.* Philadelphia: Fortress, 1974.

Herodotus. *Histories.* 4 vols. Translated by A. D. Godley. Loeb Classical Library. London: Heinemann, 1921-24.

Hill, Craig C. *Hellenists and Hebrews: Reappraising Division within the Earliest Church.* Minneapolis: Fortress, 1992.

Hillard, T., A. Nobbs, and Winter B. "Acts and the Pauline Corpus I: Ancient Literary Parallels." In *The Book of Acts in Its Ancient Literary Setting,* edited by Bruce W. Winter and Andrew D. Clarke, 183–214. The Book of Acts in Its First Century Setting. Grand Rapids: Eerdmans, 1993.

Holgate, David A. *Prodigality, Liberality and Meanness in the Parable of the Prodigal Son: A Greco-Roman Perspective on Luke 15.11–32.* JSNTSup 187. Sheffield: Sheffield Academic Press, 1999.

Horace. *Ars Poetica.* Translated by H. Rushton Fairclough. Loeb Classical Library. London: Heinemann, 1961.

Hornblower, Simon. *A Commentary on Thucydides.* 2 vols. Oxford: Clarendon, 1991.

———. *Thucydides.* Baltimore: Johns Hopkins University Press, 1987.

Horsley, G. H. R. "Speeches and Dialogue in Acts." *New Testament Studies* 32 (October 1986): 609–14.

Houlden, J. L. "The Purpose of Luke." *Journal for the Study of the New Testament* 21 (1984): 53–65.

Huber, Ludwig. *Religiöse und politische Beweggründe des Handelns in der Geschichtsschreibung des Herodot.* Tübingen: Universität Tübingen, 1965.

Humphrey, Edith M. "Collision of Modes? — Vision and Determining Argument in Acts 10:1–11:18." *Semeia* 71 (1995): 65–84.

Hunter, Virginia. *Past and Process in Herodotus and Thucydides.* Princeton, NJ: Princeton University Press, 1982.

———. *Thucydides: The Artful Reporter.* Toronto: Hakkert, 1973.

Hutter, Horst. *Politics as Friendship: The Origins of Classical Notions of Politics in the Theory and Practice of Friendship.* Waterloo, ON: Wilfrid Laurier University Press, 1978.

Immerwahr, Henry R. *Form and Thought in Herodotus.* Cleveland: Western Reserve University Press, 1966.

Iser, Wolfgang. *The Act of Reading: A Theory of Aesthetic Response.* Baltimore: Johns Hopkins University Press, 1978.

———. *The Implied Reader: Patterns of Communication in Prose Fiction from Bunyan to Beckett.* Baltimore: Johns Hopkins University Press, 1974.

———. "Interaction between Text and Reader." In *The Reader in the Text: Essays on Audience and Interpretation,* edited by Susan R. Suleiman and Inge Crosman, 106–19. Princeton, NJ: Princeton University Press, 1980.

———. "Representation: A Performative Act." In *The Aims of Representation: Subject/Text/History,* edited by Murray Krieger, 217–32. Irvine Studies in the Humanities. New York: Columbia University Press, 1987.

Jacoby, Felix, ed. *Die Fragmente der griechischen Historiker.* 3 vols. Leiden: E. J. Brill, 1923-58.

Jervell, Jacob. "The Acts of the Apostles and the History of Early Christianity." *Studia theologica* 37 (1983): 17–32.

———. "The Church of Jews and Godfearers." In *Luke-Acts and the Jewish People: Eight Critical Perspectives,* edited by Joseph B. Tyson, 11–20. Minneapolis: Augsburg, 1988.

———. "Das gespaltene Israel und die Heidenvölker: Zur Motivierung der Heidenmission in der Apostelgeschichte." *Studia theologica* 19 (1965): 68–96.

———. "God's Faithfulness to the Faithless People: Trends in Interpretation of Luke-Acts." *Word and World* 12 (1992): 29–36.

———. "The Law in Luke-Acts." *Harvard Theological Review* 64 (1971): 21–36.

———. *Luke and the People of God: A New Look at Luke-Acts.* Minneapolis: Augsburg, 1972.

———. "Paulus in der Apostelgeschichte und die Geschichte des Urchristentums." *New Testament Studies* 32 (July 1986): 378–92.

———. "Retrospect and Prospect in Luke-Acts Interpretation." In *Society of Biblical Literature 1991 Seminar Papers,* edited by Eugene H. Lovering Jr., 383–404. Atlanta: Scholars Press, 1991.

———. *The Theology of the Acts of the Apostles.* Cambridge, MA: Cambridge University Press, 1996.

———. *The Unknown Paul: Essays on Luke-Acts and Early Christian History.* Minneapolis: Augsburg, 1984.

Johnson, Luke T. *The Acts of the Apostles.* Sacra pagina 5. Collegeville, MN: Liturgical Press, 1992.

———. *Decision Making in the Church: A Biblical Model.* Philadelphia: Fortress, 1983.

————. *The Literary Function of Possessions in Luke-Acts.* Society of Biblical Literature Dissertation Series 39. Missoula, MT: Scholars Press, 1977.

————. *Sharing Possessions: Mandate and Symbol of Faith.* Overtures to Biblical Theology 9. Philadelphia: Fortress, 1981.

Jones, C. P. *Culture and Society in Lucian.* Cambridge, MA: Harvard University Press, 1986.

Josephus, Flavius. *Against Apion.* Translated by H. St. J. Thackeray. Loeb Classical Library. London: Heinemann, 1926.

————. *Jewish Antiquities.* 9 vols. Translated by H. St. J. Thackeray et al. Loeb Classical Library. London: Heinemann, 1926-65.

————. *The Jewish War.* 2 vols. Translated by H. St. J. Thackeray. Loeb Classical Library. London: Heinemann, 1966-67.

————. *The Life.* Translated by H. St. J. Thackeray. Loeb Classical Library. London: Heinemann, 1926.

Juel, Donald. "Hearing Peter's Speech in Acts 3: Meaning and Truth in Interpretation." *Word and World* 12 (1992): 43-50.

————. *Luke-Acts: The Promise of History.* Atlanta: John Knox, 1983.

Keck, Leander E., and J. Louis Martyn, eds. *Studies in Luke-Acts.* Philadelphia: Fortress, 1980.

Kee, Howard C. *Community of the New Age: Studies in Mark's Gospel.* Macon, GA: Mercer University Press, 1983.

————. "The Jews in Acts." In *Diaspora Jews and Judaism: Essays in Honor of, and in Dialogue with, A. Thomas Kraabel,* edited by J. Andrew Overman and Robert S. MacLennan, 183-95. Atlanta: Scholars Press, 1992.

Kelber, Werner H. *The Oral and the Written Gospel: The Hermeneutics of Speaking and Writing in the Synoptic Tradition, Mark, Paul, and Q.* Philadelphia: Fortress, 1983.

Kennedy, George A. *The Art of Persuasion in Greece.* Princeton, NJ: Princeton University Press, 1963.

————. *The Art of Rhetoric in the Roman World.* Princeton, NJ: Princeton University Press, 1972.

————. *Classical Rhetoric and Its Christian and Secular Tradition from Ancient to Modern Times.* Chapel Hill: University of North Carolina Press, 1980.

————. "The Evolution of a Theory of Artistic Prose." In *The Cambridge History of Literary History,* vol. 1, *Classical Criticism,* edited by George A. Kennedy, 184-99. Cambridge, UK: Cambridge University Press, 1989.

————, ed. *The Cambridge History of Literary Criticism,* vol. 1, *Classical Criticism.* Cambridge, UK: Cambridge University Press, 1989.

Klauck, Hans-Josef. *Gemeinde zwischen Haus und Stadt: Kirche bei Paulus.* Freiburg: Herder, 1992.

Klinghardt, Matthias. *Gesetz und Volk Gottes: Das lukanische Verständnis des Gesetzes nach Herkunft, Funktion und seinem Ort in der Geschichte des Urchristentums.* Wissenschaftliche Untersuchungen zum Neuen Testament 2:32. Tübingen: J. C. B. Mohr, 1988.

Knox, John. *Chapters in a Life of Paul.* Rev. ed. Macon, GA: Mercer University Press, 1987.

Koenig, John. *New Testament Hospitality: Partnership with Strangers as Promise and Mission.* Overtures to Biblical Theology 17. Philadelphia: Fortress, 1985.

Kraut, Richard. *Aristotle on the Human Good.* Princeton, NJ: Princeton University Press, 1989.

Kremer, Jacob, ed. *Les Actes des Apôtres: Traditions, rédaction, théologie.* Bibliotheca ephemeridum theologicarum lovaniensium 48. Leuven: Leuven University Press, 1979.

Krodel, Gerhard. *Acts.* Augsburg Commentary on the New Testament. Minneapolis: Augsburg, 1986.

Kurz, William S. "Effects of Variant Narrators in Acts 10–11." *New Testament Studies* 43 (October 1997): 570–86.

———. "Luke-Acts and Historiography in the Greek Bible." In *Society of Biblical Literature 1980 Seminar Papers,* edited by Paul J. Achtemeier, 283–300. Chico, CA: Scholars Press, 1980.

———. "Narrative Approaches to Luke-Acts." *Biblica* 68 (1987): 195–220.

———. "Narrative Models for Imitation in Luke-Acts." In *Greeks, Romans, and Christians: Essays in Honor of Abraham J. Malherbe,* edited by David L. Balch, Everett Ferguson, and Wayne Meeks, 171–89. Minneapolis: Fortress, 1990.

———. *Reading Luke-Acts: Dynamics of Biblical Narrative.* Louisville: Westminster/John Knox, 1993.

Lake, Kirsopp. "The Apostolic Council of Jerusalem." In *The Beginnings of Christianity,* edited by F. J. Foakes-Jackson and Kirsopp Lake, 5 vols., 5:195–212. London: Macmillan, 1933.

———. "The Communism of Acts II. and IV.–V. and the Appointment of the Seven." In *The Beginnings of Christianity,* edited by F. J. Foakes-Jackson and Kirsopp Lake, 5 vols., 5:140–51. London: Macmillan, 1933.

———. "Proselytes and God-Fearers." In *The Beginnings of Christianity,* edited by F. J. Foakes-Jackson and Kirsopp Lake, 5 vols., 5:74–96. London: Macmillan, 1933.

Lang, Mabel L. *Herodotean Narrative and Discourse.* Martin Classical Lectures 28. Cambridge, MA: Harvard University Press (for Oberlin College), 1984.

Laqueur, Richard. *Der jüdische Historiker Flavius Josephus: Ein biographischer Versuch auf neuer quellenkritischer Grundlage.* Giessen: Münchow, 1920.

Larkin, William J., Jr. *Acts.* IVP New Testament Commentary. Downers Grove, IL: InterVarsity, 1995.

Larsson, Edvin. "Die Hellenisten und die Urgemeinde." *New Testament Studies* 33 (1987): 205–25.

———. "Paul: Law and Salvation." *New Testament Studies* 31 (July 1985): 425–36.

Lategan, Bernard C. "Coming to Grips with the Reader in Biblical Literature." *Semeia* 48 (1989): 3–20.

Lateiner, Donald. *The Historical Method of Herodotus.* Toronto: University of Toronto Press, 1989.

Lear, Jonathan. "Katharsis." In *Essays on Aristotle's Poetics,* edited by Amélie Oksenberg Rorty, 315–40. Princeton, NJ: Princeton University Press, 1992.

Lentz, Tony M. *Orality and Literacy in Hellenic Greece.* Carbondale: Southern Illinois University Press, 1989.

Levinsohn, Stephen H. *Textual Connections in Acts.* Society of Biblical Literature Monograph Series 31. Atlanta: Scholars Press, 1987.

Liddell, Henry George, and Robert Scott. *A Greek-English Lexicon.* 9th ed. Oxford: Clarendon, 1940.

Lindner, Helgo. *Die Geschichtsauffassung des Flavius Josephus im Bellum Judaicum.* Arbeiten zur Geschichte des antiken Judentums und des Urchristentums 12. Leiden: E. J. Brill, 1972.

Livy. *Livy's Works.* 14 vols. Translated by W. Hamilton Fyfe. Loeb Classical Library. London: Heinemann, 1919-59.

Lohfink, Gerhard. *Die Sammlung Israels: Eine Untersuchung zur lukanischen Ekklesiologie.* Studien zum Alten und Neuen Testament. Munich: Kösel, 1975.

Longinus. *On the Sublime.* Translated by W. Hamilton Fyfe. Loeb Classical Library. London: Heinemann, 1927.

————. *On the Sublime.* Translated by James A. Arieti and John M. Crossett. Texts and Studies in Religion 21. New York: Edwin Mellen, 1985.

Löning, Karl. "Das Verhältnis zum Judentum als Identitätsproblem der Kirche nach der Apostelgeschichte." In *"Ihr alle aber seid Brüder": Festschrift für A. Th. Khoury zum 60. Geburtstag,* edited by Ludwig Hagemann and Ernst Pulsfort, 304–19. Würzburg: Echter, 1990.

Luce, T. J. "Ancient Views on the Causes of Bias in Historical Writing." *Classical Philology* 84 (1989): 16–31.

Lucian. *Lucian's Works.* 8 vols. Translated by A. K. Harmon, K. Kilburn, and M. D. MacLeod. Loeb Classical Library. London: Heinemann, 1913-67.

Lüdemann, Gerd. "Acts of the Apostles as a Historical Source." In *The Social World of Formative Christianity and Judaism,* edited by Ernest S. Frerichs, Jacob Neusner, Peder Borgen, and Richard Horsley, 109–25. Philadelphia: Fortress, 1982.

————. *Early Christianity according to the Traditions in Acts: A Commentary.* Translated by John Bowden. Philadelphia: Fortress, 1989.

Lyons, George. *Pauline Autobiography: Toward a New Understanding.* Society of Biblical Literature Dissertation Series 73. Atlanta: Scholars Press, 1985.

Lyons, William John. "The Words of Gamaliel (Acts 5.38–39) and the Irony of Indeterminacy." *Journal for the Study of the New Testament* 68 (December 1997): 23–49.

MacMullen, Ramsey. *Roman Social Relations: 50 B.C. to A.D. 284.* New Haven: Yale University Press, 1974.

MacRae, George W. " 'Whom Heaven Must Receive Until That Time.' " *Interpretation* 27 (April 1973): 151–65.

Maddox, Robert. *The Purpose of Luke-Acts.* Forschungen zur Religion und Literatur des Alten und Neuen Testaments 126. Göttingen: Vandenhoeck & Ruprecht, 1982.

Malitz, J. "Das Interesse an der Geschichte: Die griechischen Historiker und ihr Publikum." In *Purposes of History: Studies in Greek Historiography from the 4th to the 2nd Centuries B.C.,* edited by Herman Verdin, Guido Schepens, and Eugénie de Keyser, 323–50. Studia hellenistica 30. Leuven: Lovanii, 1990.

Mandell, Sara, and David Noel Freedman. *The Relationship between Herodotus' History and Primary History.* South Florida Studies in the History of Judaism 60. Atlanta: Scholars Press, 1993.

Marguerat, Daniel. "La mort d'Ananias et Saphira (Ac 5.1–11) dans la stratégie narrative de Luc." *New Testament Studies* 39 (1993): 209–26.

Marin, Louis. "Essai d'analyse structurale d'Actes 10:1–11:18." *Recherches de science religieuse* 58 (1970): 39–61.

Marrou, H. I. *A History of Education in Antiquity.* Translated by George Lamb. New York: Sheed & Ward, 1956.

Marshall, I. Howard. "Acts and the 'Former Treatise.'" In *The Book of Acts in Its Ancient Literary Setting,* edited by Bruce W. Winter and Andrew D. Clarke, 163–82. The Book of Acts in Its First Century Setting. Grand Rapids: Eerdmans, 1993.

———. *The Acts of the Apostles.* Tyndale New Testament Commentaries. Leicester: InterVarsity, 1980.

———. "How Does One Write on The Theology of Acts?" In *Witness to the Gospel: The Theology of Acts,* edited by I. Howard Marshall and David Peterson, 3–16. Grand Rapids: Eerdmans, 1998.

———. *Luke: Historian and Theologian.* Grand Rapids: Zondervan, 1970.

———. "Luke's View of Paul." *Southwestern Journal of Theology* 33 (Fall 1990): 41–51.

Marshall, I. Howard, and David Peterson, eds. *Witness to the Gospel: The Theology of Acts.* Grand Rapids: Eerdmans, 1998.

Martin, Wallace. *Recent Theories of Narrative.* Ithaca, NY: Cornell University Press, 1986.

Mason, Steve. "Chief Priests, Sadducees, Pharisees and Sanhedrin in Acts." In *The Book of Acts in Its Palestinian Setting,* edited by Richard Bauckham, 115–78. The Book of Acts in Its First Century Setting. Grand Rapids: Eerdmans, 1995.

———. *Flavius Josephus on the Pharisees: A Composition-Critical Study.* Studia post-biblica 39. Leiden: E. J. Brill, 1991.

McCord Adams, Marilyn. "Separation and Reversal in Luke-Acts." In *Philosophies and the Christian Faith,* edited by Thomas V. Morris, 92–117. Notre Dame, IN: University of Notre Dame Press, IN, 1988.

McKeon, Richard. "Literary Criticism and the Concept of Imitation in Antiquity." In *Critics and Criticism: Ancient and Modern* edited by R. S. Crane, 147–75. Chicago: University of Chicago Press, 1952.

Mealand, David. "Community of Goods and Utopian Allusions in Acts II–IV." *Journal of Theological Studies* 28 (April 1977): 96–99.

———. "The Phrase 'Many Proofs' in Acts 1,3 and in Hellenistic Writers." *Zeitschrift für die neutestamentliche Wissenschaft und die Kunde der älteren Kirche* 80 (1989): 134–35.

Meeks, Wayne A. *The First Urban Christians.* New Haven: Yale University Press, 1983.

Menoud, Philippe-H. "La mort d'Ananias et de Saphira (Actes 5. 1–11)." In *Aux sources de la tradition chrétienne: Mélanges offerts à M. Maurice Goguel,* 146–54. Bibliothèque théologique. Neuchâtel: Delachaux & Niestlé, 1950.

Menzies, Robert P. "Spirit and Power in Luke-Acts: A Response to Max Turner." *Journal for the Study of the New Testament* 49 (1993): 11–20.

Metzger, Bruce M. *A Textual Commentary on the Greek New Testament.* New York: United Bible Societies, 1971.

Meyer, R., and H. Strathmann. "λειτουργέω...." In *Theological Dictionary of the New Testament,* edited by Gerhard Kittel and Gerhard Friedrich, 10 vols., 4:215–31. Translated by Geoffrey W. Bromiley. Grand Rapids: Eerdmans, 1964–76.

Michel, Otto. "οἰκοδομέω." In *Theological Dictionary of the New Testament,* edited by Gerhard Kittel and Gerhard Friedrich, 10 vols., 5:136–44. Translated by Geoffrey W. Bromiley. Grand Rapids: Eerdmans, 1964-76.

Mitchell, Alan C. "The Social Function of Friendship in Acts 2:44–47 and 4:32–37." *Journal of Biblical Literature* 111 (Summer 1992): 255–72.

Moehring, Horst R. "The *Acta pro Judaeis* in the *Antiquities* of Flavius Josephus." In *Christianity, Judaism and Other Greco-Roman Cults,* part 3, *Judaism before 70,* edited by Jacob Neusner, 124–58. Studies in Judaism in Late Antiquity 12. Leiden: E. J. Brill, 1975.

Moessner, David P. " 'The Christ Must Suffer,' The Church Must Suffer: Rethinking the Theology of the Cross in Luke-Acts." In *Society of Biblical Literature 1990 Seminar Papers,* edited by David J. Lull, 165–95. Atlanta: Scholars Press, 1990.

———. "The Ironic Fulfillment of Israel's Glory." In *Luke-Acts and the Jewish People: Eight Critical Perspectives,* edited by Joseph B. Tyson, 35–50. Minneapolis: Augsburg, 1988.

———. "Paul in Acts: Preacher of Eschatological Repentance to Israel." *New Testament Studies* 34 (1988): 96–104.

———. "*Two* Lords 'at the Right Hand'? The Psalms and an Intertextual Reading of Peter's Pentecost Speech (Acts 2:14–36)." In *Literary Studies in Luke-Acts: Essays in Honor of Joseph B. Tyson,* edited by Richard P. Thompson and Thomas E. Phillips, 215–34. Macon, GA: Mercer University Press, 1998.

Momigliano, Arnaldo. *The Development of Greek Biography: Four Lectures.* Cambridge, MA: Harvard University Press, 1971.

Moore, Stephen D. "Deconstructive Criticism: The Gospel of the Mark," in *Mark and Method: New Approaches in Biblical Studies,* edited by Janice Capel Anderson and Stephen D. Moore, 84–102. Minneapolis: Fortress, 1992.

———. *Literary Criticism and the Gospels: The Theoretical Challenge.* New Haven: Yale University Press, 1989.

———. *Mark and Luke in Poststructuralist Perspectives: Jesus Begins to Write.* New Haven: Yale University Press, 1992.

———. "Stories of Reading: Doing Gospel Criticism as/with a 'Reader.' " In *Society of Biblical Literature 1988 Seminar Papers,* edited by David Lull, 141–59. Atlanta: Scholars Press, 1988.

Moule, C. F. D. "The Christology of Acts." In *Studies in Luke-Acts,* edited by Leander E. Keck and J. Louis Martyn, 159–85. Philadelphia: Fortress, 1980.

Moxnes, Halvor. "Patron-Client Relations and the New Community in Luke-Acts." In *The Social World of Luke-Acts: Models for Interpretation,* edited by Jerome H. Neyrey, 241–68. Peabody, MA: Hendrickson, 1991.

Müller, Dietram. *Satzbau, Satzgliederung und Satzverbindung in der Prosa Herodots.* Beiträge zur klassischen Philologie 116. Meisenheim am Glan: Hain, 1980.

Munck, Johannes. *The Acts of the Apostles.* Anchor Bible 31. Garden City, NY: Doubleday, 1967.

Neil, William. *Acts.* New Century Bible. Grand Rapids: Eerdmans, 1973.

Nellessen, E. "Die Presbyter der Gemeinden in Lykaonien und Pisidien (Apg 14,23)." In *Les Actes des Apôtres: Traditions, rédaction, théologie,* edited by Jacob Kremer, 493–98. Bibliotheca ephemeridum theologicarum lovaniensium 48. Leuven: Leuven University Press, 1979.

Neusner, Jacob, ed. *Christianity, Judaism and Other Greco-Roman Cults,* part 3, *Judaism before 70.* Studies in Judaism in Late Antiquity 12. Leiden: E. J. Brill, 1975.

Neyrey, Jerome H. "Ceremonies in Luke-Acts: The Case of Meals and Table-Fellowship." In *The Social World of Luke-Acts: Models for Interpretation,* edited by Jerome H. Neyrey, 361–87. Peabody, MA: Hendrickson, 1991.

———. "The Symbolic Universe of Luke-Acts: 'They Turn the World Upside Down.' " In *The Social World of Luke-Acts: Models for Interpretation,* edited by Jerome H. Neyrey, 271–304. Peabody, MA: Hendrickson, 1991.

———, ed. *The Social World of Luke-Acts: Models for Interpretation.* Peabody, MA: Hendrickson, 1991.

Nolland, John. "A Fresh Look at Acts 15.10." *New Testament Studies* 27 (October 1980): 105–15.

Olson, Elder. "The Argument of Longinus' *On the Sublime.*" In *Critics and Criticism: Ancient and Modern,* edited by R. S. Crane, 232–59. Chicago: University of Chicago Press, 1952.

Ong, Walter J. *Orality and Literacy: The Technologizing of the Word.* New Accents. New York: Methuen, 1982.

Orwin, Clifford. "Thucydides' Contest: Thucydidean 'Methodology' in Context." *Review of Politics* 51 (Summer 1989): 345–64.

Ostwald, Martin. *Anankē in Thucydides.* American Classical Studies 18. Atlanta: Scholars Press, 1988.

O'Toole, R. F. "Parallels between Jesus and His Disciples in Luke-Acts: A Further Study." *Biblische Zeitschrift* 27 (1983): 195–212.

———. "Why Did Luke Write Acts (Luke-Acts)?" *Biblical Theology Bulletin* 7 (January 1977): 66–76.

Overman, J. Andrew. *Matthew's Gospel and Formative Judaism: The Social World of the Matthean Community.* Minneapolis: Fortress, 1990.

Palmer, Darryl W. "Acts and the Ancient Historical Monograph." In *The Book of Acts in Its Ancient Literary Setting,* edited by Bruce W. Winter and Andrew D. Clarke, 1–30. The Book of Acts in Its First Century Setting. Grand Rapids: Eerdmans, 1993.

———. "The Literary Background of Acts 1.1–14." *New Testament Studies* 33 (1987): 427–38.

Panagopoulos, Johannes. "Zur Theologie der Apostelgeschichte." *Novum Testamentum* 14 (April 1972): 137–59.

Parsons, Mikeal C. "The Place of Jerusalem on the Lukan Landscape: An Exercise in Symbolic Cartography." In *Literary Studies in Luke-Acts: Essays in Honor of Joseph B. Tyson,* edited by Richard P. Thompson and Thomas E. Phillips, 155–72. Macon, GA: Mercer University Press, 1998.

Parsons, Mikeal C., and Richard I. Pervo. *Rethinking the Unity of Luke and Acts.* Minneapolis: Fortress, 1993.

Parsons, Mikeal C., and Joseph B. Tyson, edited by *Cadbury, Knox, and Talbert: American Contributions to the Study of Acts.* Atlanta: Scholars Press, 1992.

Pearson, Lionel. "Characterization in Drama and Oratory — *Poetics* 1450a20." *Classical Quarterly* 18 (1968): 76–83.

Pedech, Paul. *La méthode historique de Polybe.* Collection d'études anciennes. Paris: Les Belles Lettres, 1964.

Pelling, Christopher, ed. *Characterization and Individuality in Greek Literature.* Oxford: Clarendon, 1990.

———. "Conclusion." In *Characterization and Individuality in Greek Literature,* edited by Christopher Pelling, 245–62. Oxford: Clarendon, 1990.

———. "Plutarch and Thucydides." In *Plutarch and the Historical Tradition,* edited by Philip A. Stadter, 3–19. London: Routledge, 1992.

Percival, Geoffrey. *Aristotle on Friendship.* Cambridge, UK: Cambridge University Press, 1940.

Perelman, Chaim, and L. Olbrechts-Tyteca. *The New Rhetoric: A Treatise on Argumentation.* Translated by John Wilkinson and Purcell Weaver. Notre Dame, IN: University of Notre Dame Press, 1969.

Perkins, Pheme. "Crisis in Jerusalem? Narrative Criticism in New Testament Studies." *Theological Studies* 50 (June 1989): 296–313.

Perrot, Charles. "Les décisions de l'assemblée de Jérusalem." *Recherches de science religieuse* 69 (1981): 195–208.

Pervo, Richard I. *Profit with Delight: The Literary Genre of the Acts of the Apostles.* Philadelphia: Fortress, 1987.

Pesch, Rudolf. *Die Apostelgeschichte.* 2 vols. Evangelisch-katholischer Kommentar zum Neuen Testament 5. Zurich: Neukirchener Verlag, 1986.

Peterson, David. "The Motif of Fulfilment and the Purpose of Luke-Acts." In *The Book of Acts in Its Ancient Literary Setting,* edited by Bruce W. Winter and Andrew D. Clarke, 83–104. The Book of Acts in Its First Century Setting. Grand Rapids: Eerdmans, 1993.

———. "The Worship of the New Community." In *Witness to the Gospel: The Theology of Acts,* edited by I. Howard Marshall and David Peterson, 373–96. Grand Rapids: Eerdmans, 1998.

Pettem, Michael. "Luke's Great Omission and His View of the Law." *New Testament Studies* 42 (January 1996): 35–54.

Philo. *Philo's Works.* 12 vols. Translated by F. H. Colson et al. Loeb Classical Library. London: Heinemann, 1935.

Plato. *Phaedrus.* Translated by Harold N. Fowler. Loeb Classical Library. London: Heinemann, 1947.

———. *Republic.* 2 vols. Translated by Paul Shorey. Loeb Classical Library. London: Heinemann, 1930, 1935.

Plümacher, Eckhard. "Die Apostelgeschichte als historische Monographie." In *Les Actes des Apôtres: Traditions, rédaction, théologie,* edited by Jacob Kremer, 457–66. Bibliotheca ephemeridum theologicarum ovaniensium 48. Leuven: Leuven University Press, 1979.

————. *Lukas als hellenistischer Schriftsteller: Studien zur Apostelgeschichte.* Studien zur Umwelt des Neuen Testaments. Göttingen: Vandenhoeck & Ruprecht, 1972.

————. "Die Missionsreden der Apostelgeschichte und Dionys von Halikarnass." *New Testament Studies* 39 (April 1993): 161–77.

Plutarch. *Moralia.* 16 vols. Translated by Frank C. Babbitt et al. Loeb Classical Library. London: Heinemann, 1927-76.

Polybius. *The Histories.* 6 vols. Translated by W. R. Paton. Loeb Classical Library. London: Heinemann, 1922-27.

Poque, Suzanne. "Une lecture d'Actes 11/27–12/25." *Études théologiques et religieuses* 55 (1980): 271–78.

Porter, Stanley E. "Thucydides 1.22.1 and Speeches in Acts: Is There a Thucydidean View?" *Novum Testamentum* 32 (1990): 121–42.

Powell, Mark Allan. *The Bible and Modern Literary Criticism: A Critical Assessment and Annotated Bibliography.* New York: Greenwood, 1992.

————. "Luke's Second Volume: Three Basic Issues in Contemporary Studies of Acts." *Trinity Seminary Review* 13 (Fall 1991): 69–81.

————. "The Plot to Kill Jesus from Three Different Perspectives: Point of View in Matthew." In *Society of Biblical Literature 1990 Seminar Papers,* edited by David J. Lull, 603–13. Atlanta, GA: Scholars Press, 1990.

————. *What Are They Saying about Acts?* New York: Paulist Press, 1991.

Praeder, Susan M. "Luke-Acts and the Ancient Novel." In *Society of Biblical Literature 1981 Seminar Papers,* edited by Kent Harold Richards, 269–92. Missoula, MT: Scholars Press, 1981.

Price, A. W. *Love and Friendship in Plato and Aristotle.* Oxford: Clarendon, 1989.

Quintilian. *The Institutio Oratoria of Quintilian.* 4 vols. Translated by H. E. Butler. Loeb Classical Library. Cambridge, MA: Harvard University Press, 1979.

Radl, Walter. *Paulus und Jesus im lukanischen Doppelwerk: Untersuchungen zu Parallelmotiven im Lukasevangelium und in der Apostelgeschichte.* Europäische Hochschulschriften. Frankfurt: Peter Lang, 1975.

Rajak, Tessa. *Josephus: The Historian and His Society.* Philadelphia: Fortress, 1983.

Rapske, Brian. "Opposition to the Plan of God and Persecution." In *Witness to the Gospel: The Theology of Acts,* edited by I. Howard Marshall and David Peterson, 235–56. Grand Rapids: Eerdmans, 1998.

Rawlings, Hunter R., III. *The Structure of Thucydides' History.* Princeton, NJ: Princeton University Press, 1981.

Reinhardt, Wolfgang. "The Population Size of Jerusalem and the Numerical Growth of the Jerusalem Church." In *The Book of Acts in Its Palestinian Setting,* edited by Richard Bauckham, 237–66. The Book of Acts in Its First Century Setting. Grand Rapids: Eerdmans, 1995.

Rengstorf, Karl Heinrich. "γογγύζω...." In *Theological Dictionary of the New Testament,* edited by Gerhard Kittel and Gerhard Friedrich, 10 vols., 1:728–37. Translated by Geoffrey W. Bromiley. Grand Rapids: Eerdmans, 1964–76.

Rensberger, David. *Johannine Faith and Liberating Community.* Philadelphia: Westminster, 1988.

Richard, Earl. *Acts 6:1–8:4: The Author's Method of Composition.* Society of Biblical Literature Dissertation Series 41. Missoula, MT: Scholars Press, 1978.

———. "The Divine Purpose: The Jews and the Gentile Mission (Acts 15)." In *Luke-Acts: New Perspectives from the Society of Biblical Literature Seminar,* edited by Charles H. Talbert, 188–209. New York: Crossroad, 1984.

———. "Luke — Writer, Theologian, Historian: Research and Orientation of the 1970's." *Biblical Theology Bulletin* 13 (January 1983): 3–15.

———, ed. *New Views on Luke and Acts.* Collegeville, MN: Liturgical Press, 1990.

Robbins, Vernon K. "Prefaces in Greco-Roman Biography and Luke-Acts." *Perspectives in Religious Studies* 6 (Summer 1979): 94–108.

Roberts, W. Rhys. *Greek Rhetoric and Literary Criticism.* New York: Longmans, Greene, 1928.

Roloff, Jürgen. *Die Apostelgeschichte.* Das Neue Testament Deutsch 5. Göttingen: Vandenhoeck & Ruprecht, 1981.

———. "Die Paulus-Darstellung des Lukas." *Evangelische Theologie* 39 (1979): 510–31.

Rorty, Amélie Oksenberg, ed. *Essays on Aristotle's Ethics.* Berkeley: University of California Press, 1979.

Rosner, Brian S. "Acts and Biblical History." In *The Book of Acts in Its Ancient Literary Setting,* edited by Bruce W. Winter and Andrew D. Clarke, 65–82. The Book of Acts in Its First Century Setting. Grand Rapids: Eerdmans, 1993.

———. "The Progress of the Word." In *Witness to the Gospel: The Theology of Acts,* edited by I. Howard Marshall and David Peterson, 215–34. Grand Rapids: Eerdmans, 1998.

Russell, D. A. *Criticism in Antiquity.* Berkeley: University of California Press, 1981.

———. "Greek Criticism of the Empire." In *The Cambridge History of Literary Criticism,* vol. 1, *Classical Criticism,* edited by George A. Kennedy, 297–329. Cambridge, UK: Cambridge University Press, 1989.

———. "*Ethos* in Oratory and Rhetoric." In *Characterization and Individuality in Greek Literature,* edited by Christopher Pelling, 197–212. Oxford: Clarendon, 1990.

Sacks, Kenneth. *Polybius on the Writing of History.* University of California Publications in Classical Studies 24. Berkeley: University of California Press, 1981.

Salmon, Marilyn. "Insider or Outsider? Luke's Relationship with Judaism." In *Luke-Acts and the Jewish People: Eight Critical Perspectives,* edited by Joseph B. Tyson, 76–82. Minneapolis: Augsburg, 1988.

Sampley, J. Paul. *Pauline Partnership in Christ: Christian Community and Commitment in Light of Roman Law.* Philadelphia: Fortress, 1980.

Sanders, Jack T. "The Jewish People in Luke-Acts." In *Luke-Acts and the Jewish People: Eight Critical Perspectives,* edited by Joseph B. Tyson, 51–75. Minneapolis: Augsburg, 1988.

———. *The Jews in Luke-Acts.* Philadelphia: Fortress, 1987.

———. "The Pharisees in Luke-Acts." In *The Living Text: Essays in Honor of Ernest W. Saunders,* edited by Dennis E. Groh and Robert Jewett, 141–88. Lanham, MD: University Press of America, 1985.

———. "The Salvation of the Jews in Luke-Acts." In *Luke-Acts: New Perspectives from the Society of Biblical Literature Seminar,* edited by Charles H. Talbert, 104–28. New York: Crossroad, 1984.

———. "Who Is a Jew and Who Is a Gentile in the Book of Acts?" *New Testament Studies* 37 (1991): 434–55.

Satterthwaite, Philip E. "Acts against the Background of Classical Rhetoric." In *The Book of Acts in Its Ancient Literary Setting,* edited by Bruce W. Winter and Andrew D. Clarke, 337–80. The Book of Acts in Its First Century Setting. Grand Rapids: Eerdmans, 1993.

Saulnier, Christiane. "Flavius Josèphe et la propagande flavienne." *Revue biblique* 96 (October 1989): 545–62.

Schepens, Guido. "Polemic and Methodology in Polybius' Book XII." In *Purposes of History: Studies in Greek Historiography from the 4th to the 2nd Centuries B.C.,* edited by Herman Verdin, Guido Schepens, and Eugénie de Keyser, 39–61. Studia hellenistica 30. Leuven: Lovanii, 1990.

Schille, Gottfried. *Die Apostelgeschichte des Lukas.* Theologischer Handkommentar zum Neuen Testament 5. Berlin: Evangelische Verlagsanstalt, 1983.

———. *Das älteste Paulus-Bild: Beobachtungen zur lukanischen und zur deuteropaulinischen Paulus-Darstellung.* Berlin: Evangelische Verlagsanstalt, 1979.

Schmidt, Daryl. "The Historiography of Acts: Deuteronomistic or Hellenistic?" In *Society of Biblical Literature 1985 Seminar Papers,* edited by Kent Harold Richards, 417–27. Atlanta: Scholars Press, 1985.

Schmidt, Karl Ludwig. "ἐκκλησία." In *Theological Dictionary of the New Testament,* edited by Gerhard Kittel and Gerhard Friedrich, 10 vols., 3:501–36. Translated by Geoffrey W. Bromiley. Grand Rapids: Eerdmans, 1964–76.

———. "ὁρίζω...." In *Theological Dictionary of the New Testament,* edited by Gerhard Kittel and Gerhard Friedrich, 10 vols., 5:452–56. Translated by Geoffrey W. Bromiley. Grand Rapids: Eerdmans, 1964–76.

Schmidt, Karl Ludwig, and Martin Anton Schmidt. "παχύνω." In *Theological Dictionary of the New Testament,* edited by Gerhard Kittel and Gerhard Friedrich, 10 vols., 5:1022–31. Translated by Geoffrey W. Bromiley. Grand Rapids: Eerdmans, 1964–76.

Schmithals, Walter. *Die Apostelgeschichte des Lukas.* Zürcher Bibelkommentare. Zurich: Theologischer Verlag, 1982.

Schmitz, Otto, and Gustav Stählin. "παρακαλέω...." In *Theological Dictionary of the New Testament,* edited by Gerhard Kittel and Gerhard Friedrich, 10 vols., 5:773–99. Translated by Geoffrey W. Bromiley. Grand Rapids: Eerdmans, 1964–76.

Schneider, Gerhard. *Die Apostelgeschichte*. 2 vols. Herders theologischer Kommentar zum Neuen Testament 5. Freiburg: Herder, 1980–82.

———. "Zur Bedeutung von *kathexēs* im lukanischen Doppelwerk." *Zeitschrift für die neutestamentliche Wissenschaft und die Kunde der älteren Kirche* 68 (1977): 128–31.

———. *Lukas, Theologe der Heilsgeschichte: Aufsätze zum lukanischen Doppelwerk*. Bonner biblische Beiträge 59. Königstein: Peter Hanstein, 1985.

———. "Der Zweck des lukanischen Doppelwerks." *Biblische Zeitschrift* 21 (1977): 45–66.

Schwartz, Daniel R. "The End of the Line: Paul in the Canonical Book of Acts." In *Paul and the Legacies of Paul*, edited by William S. Babcock, 3–24. Dallas: Southern Methodist University Press, 1990.

———. "Non-Joining Sympathizers (Acts 5, 13–14)." *Biblica* 64 (1983): 550–55.

Schweizer, Eduard. "Concerning the Speeches in Acts." In *Studies in Luke-Acts*, edited by Leander E. Keck and J. Louis Martyn, 208–16. Philadelphia: Fortress, 1980.

———. "πνέω, ἐμπνέω." In *Theological Dictionary of the New Testament*, edited by Gerhard Kittel and Gerhard Friedrich, 10 vols., 6:452. Translated by Geoffrey W. Bromiley. Grand Rapids: Eerdmans, 1964–76.

Scott, J. Julius, Jr. "The Cornelius Incident in the Light of Its Jewish Setting." *Journal of the Evangelical Theological Society* 34 (December 1991): 475–84.

Seccombe, David. "The New People of God." In *Witness to the Gospel: The Theology of Acts*, edited by I. Howard Marshall and David Peterson, 349–72. Grand Rapids: Eerdmans, 1998.

Seifrid, M. A. "Jesus and the Law in Acts." *Journal for the Study of the New Testament* 30 (1987): 39–57.

Sheeley, Steven M. "Narrative Asides and Narrative Authority in Luke-Acts." *Biblical Theology Bulletin* 18 (July 1988): 102–7.

———. *Narrative Asides in Luke-Acts*. Journal for the Study of the New Testament Supplement Series 72. Sheffield: JSOT Press, 1992.

Shepherd, William H., Jr. *The Narrative Function of the Holy Spirit as a Character in Luke-Acts*. Society of Biblical Literature Dissertation Series 147. Atlanta: Scholars Press, 1994.

Shimron, Binyamin. *Politics and Belief in Herodotus*. Historia Einzelschriften 58. Stuttgart: Franz Steiner, 1989.

Slingerland, Howard Dixon. " 'The Jews' in the Pauline Portion of Acts." *Journal of the American Academy of Religion* 54 (1986): 305–21.

Smith, D. Moody. *Johannine Christianity: Essays on Its Setting, Sources, and Theology*. Columbia: University of South Carolina Press, 1984.

Soulis, E. M. *Xenophon and Thucydides: A Study on the Historical Methods of Xenophon in the Hellenica with Special Reference to the Influence of Thucydides*. Athens: Klapakes, 1972.

Spath, Theobald. *Das Motiv der doppelten Beleuchtung bei Herodot*. Dissertationen der Universität Wien 13. Wien: Notring, 1968.

Spencer, F. Scott. "Acts and Modern Literary Approach." In *The Book of Acts in Its Ancient Literary Setting*, edited by Bruce W. Winter and Andrew D.

Clarke, 381–414. The Book of Acts in Its First Century Setting. Grand Rapids: Eerdmans, 1993.

———. "Neglected Widows in Acts 6:1–7." *Catholic Biblical Quarterly* 56 (October 1994): 715–33.

Springer, Mary D. *A Rhetoric of Literary Character: Some Women of Henry James.* Chicago: University of Chicago Press, 1978.

Squires, John T. "The Plan of God." In *Witness to the Gospel: The Theology of Acts,* edited by I. Howard Marshall and David Peterson, 19–40. Grand Rapids: Eerdmans, 1998.

———. *The Plan of God in Luke-Acts.* Society for New Testament Studies Monograph Series 76. Cambridge, UK: Cambridge University Press, 1993.

Stadter, Philip A., ed. *Plutarch and the Historical Tradition.* New York: Routledge, 1992.

Stambaugh, John E., and David L. Balch. *The New Testament in Its Social Environment.* Library of Early Christianity 2. Philadelphia: Westminster, 1986.

Stegemann, Wolfgang. *Zwischen Synagoge und Obrigkeit: Zur historischen Situation der lukanischen Christen.* Forschungen zur Religion und Literatur des Alten und Neuen Testaments. Göttingen: Vandenhoeck & Ruprecht, 1991.

Sterling, Gregory E. " 'Athletes of Virtue': An Analysis of the Summaries in Acts (2:41–47; 4:32–35; 5:12–16)." *Journal of Biblical Literature* 113 (Winter 1994): 679–96.

———. *Historiography and Self-Definition: Josephus, Luke-Acts and Apologetic Historiography.* Leiden: E. J. Brill, 1992.

Sternberg, Meir. *Expositional Modes and Temporal Ordering in Fiction.* Baltimore: Johns Hopkins University Press, 1978.

———. *The Poetics of Biblical Narrative: Ideological Literature and the Drama of Reading.* Indiana Literary Biblical Series. Bloomington: Indiana University Press, 1985.

Suleiman, Susan R. "Introduction: Varieties of Audience-Oriented Criticism." In *The Reader in the Text: Essays on Audience and Interpretation,* edited by Susan R. Suleiman and Inge Crosman, 3–45. Princeton, NJ: Princeton University Press, 1980.

Suleiman, Susan R., and Inge Crosman, eds. *The Reader in the Text: Essays on Audience and Interpretation.* Princeton, NJ: Princeton University Press, 1980.

Sweeney, Michael L. "The Identity of 'They' in Acts 2.1." *Bible Translator* 46 (April 1995): 245–48.

Talbert, Charles H. *Literary Patterns, Theological Themes, and the Genre of Luke-Acts.* Society of Biblical Literature Monograph Series 20. Missoula, MT: Scholars Press, 1974.

———. *Reading Acts: A Literary and Theological Commentary on the Acts of the Apostles.* Reading the New Testament. New York: Crossroad, 1997.

———, ed. *Luke-Acts: New Perspectives from the Society of Biblical Literature Seminar.* New York: Crossroad, 1984.

———, ed. *Perspectives on Luke-Acts.* Danville, VA: Association of Baptist Professors of Religion, 1978.

Tannehill, Robert C. "The Composition of Acts 3–5: Narrative Development and Echo Effect." In *Society of Biblical Literature 1984 Seminar Papers,* edited by Kent Harold Richards, 217–40. Chico, CA: Scholars Press, 1984.

———. "'Cornelius' and 'Tabitha' Encounter Luke's Jesus." *Interpretation* 48 (1994): 347–56.

———. "Freedom and Responsibility in Scripture Interpretation, with Application to Luke." In *Literary Studies in Luke-Acts: Essays in Honor of Joseph B. Tyson,* edited by Richard P. Thompson and Thomas E. Phillips, 265–78. Macon, GA: Mercer University Press, 1998.

———. "The Functions of Peter's Mission Speeches in the Narrative of Acts." *New Testament Studies* 37 (July 1991): 400–414.

———. "Israel in Luke-Acts: A Tragic Story." *Journal of Biblical Literature* 104 (March 1985): 69–85.

———. *Luke.* Abingdon New Testament Commentaries. Nashville: Abingdon, 1996.

———. *The Narrative Unity of Luke-Acts: A Literary Interpretation.* 2 vols. Philadelphia/Minneapolis: Fortress, 1986–90.

———. "Rejection by Jews and Turning to Gentiles: The Pattern of Paul's Mission in Acts." In *Luke-Acts and the Jewish People: Eight Critical Perspectives,* edited by Joseph B. Tyson, 83–101. Minneapolis: Augsburg, 1988.

Taylor, Justin. "Ancient Texts and Modern Critics: Acts 15,1–34." *Revue biblique* 89 (1992): 373–78.

Thackeray, H. St. John. *Josephus: The Man and the Historian.* New York: Jewish Institute of Religion Press, 1929.

Theissen, Gerd. *The Social Setting of Pauline Christianity.* Translated by John H. Schutz. Philadelphia: Fortress, 1982.

Thomas, Rosalind. *Literacy and Orality in Ancient Greece.* Key Themes in Ancient History. Cambridge, UK: Cambridge University Press, 1992.

———. *Oral Tradition and Written Record in Classical Athens.* Cambridge Studies in Oral and Literate Culture 18. Cambridge, UK: Cambridge University Press, 1989.

Thompson, Richard P. "Believers and Religious Leaders in Jerusalem: Contrasting Portraits of Jews in Acts 1–7." In *Literary Studies in Luke-Acts: Essays in Honor of Joseph B. Tyson,* edited by Richard P. Thompson and Thomas E. Phillips, 327–44. Macon, GA: Mercer University Press, 1998.

———. "'Say It Ain't So, Paul!' The Accusations against Paul in Acts 21 in the Light of His Ministry in Acts 16-20." *Biblical Research* 45 (2000): 34–50.

———. "'What Do You Think You Are Doing, Paul?' Synagogues, Ministry, and Ethics in Acts 16-21." In *Acts and Ethics,* edited by Thomas E. Phillips, 64–78. Sheffield: Sheffield Phoenix Press, 2005.

Thompson, Richard P., and Thomas E. Phillips, eds. *Literary Studies in Luke-Acts: Essays in Honor of Joseph B. Tyson.* Macon, GA: Mercer University Press, 1998.

Thucydides. *History of the Peloponnesian War.* 4 vols. Loeb Classical Library. London: Heinemann, 1919-22.

Tiede, David L. "Acts 11:1–18." *Interpretation* 42 (1988): 175–79.

————. " 'Glory to Thy People Israel': Luke-Acts and the Jews." In *Luke-Acts and the Jewish People: Eight Critical Perspectives*, edited by Joseph B. Tyson, 21–34. Minneapolis: Augsburg, 1988.

Tissot, Yves. "Les prescriptions des presbytres (Actes, XV, 41, D)." *Revue biblique* 77 (July 1970): 321–46.

Tolbert, Mary Ann. *Sowing the Gospel: Mark's World in Literary-Historical Perspective*. Minneapolis: Fortress, 1989.

Toohey, Peter. *Reading Epic: An Introduction to the Ancient Narratives*. New York: Routledge, 1992.

Towner, Philip H. "Mission Practice and Theology under Construction (Acts 18–20)." In *Witness to the Gospel: The Theology of Acts*, edited by I. Howard Marshall and David Peterson, 417–36. Grand Rapids: Eerdmans, 1998.

Trenkner, Sophie. *The Greek Novella in the Classical Period*. Cambridge, UK: Cambridge University Press, 1958.

Trocmé, Etienne. "L'apôtre Paul et Rome: Réflexions sur une fascination." *Revue d'historie et de philosophie religieuses* 72 (1992): 41–51.

Turner, Max. "The Spirit of Prophecy and the Power of Authoritative Preaching in Luke-Acts: A Question of Origins." *New Testament Studies* 38 (1992): 66–88.

————. "The 'Spirit of Prophecy' as the Power of Israel's Restoration and Witness." In *Witness to the Gospel: The Theology of Acts*, edited by I. Howard Marshall and David Peterson, 327–48. Grand Rapids: Eerdmans, 1998.

Tyson, Joseph B. "Acts 6:1–7 and Dietary Regulations in Early Christianity." *Perspectives in Religious Studies* 10 (Spring 1983): 145–61.

————. *The Death of Jesus in Luke-Acts*. Columbia: University of South Carolina Press, 1986.

————. "The Emerging Church and the Problem of Authority in Acts." *Interpretation* 42 (1988): 132–45.

————. *Images of Judaism in Luke-Acts*. Columbia: University of South Carolina Press, 1992.

————. "The Jewish Public in Luke-Acts." *New Testament Studies* 30 (October 1984): 574–83.

————. "Jews and Judaism in Luke-Acts: Reading as a Godfearer." *New Testament Studies* 41 (1995): 19–38.

————. "The Problem of Jewish Rejection in Acts." In *Luke-Acts and the Jewish People: Eight Critical Perspectives*, edited by Joseph B. Tyson, 124–37. Minneapolis: Augsburg, 1988.

————, ed. *Luke-Acts and the Jewish People: Eight Critical Perspectives*. Minneapolis: Augsburg, 1988.

Usher, Stephen. *The Historians of Greece and Rome*. London: Hamish Hamilton, 1969.

Van de Sandt, Huub. "An Explanation of Acts 15.6–21 in the Light of Deuteronomy 4.29–35 (LXX)." *Journal for the Study of the New Testament* 46 (1992): 73–97.

Van der Horst, Pieter W. "Hellenistic Parallels to the Acts of the Apostles: 1,1–26." *Zeitschrift für die neutestamentliche Wissenschaft und die Kunde der älteren Kirche* 74 (1983): 16–26.

————. "Hellenistic Parallels to the Acts of the Apostles (2.1–47)." *Journal for the Study of the New Testament* 25 (1985): 49–60.

————. "Hellenistic Parallels to Acts (Chapters 3 and 4)." *Journal for the Study of the New Testament* 35 (1989): 37–46.

Van Ommeren, Nicholas M. "Was Luke an Accurate Historian?" *Bibliotheca sacra* 148 (January 1991): 57–71.

Van Seters, John. *In Search of History: Historiography in the Ancient World and the Origins of Biblical History.* New Haven: Yale University Press, 1983.

Van Unnik, W. C. "Luke-Acts, a Storm Center in Contemporary Scholarship." In *Studies in Luke-Acts,* edited by Leander E. Keck and J. Louis Martyn, 15–32. Philadelphia: Fortress, 1980.

————. "Luke's Second Book and the Rules of Hellenistic Historiography." In *Les Actes des Apôtres: Traditions, rédaction, théologie,* edited by Jacob Kremer, 37–60. Bibliotheca ephemeridum theologicarum lovaniensium 48. Leuven: Leuven University Press, 1979.

Verdenius, W. J. "The Principles of Greek Literary Criticism." *Mnemosyne* 36 (1983): 14–59.

Verdin, Herman, Guido Schepens, and Eugénie de Keyser, eds. *Purposes of History: Studies in Greek Historiography from the 4th to the 2nd Centuries B.C.* Studia hellenistica 30. Leuven: Lovanii, 1990.

Vielhauer, Philipp. "On the 'Paulinism' of Acts." In *Studies in Luke-Acts,* edited by Leander E. Keck and J. Louis Martyn, 33–50. Philadelphia: Fortress, 1980.

Villalba i Varneda, Pere. *The Historical Method of Flavius Josephus.* Arbeiten zur Literatur und Geschichte des hellenistischen Judentums 19. Leiden: E. J. Brill, 1986.

Von Fritz, Kurt. *Die griechische Geschichtsschreibung.* 2 vols. Berlin: Walter de Gruyter, 1967.

Von Lampe, Peter. "Acta 19 im Spiegel der ephesischen Inschriften." *Biblische Zeitschrift* 36 (1992): 59–76.

Walbank, Frank W. *A Historical Commentary on Polybius.* 3 vols. Oxford: Clarendon, 1957-79.

————. "History and Tragedy." In *Selected Papers: Studies in Greek and Roman History and Historiography,* edited by Frank W. Walbank, 224–41. Cambridge, UK: Cambridge University Press, 1985.

————. "Polemic in Polybius." In *Selected Papers: Studies in Greek and Roman History and Historiography,* edited by Frank W. Walbank, 262–79. Cambridge, UK: Cambridge University Press, 1985.

————. *Polybius.* Sather Classical Lectures 42. Berkeley: University of California Press, 1972.

————. "Polybius between Greece and Rome." In *Selected Papers: Studies in Greek and Roman History and Historiography,* edited by Frank W. Walbank, 280–97. Cambridge, UK: Cambridge University Press, 1985.

————. "Profit or Amusement: Some Thoughts on the Motives of Hellenistic Historians." In *Purposes of History: Studies in Greek Historiography from the 4th to the 2nd Centuries B.C.,* edited by Herman Verdin, Guido Schepens, and Eugénie de Keyser, 253–66. Studia hellenistica 30. Leuven: Lovanii, 1990.

————, ed. *Selected Papers: Studies in Greek and Roman History and Historiography.* Cambridge, UK: Cambridge University Press, 1985.

Walker, A. D. M. "Aristotle's Account of Friendship in the *Nicomachean Ethics.*" *Phronesis* 24 (1979): 180–96.

Walker, William O., Jr. "Acts and the Pauline Corpus Revisited: Peter's Speech at the Jerusalem Conference." In *Literary Studies in Luke-Acts: Essays in Honor of Joseph B. Tyson,* edited by Richard P. Thompson and Thomas E. Phillips, 77–86. Macon, GA: Mercer University Press, 1998.

Wall, Robert W. "The Acts of the Apostles: Introduction, Commentary, and Reflections." In *New Interpreter's Bible,* edited by Leander Keck, 12 vols., 10:3–368. Nashville: Abingdon, 2002.

Walter, Nikolaus. "Apostelgeschichte 6.1 und die Anfänge der Urgemeinde in Jerusalem." *New Testament Studies* 29 (July 1983): 370–93.

Waters, Kenneth H. *Herodotus on Tyrants and Despots: A Study in Objectivity.* Historia Einzelschriften 15. Wiesbaden: Franz Steiner, 1971.

————. *Herodotus, the Historian: His Problems, Methods and Originality.* London: Croom Helm, 1985.

Weiser, Alfons. *Die Apostelgeschichte.* 2 vols. Ökumenischer Taschenbuchkommentar zum Neuen Testament. Würzburg: Echter, 1986.

————. "Das 'Apostelkonzil' (Apg 15,1–35): Ereignis, Überlieferung, lukanische Deutung." *Biblische Zeitschrift* 28 (1984): 145–67.

————. "Christsein und kirchliche Lebensformen nach der Apostelgeschichte." In *Die Freude an Gott — unsere Kraft,* edited by Johannes Joachim Degenhardt, 157–63. Stuttgart: Verlag Katholisches Bibelwerk, 1991.

————. "Gemeinde und Amt nach dem Zeugnis der Apostelgeschichte." In *Mitverantwortung aller in der Kirche: Festschrift zum 150jährigen Bestehen der Gründung Vinzenz Pallottis,* edited by Franz Courth and Alfons Weiser, 118–33. Limburg: Lahn-Verlag, 1985.

Wenham, David. "Acts and the Pauline Corpus." In *The Book of Acts in Its Ancient Literary Setting,* edited by Bruce W. Winter and Andrew D. Clarke, 215–58. The Book of Acts in Its First Century Setting. Grand Rapids: Eerdmans, 1993.

Westlake, Henry D. *Individuals in Thucydides.* Cambridge, UK: Cambridge University Press, 1968.

Wheeldon, M. J. " 'True Stories': The Reception of Historiography in Antiquity." In *History as Text: The Writing of Ancient History,* edited by Averil Cameron, 33–63. Chapel Hill: University of North Carolina Press, 1989.

Wiedemann, T. "Rhetoric in Polybius." In *Purposes of History: Studies in Greek Historiography from the 4th to the 2nd Centuries B.C.,* edited by Herman Verdin, Guido Schepens, and Eugénie de Keyser, 289–300. Studia hellenistica 30. Leuven: Lovanii, 1990.

Wieser, Thomas. "Community — Its Unity, Diversity and Universality." *Semeia* 54 (1985): 83–95.

Wilcox, Max. "The 'God-Fearers' in Acts — A Reconsideration." *Journal for the Study of the New Testament* 13 (1981): 102–22.

Williams, David John. *Acts.* New International Biblical Commentary 5. Peabody, MA: Hendrickson, 1990.

Williamson, H. G. M. "The Historical Value of Josephus' *Jewish Antiquities* XI. 297–301." *Journal of Theological Studies* 28 (April 1977): 49–66.

Wills, Lawrence M. "The Depiction of the Jews in Acts." *Journal of Biblical Literature* 110 (December 1991): 631–54.

Wilson, John R. "Shifting and Permanent *Philia* in Thucydides." *Greece and Rome* 36 (October 1989): 147–51.

Wilson, Stephen G. *The Gentiles and the Gentile Mission in Luke-Acts.* Society for New Testament Studies Monograph Series 23. Cambridge, UK: Cambridge University Press, 1973.

————. *Luke and the Law.* Society for New Testament Studies Monograph Series 50. Cambridge, UK: Cambridge University Press, 1983.

Winter, Bruce W. "Acts and Food Shortages." In *The Book of Acts in Its Graeco-Roman Setting,* edited by David W. J. Gill and Conrad Gempf, 59–78. The Book of Acts in Its First Century Setting. Grand Rapids: Eerdmans, 1994.

Winter, Bruce W., and Andrew D. Clarke, eds. *The Book of Acts in Its Ancient Literary Setting.* The Book of Acts in Its First Century Setting. Grand Rapids: Eerdmans, 1993.

Witherington, Ben, III. *The Acts of the Apostles: A Socio-Rhetorical Commentary.* Grand Rapids: Eerdmans, 1998.

Witherup, Ronald D. "Cornelius Over and Over and Over Again: 'Functional Redundancy' in the Acts of the Apostles." *Journal for the Study of the New Testament* 49 (1993): 45–66.

————. "Functional Redundancy in the Acts of the Apostles: A Case Study." *Journal for the Study of the New Testament* 48 (1992): 67–86.

Woodhead, A. Geoffrey. *Thucydides on the Nature of Power.* Martin Classical Lectures 24. Cambridge, MA: Harvard University Press (for Oberlin College), 1970.

Woodruff, Paul. "Aristotle on *Mimēis*." In *Essays on Aristotle's Poetics,* edited by Amélie Oksenberg Rorty, 73–96. Princeton, NJ: Princeton University Press, 1992.

Zettner, Christoph. *Amt, Gemeinde und kirchliche Einheit in der Apostelgeschichte des Lukas.* New York: Peter Lang, 1991.

Ziesler, J. A. "Luke and the Pharisees." *New Testament Studies* 25 (January 1979): 146–57.

Zingg, Paul. *Das Wachsen der Kirche: Beiträge zur Frage der lukanischen Redaktion und Theologie.* Orbis biblicus et orientalis. Göttingen: Vandenhoeck & Ruprecht, 1974.

INDEX OF
ANCIENT SOURCES